LOOKING EAST TO LOOK WEST

The **Institute of Southeast Asian Studies (ISEAS)** was established as an autonomous organization in 1968. It is a regional centre dedicated to the study of socio-political, security and economic trends and developments in Southeast Asia and its wider geostrategic and economic environment. The Institute's research programmes are the Regional Economic Studies (RES, including ASEAN and APEC), Regional Strategic and Political Studies (RSPS), and Regional Social and Cultural Studies (RSCS).

ISEAS Publishing, an established academic press, has issued almost 2,000 books and journals. It is the largest scholarly publisher of research about Southeast Asia from within the region. ISEAS Publishing works with many other academic and trade publishers and distributors to disseminate important research and analyses from and about Southeast Asia to the rest of the world.

LOOKING EAST TO LOOK WEST

Lee Kuan Yew's Mission India

SUNANDA K. DATTA-RAY

INSTITUTE OF SOUTHEAST ASIAN STUDIES
Singapore

PENGUIN
VIKING
PENGUIN BOOKS
India

First published in Singapore in 2009 by
ISEAS Publishing
Institute of Southeast Asian Studies
30 Heng Mui Keng Terrace, Pasir Panjang
Singapore 119614
for distribution in all countries except India.

E-mail: publish@iseas.edu.sg
Website: http://bookshop.iseas.edu.sg

This is a reprint edition published by arrangement with the original publisher, Viking, Penguin Books India, and for sale outside the Indian Subcontinent.

All rights reserved. No part of this publication may be reproduced stored in a retrieval system, or transmitted in any form or by any means, electronic, mechanical, photocopying, recording, or otherwise, without written permission of the publishers.

Copyright © Sunanda K. Datta-Ray 2009

The responsibility for facts and opinions in this publication rests exclusively with the author and his interpretations do not necessarily reflect the views or the policy of the publishers or their supporters.

ISEAS Library Cataloguing-in-Publication Data

Datta-Ray, Sunanda K., 1937-
    Looking east to look west : Lee Kuan Yew's Mission India.
    1. Lee, Kuan Yew, 1923- —Interviews.
    2. Singapore—Relations—India.
    I. India—Relations—Singapore.
    II. Title.
DS610.47 I4D23   2009

ISBN 978-981-4279-04-8 (soft cover)
ISBN 978-981-4279-30-7 (E-book PDF)

Typeset by Eleven Arts, New Delhi
Printed in Singapore by Utopia Press Pte Ltd

Contents

Foreword by Pranab Mukherjee — vii
Foreword by George Yeo — xi
Acknowledgements — xiii

Introduction — 1
1. 'MM's Strategy, Goh Chok Tong's Stamina' — 19
2. Chinatown Spelt 'Singapur' — 46
3. Asia's 'Coca-Cola Governments' — 73
4. 'An Absolute Pariah in the Whole World' — 101
5. India's 'Monroe Doctrine for Asia' — 131
6. 'India Alone Can Look China in the Eye' — 158
7. Goh's Folly to Goh's Glory with Tata — 185
8. 'The Lowest Point in Bilateral Relations' — 212
9. 'Scent of the S'pore Dollar' — 239
10. Singapore's 'Mild India Fever' — 266
11. End of One Honeymoon, Start of Another? — 293
12. Shaping the Asian Century — 319

Notes — 346
Index — 377

विदेश मंत्री, भारत
MINISTER OF EXTERNAL AFFAIRS
INDIA

Foreword

India's Look East Policy is now a decade and half old. Its path, vigour and promise has given us renewed confidence in India's Asian destiny. Without doubt, this is Asia's century and India is proud to be part of an energetic process that has seen impressive growth across the continent. In this historical evolution in the new century, leaders across the continent have contributed, learnt with experience and evolved new approaches.

Amongst those leaders, the name of Lee Kuan Yew must rank near the top. A distinguished statesman and a system designer par excellence, Lee Kuan Yew has always impressed me with his determination, which is suffused with deep insights into the world around him. Having steered Singapore with a focus that is unique, he has today become a living legend for enabling growth through entrepreneurship and clear direction. This book throws light on Lee Kuan Yew's admiration, belief, curiosity and desire for engagement with India over the years. Undoubtedly, his abiding interest in India over the decades, tinged with expectations, finds reflection in some of the achievements that have been posted by India. A mirror image of this multifaceted expectation finds form today as components that have helped craft India's Look East Policy.

That policy, however, is predated by the much more important connection between India and Singapore, which was established more than a thousand years ago. India's ancient links with the region were nurtured on the waves of trade and culture and found both spiritual as well as concrete expression through the architecture of some of the temples in South East Asia, many of which stand to this day. The characteristic Asian treasure of spirituality is one of the strongest contributors to our links. In the current context, this has found expression in the significant

प्रणव मुखर्जी
PRANAB MUKHERJEE

विदेश मंत्री, भारत
MINISTER OF EXTERNAL AFFAIRS
INDIA

: 2 :

support being shown by Singapore for the revival of the Nalanda University. In a way, this is the completion of a virtuous circle enabling us to begin the second chapter of our relationship with greater confidence.

Relations between India and Singapore have always been marked by a significant degree of closeness, not only at the Government level, but in the private sector too. It is well known that the foundations of Singapore's industrialization were laid in 1972 when the Tatas helped in setting up the first technical training institute and a precision tools manufacturing plant in the island. In fields as widely separated as diplomacy and airline management, India has had the opportunity to assist Singapore in capacity building.

Today, we see the visible effects of the process started then. The recently concluded Comprehensive Economic Cooperation Agreement concluded in 2005 arose as a result of the development of close relations with ASEAN in general and Singapore in particular. One example would suffice: today, there are 172 flights that connect Singapore to various cities in India per week. This is the result of the persistence in vision and the focus that Minister Mentor Lee Kuan Yew personifies.

To bring together the multiple strands of this complex relationship, there is no better a person that Sunanda K. Datta Ray. Sunanda is distinctly qualified to write this book. As Editor of The Statesman, one of the leading newspapers published from Kolkata, Sunanda made sure that the newspaper gave adequate space to cover news about countries east of India. The Statesman itself has a hoary tradition, having been originally incorporated as "The Friend of India" in 1818 one year ahead of the establishment of Singapore as a trading post in 1819. Incidentally, the business affairs of Singapore were conducted till 1867 from Kolkata!

प्रणव मुखर्जी
RANAB MUKHERJEE

विदेश मंत्री, भारत
MINISTER OF EXTERNAL AFFAIRS
INDIA

: 3 :

The experience has stood Sunanda in good stead. Now, having lived for nearly a decade in Singapore as a journalist and a researcher, the message of his book is that even if friendship takes time to crystallize, it is the foundation that lends it the energy. The contributions of India's political leaders over the years, as brought out in the book, constitute these foundational elements. The launch of the Look East Policy was perhaps "the decisive moment", to borrow a phrase from photographer Henry Cartier Bresson. With this book by Sunanda, we now have a volume that starts today, reveals the past, and points to what new heights can be attained.

Pranab Mukherjee
Minister of External Affairs
Government of India

New Delhi
9 June 2008

MINISTER FOR FOREIGN AFFAIRS
SINGAPORE

FOREWORD

1. After meeting Rahul Gandhi in October 2007, Lee Kuan Yew remarked thoughtfully to some Singapore ministers that he knew Rahul's father, grandmother and great grandfather. Having lived so long and observed at close range India's complex recovery of its sense of self after independence in 1947, Lee Kuan Yew has a unique longitudinal perspective of India's development in the last 60 years. He was happy to give extended interviews to Sunanda Datta-Ray for this book.

2. Singapore's relationship with India of course goes back much longer. The name Singapore itself is of Sanskrit origin. Singapore is at the heart of Southeast Asia. Located at the southernmost tip of Eurasia, it is where ships sailing beneath the trade winds between the two oceans have to turn. As the flows of trade ebbed and flowed over the centuries, they left on the shores of Southeast Asia aspects of Indian civilization. Southeast Asia is where the traditions of the Ramayana and Mahabharata remain alive and thriving outside India, albeit in somewhat different forms. It was through Southeast Asia that Buddhism travelled by sea to China, Korea and Japan. It was for the China trade that the British East India Company established Singapore as a trading post in 1819. Modern Singapore is a daughter city of Kolkata from where Singapore was administered until 1867. That Bengali link was reactivated when Subhas Chandra Bose established the Indian National Army in Singapore during the Second World War. In a new age of globalisation in the 21st century, it should not be surprising at all that an old but persistent relationship should be refurbished and refreshed. When explaining the reasons for the Comprehensive Economic Cooperation Agreement with India, I tell my Indian friends half in jest that all it does is to restore the position of the Raj when trade flowed freely, standards were similar and professionals were able to move across jurisdictions with relative ease.

3. In Lee Kuan Yew's India, Datta-Ray chronicles Singapore's re-engagement of an India which, after decades of introspection, is once again looking outwards. Years ago, Lee Kuan Yew knew instinctively that India

would one day open up and recover its position on the global stage but the question was always when? That Singapore took an early position on India before many other countries did was not because we were smarter or had better information but because India has always been a part of us. We could feel it in our bones. Having lived many years in Singapore, Datta-Ray understands this and it shows in the way he tells the story. As a relatively late participant, I could relate to many of the observations he makes but it is perhaps only to be expected that the images that come through the lenses of another person should sometimes look a little different from those I myself registered.

GEORGE YEO

Acknowledgements

A book like this, drawing heavily on interviews and informal chats, is something of a collective effort. The list of persons in Singapore and India to whom I am indebted is, therefore, enormous. Some of them may not even have been aware of dropping pearls of wisdom that were picked up and pocketed. It would be invidious to publish their names. But it is only right to admit that much of the flavour of the India–Singapore dialogue over the years derives from these conversations.

It all came about quite fortuitously because of a call on Minister Mentor Lee Kuan Yew in 2005. A generous fellowship at the Institute of Southeast Asian Studies, for which I am deeply grateful to the director, Ambassador K. Kesavapany—universally known by the affectionate diminutive of Pany—made it possible for my wife and me to return to Singapore for eighteen enjoyable months during which, thanks to Colonel Lee Seow Hiang, then MM's Principal Private Secretary, I was able to engage MM in seven long, informal, free-ranging, recorded conversations. Including the first unstructured but also recorded chat, there were thus eight sessions. That made a change from my first visit to Singapore in 1976 (for London's *Observer* newspaper to the fury of the paper's resident correspondent, Dennis Bloodworth, whose bitterness over my assignment was simmering even twelve years later when he wrote his memoirs), when I cooled my heels for a week in Raffles Hotel without being granted an interview by Prime Minister Lee Kuan Yew, as he was then. I did, however, meet Foreign Minister S. Rajaratnam, who was dismissive about non-alignment. Taking me to the window, Rajaratnam pointed to the harbour and said Singapore would be lost if the Americans didn't keep her informed about possibly hostile vessels that berthed there. That is the raw material of this book. Only Colonel Lee sat in on the meetings, though my son, Deep Kisor, joined us for the last session and MM responded to his inputs with the gracious forbearance with which he put up with my inquisitiveness about times long past. Only once did he explode, exclaiming that I was prodding him about things that had happened forty or fifty years ago. Otherwise, he was unreservedly patient and forthcoming about what might be called the software of contemporary history.

It is generally assumed that files hold the key to understanding how governments think and act. B.V.R. Subrahmanyam, then a senior member of Prime Minister Manmohan Singh's office, says files do not disclose intent. That emerges only from conversation with people, something that many academic researchers tend to overlook. People animate government. Some people are more powerful than others, and a few are powerful enough to make and execute policy. But even the most powerful do not operate in isolation. And so, I have supplemented Lee Kuan Yew's obiter dicta with an exhaustive series of interviews with officials and politicians in India and Singapore who fleshed out the relationship. At the same time, I have not neglected other evidence, spending many months scanning official documents, newspaper records, and the books and other paper traces left by the men and women who played some part in the story.

Most of the people I interviewed appear in the pages that follow; the endnotes acknowledge their wisdom and insight. Not thanking them individually does not mean I do not appreciate the time they gave me or the care with which they answered questions. Only a very few of my informants are not named, and that is entirely their choice. There are others, like Gopinath Pillai, businessman, diplomat and raconteur, whom I did not ever specifically interview but who is one of those who bring colour and liveliness to any subject they discuss. Just chatting with Gopi filled many gaps in my knowledge and supplied many unsuspected details. How else would I have known that *congee*, Chinese porridge, is also an Indian word like Mandarin (*mantri*), being derived from our *kanchi*, starch? I had been unaware till then of the Chinese debt to India! There was much else in that vein.

Named or not, my informants are the supporting cast around

MM. Non-players were also invaluable. Apart from the service that the ISEAS library assistants readily provided, a working day at the institute would have been dull indeed without the cheerful radiance with which Kamala and Mr Tee (no other names were ever used for these two delightful and indispensable persons) enlivened routine. A special thank you is due to the Singapore Press Holdings Resource Centre. With no obligation save of long association, Gokelam Ponniah Achary was like a personal research assistant, looking up and e-mailing back to me within minutes of my mentioning some story that had appeared in the *Straits Times* (or some other publication) many years ago, and of which I had only a vague recollection. She continued her help even after my ISEAS fellowship ended and I returned to Calcutta to continue working on the manuscript, and then in London where I read the proofs. Sonny Yap Thiam Por, friend and colleague, was also unstinting with information, though immersed in his own labours over a history of the People's Action Party.

None of this would have happened if President S.R. Nathan of Singapore ('smooth, soft and suave' in the words of an Indian diplomat) had not taken an interest in the project even before it began. His encouragement and the hospitality he and Mrs Urmila Nathan, whose family had migrated to Malaya from our part of India, extended, made a great difference to my wife and me during our stay in Singapore.

Being a scholar, unlike his father, Deep Kisor gave me the benefit of his academic insights. But there would have been no book without my wife's contribution. While some ISEAS colleagues urged me to engage a student aide (at my cost!) Sumita plugged in a pair of earphones, inserted the tapes and sat for hours on end, day after day, listening and transcribing. Not only tapes of long interviews with Lee Kuan Yew but of all my conversations in India and Singapore. By the end she must have trumped the expertise of Henry Higgins in *My Fair Lady* in being able to detect and decipher the many distinctive accents that give Singlish, Hinglish and all the other Englishes of our two countries a special resonance.

Several friends read parts of the manuscript and made useful suggestions. The one to whom I am especially grateful is Kanti Bajpai for taking time off from packing for Oxford to pore over every line and word. His advice helped to iron out many infelicities that affected the theme as well as the conclusions for which I alone bear responsibility.

'Stand up'

Courtesy *Hindustan Times*

(See pages 151–52)

Introduction

Within moments of proclaiming Singapore independent on 9 August 1965, Lee Kuan Yew, the tiny island republic's first prime minister and architect of its phenomenal growth, wrote to India's prime minister, Lal Bahadur Shastri, seeking military assistance. Shastri, whom he had met in New Delhi three months earlier, ignored the appeal. Other rebuffs followed. Singaporean fishing craft were routinely arrested for straying into Indian territorial waters. India turned down Singapore's request to use the Nicobar Islands for defence training. A proposal to import sand from the Andaman Islands was similarly rejected. India sold arms and ammunition to Malaysia during anti-Chinese rioting there when Singapore feared an influx of refugees across the Causeway linking the two countries. India also questioned Singapore's decision to provide facilities to American troops when the Philippines bases were closed. Mistrust and misgivings were not confined to one side. Goh Chok Tong, who became prime minister in 1990 when Lee 'stepped aside' with the designation of Senior Minister or SM, warned twice that an American withdrawal from Asia would encourage hegemonic India with an increasing military reach.

Four decades after the abortive appeal to Shastri, India and Singapore are poised to realize Lee's early vision of restoring the seamless unity of what the Ramayana called Suvarnabhumi, Land of Gold (also known as Suvarnadwipa, Isle of Gold). His unspoken Mission India, which inspired and guided his successors, eventually also struck a responsive chord in New Delhi. Four unprecedented agreements promise to erase strategic and economic boundaries, and transform the Little Red Dot (an Indonesian president's derisive term for the Chinese island in an Islamic sea) into the doorway to a huge Indian hinterland and India's springboard for the world. Three defence agreements provide for joint military training, exercises and other professional exchanges between the Indian and the Singaporean armed forces. The arrangement might be 'a small step for dynamic little Singapore whose military units are scattered around the globe' but represents 'a giant step for India's relatively opaque, inflexible and bureaucratic defence sector.'[1] It is 'certainly . . . a major, major step' for India, agrees Prime Minister Lee Hsien Loong, because 'India never used to allow such things.'[2] The younger Lee succeeded Goh in 2004 as Singapore's third prime minister when his father, Lee Kuan Yew assumed the style of Minister Mentor, MM, and Goh became the new SM.

As momentous as the defence agreements of 2003, 2005 and 2007, the Comprehensive Economic Cooperation Agreement signed in 2005 heralds 'a larger process of Asian integration'.[3] Ceca's 'pre-establishment' clause—entitling Singapore-registered enterprises to be treated at par with Indian companies—can revitalize India's economy with a flood of funds from abroad while guaranteeing Singapore permanent middleman's fees. The agreement is expected to push up bilateral trade to more than US$50 billion by 2010, increase Singapore's cumulative investment in India to US$10 billion by 2015, and enable more Indian firms to follow the Tatas and Punj Lloyd in acquiring companies in Singapore.[4]

Historians are silent about this revolutionary transformation after decades of hesitation, suspicion and misunderstanding. The saga of a relationship that straddles the frontiers of foreign and domestic affairs, history and culture, politics and personality, public and private life, remains an untold story. It challenges established perceptions, dissolves prejudices and dispels the notion that international relations is the product of textbook theories and calculations. This book demonstrates that international relations are also determined by individuals, as much to meet national requirements as to realize their own ideals. The title, *Looking East to Look West: Lee Kuan Yew's Mission India*, reflects both the sophistication of P.V. Narasimha Rao's Look East strategy and Lee's vision of India as an Asian player long before Indians turned again to their ancient footprints in the Sri Vijaya and Majapahit empires. Indeed, Singapore looms so large today in India's public consciousness only because of Lee's robust proselytization. As Sellappan Rama Nathan, a former civil servant who became president of Singapore in 1999, says, he 'was trying all along to woo India to play a bigger role in South-east Asia.'[5] He constantly badgered India's leaders to activate India's historical involvement in Asian affairs.

Predictably, many Indians and Singaporeans alike dispute Lee's leading role that this book describes. An Indian high commissioner warned that I was 'in a minority of one' in crediting him with any part in the developing equation between the two countries. Another was even more dismissive. 'LKY will try and say he was always a friend of India. He will also suggest it was a case of tough love. Don't buy it!' The most scathing comments came from Singaporeans: 'LKY's a racist you know! You should write that,' said a colleague at the Nanyang Technological University where I taught in 2001–02. I assured him I would if he provided the evidence, but he had none beyond rumour and a stock of well-worn stories of dubious authenticity. All three—and others—insisted that the present exuberance between India and Singapore is entirely Goh's handiwork. The superficial evidence certainly appears to support this simplistic popular version. Goh lent credence to it by telling the Singapore–India Partnership Foundation in Calcutta in 2006 that he derived 'tremendous personal satisfaction' from being 'able to convert . . . sceptics'.[6] In proof, he quoted Lee's admission that 'he had given up on India long ago . . . [but] was happy to be proven wrong'.

This book cites evidence to explode that myth. The 'conversion' of which Goh spoke was no more than a return to the faith that had inspired Lee in the 1950s when Rajabali Jumabhoy, a prominent member of Singapore's Indian community, complained in the Legislative Assembly of which he was a member, that Lee 'constantly quotes India.'[7] So he did for, as he says, India and Indian nationalists were the only models he had as a young man fired by patriotic fervour. But as India floundered, his enthusiasm waned: 'The interesting part is I started off with high expectations. I tailed off, and now it's being revived, but in a more realistic appraisal of what is possible. I mean no flights of fancy—because I know this is the system. This is the culture and in spite of all this slowness, India is going to make the grade. It can make the grade.'[8]

The second fallacy the book destroys is that India was not interested in Asia until 1991. Chandrasekhar Dasgupta, India's high commissioner to Singapore in the early 1980s, argues it is a total misperception to imagine that everything was frozen until then.[9] India's historical commitment to Asia was emphasized soon after the First World War when the Indian National Congress spoke of an Asian federation.[10] Indians share the conviction of the then external affairs minister Pranab Mukherjee that 'Asia minus India is like *Hamlet* without the Prince of Denmark.'[11] Why nothing came of scores of ministerial visits, dozens of trade delegations and any number of industrial exhibitions, promotional campaigns, memoranda of understanding, feasibility studies, joint venture businesses, double taxation agreements, and technical assistance programmes, both bilateral and through the Colombo Plan, is another story. It is discussed in the succeeding pages.

The title, *Looking East to Look West,* also highlights a third point this book makes. In looking East and beyond, across the Pacific, Narasimha Rao's Look East policy brought back into focus a region that India had perforce neglected in recent centuries. His original target was the West. The West was the world. As Lee Hsien Loong knows, India's 'reforms started because the country had got into such dire straits that the IMF had to be called in. In those circumstances, with your feet to the fire, you had to do something decisive.'[12] Narasimha Rao's well-crafted response was to break out of the prison of self-sufficiency and move closer to countries with which India could establish substantial trading, investment and security links. That meant the United States and its partners. Singapore was the first stop on the road to America, a major break that came to be a destination in itself when India rediscovered Jawaharlal Nehru's realization that the world converged in Singapore.

Fourth, the book explains that in many respects India's relations with Singapore are an extension of her domestic governance. Lee the pragmatist recognized long ago that India would have to build up her strength before she could become a major player in the 'Concert of Asia' and keep her 'Tryst with Destiny' in the new millennium. His prescription called for clean politics, secular egalitarianism, a unifying language that permits unhindered access to the storehouse of global knowledge, economic opportunities, and an honest, efficient and impartial administration. When he sounded most carping, it was because of the fear that an enfeebled India shackled by the Hindu rate of growth and wracked by caste and communal conflict could never match the grandeur of his dreams. When he appeared to eulogize China at India's expense, it was because of the fear that unless India became strong and powerful, China would steal a march to 'become the dominant power in Asia'.[13]

That leads to the fifth point. Lee has never wavered in his conviction that South-east Asia needs India to cope with China. In the 1960s he thought of a military partnership. Now, the focus has shifted to economic cooperation. Asean (the Association of South-east Asian Nations) alone cannot contend with China's growing might as one of the world's most significant trading and manufacturing powers. But Asean plus India commands impressive weightage. Like Manmohan Singh, however, Lee believes that Asian stability demands competition and cooperation, not confrontation, between the two giants; it calls for a trust-building process, the Indian leader's 'Asian Way', leading to an 'arc of advantage and prosperity across Asia' and 'an Asian economic community.'[14] Though Lee perceives that as Washington's strategy too, he adds a refinement: India and China must recreate the synthesis of the past.

Historically, these two great countries have influenced the economies, religions and cultures of South-east Asia. Hence the name Indo-Chinese peninsula and its mix of Indian and Chinese culture.[15]

Finally, the book discusses Lee's concept of Singapore's special responsibility for engaging India and bringing about a harmonious replication of the encounter with China that created one of the world's most enduring cultural fusions. He told Jaswant Singh—a courtly Rajput who was commissioned in the Indian army and served as India's defence, external affairs and finance minister before the Bharatiya Janata Party expelled him in August 2009 for not being sufficiently zealous in the cause of Hindu nationalism—that Singapore's survival depends on the equation between the two great civilizations whose symbolic confluence lay in Laos's mysterious Plain of Jars.[16] Atal Behari Vajpayee paid tribute to Singapore's 'energetic espousal' of India's dialogue with Asean.[17] Manmohan Singh admits that India's 'engagement with South-east Asia owes a great deal' to Singapore's support.[18] Pranab Mukherjee too acknowledges that Singapore is 'a strong partner and an enthusiastic advocate of India' and that 'its political and corporate leadership have engaged Indians across a very broad spectrum of issues.'[19] Singapore has been called a 'Mother Hen' promoting India in Asian affairs.

Nehru was Lee's political inspiration. Nehru visualized Singapore as the hub of a new Concert of Asia in which a regenerated India would be a vigorous player. Visiting Singapore in 1946, he prophetically told members of the Ee Hoe Hean Club, comprising Chinese millionaires, 'Singapore can well become the place where Asian unity is forged, for in the future the peoples of Asia must hold together for their own good, and for the good and freedom of the world.'[20]

****

This book describes in Lee's own words his fluctuating relationship with India—the journey from the sunlit peaks of hope into valleys of dark despair and, now, towards the radiance of a new dawn. Kamal Nath, now India's minister for road transport and highways, was a young man when he encountered Lee at the New Delhi Commonwealth summit in September 1983.[21] Having got to know him and Singapore since then, Nath sums up Lee's changing attitude: 'The difference between the acerbic and sharp speech from Prime Minister Lee Kuan Yew in his heyday [in 1983] and the fulsome confidence that this retired, wise statesman expresses for India today is the visible aspect of India's transition from its past to modern India.'[22]

Lee kept his Mission India to himself. He did not publicize the passionate interest that took him there year after year for three decades in search of economic space, political options and strategic support—pursuing and prodding the somnolent Indian giant to emerge from the ramparts of its South Asian bastion. Senior Singaporean officials were taken aback when I listed fourteen trips between 1959 and 2005. Even a minister who had to accompany him found the journeys as baffling as the Hindu god that keeps vigil outside his study in the Istana Negara Singapura—palace of the state of Singapore, the president of Singapore's official residence, where Lee has his office. Hardly anyone knew that on his first visit to China in 1976, he snubbed Premier Hua Guo Feng by refusing to accept his gift of Neville Maxwell's controversial book, *India's China War*, which blames India for the 1962 Himalayan conflict. Lee thinks it a partisan account that tries to exonerate misguided belligerence.

The scanty literature on India–Singapore relations is severely academic and rarely ventures beyond economics or strategy. History and humanity play little part in these dissertations. The unsuspected vision that prompted Lee to seek invitations from successive Indian governments received even less attention. But Ong Keng Yong, a Singapore diplomat who witnessed the evolution of bilateral relations from the inside, put it in a nutshell, summing up the contributions that Lee and Goh made. The first chapter fleshes out his claim that 'the strategy was MM's. The stamina is SM's'. Ong also cites a perspicacious Westerner who drew a distinction between a 'racialist', someone who understands and appreciates ethnic differences, and a 'racist' who is driven only by prejudice.

Lee's geostrategic thinking was powerfully influenced by Kavalam Madhava Panikkar, the Indian historian and diplomatist who coined the term 'South-east Asia' for what had been known until then as Further India.[23] India was the first name that came to Lee's lips when he was asked about his infant republic's diplomatic relations on that historic day when he wrote to Shastri. He thought of India again the following year as soon as he learnt of Britain's planned force withdrawal from east of Suez, and flew to New Delhi to ask Indira Gandhi, who had succeeded Shastri, to become the new 'guardian' of South-east Asia.[24] As he confessed to the doyen of Indian industrialists, J.R.D. Tata, in a long recorded conversation on 18 May 1974 (but not published in Singapore until 1995), he had 'a selfish motive in wanting India to emerge as early as possible as a major economic power in world politics'.[25] If India did not 'emerge', Lee warned, Asia would be 'submerged'.[26] He based his case on Panikkar's thesis that 'the power which controls India can at all times control the East Indies' and must, therefore, play an active part in the ocean that bears her name.[27]

Indian officials and politicians confirm his regular refrain, 'Why is India holding back?' He grumbled about Indians living in a 'dream world'. He criticized India's politicians for pampering vested interests in the name of socialism. He blamed Indian bureaucrats for serving themselves at the cost of the nation. He saw the decline of Air India, once one of the world's finest carriers, as symptomatic of the Indian state. He said everything that many Indians grumbled about, and more. He stayed away for years. But he did not ever abandon the idea of India. The myth of his aversion to India is really a distillation of the Singaporean bias that is neatly captured in *Raffles Place Ragtime*, a novel by Philip Jeyaretnam, a second-generation Singaporean of Ceylon Tamil descent. When Connie, a Chinese Singaporean girl trying to recover from an unhappy love affair, says she might 'travel round India', her friend Audrey, also of the same ethnicity, replies, 'So dirty. You'll catch hepatitis.' The tone of media coverage did not help. India was not part of Singapore's general discourse, as China was.

The most conclusive evidence against Lee, apart from his rather austere manner, is that so little happened bilaterally during his thirty-one years as prime minister. There is no denying that every substantive development started only after he selected Goh to carry on his work. Though Lee Hsien Loong modestly disclaims credit, the relationship gathered further momentum after he took over, prompting irreverent Singaporean jokes about 'the Father, the Son and the Holy Goh'. Two perceptive local politicians, Shunmugam Jayakumar and George Yong-Boon Yeo, who can themselves claim considerable credit for furthering ties, advance the most convincing explanation for the breakthrough not taking place earlier. As Mukherjee says in his Foreword, it was like Henri Cartier-Bresson's inspired photography: there had to be a 'decisive moment' for an exhilarating union of local and global circumstances.

The Cold War was the global factor that ruled out an earlier reconciliation of local interests. Jayakumar, lawyer, diplomatist and deputy prime minister, stresses that Lee's personal interest in India and familiarity with her leaders were not matched by a 'convergence of strategic or economic interest between India and either Singapore or Asean.'[28] In other words, Lee was a man before his time. There could be no meeting ground at the national political level so long as India and Singapore belonged to different international camps. Despite India's commitment to Asia as reflected in the two epochal conferences in New Delhi that paved the road to Bandung, the Cold War forced her leaders to negotiate a delicate course between and with the superpowers. Only the concatenation of international events triggered by the end of the great global polarization made understanding possible. Lee's comparison of Indian recognition of Cambodia's Vietnam-backed Heng Samrin regime with Singapore's endorsement of the American invasion of Iraq acknowledges that both had to adjust to the superior force of international alignments.

As for local factors, George Yeo, who, like Lee, leavens politics with philosophy, identifies two equally significant reasons why the seed Lee sowed took so long to bear fruit. First, a 'fossilized' India saw no reason to undertake the domestic reforms without which there could be no meaningful relationship with a Singapore that rated economic vibrancy above all else. Second, India had to make the first move. 'If India turns inwards, we can wave, we can jump up and down, flash a light, but I don't think we'll receive much notice. It's only when India decides to look outwards, particularly when it looks eastwards, that Singapore comes into view.'[29]

India did that in July 1991 when Narasimha Rao and Manmohan Singh revolutionized national priorities. 'Let the world hear it loud and clear, India is now awake,' the finance minister proclaimed.[30] Lee heard, as he had heard Nehru's 'Tryst with Destiny' pledge forty-four years earlier, and was again enthralled. But he 'was already pretty elderly' he says, and 'didn't have the energy to go travelling'. 'So I said [to Goh] you chase it.'[31] Michael Leifer of the London School of Economics suggests that Goh also had personal reasons for responding to India's signal with his 1993 National Day Rally promise to spark 'a mild India fever'.

The partnership was still delayed because of a host of reasons. Despite her technical advance and huge market, India put off foreigners with what Lee calls her 'thicket of rules and regulations and bureaucracy'.[32] Mukherjee ('a very able fellow,' says Lee, 'I'm impressed with his intellect.')[33] has a psychological explanation. He says that centuries of foreign domination have left India with fear and suspicion of the rest of the world so that her quills bristle like a porcupine's when an outsider approaches.[34] While Indians conceived of international relations in terms of the brotherhood of man,

Singapore thought of foreign policy only as a business proposition. Lee's economic pragmatism clashed with India's socialist benevolence. His unabashed focus on wealth generation offended the Gandhian sense of virtuous poverty. Nehru's India firmly rejected notions of balance of power and spheres of influence that contradicted the idyllic vision of non-aligned brotherhood.

Moreover, the Asian role Lee outlined seemed unnecessary because, in her own estimation, India was always a world power. Indira Gandhi's favourite Peter Sellers line was a riposte from the comedy, *The Party*, where an Indian who is asked, 'Who do you think you are?' retorts, 'In India we don't think who we are, we know who we are.' India was so wrapped up in India, said John Gunther Dean, the German-born American ambassador, that foreigners were irrelevant. Singapore, groping in the Afro-Asian jungle, had little 'to bring to the table'.

****

Lee was not the first Singaporean leader to look to India. That credit goes to the first chief minister, David Saul Marshall, a Baghdadi Jew with family connections in India, who was described at a symposium on the centenary of his birth as 'Singapore's first nationalist'. Marshall famously declared in the mid-1950s that he would place himself 'at the feet of Mr Nehru' before demanding self-government from the British. But Lee tried to give the relationship a depth and weight that was without international precedent. His intimate knowledge of India's history, culture, political and social institutions, and of individual players like Indira Gandhi's planning minister, Asoka Mehta, gave him the confidence to try to change the ideological constraints to which he himself had once paid lip service. This is, therefore, as much a book about multiracial Singapore and the enigma that is Lee Kuan Yew as about India's domestic developments in which Lee took a keen and informed interest. India, Singapore and Lee are details of the larger motif of an evolving Concert of Asia shaped by internal impulses and external pressures.

The combination of India's reluctance to become involved and China's 'unstoppable' (Lee's word) rise prompted him to think in terms of a multi-power solution for Asia's security problem in which India would play a crucial part. K. Kesavapany referred to that goal in his Eminent Person's Lecture in New Delhi in March 2005 as the joint stake 'India and Singapore have in shaping the architecture of the new Asian regionalism.'[35] Even after helping India into Asean and the Asean Regional Forum, Singapore 'had to intervene', Lee says, to 'stop' China 'from hijacking the East Asia Summit' so that India was assured of her role there too.[36]

The mysterious bronze Nataraja, king of dance, outside Lee's door, is an apposite symbol of these complexities in a relationship that Yeo says is 'almost like a love affair'.[37] Even an old friend like Indian diplomat Thomas (Tom) Abraham assumed the image was another of those useless presents national leaders dump on each other. Few suspect that this depiction of Siva performing the *tandava nritya* or the Cosmic Dance of the Universe within a ring of fire has deliberately been placed there next to a boldly executed scroll by Zheng Bijian, friend and adviser of Hu Jintao and interpreter of China's 'peaceful rise'. Malacca-born Chingara Veetil Devan Nair, a trade unionist who became Singapore's third president and the first Indian in that position, bought the Nataraja when he lived in the Istana. In 1991, five years after Devan Nair's tempestuous exit, Lee had the figure moved to his anteroom.

Nataraja's religious significance cannot mean anything to an anglicized Chinese agnostic. Perhaps Lee likes the bronze just as a decorative piece. A Hindu deity amidst the Istana's Chinese scrolls and porcelain can also be a politically tactful gesture to the Indian element (8 per cent) in multiracial Singapore. It is especially meaningful to Tamils who dominate the Indian community (70 per cent) since this manifestation of Siva is identified with the tenth century Chola dynasty which emerged from Tamil Nadu's fertile Kaveri valley to leave a strong imprint on South-east Asia's life and culture. The Chola Nataraja is said to be the supreme statement of Hindu art.

Dare it be suggested that Lee's own achievement in fashioning a glittering modern metropolis out of a ramshackle colonial settlement without running water or electricity for most inhabitants, and where the people could only 'grow tapioca, make children and drink', may have looked like an earthly parallel of Siva's whirlwind dance to create the universe? 'We went through fire!' he says of the hazards the pioneers suffered. Nataraja's ring of flames could indicate just that.

A fifth possibility is that the image is a mute link with a man whose life and work were so closely connected with his but from whom he was rancorously estranged at the end. If so, it would suggest that the early associate who said there was not 'an ounce of sentiment' in Lee was mistaken. That was confirmed again in January 2008 by his whistle-stop trip to Jakarta to spend fifteen minutes at the dying Suharto's bedside.

Singapore's creator can be exasperatingly contrary, 'the most puzzling politician' Vernon Bartlett, the British socialist writer, had ever met.[38] When Lee denied being 'emotional' ('I do not usually cry, or tear my hair . . . '), he was obviously unaware of the number of times he has broken down and wept in public. It was especially ironic that he staked the claim vis-à-vis the utterly phlegmatic Nehru. Though Lee also declared more than once that independent Singapore would not need Gurkha troops, he could not forget their stoic march to prison in 1942. 'As a result, the Singapore government has employed a Gurkha company for its anti-riot police squad from the 1960s to this day.'[39]

The world knows Lee as the champion of Asian values. But to Harold Wilson's maverick foreign secretary, George Brown, Kuan Yew Lee, GCMG, CH (as an honorary knight he cannot use the 'Sir' prefix that other Grand Companions of the Most Distinguished Order of St. Michael and St. George can) was 'the best bloody Englishman east of Suez.'[40] Singaporean critics sometimes rudely apply to him the American-Chinese slang of 'banana' (yellow outside, white inside) which has given rise to the 'coconut' (brown outside, white inside) jibe for Westernized Indians. Yet, this supposed Englishman manqué astounded Commonwealth leaders by declaring that only two battalions and five divisions of Vietcong-style guerrillas could put down Ian Smith's white rebellion in Rhodesia, while India's Swaran Singh and Malaysia's Tengku Abdul Rahman were advocating talks with the rebels. Lee can criticize the United States as sharply as Indira Gandhi.

The ultimate paradox was the spectacle of a Chinese politician making overtures to China's rival, an unabashed capitalist playing footsie with strident socialists, an American ally cosying up to the Soviet Union's friends, a fervent democrat paying implicit tribute to

India's caste and class hierarchy. But, then, it would be idle to expect consistency from 'one of the few Confucian emperors to ever step down voluntarily.'[41] Tom Abraham quotes Ralph Waldo Emerson, 'A foolish consistency is the hobgoblin of little minds, adored by little statesmen and philosophers and divines. With consistency a great soul has simply nothing to do.'

****

The story falls into three phases. The first reaches back into the mists of antiquity. As Lee and his son repeat, the Lion City's Sanskrit name is a permanent reminder of India's *mission civilisatrice*. Lee Hsien Loong elaborates: 'Historically India has had an enormous influence on South-east Asia; economically, and culturally too. The Ramayana story is present all over South-east Asia in different versions. The civilizations in the region were really Indian in origin—Sri Vijaya, even the Majapahit empires, and along the Malay peninsula and Singapore too.'[42]

The second phase began in 1819 when Stamford Raffles arrived in the appropriately named *Indiana,* and continued to the mid-1960s. Singapore was administered from Calcutta between 1819 and 1867. History in the guise of Pax Britannica reinforced the eternity that is Suvarnabhumi. Lee says 'the underlying ties were of an enduring nature . . . We read similar books and shared similar thought processes . . .'[43]

Colonial rule gave ethnic Indians an edge over the majority Chinese in this second phase. Though demographic reality took over, laws and banks, Godrej cupboards and Usha fans, manhole covers from Calcutta and schoolmasters from Madras or Kerala kept alive the common heritage. Ng Pock Too, a smart globetrotting businessman who was a member of Parliament (MP) from the ruling People's Action Party (PAP), Lee's political secretary and a key player in Tata's pioneering Singapore venture, speaks with affection of the Malayali 'Mr Vincent' who taught him mathematics. An elderly Chinese Singaporean told me he saw *Mother India* nine times in the *kampong* (the semi-rural settlements in which poorer Malays and Chinese lived) of his youth. Those links fell out of fashion. A PAP MP offered a partial explanation from Lin Yu-tang's *My Country and My People*—'Some people even regard the Moon as more beautiful if you look at it from the West.'[44] But fashion also has logic. India lost out by failing to keep pace with the global best. She and her products were identified with Singapore's early poverty-stricken days. As India forges ahead again, her ties with prosperous Singapore, sitting astride the crossroads of Asian, indeed global, culture, as Nehru appreciated, are coming back to life.

Despite huge disparities of size, numbers and economic status, India and Singapore have much in common. Both are multiracial, multi-religious, multilingual secular democracies, members of the Commonwealth, non-aligned and G77 clubs. Singapore's first foreign minister, Sinnathamby Rajaratnam, remarked after a meeting with his Indian counterpart, Dinesh Singh, that there were no bilateral issues to sort out.[45] Everything they 'discussed related to other people's problems in whose making we played no part.' The downside of this 'happy state of affairs' was that there were no stakes either. Lee crusaded relentlessly to change that. In consequence, linkages range from Buddhism to banking, military to museums, terrorism control to technology transfer, investment to infrastructure, ports to piracy. Economic, strategic, social and cultural ties are developing so rapidly that no book can keep pace with them.

Common features and interests, and the absence of quarrels do not simplify the task of chronicling this third phase of a relationship that operates at many levels. Neither country is liberal about granting access to its archives. Because of the personal friendship between their leaders, many exchanges bypassed formal channels. Recollections can conflict and memory play tricks. One side's version is not always the other's. Even different people on the same side sometimes remember the same event differently. Inevitably, there are many grey areas, big and small, that lend themselves to conflicting interpretations— Singapore's response to India's Himalayan war; the Israeli connection; Asean's American provenance; Air India's role in setting up Singapore Airlines; or whether news of Pokhran I (India's first nuclear explosion in 1974) broke in Lee's office or the Mandarin Hotel, the list goes on. I have been given different versions of the meanings of even the defence and economic pacts that the two countries have signed.

Indians were baffled and disturbed by Goh's suspicions since Lee always described an Indian presence in South-east Asia as essential for the region's security and stability. A popular Indian fallacy is that India was the first country to recognize Singapore. Lee's conviction that China was Vajpayee's road to Damascus where he saw the light of liberalization is another puzzle. Lee's relationship with Indira Gandhi remains the ultimate enigma.

This book tries to steer through discrepancies and differences to recount how India and Singapore rediscovered each other in the endeavour to create a new Asia. Kunwar Natwar Singh's comment that India is pro-America because the children of eight out of ten Indian diplomats are studying or working in the United States is another way of repeating the famous claim by Thomas (Tip) O'Neill, speaker of the American House of Representatives, that all politics is local. So is all diplomacy. Singapore is fast becoming the new America for Indians, but with a difference. While only top-end professionals go to the United States, Indians from both extremes of the social spectrum can be found in Singapore. A later chapter describes how thousands of 'foreign workers' drawn by 'the scent of the S'pore dollar' as well as high-powered executives and consultants can in their different ways both strengthen and weaken the bond. Zheng Bijian's calligraphy in Lee's anteroom says it all: 'Raising one's head to view the vastness of the universe, lowering one's eyes to inspect the intricacies of things.'

****

The genesis of this project lies in the old *Straits Times* office on Kim Seng Road where I worked for most of the 1990s. Rummaging in the library one lazy afternoon, I came upon a speech Lee had made in 1959, when Singapore still saw itself as an organic part of Malaya. Inaugurating an exhibition of Moghul and Rajput miniatures organized by India's representative, S.K. Banerjee, Lee compared India's imprint in South-east Asia with Greek and Roman influence in Europe.[46] He thought that India's cultural heritage was still 'glowing like a jewel in Malayan folklore, language, customs, court rituals, dances and music', and should inspire scholars to rewrite history 'not in terms of Western empire builders, but from the standpoint of a Malayan nationalist'. It intrigued me that an ethnic Chinese born of immigrant stock, not a natural heir to the Suvarnabhumi tradition, should so ardently exalt a legacy that many South-east Asian leaders would rather forget. After meeting Nehru for the first time three years later, Lee paid enthusiastic tribute to India's 'machine age'—steel mills, giant hydroelectric projects and Five-Year Plans.

Compliments to India were so unusual in Singapore at that time, and local gossip so firmly branded Lee anti-Indian that my curiosity was aroused. I read many other speeches in the same vein that Lee had delivered all over the world, in Uppsala, Auckland and Lehigh universities, at the East-West Center in Honolulu, in London, Melbourne, Kuala Lumpur, New Delhi and, of course, Singapore. Apart from a reverence for Nehru, they expressed appreciation of India's ancient cultural roots, political stability, administrative efficiency and economic planning, as well as sympathetic understanding of the challenges India faced. Lee also paid Indian politicians compliments that sounded bizarre to an Indian ear. India was heir, for him, to an ancient civilization that continues to influence the contemporary world, even to the extent of explaining crucial differences between modern Malaysia and Indonesia. His expositions demonstrated a familiarity with India that no other foreigner can match. They also unfolded a vision of the future that draws sustenance from the past.

Some caveats must be entered. There are still problems of perception, more in Singapore than in India; and of indifference and suspicion, more in India than in Singapore. Lee Hsien Loong describes differences between India's central and state governments, between politicians and bureaucrats, between different arms of the same political party. In his view, West Bengal's chief minister, Buddhadeb Bhattacharya, 'says the right thing, but in Delhi, the Marxist party doesn't sing the same tune.'[47] Any disruption of the liberalization process would diminish India's attractiveness for Singapore; rationalization of a bureaucracy that, as a Singaporean investor found, never misses a chance of saying 'No', would facilitate cooperation. Finally, India needs a settled neighbourhood to live up to Lee's expectations. The Concert of Asia of his dreams will lack balance and harmony if a China that has twice in twenty years felt called upon to 'teach' a neighbouring country a lesson (to quote the imperious language of Chinese leaders) continues to see itself as more equal than others.

Assuming all goes well, two questions should be asked. First, where is the relationship heading? Second, what keeps it going? Some of the pioneers of India's Information Technology industry who have set up global disaster recovery centres in Singapore feel the island could be to India what Hong Kong is to China. That is another way of repeating Badr-ud-din Tyabji's proposal in 1954, when he was ambassador to Indonesia, that Indian diplomacy in South-east Asia should be managed from Singapore.[48] There is also Lee's standing invitation to India to treat Singapore as the hub of her interests and activities in the region. Recalling the many proposals for novel forms of cooperation floated over the years, one can only speculate on some unique and as yet undefined multi-sided association that cannot be confined in the straitjacket of foreign relations. It may be pertinent to note in this context that Jaswant Singh, with his passion for antiquity, reminds us that India has never had a sense of territory. She has always been a nation but not a state. 'You can't find a single map of India before British times.' Asia is for India a borderless world.[49]

As for the second question, it might well be asked, two prime ministers down the road in Singapore and five in India, whether Lee's love affair still sustains the relationship. Or fuelled by mutual self-interest, has it acquired a momentum of its own? Something of both, I would say. Singapore's substantial investments, whether of Temasek Holdings in ICICI Bank or CapitaLand's in Pantaloon, are, as Lee stresses, a vote of confidence in booming India. No outsider can assess the octogenarian Lee's reach within the government, but the evidence suggests that his vision still shapes official thinking. He attends every Cabinet meeting. In fact, the ground floor Cabinet room in the Istana, with its long board table, ranks of chairs and impassive Gurkha guard, provides the entrée to the lift that leads to Lee's suite. No one can tell how long his influence will continue before mortality introduces a new order, but so far, Singapore has not deviated from his blueprint. One remembers in this context his warning in 1988 that anyone who imagined he would go 'into permanent retirement really should have their heads examined.' The phenomenon of the Singaporean taxi driver whose garrulousness provides inquisitive foreigners with what sociologists call the 'Other' does not suggest that many people do. My wife and I were returning home late one night when the cabbie took the wrong exit. He promptly realized his mistake, braked, and backed out into the main road, saying, 'It's all right lah, Lee Kuan Yew sleeping now!'

Lee might have been unaware of that minor transgression but his two visits to India late in 2007 confirmed he definitely was not sleeping on a burgeoning relationship that seems likely to alter Asia's strategic contours.

{1}

'MM's Strategy, Goh Chok Tong's Stamina'

When Lee Kuan Yew met Rahul Gandhi for the first time, the veteran Singaporean told India's political fledgling, 'I knew your father, your grandmother and your great-grandfather!' Lee was eighty-three; Rahul thirty-six. History was repeating itself—almost—after a forty-three year interlude. 'Seventy-three-year old leader got on very well indeed with thirty-eight-year-old Kuan Yew, and Lee was shocked, pleasantly so, to discover how well Nehru had been briefed about Malaya and Singapore,' wrote Alex Josey, his British press officer who accompanied Lee and his ever-supportive wife, Kwa Geok Choo, on their first official trip to India in 1962.[1]

Unusual in global diplomacy, familial links are especially rare in Asia's volatile politics where leaders come and go like Monsoon storms. Lee is the exception in being able to count four generations of the Nehru–Gandhis as personal friends. Jawaharlal Nehru's India, blazing a political and economic trail from colonialism to self-sufficient Independence, occupied a central place in the vision of a renascent Asia that took him privately to Calcutta, Delhi and Agra three years before the 1962 visit. 'Amongst the politically aware—what were our models?' Lee asks forty-seven years after that first visit in 1959 and answers his own question: 'First, India and Indian nationalists, the Congress Party, and the writings of Nehru and people like Panikkar. We used to get all the books and pamphlets that came out.'[2]

His old friend and colleague, Maurice Baker, Singapore's first high commissioner to India, agrees. Born of an English father and Tamil mother, Baker was at school with Lee and a corporal in the wartime medical unit in which Lee served as a private. While studying in Britain in the 1950s he helped to found the Malayan Forum which catered to students from the entire Malay Peninsula including Singapore. 'India inspired us,' Baker says.[3] No wonder the colonial authorities refused to let him teach in any government institution on his return. They regarded him as a subversive.

Lee proudly reminds people how different colonial Singapore was from the spanking new city-state he created. A British politician called it 'a pestilential and immoral cesspool'. Despite a substantial number of Indian settlers, comprising about 7 per cent of the population, no Indian of any consequence spared Singapore a passing thought. Singapore's response was more complex. Lee, Baker and other veterans were obviously acutely aware of all that India had achieved and stood for. But they represented a dwindling minority as Singapore reinvented itself as the showpiece of Asia while India seemed to be grappling ineffectively with the age-old problems of poverty, disease and illiteracy.

The girl in Philip Jeyaretnam's novel mentioned in the Introduction reflected a point of view that drew as much on mainland China's traditional sense of superiority as the Singaporean Chinese attitude to local Indians. Chinese and Indians did not mix much, as visitors like Charles Freer Andrews, Gandhi's colleague whom Indians called 'Deenabandhu', friend of the poor, observed. Ironically and unfairly, Lee was identified with this exclusiveness. India was dirty, overcrowded and poor, Singapore's rundown Little India district writ large. Shashi Tharoor, the minister of state for external affairs, who represented the United Nations High Commission for Refugees in Singapore from 1981 to 1984, recalls that Singaporeans saw India 'as a country mired in despair and disrepair'.[4] Political analyst Kripa Sridharan holds media coverage (which means Singapore's flagship newspaper, the *Straits Times*) responsible for a perception that 'was negative on most counts'.[5] A 'less than complimentary press' was responsible for 'the generally poor opinion in Singapore of India's management of its economy and its inability to handle the various domestic crises that rocked it periodically.' India was of 'marginal utility to South-east Asia.'[6] As the next chapter shows, the colonial *Straits Times* had close links with British India. But Han Suyin thought the paper 'hates anything Asian'.⁷ After the paper passed into local hands, it either ignored India or despatched Asia's second-biggest country in a few quirky reports that provoked much gnashing of teeth and frustrated muttering. Some official nudging probably persuaded the *Straits Times* finally to post a correspondent in New Delhi in July 1999. Another three years elapsed before the paper discovered that India was in Asia and rearranged its foreign news pages accordingly. Both editorial decisions followed the government's revived pursuit of Lee's Mission India giving priority to Singapore's economic and strategic interests in India.

Trapped in their own cultural time warp of language, caste and class, Indian Singaporeans had to find space for themselves within these parameters set by the authorities and the Chinese majority. A prominent local businessman says in matter-of-fact tones that it was not socially acceptable to talk of holidaying at Kanyakumari or visiting the Tirupati temple, except perhaps among close intimates who were also, of course, Indian. When an Indian needed any kind of governmental help, he preferred to go to a Chinese MP rather than an Indian one. Chinese politicians were more responsive while Indian members of Lee's ruling People's Action Party tended to distance themselves from their compatriots. They were also usually in the forefront of publicly applauding China and denigrating India.

Some local Indians may genuinely have lost interest in India. Remembering the circumstances of their migration, others may have had no reason to look back with fondness. A few among the more successful were possibly apprehensive that tradition-bound India would not acknowledge the status they had achieved. Or like minorities the world over, they tried to adopt what they thought was the majority position. Whatever the reason, it was not uncommon to find Indian Singaporeans affecting an exaggerated version of the disregard for India of which Lee was accused. 'Indian culture, yes! Indian toilets, no!' exclaimed Devan Nair, echoing the impatience that marked the Jeyaretnam character.⁸ At the same time, Singapore's first Indian president saw no paradox in boasting of being steeped in India's twin traditions of revolution and philosophy. He claimed to have grown up in the ambience of Gandhi, Nehru and Rabindranath Tagore whom he called 'a poet of liberation'.⁹

Badr-ud-din Tyabji of the Indian Civil Service recalls an encounter with Rajabali Jumabhoy, a successful businessman of Kutchi origin, when he stopped by in Singapore in 1954 on his way to Jakarta to take up his post as India's ambassador. Jumabhoy had fled to Bombay during the Second World War and pulled strings there to become Tyabji's assistant in the wartime supplies office. Back in Singapore, he treated his former boss to a banquet that was so sumptuous as to be 'in rather bad taste'. When the patrician Tyabji 'commented on its extreme lavishness', Jumabhoy's 'complacent' reply was, 'You see sir, you only exist in India, we live in Singapore!'[10] Jumabhoy's slightly different version admits to telling Tyabji in Bombay that 'we live in Singapore and here Indians only exist' but claims that having sampled his hospitality, it was the ambassador who gushed, 'Mr Jumabhoy, you were right, you people live, we only exist in India.'[11]

The smugness is unmistakable in both accounts. Variations of it can still be found at all levels. India is the symbol of all that many members of the diaspora have risen above, and seek to both impress and disown. A young taxi driver rattled off in Singlish, the graphic local dialect, that he had written off the three houses he had inherited in Tamil Nadu because his 'mammy' had warned him his Indian relatives were so poor they would murder him if he tried to claim his inheritance. At a higher level, an ethnic Indian emissary sent to forage among British Indian archives did not hide his contempt for India's storage and research facilities. 'Any secondary school in Singapore is better equipped!'

But the discerning few at the top did not miss more fundamental similarities. In Singapore as in India, political emancipation did not mean a drastic transformation of state or society, as in China or Vietnam. The two Labour Front chief ministers who preceded Lee, David Saul Marshall and Lim Yew Hock, were as much children of empire as Gandhi or Nehru. Marshall and Lim governed Singapore from 1956 to 1959, when Lee became the first prime minister of a self-governing colony. It was the year in which Indira Gandhi, the Indian leader with whom Lee interacted most closely, made her political debut as president of India's ruling Congress Party and took her first step in the international arena as a member of the United Nations Educational, Scientific and Cultural Organization's executive board. Indira Gandhi's two stints as prime minister were from 1966 to 1977, and from 1980 to her assassination in 1984. Lee ruled without a break from 1959 to 1990 when he became Senior Minister, a title he held for fourteen years before designating himself Minister Mentor or MM in 2004.

Foreign policy in both countries was almost the monopoly of individual leaders. Like Lee, the three principal Indian players, Nehru, Indira Gandhi and P.V. Narasimha Rao, had a firm grasp of international affairs. Lee and Indira Gandhi shared a commitment to power, an almost brutal pragmatism and a fascination with mystic predictions of the future. Both dominated the scene around them. So much so that though lacking the alliterative resonance of the loyalist chant during the Emergency, 'Indira is India, India is Indira', it might be more accurate to recite 'Kuan Yew is Singapore, Singapore is Kuan Yew'. He is probably the world's only democratically elected leader who can boast, as France's Louis XIV is believed to have done, '*L'état c'est moi*' (I am the state). That, too, has an Indian parallel. It was only half in jest that British newspapers bestowed on Indira Gandhi the 'Empress of India' title invented for Queen Victoria.[12]

Brahmins, Officers and Gentlemen

Lee knows that people deny him any part in shaping the current close and growing ties between the two countries. But no one with experience of the Singapore system can doubt Ong Keng Yong's assessment that Lee laid the foundations of the relationship. As Singapore's high commissioner to India (1996–98) and Prime Minister Goh's press secretary (1998–2003) before becoming Asean's eleventh secretary-general, Ong closely observed and participated in the sudden dramatic upswing in a relationship that had remained static for decades before concluding that 'the strategy was MM's; the stamina Goh Chok Tong's'.[13] Whatever Lee's title, no significant move could have been made without discussion in Cabinet (of which he remains the most important member) or his express approval.

A Western newspaperman told Ong that Lee was 'a very good racialist'. Baffled, he asked if that meant racist. No, the journalist did not think Lee was a racist but repeated that he was a good racialist. 'He understands the reality, the differences between races, and can draw very clear lines,' explained the journalist. Lee 'is very acutely aware of racial differences' but is not swayed by them. 'I think he has strong views about certain specific instances of racial policy elsewhere,' Ong says, referring to Lee's distaste for South African apartheid and the white Rhodesian rebellion. 'But he is not the kind of guy who says these people are like that because they are non-Chinese or these people are better because they are Chinese.'[14] Baker, whose features betray his Indian blood, has something to say about that: when they were both students at Raffles College, the young Lee furiously took up cudgels because Baker was not allowed into a swimming pool open to Europeans and Chinese.[15] To complicate matters, the pool's manager was Lee's uncle.

But the stories still circulate. The one most often repeated is of Lee disqualifying a PAP loyalist, Suppiah Dhanabalan, as his successor on grounds of race. Dhanabalan, a banker who started with Singapore's Economic Development Board from 'the first day minus one' and was foreign minister from 1980 to 1988, became chairman of Temasek Holdings where Lee's daughter-in-law, Ho Ching, was managing director. He points out that what Lee actually said was that Singapore was not yet ready for an Indian prime minister. In the next breath Lee ruled out another Cabinet member, Ong Teng Cheong, for being too Chinese.[16] Lee also helped Shridath (Sonny) Ramphal, a Guyanese of Indian descent and one of his closest friends, get an extension as Commonwealth secretary-general.[17]

Lee grew up in a Singapore that was in microcosm the empire on which the sun was supposed never to set. Imbibing his knowledge and ideas about the brightest jewel in the imperial crown from British sources, he became remarkably well-informed about India's social structures and institutions. Her history, culture and politics excited his intellectual curiosity. Understandably, he emphasizes those factors—caste, martial races, regional stereotypes—that most intrigued the British. It is another matter that they are not the most relevant to contemporary India, and confuse outsiders who do not grasp the extent to which usage and convenience mutate theory. Lee even lapses into the archaic lingo of the Raj, incorrectly saying *punkhawallah*—a word and function that died out a century ago—for peon. No other foreign leader is as conversant with India, past and present. He is also the only Asian politician with whom Indians can chat without constraint. Shaped in the same crucible, he can say, 'It so happens that my political beliefs are fairly akin to India's and, therefore, I find the dialogue easy to maintain and we use the same vocabulary.'

As Lee noted, India offered lessons in combating colonialism and managing the transition. She was a model for domestic governance, economic development and foreign relations. Some of his early comments on Indian politics and politicians are generous by the stringent standards of India's own commentators. His appraisal of Congressmen is an example. 'Without them India would not have emerged the way it did,' he told the Malayan Forum in London in 1950, adding that 'a whole generation (of ordinary Congress workers) paid a very heavy price' for freedom: 'Without the countless unnamed Indian patriots who did their share in awakening a sense of national pride and dignity and independence, there could have been no Congress Party, no Gandhi, no Nehru and no Indian republic.'[18]

Lee was twenty-seven when he made that claim. Baker, who was in the chair that day, regards this as his first major political exposition. But Lee's sting was in the tail. 'Alas, they didn't deliver,' he laments of the Congress pioneers. 'They did not live up to the opportunities that could have been exploited.'[19] He is merciless with failure. But he respects the Hindu genius that inspired Suvarnabhumi. The modern Indian's DNA is the same, he says, as that of his ancestors, which is one reason why the democracy that has faltered and failed in so many parts of Asia flourishes in India. Asked where in the global hierarchy of talent he would place Indians, he replies without a moment's hesitation, 'I would say in your upper class, equal to any in the world.'[20] He might as well have said 'caste' as he talks enthusiastically about a faithful aide:

> I used to have a personal assistant. He was the son of the chief priest in a temple down the road, a very able man, didn't go to university because it was before his time. But apart from that, he was the equal of any other administrative officer. The things he could cope with! He was a Brahmin. Sankaran was his name. And when we went to India—we were staying at the

Rashtrapati Bhavan—the bearers immediately recognized him as a Brahmin, and he ordered them around. He spoke as a Brahmin. I suddenly saw a different Sankaran.[21]

Ayyavier Sankaran had grown up with a consciousness of his *dwija*, twice-born, identity since his father was a priest in the Thendayuthapani Temple in Tank Road with its two sanctum sanctorums. Non-Brahmin priests were allowed to worship in one but the other, where Sankaran's father served, was strictly only for the most exalted Brahmins. Recognizing no higher rank, Sankaran was not awed by the pink sandstone viceregal palace with 340 rooms that had become Rashtrapati Bhavan, the President of India's official residence: 'He told them, "Do this, do that, don't do this. I like my yoghurt this way and so on." I was most impressed because they recognized probably from his name and his bearing and his features that he was a Brahmin.'[22]

People who knew the modest Sankaran say no one was less likely to throw his weight around, though he was the only man who dared correct Lee's grammar and punctuation. Working for such an exacting master, and the long hours it entailed, reduced him to a nervous chain-smoking wreck. In his fondness for the man, however, Lee will not consider that Rashtrapati Bhavan flunkeys are too familiar with the currency of power to bother with traditional hierarchies and that they deferred to Sankaran only because of his master. Lee and his wife were among the first to reach the public housing estate flat when Sankaran died.

With his interest in caste and class, Lee at once identified a new Indian diplomat as a Brahmin from his name. Another diplomat's polish indicated the exclusive Doon School in Dehra Dun town in the Himalayan foothills where Indira Gandhi sent her sons. A successful Bengali barrister who himself went to public school in England, as did his two sons, founded Doon so that later generations of upper class Indians did not risk becoming deculturized in boarding schools abroad. Doon's first headmaster and his deputy, both British, were imported from Eton and Harrow. When the Sultan of Johor said his grandson was in Dehra Dun, Lee's immediate reply was, 'There is something unique about Dehra Dun. I have met a lot of people who are graduates of Dehra Dun, they are of a different calibre. I must visit the place one day.'[23] Though the Sultan meant Dehra Dun's Indian Military Academy where his grandson was a 'gentleman cadet' and Lee was thinking of Doon School, both had in mind the same Indianized version of England's officers-and-gentlemen ethic.

Democrat Who Could Have Been Dictator

Lee's perception of India through the prisms of caste and class was influenced by his veneration for her first prime minister. He admired Nehru for successfully adapting Westminster's noble principles to Asian reality. Nehru could rouse mobs like any demagogue but treated the protocols of governance with fastidious deference. His moneyed background, the ease with which he took to anti-colonial politics, his charisma, long-term vision and, most of all, the limitless power he epitomized but chose to rein in with self-imposed constitutional limitations still mesmerizes Lee. Nehru was a democrat who could have been a dictator, someone who would always win a popular mandate by a handsome majority which no other Asian leader could do. Lee thinks Mao Zedong would undoubtedly have lost his deposit if he ever gambled on an election.

Clearly, this admiration held a strong element of self-identification. The anglicized Brahmin, the socialist educated at Harrow and Cambridge, bristled with as many contradictions as Lee himself. He had 'dipped into' all Nehru's books: 'When I read Nehru—and I read a lot of Nehru—I understood him when he said: "I cry when I think that I cannot speak my own mother tongue as well as I can speak the English language."'[24]

It was a sore point with Lee even in 2007 that he could read the English translation of Chinese Chairman Hu Jintao's speech on relations with Japan more easily than the original.[25] He must have squirmed when his Chinese-educated opponent from Tanjong Pagar constituency challenged him to a debate in Mandarin during the general election of 1955 which marked the beginning of serious politics. Later, in the Assembly, when he translated 'Independent' (for a non-party MP) as '*wu tang wu pai*' (literally, no party, no faction), another MP yelled, 'Nonsense! Go and learn some more Chinese.'[26]

Nehru had struggled with a similar disadvantage. So much so that Jaswant Singh says he was utterly confused by a letter Nehru wrote in Hindi to his young daughter:

> I wondered whether it was the child that had written to the father or the father to the child! It's astonishing how childish were Nehru's writing, script and indeed his use of Hindi words. I believe nothing Indian infused his spirit with the result that he always looked West.[27]

Lee's admiration for Nehru turned to awe when Devan Nair told him that come election time even Communist trade unionists voted for the Congress. It was proof of a prestige that transcended party labels to embrace the entire nation. As a Cambridge undergraduate Lee was struck by journalist Patrick O'Donovan's argument in Britain's *Observer* newspaper that Asians who studied in the West were 'emotionally and psychologically unprepared for independence and what it entails, and therefore it (the leadership) has to go to the next generation.'[28] It was a perceptive comment, Lee says, harking back to the great caste divide in all colonial societies between the 'England-returned' and those who went through the mill of school and college at home: 'The common man in Malaya rightly or wrongly associates intelligence and ability with an education in England, perhaps for the reason that such an education makes possible a greater and more rapid acquisition of wealth in British Malaya.'[29]

What counted even more than money was the glamour of the metropole that enveloped 'The Returned Student', the title of Lee's talk to the Malayan Forum. He understood the social significance of a phenomenon that gave rise to much jealous mockery in India where *belait-pherat* (England-returned in Bengali) sahibs were the secretly-envied butt of countless jokes. Similarly, the Chinese play, *The Peking Man*, was 'a satire on the returned student who was so well educated that he could not adjust' to China's social revolution.[30]

The Chinese were more honest than Indians in appreciating foreign training, witness the paper, 'The Influence of Foreign Educated students in China', that Sun Yat Sen's wife, Soong Ching Ling, wrote in 1911.[31] Deng Xiaoping's message that China would be transformed when thousands of Chinese students abroad returned home reiterated her conclusion. Lee told the Malayan Forum that returned students had already taken the lead 'in British-dominated India, Dutch-dominated Indonesia, and American-dominated Philippines'. They spearheaded national movements throughout Asia.[32] He listed Nehru (Harrow and Cambridge), Burma's Thakin Nu (also Cambridge), Liaquat Ali Khan of Pakistan (Oxford) and Indonesia's Mohammed Hatta (University of Leyden). Even Ho Chi Minh saw the light in Paris.

The British wanted to hand over power to the Nehru generation which they had nurtured, not to nationalist movements gathering strength on the ground, but did not expect someone from Nehru's background to identify so completely with popular aspirations. Nehru's idealism shone all the brighter when contrasted with the manoeuvrings of Pakistan's founder, Mohammed Ali Jinnah, whose 'nationalism, or Muslim separatism' did not grow out of any nationalist feeling, and who did not even 'believe in an Islamic state'. Unlike Nehru, Jinnah was 'enthralled by the British'.[33] The tentativeness with which Lee offers his views—referring to Stanley Wolpert's *Jinnah of Pakistan*—contradicts his reputation for certitude.

Nehru and Jinnah went to England, he says, in the heyday of the Raj. But the empire was crumbling by the time it was his turn to make the pilgrimage. 'It died the day they lost Singapore. You can never erase that humiliation.' Baker recalls the whole island being shaken by a thunderous explosion when retreating British forces blew up the Causeway linking Malaya and Singapore. 'That is the end of the British empire!' Lee had exclaimed. They were in Raffles College and the British principal standing nearby pretended he had not heard.[34] 'But,' says Lee, 'the empire looked like lasting another few hundred years when Nehru was in England.'[35]

Sitting by the radio in his rooms in Fitzwilliam College, Lee listened spellbound as the eloquence of Nehru's 'Tryst with Destiny' speech rolled out through the ether. The evocative phrase caught his imagination and he has returned to it many times over the years. Some of the magic Nehru exercised on him on 15 August 1947—midnight in New Delhi but late the previous evening in England—lights up his features as Lee savours the phenomenon of an elitist mass leader. It is unfair to suggest the aphrodisiac of power was the only attraction. Or that he regarded himself, Nehru and Sukarno as an exclusive trio of first-generation Asian leaders. But yes, British education did create a special bond with Nehru. They had imbibed the best of colonial culture and turned it to patriotic service. They shared a great faith in Asia's future. Both men believed in the primacy of foreign policy. Both saw the one-man-one-vote mantra as the means to an end. The priorities that India's leader, also an ardent modernizer, professed, appealed to Lee, especially his declaration that 'without an economic content, democracy has no meaning.' Josey noted that Nehru

> . . . insisted that, in the final analysis, everything that stands in the way of achievement of economic democracy must be removed—removed in a friendly way; removed in a cooperative way; removed by state pressure; removed by law—because nothing should be allowed ultimately to come in the way of achieving that social objective.[36]

That exaltation of economic needs above political rights could be taken to lengths that would have distressed Nehru.

'Mister Panicky' Creates South-east Asia

Lee's other Indian inspiration, Kavalam Madhava Panikkar, was an erudite, Westernized Malayali nationalist whose Oxford tutor, the historian Arthur Hassall, thought he had 'never had a more brilliant student' in his long career teaching at Christ Church.[37] Nehru appointed him ambassador to China (1948–52), Egypt (1952–53) and France (1956–59). It was from Paris that he graciously accepted my invitation to cross the English Channel and be chief guest at a gathering of Indian students in a country house in the Derbyshire Dales. I remember him as a plump man with a touch of vitiligo, a little imperial and a fob chain looping across his waistcoat. Zhou En Lai summoned him on 3 October 1950 to warn that China would send troops to defend North Korea if United States—and not South Korean—forces crossed the Thirty-eighth Parallel. He might have succeeded in averting

Chinese involvement the Korean War if American officials had not dismissed the message and derided Panikkar as 'Mister Panicky'.

Panikkar coined the phrase South-east Asia for the scattering of British, Dutch, French and Portuguese colonies whose only common link was their Hindu heritage. Sinnathamby Rajaratnam, who became Singapore's culture minister in 1959, and first foreign minister on independence six years later, says the region was known 'as Further India, the Indian Archipelago, the Indies and Indo-China'. Lord Louis Mountbatten's South-east Asia Command came after Panikkar's book, *The Future of South-east Asia: An Indian View*, reinvented Suvarnabhumi in modern terminology. Russell H. Fifield, a key figure in the American strategic establishment who wrote extensively and with uncanny prescience on post-Second World War South-east Asia, acknowledged Panikkar's innovation. Fifield was a member of the faculty of the National War College and visiting research fellow at the Council on Foreign Relations. He thought Panikkar 'may have chosen the term South-east Asia instead of Further India in order to take into account the rising nationalism in the area and thus avoid the embarrassment to his country the term Further India might bring'.[38]

Panikkar looked to the past, ancient as well as colonial, to argue—the first historian to do so—that India and South-east Asia are 'connected integrally in their political, social and economic life.' The Second World War had confirmed that a region that borders China and links the Indian and Pacific oceans is essential to India's defence. If Rajendra Chola could cross the seas in the eleventh century to attack the Sri Vijaya kingdom in Sumatra and establish dominion over the Malayan peninsula, some ambitious South-east Asian potentate, or an outside power with a foothold in the region, could repeat the adventure in reverse. No wonder Whitehall saw the arc from Suez to Singapore as India's protective glacis. It treated the Indian Ocean like a 'British lake'. The tsunami that devastated hundreds of thousands of lives, from India's Coromandel Coast to Aceh in Indonesia, on Boxing Day of 2004, further underlined the Indian Ocean community's essential unity.

Lee appreciated Panikkar's concept of geopolitical security and agreed with his prediction that China would emerge as 'a first-class Asiatic power'.[39] What he liked most was the underlying nationalism, the conviction that while taking the best the West had to offer, Asia should make its own decisions. Panikkar

> ... espoused a point of view which I shared at that time. An Afro-Asian point of view, that we have to assert ourselves, that we have a history, we have a culture, we are not monkeys come down from the trees, which is what the British and the French thought we were, treated us as if we were.[40]

And so he inflicted lengthy extracts from Panikkar's ruminations on imperialism and governance on bemused Singapore legislators. White supremacism notwithstanding, the ICS, the heaven-born service as it was called ('an Indian had to be outstanding to be admitted into this elite British service', Lee says), had established a reputable and responsible mandarinate. Its excellence had to be extolled for the benefit of bored PAP radicals, 'Chinese-educated pro-Communists', before they hived off in 1961 to form the Barisan Socialis (Socialist Front). In Lee's words, 'They were not interested in India, they were interested [only] in the great deeds of China, the new revolutionary China.'[41]

Even Lee felt the war and Britain's humiliation in South-east Asia had overtaken some of Panikkar's ideas. But he sought an alliance with India because like Panikkar, he saw India playing a crucial part in the Concert of Asia.

No Time for Netaji

The one prominent Indian for whom Lee has no time was the only one who soared physically into his horizon and may thus have been an unlikely and unwitting catalyst for his interest in India. Though Lee did not know it, Subhas Chandra Bose, Netaji (Respected Leader) to millions of Indians at home and throughout the diaspora, had another claim on his attention: he was one of a handful of Indians to qualify for the charmed ranks of the ICS but threw it away for a cause.

As a boy Lee had little personal contact with Indians. Those he met later at Cambridge were too absorbed in their country's newly acquired independence to bother with a Chinese Malayan still chafing under colonial rule. But he had already experienced the flamboyant Netaji legend that touched the hearts and minds of Indians in Singapore and Malaya who called their sons 'Chandra Bose' and reiterated the Indian National Army's rallying cry of 'Blood! Blood! Blood!' Lee was nineteen when Bose proclaimed the Azad Hind (Free India) government in Singapore's Cathay Cinema and reorganized the men and women fighters for whom the city was going to be the launching pad for Asia's deliverance from colonialism: 'I watched him parading on this little field opposite what is now our museum—St. Joseph's Institution. There was an open field, and he used to march back and forth with the Rani of Jhansi regiment . . .'

He remembers the parades and Lakshmi Sahgal but felt that INA recruits who had been trained by the British and sworn fealty to the Raj switched sides only for personal gain.

> The Japanese maltreated them as prisoners of war, and if you joined the Indian National Army, then you got all the rations and everything, you were part of the Greater East Asia Co-Prosperity Sphere. The Japanese said for political reasons, 'Right, if you join this then you get full rations.' So I was ambivalent.[42]

Lee admits that civilian recruits (President Sellappan Rama Nathan's brother and Dhanabalan's sister among them) were, indeed, fired by patriotism but 'the bulk was just the captured prisoners of war' who escaped the horrors of Japanese labour camps by throwing in their lot with Netaji.

Those turbulent years gave Singapore two memorials without any equivalent in India. One is a life-size figure of General Kodandera Subayya (Timmy) Thimayya in the tableau depicting Mountbatten and his colleagues accepting the surrender of General Seishiro Itagaki, representing Field Marshal Count Hisaichi Terauchi, who had suffered a stroke. The actual ceremony was in City Hall but the twenty-seven waxworks are now in the air-conditioned glass-sided Surrender Chamber in the Sentosa island resort. The other is the National Heritage Board's plaque on the Esplanade, across the Padang from

City Hall, marking the site of the monument to fallen INA soldiers. Bose laid the foundation stone but Mountbatten had the monument blown up when the British recaptured Singapore.

As a cable editor in the Japanese propaganda office on the top floor of the Cathay Building, Lee tracked the course of the war and the Japanese advance through Burma to Imphal and Kohima in India. He did not think they were going to make it 'because the logistics were too stretched, the railway was too tenuous, and the Japanese ships were being sunk.' The pessimism of all those years ago surged back when Nathan lent him *Breakthrough in Burma: Memoirs of a Revolution, 1939–1946*. Ba Maw, the author, was a colourful figure whose dedication to Asian liberation has not received adequate recognition. The son of an official at the royal court of Mandalay, he studied at the Calcutta and Cambridge universities and was called to the Bar from Gray's Inn. His unique distinction was to have been prime minister under both the British and the Japanese. 'Bose was a man you could not forget once you knew him; his greatness was manifest,' wrote Ba Maw. He saw Netaji as the real author of India's independence. 'Only the usual thing happened: one man sowed and others reaped after him.'[43]

Bose's ill-starred career held a warning for Lee about methods and allies. It was the Japanese he doubted.

> They dominated the place, they made no bones about it, that 'We are the masters.' I never doubted that Bose was a patriot, but what could he do? That was what the Japanese offered him. He was like De Gaulle under British and American patronage. De Gaulle chafed but the Americans wisely allowed him to enter Paris.[44]

INA troops wanted to be on the front line which would have embarrassed the British Indian army. 'But the Japanese never allowed that.' Japan's 'intention was to be the boss, remain the boss.'[45] A reassessment was to wait more than sixty years when George Yeo, Singapore's fifth foreign minister, announced that he and Pranab Mukherjee, then his Indian counterpart but now finance minister, had discussed 'the formation of a group to study, in a contemporary context, the heritage of Bose and the Indian National Army in Singapore'.[46]

Sixteen Visits to India

Lee 'understood India's potential importance before we did' says Jagat Mehta, a former British public schoolboy who headed India's foreign office from 1976 to 1979.[47] 'Our main drawback was our preoccupation with Pakistan.'[48] The mystery is that Lee took so few Singaporeans into confidence over his Mission India. Diplomats had instructions to send him any literature they could find on India's politics and economics but no one outside the MFA, Singapore's ministry of foreign affairs, knew this. J.Y. (Joe) Pillay, a civil servant whom Lee regarded as the 'equal of the best brains in America', says Lee's repeated visits to India 'didn't register!'[49] Dhanabalan, who could not help but know since he accompanied Lee several times, could not understand the reason for the trips. 'It was always a bit of a puzzle to me,' he says.[50] Only Nathan, second of the two Indians to become Singapore's president, had some understanding of Lee's interest. A Colombo Plan award to study ports and seamen's welfare services took him to India for the first time in 1957; subsequently, Nathan did his best in his various incarnations in the defence and foreign ministries, as head of intelligence, and Singapore's representative in Malaysia and the United States, to further the connection. Few others were as sympathetic or even as perspicacious.

Since prime ministers don't drop in informally on each other, there was always an official invitation. But Lee has no qualms about admitting he sought them: 'I was interested to see how India was progressing. In the old days I used to travel a lot to Europe, so on the way to Europe, I would drop by. Or on my way to Africa I would drop by to see how India was progressing. I'd get a few lessons. I would pick up points.'[51]

He told Jaswant Singh the visits were always instructive. 'He said, "I was learning from India, you had so much talent. I also came to tell you that you had so much to teach me. Your officers taught me so much. I would take them out to golf and talking to them was a great help for me." He spoke glowingly of K.B. Lal and other senior civil servants.'[52] The absence of reciprocation did not worry Lee. 'You are a big country preoccupied with so many problems. I was always well received. I had access to all your leaders.'[53]

The journeys were reported discreetly for the *Straits Times* did not in those days splash the travels of the great across the front page, certainly not to countries of little consequence. Nor did it routinely reprint their speeches as special articles. Lee's tours were such low-key affairs that All India Radio's Deepankar Mukhopadhyay thought in 1988 he was going officially for the first time. Lee corrected him with a gentleness that Singaporeans would call uncharacteristic. True, the last official visit was a decade earlier, but Commonwealth conferences had taken him to India in 1980 and 1983. And the year 1962 saw him twice in New Delhi.

Even High Commissioner Baker overlooked the second visit.[54] Lee, too, is hazy. Asked if he went back that year he blurts out an emphatic, 'No, I did not!' Then, after a pause, 'Ah... Oh yes, I did!' He is vague about the month, remembering only that he flew Air India from Moscow and that it must have been before November when it would have been 'beastly cold'.[55] Actually, it was late September; Lee's memoirs mention the furore his Soviet trip on the eve of merger with Malaya caused in Kuala Lumpur, but not the detour to New Delhi on the way back. Confusion about his itinerary is excusable, for who would expect tours of seventeen African countries or of five in Europe to terminate in India? New Delhi might be a natural stop after Rangoon or en route to London, but Lee also found himself there when returning from Cairo and on his way to Lusaka. India's capital was the new Rome to which all roads led.

Probably only two cabinet colleagues—Goh Keng Swee and Rajaratnam—came close to understanding this interest. With Lee and Toh Chin Chye they comprised the Gang of Four that founded the PAP. Neither man owed his awareness of India to his prime minister. Dr Goh had been friendly at the London School of Economics with Freddie A. Mehta, a fierce free marketer who rose high in Tatas, one of India's largest business houses. 'Goh Keng Swee was very interested in India,' says Lee.[56] On Nathan's recommendation Dr. Goh invited Manoj Das, a teacher in the Sri

Aurobindo Ashram in Pondicherry, to work on a new school textbook on Hinduism. Das 'was amazed by GKS's detailed knowledge of the Ramayana and the Mahabharata.'[57]

As finance minister, Dr Goh, who was much taken with India's Five-Year Plans, lauded India's efforts 'to lift her citizens from age-old and dire poverty' two years before Lee's first official visit to New Delhi. Indians would have been gratified to know that the man who pioneered Singapore's industrialization held up their country as an example for Asia. Reviewing regional economic developments in his 1960 budget statement, Dr Goh eulogized India's massive Five-Year Plans, financial allocations, large new industries and extensive community development schemes. Though other Asian countries also accepted the overriding importance of economic development as a national objective, few had achieved 'the success in planning and execution that India has.'[58] Alas, roles were soon to be reversed.

Rajaratnam's response was more complicated, as was to be expected of a Jaffna Tamil from Sri Lanka (Singapore counts them as Indian) who had spent thirteen years in London where he 'fervently attended' meetings of the Fabian Society and Left Book Club (the Hampstead branch naturally!) which Indira Gandhi and her circle also patronized. Rajaratnam hobnobbed with intellectuals like Kingsley Martin, the celebrated *New Statesman* editor, and Harold Laski whose impact on an independent India supposedly prompted an Indian prime minister to remark that 'there is a vacant chair at every Cabinet meeting reserved for the ghost of Professor Laski'. Rajaratnam claimed as gurus fashionable fellow-travelling Indians like the novelist, Mulk Raj Anand, and Nehru's protégé, the gadfly V.K. Krishna Menon who was 'in manners far more English than any Englishman'.[59]

The kinship was of the spirit. Rajaratnam's comment, 'I don't care if you call me an Indian or an Eskimo', rejected ethnicity. He gloried in the non-denominational ideal of 'one united people, regardless of race, language or religion' enshrined in the Singapore Pledge he had crafted. Like many subcontinental emigrants, he had no yearning for all that Lee was enjoying discovering. 'If there is such a thing as a Singapore identity, the British journalist, Ian Buruma, says, 'Raja' is its author.'

Politics but Never Business

Dhanabalan was surprised that Lee met no businessmen on his Indian journeys, especially since Dr Goh had told him of India's sizeable industries. 'They came here,' Lee explains. Jehangir Ratanji Dadabhoy Tata—JRD—head of Tatas, was a frequent visitor. So were Ashok and Aditya Birla, representing a politically powerful clan with 560 industrial units in India. Yogendra Mafatlal, who sprinkled crushed tulsi into his Scotch to purify it, and the members of the Godrej clan, whose manufacturing empire dated back to 1897, also came. These were courtesy calls. Lee's dialogue was with India's political leaders and they were tête-à-tête, *empat mata,* Malay for what intelligence-speak calls 'four-eyes only'.

Lee has known most of India's twelve prime ministers since Nehru, from the austere Morarji Desai to 'calm and quiet' Atal Behari Vajpayee who 'seemed to be just presiding but was setting a firm direction', according to Lee's son, Prime Minister Lee Hsien Loong.[60] Though Lal Bahadur Shastri was only a ship that passed in the night, Singaporeans have good reason not to forget Nehru's diminutive successor. Lee hailed Narasimha Rao as India's Deng Xiaoping, founder of modern China, and quotes Inder Kumar Gujral on corruption. Manmohan Singh became and remains a special favourite. Outside their ranks, young Rahul, his guest in Singapore in November 2006, boasts he 'could have been PM at twenty-five if [he] wanted to.'[61]

Hardly any state business was transacted on Lee's trips though he sometimes briefed his Cabinet afterwards or circulated a summary of his impressions. The governmental apparatus on either side was not usually involved beyond the demands of protocol. The tours looked like relaxed holidays. He went sightseeing and played golf, though never, alas, in Kashmir where the ball flies so high, he says, eyes sparkling as he throws up an arm, it's lost in the snowline. The unfulfilled ambition, nursed since before he set foot in India, was abandoned when a frozen shoulder forced him to give up the game. Pilgrimages to the temples of modern India—Bangalore's watch factory and the Okhla industrial estate near Delhi—were more duty than pleasure.

In this third phase of the relationship, India was becoming less attractive technologically for worldly Singaporeans. There was no dismissal, however, of India's past. Lee recognized Indian, especially Hindu, civilization as the creation of people with considerable talent, a capacity for organization and administration, and the ability to sustain cultivated living over long periods of time. Indians would not have been able to foster music, literature, painting, sculpture and architecture without surplus agricultural and pastoral production.

The genius expressed in solid granite chiselled and carved into the Ellora caves near Aurangabad in the sixth to seventh centuries, the temples of Mahabalipuram near Madras in the seventh and eighth centuries, or more recent, in the seventeenth century under the Mogul emperor Shah Jehan, the Taj Mahal, these monuments surpass any architecture of the same period in the West.[62]

Khajuraho's erotic sculptures may have shocked 'the last Victorian' as he calls himself but Lee sounded wistful as he admitted, 'I come from a nation which, by Asian standards, has a very short history, just over 150 years. We have no ancient monuments, temples and other glorious antiquities. As a result, we are only too eager to innovate and even to change our way of life.'[63] Was it boast or lament? He felt that the lack of historical baggage could be dangerous because 'there is not the assurance of a long and splendid history to provide the confidence that destiny is on our side in coping with the next ominous crisis.'[64] He recalled Tagore's 'tear drop on the cheek of infinity' at the Taj Mahal. As he said in his 1970 Dillingham Lecture at the East-West Center, 'in modern times, the poetry of Tagore bears witness to Bengali artistry in both English and Bengali, whilst India was still under the British Raj.'

Bengalis, from Tagore and the first Lord Sinha (Satyaprasanna Sinha, Baron Sinha of Raipur, the only non-white hereditary peer and member of Britain's 1914–18 wartime Cabinet) to Amartya Sen and Pranab Mukherjee, fascinate him. 'Why are Bengalis the brightest chaps in India?' he asked when I called on him at the Istana for the first time on 4 August 2005. His law firm had a Jewish client litigating against another branch of the family in Calcutta and the latter often brought Bengali lawyers with 'great stacks of books', always chasing up new authorities as new arguments came up. Lee found them very capable: 'They are the tops.'⁶⁵

> Bengalis are the best for words; the facility to put ideas into words. That's a very important gift. That is a special part of the brain according to neurologists. The Chinese are poor at that. When they do this SAT test, our students score very high in mathematical and numerical tests but on the literary side they cannot rival the Indians who always score higher. It is just a natural facility.

In law, the Chinese prefer corporate work while Indians are the best litigators. It just happens that way, he says, demolishing popular suspicions of academic manipulation to discourage Indian Singaporeans from reading law: 'The strange thing is that for one Indian graduate in law there are about eight or ten Chinese graduates. Yet, our top litigators are Indians. I think it is a genetic trait.'⁶⁶

How Did the Hindus Do It Without Air Conditioning?

Seeing Singapore as 'a parvenu society consisting mainly of migrants', Lee went to great lengths to claim an Indian lineage by way of Malaya:

> When future generations write the history of Malaya and Malayan culture, they will have a difficult task tracing the many fine threads that go to make its fabric. But we should have no difficulty in recognizing one of these strands. It is not only the oldest of our cultural strands but also the longest, the most illustrious, that which leads to India.⁶⁷

The official style for Singapore's prime minister—*perdana menteri* (India's *pradhan mantri*)—could have been plucked out of one of the royal courts of Suvarnabhumi. But other regional leaders deny the heritage or claim it as their own. In a conversation with this writer in Bangkok's Chitralda Palace, Thailand's Princess Maha Chakri Sirindhorn, with a degree in Oriental epigraphy, learned in Sanskrit and Pali, and a regular and friendly visitor to India, warned that South-east Asia prefers the neutral 'Indic' adjective to Indian. Many Thais probably believe the Buddha was born in the kingdom that has reinvented itself as Ayodhya and its monarch as the Hindu god-king Rama.[68] Her father, King Bhumibol Adulyadej, is King Rama IX.

Malaysia's Hindu past marches with the present. The *Sejarah Melayu* (Malay Annals) traces the ancestry of the country's nine sultans through Malacca's Iskandar Shah, previously Singapore's Sri Tri Buana, to Raja Chulan of Kalinga whom some scholars identify with Rajendra Chola. According to one writer, '*All* the Malay sultans are descended from Indian Muslims'.[69] That makes them Klings, a controversial term of which more in the next chapter. The ancestors of the Sultan of Johor—'His Majesty Sultan Iskandar Ibni Almarhum Sultan Ismail, Sultan and Sovereign Ruler of the State and Sovereign Territories of Johor Darul Ta'zin'—bore the simpler Hindu title of Maharajah of Johore until 1885. The first eight rulers of Kedah, which claims to be one of the oldest extant states in the world with the world's second longest reigning dynasty, were styled maharajah. A Muslim raja still reigns in Perlis.[70] Many court rituals are identifiably Brahmanic.

This Hindu ancestry leaps out at Bujang, a fourth century trading and migration port within sailing distance of India, where more than fifty temple ruins were excavated in the 1930s. But an American writer who visited the site in 2000 felt that the Hindu past had been so downplayed and even denigrated that an Indian 'visiting the Bujang Valley might come away feeling demeaned rather than proud—and that would be no accident.'[71]

Malaysia, 'going green', in Lee's words, might downplay Hindu artefacts but cannot exorcize the living evidence since 'for more than 2000 years, words of Indian origin have been insinuating themselves into the Malay language.'[72] Some 40 per cent of Malay words are so derived.[73] Not words alone but ideas, institutions and political concepts like *bumiputera* (from the Sanskrit *bhumiputra*, son of the soil) on which Malaysia stakes its existence. Even Islam came with thirteenth century Indian merchants, mariners and maulvis.

If Malaysia belittles the past, Muslim Indonesia has thoroughly internalized the Ramayana through its *wayang kulit* puppeteers. A story goes that a visiting Indian dignitary was asked after a performance, 'I believe you have something like it in your country too?' Sukarno's folie de grandeur exploited the past, claiming the Sri Vijaya empire as the first Negara Indonesia, state of Indonesia. Lee had no time for such pretensions and told a seminar at the University of Singapore 'that it was really Hindu culture and civilization that made these (empires) possible.' He returned to the theme at New Zealand's Canterbury University, saying that though the Indonesian archipelago had enjoyed 'periods of greatness when the Hindus came in the seventh and again in the twelfth centuries,' the ruins of Borobodur suggest that 'a people (who are) primarily self-indulgent' could not maintain their heritage.[74] Especially in Indonesia's humid heat. He had found it difficult enough running his lawyer's office when only the partners sat in air-conditioned comfort. Recalling the hubbub, the dust, the heat and the mistakes people made in the humid afternoons, Lee, who calls air-conditioning the twentieth century's most significant invention, is amazed at what the Hindu pioneers achieved without it. As a young legislator he installed an air-conditioner in his car at his own expense because it 'helps in clear thinking'.[75]

He maintains there would have been no modern Singapore without air-conditioning: 'You cannot work if you have to worry about your papers flying away. We cannot do the computer chips and biotechnology and so on with the fans blowing and high humidity. It's not possible, and in the afternoon after lunch you need to rest. It's not dry heat like in Delhi. It's moist heat,very trying.'[76]

But not only did the Hindu pioneers manage, they left behind a legacy that saves present-day Indonesia from being caught up in religious extremism like the Achinese or the fundamentalism that Malaysia's Parti Islam SeMalaysia peddles: banning yoga and chopsticks as un-Islamic. The 'underpinning of Buddhism and Hinduism gives Indonesians, particularly the Javanese, a certain balance, a certain ability to resist the inclination to extremism' that is evident in Malaysia.[77] Lee contrasts political styles. Election rallies are solemn affairs in Malaysia 'starting with a prayer, the blessings of God, and so on.' But in Indonesia, the campaign is still fun with attractive girls in T-shirts and jeans playing the guitar and singing. 'I am not sure whether it will continue though I think the chances are that it will. It's a different culture that must upset all the orthodox Muslim radicals.'[78] Lee repeats that 'as a people the Javanese are not easily attracted to extremism.' The terrorists who killed more than 200 people in a Bali discotheque in 2002 and exploded bombs in Jakarta were foreigners who corrupted some locals: 'You look at Bali! It is a completely different culture. The Balinese were not responsible for the bombings. It was a Javanese who had been trained by people like Abu Bakr Bashir whose DNA is Arab.'[79]

If Jemayat Islamiyah leaders of Middle Eastern origin are Indonesia's Islamic future, Bali is its Hindu past.

Travelling in India, Lee constantly searched for contrasts and complementarities that might be useful to Singapore. No detail was too petty to engage him. How did the woman hawker in Calcutta make a living with so few mangoes to sell? A cobbler's mess on a New Delhi pavement reminded him of Singapore's banished five foot-way (arcades) trades. The magnificent horses in the President's Bodyguard caught his fancy and there was talk of a cavalry regiment and ceremonial escort in Singapore. But why were the bodyguards, so resplendent in scarlet and gold when on duty, allowed to dry their underpants on clothes lines for every Rashtrapati Bhavan visitor to see?

Lee's knowledge of India came from such observations, not only official briefings. He watched changes, studied India's administration as well as administrators and asked searching questions. On a free evening he invited officials to his suite for a drink. Or he got up at dawn to play golf with India's champion golfers, diplomats and senior army and police officers. He did not ever miss an opportunity of developing contacts with people in responsible positions. Successive high commissioners record his readiness to meet with Indians of note passing through. They gave him a feel of India, past, present and future. He wanted information about economic plans and defence strategies. He probed how libraries and museums inherited from the British Raj were faring. And as always, he compared them with their counterparts in Singapore. It was all grist to his mill.

Nehru: Rule of Law and Rule of Life

In January 1959, two years after Nathan's visit, Lee was one of nearly 200 lawyers, judges and law professors from fifty-two countries who gathered in New Delhi for the Congress of the International

Commission of Jurists. The conference theme, Rule of Law in a Free Society, prompted Lee to wonder how the English rule of law with its stress on individual rights, liberties and freedom could operate within the context of the Asian revolution. He wanted to experience India. He was anxious to see and hear Nehru.

A British law professor at the University of Malaya led the delegation. Lee, his wife who was also trained in law, and a rising young Kuala Lumpur lawyer, Yong Pung How, who had been at Cambridge with them and later became Singapore's chief justice, were members. They flew to Rangoon and from there took the BOAC flight to Calcutta where they stayed at the Grand Hotel overlooking the Maidan. Wandering about British India's original capital, long reduced to provincial status, Lee was struck by the beautiful colonial architecture that 'deserved to be preserved'. He thought the buildings were built to last; they were 'well sited in historical parts of the city, and represented massive investment'. But Calcutta was teeming with people even then.

The group went to Delhi, took the night train to Agra where they saw the Taj Mahal by day and at night. Lee was impressed by everything. If Calcutta, Delhi and Agra were any indication, Nehru's India 'had the promise of a country that could grow'. The many British and American jurists he met, some of whom he knew already, 'were also optimistic about India'.

Lee found it curious that delegates from Asian countries where 'the rule of law has disappeared and where it is rule by the gun rather than rule of law' held forth most stridently on the rule of law. The *Straits Times* reported his views but he was then only 'a Singapore lawyer, Mr Lee Kuan Yew'.[80] He still sat on the Opposition benches. Hsien Loong, then aged seven, remembers his parents returning with a model of the Taj Mahal, 'a beautiful white marble miniature, little thing with coloured stones, and a guide book telling all the cities and places in India which I pored through'. The little boy 'didn't have any feel for the place but was fascinated'.[81] His own visit to India thirty-three years later as deputy prime minister set the ball rolling for the current series of high-powered exchanges.

In New Delhi Lee at last saw and heard the man who had captured his imagination: 'Nehru, he came in your Hindustan, the Morris Minor, no Morris Oxford, which really symbolized his modesty, and the realistic targets that he set for India at that time. And as he usually does, he spoke off the cuff, a philosophical speech, coherent.'[82]

Lee told Inche Baharuddin of the Malay newspaper *Utusan Melayu* that everyone had agreed that the law must change with changing societal conditions because, 'as Jawaharlal Nehru said at the inaugural meeting, the rule of law must conform to the rule of life.' It was a portentous comment. Looking back, he reflects on Nehru, 'I liked his style, I liked his sentiments. He resonated with me.'[83]

{2}

Chinatown Spelt 'Singapur'

Despite its geographical location at the tip of Malaya, historical links with Britain and an overwhelming Chinese majority, Singapore 'grew up in the image of Calcutta'.[1] The Indian association was so strong that when Peter Chan Jer Hing was posted in the Singapore high commission in New Delhi in the early 1970s he received letters from simple Indians who spelt 'Singapur' like Kanpur, Udaipur or any other town in India.[2] Indians have a sense of eternity but not history, says Lee's old associate, Natwar Singh, diplomat and politician, whose Kunwar prefix speaks of his lordly lineage. And so they looked beyond the recent connection to Suvarnabhumi which gave Singapore its name. The willing retention of the name was, in Rajaratnam's view, the 'best tribute' Chinese Singapore could 'pay to India and her civilization'.[3] He might have mentioned another Lion City (Simhapura), capital of the Hindu kingdom of Champa that flourished between the seventh and fifteenth centuries, now lost under a Catholic church in the provincial bustle of Tra Kieu in central Vietnam. Stranded in an Islamic sea after the tide of Indian culture receded from the Malayan peninsula, Singapore might also have been obliterated but for British rule followed by the Chinese energy and initiative that became the economy's driving force.[4]

The British treated Singapore as a fragment of the Bengal Presidency, the human capital of thousands of Indians who went there under British aegis sustaining a sense of familiarity. A 'wizened and white-haired' ancient, who claimed to be 102 years old, the son of an early convict, proved Natwar Singh's point when David Marshall was threatening to resign as chief minister if Britain did not grant Singapore independence. The old man pleaded with him to stay on. 'Indians built up Singapore and it belongs to Indians,' he said. 'As a descendant of our race, you should not resign!'[5] The emotional and excitable Marshall was not Indian though his folk 'were an extension of the long-established Jewish community in Calcutta'.[6] Nor did Indians build Singapore except in the strictly literal sense of convicts from the former penal settlement of Bencoolen (transferred to the Dutch in 1824) shovelling brick and mortar to erect the Istana, St. Andrew's Cathedral and several Hindu temples. But the Indian presence was so vibrant until Singapore became independent that the feeling persisted that it was part of British India.

Indifference to history may explain the agitation in the early 1920s to rename Kling Street, near Raffles Place, Chulia Street, as it is still called. Popular lore ascribed 'Kling' to the convict's clinking ball and chain, and Malays especially used it as a derogatory word for Indians (as indicated in the previous chapter). Chulia was seen as a neutral term for Tamils (for whom Raffles reserved that part of town) though few locals immediately recognized it as a corruption of Chola, the Tamil dynasty that ruled much of south India until the thirteenth century. It took a British reporter to argue that Kling 'was really a local name of great historical interest' derived from 'Kalinga, the ancient empire of southern India which had trading connections with the Malay peninsula and Java and Sumatra in the early centuries of the Christian era, and was the first to plant higher civilization in that region.'[7] Kalinga encompassed present-day Orissa on the Bay of Bengal.

The link is not forgotten, as Bijayananda (Biju) Patnaik, a flamboyant Orissa politician whom Nehru called 'India's Buccaneer', told me many years ago as we bowled along the Bay in his jeep. Driving from the pilot's cockpit seat he had installed behind the wheel because he felt more comfortable flying, Patnaik described the full moon festival when women set afloat oil lamps in hollowed-out plantain trunks symbolizing boats, singing to their menfolk as the twinkling lights fan out across the waters of the Bay of Bengal to bring back golden ornaments from Suvarnadwipa. As I will show in the next chapter, he played a heroic role in modern India's interaction with South-east Asia.

Eternity merges into modernity. Vivian Balakrishnan, a young Singapore doctor turned politician, quotes Confederation of Indian Industry president Anand Mahindra as saying that 'an Indian businessman coming to Singapore must be able to say, "I have seen the future, and it works."'[8] It is a future that grows out of the past which gives India what Lee calls 'a long view of history' and enables her to 'weather many a crisis with equanimity and quiet resolve'. In 1926, this 'long view' inspired Calcutta scholars like Ramesh Chandra Majumdar, Kalidas Nag and Suniti Kumar Chatterji to form the Greater India Society with Tagore's blessings. The following year B.R. Chatterji wrote a trifle condescendingly in *India and Java* that though 'Hindus had lost their independence in their own home,' India's religion, culture, laws and government 'moulded the lives of the primitive races all over' Suvarnabhumi so that 'they imbibed a more elevated moral spirit and a higher intellectual taste . . . [and] were lifted to a higher plane of civilization . . . A greater India was established by a gentle fusion of races, which richly endowed the original inhabitants with the spiritual heritage of India.' Chatterji called this 'colonial and cultural expansion . . . one of the most brilliant, but forgotten, episodes of Indian history, of which any Indian may justly feel proud.'[9]

The principal reminders today of that empire of the mind are place names whose context has been forgotten, customs whose provenance is not known and scattered places of worship that bear out Lee's frequent but not always complimentary references to Indian spirituality. It took more than two centuries to complete the Preah Vihar temple over which Thai and Cambodian troops came to blows in late 2008. The magnificent monuments of Borobodur and Prambanam in Java, Bali's profusion of smaller temples, the stupendous pile of Angkor Wat in Cambodia, Thailand's Prasat Hin Muang Tum temple and South-east Asia's oldest Hindu architecture, Vietnam's My Son sanctuary not far from lost Simhapur, speak of the values with which Further India was imbued. 'It was from India, especially from the south, that the people of South-east Asia learnt the art of writing' wrote an eminent British Indologist who declared that 'the whole of South-east Asia received most of its culture from India.'[10]

The Raj bridged the gulf between eternity and history. Raffles's boast that Singapore 'bids fair to be the next port to Calcutta' and a British official's comment that many in Britain thought the town was somewhere near the centre of India confirmed India as a constant point of reference. The process of leapfrogging the neighbourhood to which Lee attributes his economic miracle has always been a feature of South-east Asian life. It was reinforced when colonial Singapore looked to Britain's base in India—regarded then as geographically contiguous—for ideas and expertise because the surrounding countries had little to offer.

Early parliamentary debates reveal the extent to which Indian examples and parallels, institutions and personnel dominated Singapore. G.D. Coleman, the director of public works, who had gone there from Calcutta, 'graced the infant port with a lovely series of Tank Square (the old name for Dalhousie Square, now BBD Bag, Calcutta's business centre) public buildings, Chowringhee godowns, and even a proxy South Park Street cemetery.'[11] The Padang, smaller and neater than the tattered sprawl of Calcutta's Maidan, also recalls that connection. Both parks are similarly ringed by the monumental staple of colonial cities—cathedral, court and council. Thanks to Coleman who is immortalized in a busy commercial street in Singapore, older Housing Development Board flats faithfully replicate the architectural drabness of India's Public Works Department. Singapore adopted and adapted the Indian Penal Code, and derived many of its early legal and administrative structures from British India.[12] Indian mints struck Singapore dollars and the Union Bank of Calcutta started Singapore's first bank in 1840. A Calcutta Armenian, Catchick Moses, founded the *Straits Times* five years later.[13] Its first editor, Robert Carr Woods, was also from Calcutta.[14] So, the *Bombay Times* was taking a swipe at a rival Indian city when it expressed snooty 'surprise that a little Singapore newspaper should be given the pretentious title of *Straits Times*'. It added cuttingly that '. . . nothing perhaps could be better adapted for the community of Singapore where, as everybody knows, the people are only half-civilized, and refined wit, even if it could be obtained, would be "caviare to the general".'

Calcutta remained a point of reference for the new paper whose later editors included at least two Englishmen from the *Statesman* in Calcutta. One of the young Peet's chores was to cull news from the *Statesman,* the *Madras Mail* and other British Indian newspapers with no question of affecting superior airs. Another Indian link is a bright red poster on sale at the Singapore Zoo. Titled The Value of a Tree and published by Update Forestry, Michigan State University, it quotes 'Professor T.M. Das of the University of Calcutta' to value a tree at $196,250, breaking that down into precise figures for oxygen generation, air pollution, erosion control, improved fertility, recycled water and a home for animals, but excluding the value of fruit, timber or beauty.

When Francis Thomas, Singapore's British minister for communication and works, sought help from 'our great neighbour and friend, India' for the Royal Singapore Flying Club, Lee jumped up to contrast teetotal Indian clubs where Indians learnt to fly with the Singapore counterpart where whites propped up the bar. India lent a Chipmunk as well as a flying instructor. Not unexpectedly, Thomas, who had a Malaya-born Chinese wife and was domiciled in Singapore, thought Lee was 'obsessed with what he calls white races.' He was 'not prepared to accept anybody who has not got certain pigments in his skin, either as a fellow being or a friend.' Another Caucasian legislator, G.A. Sutherland, accused Lee of carrying on his shoulder not a chip about whites but a marble slab.[15]

The jibes placed him in good company. In New Delhi, United States Ambassador Loy W. Henderson belittled Nehru's commitment to Afro-Asian solidarity as only an attempt to 'lead a global union of coloured peoples'.[16] It was more grist to the race mill when Lee protested that Air India had not been offered shares in the new Singapore-registered Malayan Airline in which BOAC and Qantas held 51 per cent equity. Singapore dignitaries flew Air India because it was the best. Yet, it was excluded in favour of the white-owned airlines when it came to ownership.[17]

Singapore's Indian community greeted the Second World War with mixed feelings. K.S. Sandhu and A. Mani claim in their monumental work on Indians in South-east Asia that 'it was the only time in the history of Indians in Singapore (and Malaya)' that linguistic differences were buried and 'a unified identity prevailed'.[18] Many joined Bose's Indian Independence League or rallied round the INA. Many also rushed to escape. Jumabhoy, a municipal commissioner and president of the Indian Chamber of Commerce, cabled Lord Wavell, the viceroy, and Gandhi, complaining that only Europeans were being evacuated. The Indian government sent four ships, and though the Japanese radioed from Malaya asking Jumabhoy to stay—their strategy needed well-placed Indian protégés—he and his family sailed on the *SS Ho Sang* with a thousand other evacuees.

The Chinese who fled with them were also men of substance with influential Indian friends or contacts in Chiang Kai-shek's Kuomintang regime which had 30,000 troops in India and a consulate-general in Calcutta. The writer Yang Sou Mer worked with Force 136, an underground resistance outfit that the British launched from Meerut in northern India to operate behind enemy lines.[19] Loke Wan Tho, a colourful businessman and philanthropist educated at Montreux, Cambridge and London, became friendly with the distinguished Indian ornithologist, Salim Ali. He sold the Indian government the bungalow on Peirce Road that became its representative's residence, to the annoyance of successive envoys in Kuala Lumpur who ranked higher in the diplomatic pecking order but had to be content with a smaller house. Siew Qui Wong was a Cambridge-trained lawyer and municipal commissioner as well as a member of Johor's state council. Two distinguished bankers, Lien Ying Chow of the United Overseas Bank and Tan Chin Tuan of the Overseas-Chinese Banking Corporation, also took refuge in India. The latter was known as 'Mr OCBC' and his nephew, Tony Tan Keng Yam, later became Singapore's deputy prime minister.

Tan Chin Tuan registered the OCBC in Bombay but had a tempestuous time in Calcutta because of the Kuomintang regime's citizenship law based on the *lex sanguini* theory of an indivisible and indissoluble Sinic nationality which held that though the Chinese are of mainland China, its offshore islands and diaspora are separated by seas and frontiers, they are 'essentially one people with a shared heritage, the Chinese civilization'.[20] Hong Kong and Macau were the

Second China; Nanyang, region of the southern seas where Singapore is located, the Third.²¹ British India retaliated by requiring all Chinese refugees to register under the Registration of Foreigners Act. When Tan Chin Tuan refused, the British police officer in Calcutta barked, 'purple with rage', that the Chinese were shoemakers, restaurateurs and black marketeers! The situation was saved only through the intervention of another Briton whom Tan had known in Singapore as a commercial artist but whose Cathay Building office (where Lee also worked for the Japanese) was a front for the notorious Special Operations Executive charged with sabotage missions in enemy territory.²² The SOE, by the way, was also instructed to liquidate Bose.²³

Another refugee, Sir Tan Cheng Lock, who spent four years in Bangalore, was, in Lee's words, 'a grand old man of the Straits Settlements and the patriarch of one of Malacca's oldest and wealthiest families.'²⁴ The Congress Party's successful mass mobilization inspired Sir Cheng Lock to launch the Overseas Chinese Association which became the MCA (Malayan Chinese Association).²⁵ His biographer, K.G. Tregonning, wrote with perceptive understanding of Chinese race attitudes:

> It may have been hard for Tan Cheng Lock, a Chinese, to learn from India, but the unexpected impact of India, bypassed always before on visits to Europe, was unmistakable ... Among Tan's files was preserved a voluminous collection of Indian newspapers of the 1943–45 period. The speeches of Nehru, Jinnah, Gandhi, etc., were underlined in red pencil.²⁶

His son, Tan Sew Sin, independent Malaya's finance minister, retained his father's wartime links with the Birlas in India. Xu Beihong, the artist best remembered for his 'Galloping Horse', was a wartime visitor to Santiniketan and Darjeeling where he worked on his large masterpiece, 'The Foolish Old Man Who Removed the Mountains'. Xu Beihong also painted Tagore, Gandhi, Maharani Indira Devi of Cooch Behar (whom he called 'Queen-Mother of Bihar'), and a number of Indian landscapes. His other portraits include Loke Wan Tho's first wife.

Fateful Encounter: Jawaharlal and Edwina

The boy Nathan's first glimpse of Nehru and his daughter was in Johor Bahru in May 1937. He saw them again in Singapore later during that trip and remembers Nehru's 'fiery temper' when his car stalled on its way to the old racecourse in Little India where a crowd of more than 15,000, including Chinese and Europeans, was waiting. Indira Gandhi recalled in 1968 the 'tumultuous welcome' she and her father had received but that first visit was not altogether propitious for the young Indira. First, the car in which she was travelling from Tanjong Pagar station with Mrs A. Abisheganaden, secretary of the local Lotus Club for South Asian women (the *Indian Daily Mail* called her 'Mrs Abishagam') skidded at the corner of Cavenagh Road. The *Indian Daily Mail* noted, 'Miss Nehru sustained a slight cut on her scalp and under the chin and her dress was soiled by a few drops of blood. She received medical treatment after she arrived at their temporary residence.'[27]

Then the Namazie family's seaside bungalow in Siglap where the Nehrus were to stay as guests of the Indian Association was not to her liking and they moved to the Sea View Hotel.[28]

As soon as the war ended Nehru wanted to visit Singapore again to see how disbanded INA troops were faring under Mountbatten's British Military Administration, and to arrange for their legal defence. Burma's British governor refused to let him set foot in Burma, the BMA's director of intelligence, Air Vice Marshal L.F. Pendred, thought the request 'should be refused', and Mountbatten's own staff decided to make things uncomfortable if Nehru insisted on coming by denying him official transport, confining Indian troops to barracks, and playing down his presence in every way. However, Mountbatten jumped at the chance of hosting a future world leader. The two men had nearly met in January 1944 when Mountbatten was visiting Bombay and Nehru writing *The Discovery of India* as a prisoner in the nearby Ahmadnagar Fort. Now, the supremo declared himself 'extremely displeased' with the BMA for not realizing that Nehru was 'one of the most important political figures in the world'. Not only was their action 'disloyal' to him 'personally,' but the cancellation of the visit 'would invite worldwide criticism which Nehru would not fail to exploit.'²⁹ Mountbatten wrote to S.K. Chettur of the ICS, India's official representative in Singapore with an office in Robinson Street, 'I am not as foolish as to imagine that there will be no political significance attached to his visit but I know that he is a man of honour and that he will not place me in an embarrassing position by carrying out any agitational activities during the period I am responsible for the administration of this country.'³⁰

His formal invitation to Nehru to visit Malaya and Singapore 'as an official representative of the All-India Congress' apologized for the rudeness of his officers and made up for it by laying on almost head of government honours.³¹ Two senior British staff officers were waiting for Nehru's plane at Kallang airport with Brigadier J.N. (Muchu) Chaudhuri, later independent India's Chief of the Army Staff, who was attached to him for the duration. Among the other notables who received Nehru were Chettur, Jumabhoy and Tan Kah Kee, leader of the overseas Chinese. Tan Kah Kee was a man of consequence. Zhou personally supervised his state funeral when he died in Beijing in 1961.³² The garlanding and welcome addresses over, Chaudhuri took Nehru through a crowd of 2000 men in INA uniform with tricolour badges (Mountbatten had permitted this) to the Istana, then Government House, where the future (and first) prime minister of India met the future (and last) viceroy of India over tea. Not at all disconcerted when 300 INA men marched up to Government House shouting revolutionary slogans, Mountbatten 'rode in state' with Nehru in an open car to the Indian YMCA Welfare Centre. The *Tamil Murasu* newspaper was profoundly impressed: 'It was the neatest diplomatic stroke and so casually executed that Lord Louis Mountbatten displayed real genius in ensuring smoothness and success in Nehruji's visit and stay in this country.'³³

The cheering throngs in the packed streets included many 'former Indian soldiers', the official euphemism for the INA. Their 'Nehruji *ki jai*!' was expected but surprising cries of 'Lord Louis Mountbatten *ki jai*!' set the precedent for India's adulatory mobs. Contemporary newspaper accounts and intelligence reports say the crowd in the streets was nothing compared to 'the seething and bubbling mass... (that) just boiled all round the YMCA' in Stamford Road where

Edwina Mountbatten, Lady Louis as she was then, waited with Indian Red Cross workers.

Mountbatten's diary records that he and Nehru were inside the YMCA when 'a roar as of a dam bursting fell upon our ears, and the crowd burst through every door and window . . . in no time they were upon us.' Edwina was knocked down and disappeared under the mob. 'The Pandit screaming: "Your wife; your wife; we must go to her", linked arms with me and together we charged into the crowd in an endeavour to find her. Meanwhile, she had crawled between the people's legs and had come out at the far end of the room, got on a table and shouted to us that she was all right.'[34] Nehru's own account to Dorothy Norman seventeen years later was more subdued.

> We arrived at the canteen and I met Lady Mountbatten there. We then moved in from the porch or portico to a room inside. Just then there was a wild rush of Indian soldiers, presumably wanting to see me. When we reached the room inside, Edwina Mountbatten was nowhere to be seen. I think I got up on a chair to have a look around. Soon Lady Mountbatten crawled out of the milling crowd. She had evidently been knocked down by the solders rushing in. That was an unusual introduction for us.[35]

Some might discern fate's hand in such a dramatic first encounter. Mountbatten gave a small dinner party that evening for Nehru who told 'Chaudhuri on his way back that he hadn't enjoyed an evening with English people so much since he had come down from Oxford [sic], [Nehru was at Cambridge] more than thirty years ago.'[36] Mountbatten writes that he made just one request.

> I asked Nehru to cancel only one item of his programme; namely, the laying of a wreath on the War Memorial for the Indian National Army, since they had fought not only against us but against the local people of Malaya. He agreed to do this. I also asked him to avoid incurring any indiscipline among

the Indian troops and this he undertook to do. I found him most reasonable.[37]

Whatever promise he gave, Nehru could not afford to disappoint a significant political constituency. 'He slipped away quietly the following day and left his personal wreath'—a bunch of roses that people thought he had bought for Lady Louis—at the INA memorial.[38] The makeshift wooden replica of the original monument that had hastily been erected at the site was quickly dismantled after Nehru's car sped away and the crowd of some 300 people dispersed. Pranab Mukherjee made up for that hole-and-corner affair sixty-one years later, beginning his visit to Singapore by paying his respects at the INA memorial.[39] He was the first senior Indian dignitary to do so though Nehru did do his duty by Bose by instructing a promising local lawyer, Radhakrishna Ramani, to see to the INA personnel's legal needs.

To do Mountbatten justice, he was never a prisoner of conventional prejudice. His wife was even more oblivious of differences and could not remember once whether the 'lively' man next to her at dinner was black or white.[40] But Mountbatten was also a political operator. His graciousness, including turning a blind eye to Nehru's truancy (and even colluding with it since the wooden replica could hardly have been built and dismantled so swiftly without a nod from him), was not disinterested. Nehru was already a global star. Britain's prime minister, Clement Attlee, viewed him with favour. Wavell regretted that subcontinental politics made it difficult for him to socialize with the Congress leader. Warned of the tremendous fund of goodwill for Nehru, Mountbatten 'believed he could lose nothing by sharing the crowd's enthusiasm and taking half the wind destined for Nehru's sails'. More deviously, he hoped his public display of friendship would diminish Nehru in the eyes of ardent nationalists and encourage them to suspect 'that one who fraternized openly with representatives of the British Raj was a bit of a Quisling' which might help to temper Nehru's radicalism.[41]

The gambit was rewarded when Nehru rebuked the crowd of 100,000 people in the Jalan Besar Stadium for raising the old INA chant of 'Blood! Blood! Blood!' Netaji had done great work but the time had come for peaceful, disciplined and constructive effort to achieve freedom. Slogans that were 'provocative and unwise' should be abandoned. Nathan, catching a third glimpse of Nehru, found him 'a much mellowed' man. The British were gratified to note that INA soldiers in the stadium gradually slipped away as Nehru spoke in generalities instead of hurling abuse and defiance at the Raj.[42] The rally could easily have turned into an anti-British scrum for the INA was out in full force with a profusion of tricolour flags, a large portrait of Netaji in military attire, uniformed guards of honour and a brass band playing martial Azad Hind tunes like the popular '*Dilli chalo!*' (march to Delhi). It was not an exclusively Indian affair for Chinese (including Communists) and Indonesian groups also marched to the stadium bearing banners and flags.[43]

Looking to the future, Nehru said that the Chinese, Malays and Indonesians in the audience reminded him of an old dream: 'A dream of one united Asia! Asia against the other peoples.' He returned to the theme at dinner at the Ee Hoe Hean Club for Chinese millionaires that Tan Kah Kee hosted, telling the gathering, as *Nanyang* reported, that free India and free China 'should work for the good and weal of the world'. His words would also have 'resonated' with Lee who was then studying in England but articulated the Nehruvian dream thirteen years later, hoping that 'a vigorous, vital and cultural civilization' would emerge from the Malayan peninsula's 'boiling pot' of Indian, Chinese and European cultures.[44]

Mountbatten's concerns were more immediate and tactical. 'Altogether we must have stolen part of the old boy's thunder, besides publicly linking him up with us . . .' was his self-satisfied comment afterwards.[45] There is no reason to believe he had any notion then of the imminence of change in India or that Nehru himself would recommend him for the post of viceroy.[46] But that day's happenings forged a lifelong friendship. Nehru's biographer says Mountbatten 'bewitched' him.[47] The viceroy's daughter, Pamela, believes her mother and Nehru fell deeply in love in Singapore but that the relationship was platonic.[48] A packet of Nehru's letters was found by Lady Mountbatten's bedside when she died in her sleep in Borneo in 1960. She willed the entire collection of his letters to her husband who had pragmatically accepted the intimacy and used his wife as a political bridge to Nehru.⁴⁹ Much has been written about this extraordinary ménage à trois. Nehru and Edwina stumbled into it unawares but the record indicates that Mountbatten had an eye to the future. His machinations yielded handsome dividend for him personally and for the British Crown, giving the Commonwealth a new lease of life when India became independent. Nehru visited Singapore again in 1950 and stopped there five years later on his way to Bandung. The visits were still under British auspices and thus reinforced a sense of continuity as he laid the Indian Association's foundation stone in Balestier Road, addressed the usual huge crowds at the Jalan Besar stadium and Farrer Park, and graciously consented to the Lotus Club being renamed after his dead wife Kamala. He lectured the Ramakrishna Mission into calling its Orphanage Dormitory the Boys' Home because orphanage was an unfeeling word, inspected a children's guard of honour and presented the swamijis with a purse from a Calcutta businessman. Singapore might, indeed, have been Singapur.

Illusion of Indian Leadership

Stamford Raffles arrived in 1819 with 120 Indian sepoys, lascars, assistants and servants. A Penang trader called Narayana Pillay was also of the company. They found '120 people living at subsistence level on fishing, root-staples and piracy'. About fifty of them were Chinese, but the bulk of Singapore's Chinese came later, fleeing flood and famine, riot and revolution. A succession of crises captured in the Chinese saying, *guo po jia wang* (the country is defeated and the home lost), propelled them in such massive numbers that they soon overwhelmed all other races and became a firmly-entrenched majority, accounting for 75 per cent of the population.

Thus did Chinatown take shape in the heart of Islam. But despite looking Chinese, Singapore sounded Indian as Mountbatten gave way to civilian rule a month after Nehru's second visit. The Straits Settlements were dissolved, Penang and Malacca joined Malaya, and Singapore became a standalone colony with a governor and advisory council. Only British subjects could vote in the first Legislative Council election for six members in 1948, explaining Lee's grumble about 'Indians from India who had become "Singapore leaders" by reason of their British passports and the political vacuum the MCP (Malayan Communist Party) revolt had created'.[50] Although they were mainly Chinese, MCP members celebrated Nehru's birthday while ignoring Sun Yat Sen's.[51] But it rankled with them that the British made it hard and humiliating for the Chinese to become citizens by insisting on testing their spoken English, as Marshall told historian Tudor Parfitt: 'Each time they took the test, the British "slapped them down with words they did not understand" . . . Their proud reaction was to stop trying and reject citizenship in British Singapore out of hand.'[52]

Elections were in any case an alien rite for the Chinese who dismissed politics as 'the Indian's business', hinting at the more fundamental nature of their own interests. They were also shrewd enough to know that a few elected members merely gave a thin democratic patina to the substance of colonial power.

But the tiny Indian middle class loved the make-believe world of colonial politics. In August 1946, a British-trained lawyer, John Aloysius Thivy, founded the Malayan Indian Congress whose commitment to India's independence underlined that Indians still saw Singapore as an extension of India. Thivy had met Gandhi in London, listened to Bose's speeches in Singapore, joined the INA and was imprisoned in Changi prison after Japan surrendered, one of the very few Christians the British jailed. Other Indians were involved in the multiracial Malayan Democratic Union, the Progressive Party, the Singapore Labour Party and the University of Malaya Socialist Club whose newsletter *Fajar* (Dawn) became a cause célèbre. The PAP had its Indians, too, and a photograph of the 1955 election from Tanjong Pagar shows one of them delightedly carrying a victorious Lee on his shoulders.

As India's independence drew nearer, 'Westernized Indians showed an increasing desire to ensure an adequate role for Indians in public life.'[53] They were not worried about Singapore's overwhelming Chinese majority because they misinterpreted Chinese apathy towards politics. Moreover, they were convinced like Lee that Singapore would sooner or later merge with Malaya which meant that the Chinese too, would be a minority. Comfortable in the knowledge that, whatever the present and future might bring, eternity was theirs, Indians were not perturbed as, thanks to Marshall's democratic liberalism, the island that might have been Little India moved inexorably towards the demographic logic of its destiny as Chinatown. It was the rise of a strong post-war Malay nationalist movement that instigated the Indian elite's 'remarkable drive' for 'positions of public eminence and influence' in the federal state they expected to encompass the entire peninsula.[54]

As Singaporeans awaited the 1948 election, described as 'dull and insipid', a group of men and women assembled in Calcutta for a purpose that was neither dull nor insipid and which convulsed the Malayan peninsula for twelve years. The Conference of Youth and Students of South-east Asia Fighting for Freedom and Independence promised to ignite the flames of revolution throughout the east. Calcutta was an appropriate setting, for radical Bengalis clung to the belief that the great Lenin had predicted that the road to world revolution would run from Peking to Paris via their city. The meeting was held under the auspices of the World Federation of Democratic Youth and the International Union of Students but the fraternal delegates housed in a cluster of rundown hutments that American troops had used as their wartime hospital were hardly youths or students. There were commissars from the Soviet Union, Australian ideologues, French trade unionists, battle-hardened Vietminh officers, Yugoslav revolutionaries and Malayan Chinese guerrillas.

The MCP's Lee Siong 'who had been chosen to attend because he spoke good English' was among these torchbearers of revolution.[55] From Calcutta he went to Rangoon for a peasants' congress and thence by boat to Singapore, arriving a day after the MCP's fourth plenary meeting ended. But Lawrence Sharkey, president of the Australian Communist Party, who travelled direct to Singapore on 9 March and stayed there until 20 March, attended the plenary where the crucial decision to revolt was taken.[56] He probably conveyed to the Malayan (Chinese) comrades the Calcutta conference's secret recommendation of armed struggle. Revolution being an early manifestation of globalization, insurrections broke out almost simultaneously in India, Burma, Indochina, Indonesia, the Philippines and of course Malaya. There were additional local reasons for each uprising but the Calcutta gathering, egged on by Le Tam, leader of the Vietnamese delegation, and two militant Yugoslavs, could have been the common ignition.[57]

B.V. Keskar, India's deputy minister for external affairs, reported after touring South-east Asia, that far from being freedom-fighters, the Communists were outright bandits.[58] The British called them terrorists. Indians, who helped to kindle their insurgency, played only a minor part in it, also because of the long-range effect of events in India. Tensions in India's body politic were reproduced in Malayan Indian politics, and the Labour Department noted that shocked by Gandhi's murder in January 1948, Indian workers, many of them INA veterans who had drifted into the MCP, repudiated violence.[59] The MDU's complaint to Nehru that Indian candidates in the election held only a month after the Calcutta conference were indulging in 'opportunism and personal aggrandizement' and colluding with the British 'to perpetuate colonialism'[60] vested India's prime minister with extra-territorial jurisdiction. Or, perhaps, the MDU believed with Jaswant Singh that the Indian nation was not a state hemmed in by geopolitical boundaries.

Forty-five per cent of the eligible voters who registered were Indian, and only 25 per cent Chinese. There were 1811 Indian voters against 1001 from other communities in the Rural West constituency where S.C. Goho, a Bengali barrister with his Chinese second wife and a stock of goodwill from his wartime role in the IIL, 'put on an Indian dress to canvass for votes' (photographs show him wearing a Gandhi cap like Thivy) and defeated a prominent social worker, Malati Pillai, whose husband owned two Malayali papers catering to employees of the British base.[61] Their son Gopinath is today a prominent businessman and diplomat. Goho's relatives in Calcutta were convinced he had become 'governor of Singapore'. Legend dies hard and 'Barrister Goho' was recommended to me as late as 1993 when I was setting out for Singapore.

Three of the six elected councillors were Indian, the others being Chinese, British and Malay. The imbalance remained when Singapore went to the polls in 1951, this time to elect nine councillors. Voting took place only four months after the Maria Hertogh riots (over a Dutch girl's conversion to Islam) and under 53 per cent of the 48,155 registered voters participated in what Lee called 'a genteel affair with tea and dinner parties'.[62] With the Chinese still standing aloof, Indians fielded fifteen of the twenty-two candidates and won four seats. Every municipal or city council election between 1949 and 1953 resulted in disproportionately high Indian representation.[63]

The next election in 1955—the first for a Legislative Assembly under a new constitution—was also 'the first lively political contest in Singapore's history'. Indians were losing their advantage since a new rule automatically registering everyone who was born in Singapore meant that 60 per cent of the 300,000 voters were Chinese. Marshall's Labour Front won ten out of twenty-five seats, enabling him to become chief minister at the head of a coalition with the United Malays National Organization and MCA. Lee, sole survivor at the time of writing of that exercise, was one of three successful PAP candidates. His passionate commitment was very different from the gentlemanly avocation of Indian councillors and he scornfully dismissed the advice of Bashir Mallal, a lawyer's clerk whose son was his schoolmate and whose brother, N.A. Mallal, founded the *Malayan Law Journal* in 1932, to make his name and fortune in law and then go into politics. That was the conventional wisdom for India's Congress politicians. Bashir 'didn't understand that something dramatic had happened to my generation, that making a fortune, playing safe, doesn't add up when the system is wrong. I was dead set against the system.'[64]

Lee was outraged when Singapore's first woman legislator, Velasini Menon, who was elected with him, and her lawyer husband 'absconded' to India with a large sum of clients' money: 'That did no good to the standing of India-born Indians in Singapore, who were regarded as birds of passage.'[65] The reputation stuck, and Dhanabalan says locals spoke of 'Air India Indians' because of the return tickets supposedly in their pockets. Preet Mohan Singh Mallik, an Indian diplomat who was in Singapore in the late 1960s (and was maried there) and high commissioner to Malaysia (1986–90) corroborates that even salaried employees took their pensions back to India when they retired. The Velasini Menon episode, precursor to the 'expats vs. locals' controversy half a century later, drew attention to the absence of Singaporean roots. It also highlighted factionalism among Indians chasing the will o' the wisp of political power. The unity Sandhu and Mani had spoken of in their book on the diaspora died with the war. Thivy's appointment in 1948 as independent India's first commissioner provoked heartburn among other prominent expatriates. Several organizations represented Indian commercial interests, and when chambers of commerce were empowered to send nominees to the Legislative Council, the south Indian chambers were left out, compounding the sense of grievance.[66]

This north–south divide coincided roughly with socio-economic status. Community leadership 'lay in the hands of the urban middle-class Indians who drew their inspiration chiefly from the Indian National Congress' while the rank and file were labourers. Gujaratis, Sindhis, Punjabis and Marwaris boasted the highest literacy rate among Indians and held the best jobs.[67] They 'were generally divorced from the Indian working class who were predominantly Tamil . . . The majority were illiterate or semi-literate labourers emasculated by years of paternalistic supervision by the government, the employers, and the agents of the Indian government.'[68] Tamils regarded 'the Singapore Indian Regional Congress (originally a branch of Thivy's MIC) as a tool of Indian commercial interests.'[69] They themselves were not welcome in Singapore's Indian Association: 'Some said that if the labourers were admitted, they would come half-naked to the meetings. Others were reluctant to mix freely with the "lower orders" as the coolies were referred to.'[70]

Most Tamils were in the peninsula where a Malaysian human rights lawyer, Ponnusamy Waytha Moorthy, filed a US$4 trillion suit against the British government in 2007 for atrocities allegedly suffered by their forefathers who had been taken to Malaya as indentured labourers (migration was banned in 1938). He claimed that this 'colossal' sum reflected 'the years of pain, suffering, humiliation, discrimination and continuous colonisation'.[71] The political action that followed the suit, with the Hindu Rights Action Force organizing protests, led to sharp clashes with the Malaysian government, encouraged fears of a spillover into Singapore and prompted indignant questions in India's Parliament.

But as with India, so with Indians. Though the divisions and differences may be more noticeable, the unifying bonds are stronger.

The protection of the Raj, the assurance of a place of ultimate refuge and cultural confidence—the belief in eternity—gave the community strength and resilience. Lee was right in telling Singapore undergraduates that Indians 'attend their temples, keep to customs' more than the Chinese.[72] Indian Singaporeans are more Indian than Chinese Singaporeans are Chinese, reiterates Dhanabalan who himself is the exception that proves the rule. His father acquired fame as founder of a Hindu cult, Krishna Our Guide, but Dhanabalan broke away to become a fervent Christian and marry a Chinese wife. Indian conformism was cause and effect of another distinction. Until Singapore became an economic powerhouse, Chinese immigrants, cut off from China by the turmoil that the Communist revolution aggravated, had no entrée to China's new elite. Though Rajaratnam noted after a visit in the early 1960s that despite political hostility for the 'LKY clique', Chinese looked on Singaporeans as 'kinsmen', it was some time before the Chinese Singaporean community evolved an equivalent of the prominent Indians who enjoyed or had developed high connections in India.

The PAP's bluff and breezy S. Chandra Das, whom officials at the Trade Development Board he headed called 'Mister India' (his first official trip abroad was to represent Singapore at Unctad Two in New Delhi in 1966), was one. Others included businessmen like Gopinath Pillai, the Jumabhoys, Satpal Khattar, Kartar Singh Thakral, and the Melwani and Chanrai merchant clans as well as a number of Bengali lawyers and doctors. This small milieu could bridge the gulf because there was no break in continuity. Caste and community bonds endured under British rule and a flow of celebrities kept alive social and political contact. China sent no visitors to match the stream of Indian monks, ministers and maharajas.

Rajabali Jumabhoy epitomized Indian duality. He told a Chinese audience in Hong Lim Green that he was 'a better Chinese' than them because he had donated a thousand dollars to the Sinocentric Nanyang University and his grandson Rafiq called himself a 'chocolate Chinaman'.[73] But the senior Jumabhoy was also conscious of his access to India's rulers. He entertained every important Indian visitor, and recounted how, as a youth, he had flagged Gandhi down in Bombay to harangue the great man about riding a British car while preaching the boycott of British goods, 'He [Gandhi] promptly replied, 'Yes, if cars were manufactured in India, I would not sit in such a car, but as I have to go here and there very quickly, I have to utilise this motor-car instead of a bullock cart.'[74]

The disadvantage of connectivity was that it fuelled charges of extra-territorial loyalty against Singapore's Indians as the British retreated and Chinese influence strengthened. Understanding local sensitivities, Jumabhoy tried to anticipate future suspicion by proposing as long ago as 1939 that Indian Association members dissociate themselves from India's politics, but his resolution was defeated by forty-five votes to five.[75] Middle-class Indians were not ready to sever the umbilical cord, justifying Rajaratnam's complaint that they used 'Singapore politics as extensions of Indian politics'.[76]

Indians saw no contradiction in flaunting several labels because nothing could erode an identity that was for eternity. Amarendra Nath Mitra, another Bengali barrister, headed the MIC, represented the Citizens of the United Kingdom and Colonies, and chaired a meeting at the Kerala Samajam in 1959 to demand that 'Singapore, being now a free country . . . the War Memorial known as the "Martyrs Tomb" which was erected by Netaji Subhas Chandra Bose' should be rebuilt. Lee, 'well known as a fighter for freedom', was implored to respect 'the spirit of sacrifice, sufferings and dedication for the cause of liberation of South-east Asian peoples' that the memorial symbolized.[77] A prominent Indian MP, Samar Guha, was in Singapore at the time also to request Lee to rebuild the INA memorial and extend moral support to Tibetans at the next Afro-Asian conference in New Delhi. Lee's secretary warned Guha that Singapore 'did not encourage visitors to play politics while visiting the state'.[78] It was not clear whether the objection was to Netaji or Tibet, but Guha did not get to see Lee.

Tamil mobilization was more serious, especially after two visits (1929 and 1954) by E.V. Ramasami Naicker, the iconoclastic social reformer and founder of Tamil Nadu's Self-respect Movement, resulted in a crop of *kalagam*s (associations) and two publications, the weekly *Ina Mani* in Malaya and the monthly *Dravida Murasu* in Singapore. Predictably, it took a local Indian MP, the PAP's S.V. Lingham, to draw attention to the supposedly dire threat of Singapore's

Kolhai Muzhakkam using the same name and rising sun symbol as a publication by India's Dravida Kazagham party. While DMK politicians in Madras ridiculed the peril, Lingham's disclosure enabled an indignant Defence Minister Lim Kim San to warn that he would 'watch with a hawk-like eye' for signs of Indian links. The evidence of 'a very clear connection between the DMK here and the DMK in Madras' was 'quite disturbing'. Singapore's DMK was supposed to be a purely cultural organization, and here it was 'indulging in political activities'![79]

First Marshall Plan but after Marshall

Marshall inspired the legislation that transformed a British colony into a Chinese republic. Brought up in Baghdad, Switzerland and Singapore, fluent in French and German, with relatives in Australia, and an English wife, he was a man of the world. He had been called to the Bar in London, slaved in a Hokkaido coal mine as a Japanese prisoner of war and popularized the then unorthodox safari suit. The Marshalls holidayed in Kashmir, mixed with the top echelons of Indian society, and sent orchids to Indira Gandhi, her aunt, Vijayalakshmi Pandit, and President Rajendra Prasad. Mulk Raj Anand, back from flirting with London's literary left, was friendly with Marshall's uncle in the hill station of Khandala near Bombay.

But David Marshall's entire commitment was to Singapore and he persuaded Zhou Enlai to issue a proclamation in October 1956 urging Chinese settlers to become Singapore citizens. Zhou obliged, adding a rider that Chinese Singaporeans should be allowed to return to China to 'bury their bones in the ancestral country.'[80] Grateful taxi drivers refused ever afterwards to charge Marshall for rides. Cynical Caucasians may have thought Marshall was identifying with the majority when he had his grey Jaguar painted yellow but he did so out of devilment to mock official propaganda against 'Yellow Culture'. Yellow the Jag remained, its number SF 1171 popular with Chinese gamblers, until 'it died of old age in the 1970s'.[81]

The MDU was not alone in vesting India and her prime minister with jurisdiction over Singapore. Others too looked on India as a Delphic oracle whose blessings had to be obtained for every endeavour.

Nehru was the high priest of that temple of the gods. Lee's caustic comment that 'former chief ministers used to go to Delhi for solace and comfort whenever they failed in diplomatic and constitutional discussions in London' was a dig at Marshall who matched him in praising the 'ascetic self-discipline' of the 'old guard of the Congress movement' and the 'clean, unflinching, absolute dedication' which had won them 'moral power and prestige'.[82]

Learning in New Delhi of the furore his mission had caused at home, Marshall retorted acidly that Lee and the PAP would probably prefer he sat at the feet of British Prime Minister Anthony Eden and his colonial secretary, Alan Lennox Boyd.[83] Lee was not denigrating India's leader when he mocked Marshall's 'abject humility at the feet of Pandit Nehru'. The taunt that 'in three days of banqueting in New Delhi, the chief minister of Singapore will imbibe his (Nehru's) wisdom and statesmanship' implied that Marshall, whose travels and pronouncements Lee dismissed as 'an extravaganza from the Hollywood studios of Walt Disney,' did not have the intellectual capacity or political acumen to absorb anything from Nehru, no matter how long he grovelled at the master's feet.

Rajabali's estranged nephew, Jumabhoy Mohammed Jumabhoy, a member of Marshall's Cabinet, who accompanied his chief to New Delhi, declared exultantly that 'with Mr Nehru's help, the battle (for home rule) would be won immediately.'[84] Though striking a more cautious note, Nehru did offer to talk to the British and bring up the question of Singapore's independence at the next Commonwealth conference. More philosophically, he advised Marshall, as he told Leslie Hoffman who was covering the tour for the *Straits Times*, 'There are no failures in a right cause; only setbacks.'

Marshall finally carried out his threat to resign in June 1956. On the eve of setting out for London for the second constitutional conference the following March, his successor, Lim Yew Hock, startled other MPs by reciting Tagore's *Gitanjali*. For him, the Nobel Prize-winning poem defined Singapore's sense of high endeavour as it faced the next stage of political evolution.

> Where the mind is without fear and the head is held high;
> Where knowldege is free;

> Where the world has not been broken into fragments by narrow domestic walls;
> Where words come out from the depths of truth;
> Where tireless striving stretches its arms towards perfection;
> Where the clear stream of reason has not lost its way in the dreary desert sand of dead habit;
> Where the mind is led forward by thee into ever-widening thought and action;
> Into that heaven of freedom, my Father, let my country awake.[85]

Supporting the chief minister, Lim Choon Mong, member for Serangoon Gardens, urged the 'few timid people who were afraid of *merdeka* [freedom in Malay, like India's *swaraj* and *uhuru* in Swahili] . . . to come out of their cosy holes' and learn from the journey Singapore's 'great neighbour, India' had made. A merry mix of genders spiced his Singlish effervescence.

> She has come out and become an independent nation. She is today one of the leading nations of the world. Everything that is done there is peaceful and progressive, and we know that we certainly will follow that great brother through that road of independence and progress.[86]

The third constitutional conference the following May finally led to a settlement that Lee, who was again a member of the negotiating team, hailed as *tigu suku merdeka,* Malay for three-quarters independence. Lim, who was destined to end his days in Saudi Arabia as Haji Omar Lim Yew Hock, a Muslim convert, had other innovations up his sleeve. He engaged Dr Goh as economic adviser, and Dr Goh made India-born James Puthucheary, a political romantic like his younger brother Dominic, head of the Singapore Industrial Promotion Board. Puthucheary studied at Santiniketan, helped to found the University Socialist Club, fought the colonial regime, joined the INA, joined the Communists, was in and out of prison and helped Lee form the PAP. In between, he found time to collect degrees and write a socialist tract, *Ownership and Control in the Malayan*

Economy, while a prisoner in Changi jail. He seemed the ideal man to supervise growth with equity.

Singapore and Lee owe much to Chief Minister Lim who used army helicopters and armoured cars to suppress the rioting that broke out in October 1956 when the government ordered two Chinese schools to expel 142 students suspected of being Communist agents. But the real debt is to Marshall who planned the demographic revolution, though the laws he conceived and his successor pushed through, militated against his own multiracial party and laid the permanent foundations of the Chinatown of the spirit that became the PAP's vote bank. Singapore had a little over a million Chinese and 124,000 Indians in 1957. Lim's Citizenship Bill created 325,020 citizens by February 1958. From only 72,000 in 1952, the electorate jumped to half a million. These new Singaporeans were mostly Chinese-educated, dialect-speaking working-class people emotionally drawn to China and ideologically to the Left. Compulsory voting obliged them to take over what had previously been spurned as 'the Indian's business'. Abolition of the English language requirement for citizenship or speaking in the Assembly hammered the last nails into the coffin of the middle-class Indian monopoly over politics. Ignoring the advantage this gave his political opponent, an ecstatic Lim declared that 'the dividing attitudes of class, communalism and creed' would 'give way to the unifying attitude of "All Citizens Together"'.[87] That balmy spring prompted some optimists to declare there was no minority in Singapore.

While India ignored these changes, it is doubtful if local Indians grasped their full implications. Some simple members of the community rushed to file citizenship papers, fearing they might lose their jobs or even be deported. A few middle-class professionals anticipated being driven to the margins and packed their bags for India. Most stayed on, seeing in the changes no more than de jure recognition of the de facto position. But few can have been as lyrically supportive as the India-born editor and social activist Govindasamy Sarangapany who had arrived in Singapore at the age of twenty-one, married a Chinese, founded and edited two news bulletins in Tamil (*Munnetram* and *Seerhirutham*), and in 1935 launched *Tamil Murasu* which is now part of the *Straits Times* group. In 1954 when the colonial government allowed Commonwealth immigrants to become citizens, Sarangapany single-handedly persuaded 20,000 Tamils to register. Commenting on Lim's Bill on behalf of fifty Tamil organizations, he declared:

> Those who came here as settlers did so treating this land as a HOTEL; it took some time for them before they regarded this land as HOSTEL; the interests and stakes they have acquired in this land have induced them to make this land their HOUSE; it is the honest hope and prayer of the Tamil Representative Council that the Singapore Citizenship Bill will encourage them to adopt this land as their sweet HOME.[88]

Thus was Lee's 'Singaporean' born. Until then, as Peet records, the most that the 1954 law entitled was for some people to speak of themselves as 'citizens of Singapore'.[89]

Lee might mock his rivals for deferring to India and Nehru but was properly mindful of his own obeisance. He told British businessmen who feared for their capital and factories that a PAP government would do exactly what India had done: 'We do not want to expropriate you. We do not want to act illegally, or act against the principles of good conduct which all nations in this world wish to observe. We shall allow you to carry on so long as it is in our interest.'[90]

That was 'exactly the trouble' the British countered. 'In India, they are demanding more and more directorships and they are taking over our companies.' Though Lee had already rejected the Chinese road where 'the state takes over the whole machinery', British businessmen were unsure how much credence to attach to his stated preference for the alternative system 'where Indian capitalists go into partnership with foreign capital.'[91]

Singaporeans may have noted another Indian precedent when the PAP swept the polls in 1959, and like Mountbatten in New Delhi, Sir William Goode, the last British governor, stayed on for six months as head of state but with the Malay title of Yang di-Pertuan Negara. The PAP victory made headlines in India. But the *Tribune* newspaper in the Punjab was premature in declaring that the outcome mattered to India because of Singapore's 'hundred thousand Indians who live in relative prosperity in the land of their adoption'.[92] India championed victims of South African apartheid because of Gandhi but as described in the eighth and ninth chapters, was not overly concerned about her scattered seed. There was no Indian equivalent of Kuomintang China's citizenship law. Nehru would have regarded a variant of Zhou's proclamation about funerals as superstitious nonsense. Unlike Malaysia which protested to Burma in 1992 against its treatment of Muslim Rohingyas, India did not champion any religious group. Unlike China which expressed concern during Indonesia's 1998 ethnic riots, India did not take up Malaysia's treatment of its Tamils with Kuala Lumpur though Prime Minister Manmohan Singh was under considerable domestic pressure to do so. Unsurprisingly, many members of the diaspora feel let down, and the INA's Rani of Jhansi Regiment veteran, Malay-born Rasammah Bhupalan, who yearned to 'die for India' refuses to live there. 'This is not the India we fought for', she says.[93] Preet Mallik thinks New Delhi was not interested in Indians in the Malay peninsula because of their socio-economic profile and south Indian roots.

They did not wield the clout of today's ethnic Indian millionaires in the Silicon Valley of whom an Indian journalist wrote, 'When half-a-dozen Indian-Americans sneeze, it is not unusual for official New Delhi to catch a cold.'[94] The website of the ministry of overseas Indian affairs flaunts pictures of celebrities like V.S. Naipaul and Lakshmi Mittal. It was only pressure from influential Indian-Americans and the example of China's rich investment haul from overseas Chinese that changed New Delhi's thinking. Indian governments were content to argue until then that emigrants should make the best of the circumstances in which they found themselves without expecting a Bharat Mata they had abandoned to bestir herself on their account.

Lee would not have welcomed New Delhi's interest in Indian Singaporeans. He neatly rebuked AIR's Mukhopadhyay for suggesting an ethnic bond with the comment that Singapore had strong ties with the United States and Japan without American or Japanese settlers. Nor, he said, was there any contact with China for thirty years though three-quarters of Singapore's population was Chinese. 'The fact that we have a substantial Indian population here is not the indicator or the determinant of our official level contacts,' he added. His Asian Dream was not of flesh and blood. That was to change, but not yet.

The 1959 election results had far-reaching racial and ideological implications. One effect was that 'the large bloc of Chinese voters became a significant factor in determining the outcome' of future elections. Another was to increase 'the political clout of the pro-Communist faction in the PAP led by Lim Chin Siong and Fong Swee Suan.'[95] The results also encouraged Lee to demand that Singapore should join Malaya—he saw the two as an organic whole—but without surrendering its distinctive identity.

Nehru, whose 'foreign policy (was) that no foreign power should rule over any Asian country', had welcomed Malayan independence.[96] Despite his opposition to foreign military bases, he acquiesced in the 1957 Anglo-Malayan Defence Agreement which covered Singapore and provided for British outposts and soldiers. He also approved of the federal plan for a greater Malaysia incorporating British-ruled Sarawak, the Crown colony of North Borneo (Sabah) and Singapore under the resolutely anti-Communist 'Bapa Malaysia', Prime Minister Tengku Abdul Rahman, twentieth child of the Sultan of Kedah. Nehru had shared platforms with the Tengku, who called him his model and 'favourite politician', during his South-east Asian tours in 1937 and 1946.[97] Indira Gandhi addressed the Malaysian leader as 'Uncle'. Malayan defence personnel and civil servants were trained in India, and all Malayans, not just Indian settlers, benefited from India's scholarships for medical and other studies. India had helped build railways in Malaya and Indian companies invested there. But not everyone was as enthusiastic about merger as Lee and Nehru, and the bitter opposition of Singapore's Barisan politicians who knew that a Malaysian federation would be a further bulwark against Communist insurgency and Chinese subversion, found powerful support in Sukarno's great archipelago of thousands of islands across the Straits of Malacca.

{3}

Asia's 'Coca-Cola Governments'

Indonesian Foreign Minister Subandrio warned Krishna Menon that an enlarged Malaya would make 'Konfrontasi' inevitable. 'There's no such word in the English language!' snapped the pedantic Menon who had been an editor with Penguin Books in London. 'Mr Menon,' Subandrio replied, 'in one year's time there will be a word called Konfrontasi in the English language. We will see to it!'[1] Subandrio was out by only four months. He formally announced Konfrontasi—confronting Malaysia—on 20 January 1963, sixteen months after the exchange with Krishna Menon at the non-aligned nations (NAM) inaugural summit in Belgrade in September 1961.

The decade of the 1960s was a happening time for both India and Singapore. Though both faced problems with neighbours, and Nehru took a liking to Lee, wariness at the official level in New Delhi ensured a restrained response to Lee's overtures and prevented wholehearted support being extended to his cause. For India, those years of change, marking the end of the Nehru era, saw the fading of the Asian dream that had inspired the Indian National Congress soon after the First World War when Congressmen spoke of the 'Asiatic Federation of Nations'.[2] For Singapore, they witnessed a new beginning in which the brief unhappy interlude of merger with Malaya was a stepping stone to a unique global position.

Friction between Malaysia and Indonesia and reverberations of 'Ganjam [Crush] Malaysia!' and 'Ganjam Indonesia!' placed India in a quandary. Despite interaction with Malaysia at many levels, India's closer political links with Indonesia were integral to the Asian dream that had inspired Indian leaders long before Narasimha Rao made Look East the apparent centrepiece of his pro-Western foreign policy. Subhas Chandra Bose had reminded the Assembly of Greater East-Asiatic Nations in Tokyo on 6 November 1943 that Indian nationalists 'nursed the dream' of a 'Pan-Asiatic Federation' before it became a Japanese construct. Nehru was outraged in September 1945 when Britain deployed Indian troops against Indonesian and Vietnamese nationalists. He spoke of 'a common nationality for India and all these regions of South-east Asia' during the tour of Malaya and Singapore described in the previous chapter.[3] The British, too, thought of a linkage that may not appear so far-fetched in the light of Rajendra Chola, the Second World War, and Singapore's current defence arrangements with India. The Attlee government instructed the Cabinet Mission under Sir Stafford Cripps, sent to India in March 1946, to make India's assistance in defending the 'South-east Asia area' a condition of independence.[4]

Nehru's pan-Asianism was tempered with realism. Nothing came of the Asian Relations Organization that his 1947 Asian Relations Conference set up, and the South-east Asian League that was born in Bangkok some months later, soon fell foul of the authorities and was banned as an instrument of Communist subversion. Nehru explained to the Americans in 1948 that he had no intention of acceding to Thakin Nu's proposal for a 'United Nations of South Asia' which would detract from United Nations' authority, inject a racial and regional element into world affairs, and distract attention from the economic development that was India's first task. Nevertheless, a 'Federation of South-east Asia' continued to be discussed, and Thanat Khoman, who opened Thailand's New Delhi embassy in 1947 and was chargé d'affaires and acting ambassador for two years, 'wrote a few articles advocating some form of regional cooperation in South-east Asia'.[5]

When the Dutch tried to reconquer Indonesia, Nehru sent the strapping young Biju Patnaik, who had helped to evacuate British families from Rangoon when Burma fell, to bring Indonesia's leaders to New Delhi. Patnaik piloted his single-engine Dakota to Java, snatched Vice-President Mohammad Hatta and Prime Minister Sutan Sjahrir from under the nose of the Dutch army, and smuggled them to Singapore disguised as crew members.[6] A grateful Sukarno made him a 'Bhumi putra', son of the soil, Indonesia's highest civilian honour, and asked him to choose a name for his newborn daughter. 'Patnaik, the romantic hero, called her Megawati, or Goddess of the Clouds ... So longstanding was her gratitude to India that Megawati named her own daughter Orissaputri, or Daughter of Orissa.'[7] Mindful of his country's debt, Suharto, too, honoured Patnaik in 1995 with the Chin Tunga Yashottam title.

Renewed Dutch aggression against Indonesia prompted Nehru to organize another conference in January 1949 in the teeth of American opposition. Carlos P. Romulo, leader of the Philippines delegation, who referred to India twenty years later as 'the Guru in the noble tradition of Buddha and Gandhi', assured the Americans he would allow no 'yelling' or division along the 'colour line'. Ambassador Henderson also took a hand and the Americans boasted afterwards that only his 'exceptionally skilful diplomacy' kept the conference resolution 'comparatively moderate.'

When he was not trying to thwart India's diplomatic initiative, Romulo sounded out conference participants on 'a permanent organ of consultation on problems of common interest among the countries of South-east Asia within the framework of the United Nations' and reported that they 'exhibited keen interest in establishing a permanent organization to safeguard their common interest.'[8] But differences over defining those interests surfaced when President Elpidio Quirino called a conference at Baguio in May 1950 to discuss the proposed South-east Asia Union, changed three months later to the Pacific Union. India insisted on an economic agenda while the Filipinos and the Thais wanted an anti-Communist front. The Americans feared that the Soviet Union would exploit an Asian bloc, and any attempt 'to prevent its formation would probably be ineffective and would certainly intensify anti-United States sentiment in Asia'. They went ahead, therefore, with their own plans and launched the eight-nation South-east Asia Treaty Organization in Bangkok with three Asian members 'to protect Asian collective interests'. Lee recognized that 'nobody really believed the Thais, the Filipinos and the Pakistanis were conscious of their joint interests.' They joined for domestic reasons, and 'partly to get American arms like Pakistan.'[9] There is an amusing story of Seato's architect, the redoubtable John Foster Dulles, telling Walter Lippmann, the renowned American columnist, that he had roped in Pakistan to supply 'some real fighting men' since the Gurkhas were Asia's best. When he was told they were Indian, Dulles retorted blithely, 'Well, they may not be Pakistanis, but they're Moslems!'[10]

Asia's cooperative efforts had continued meanwhile. The Tengku's visit to Manila in 1959 led to the South-east Asia Friendship and Economic Treaty or Seafet which was uncomfortably reminiscent of Seato. When Thai initiatives produced the Association of South-east Asia in July 1961, one of the founders remarked that the Asa acronym meant 'hope' in the language of all three member states (Malaysia, Philippines and Thailand) without realizing the word was another Indian gift. Maphilindo—Confederation of Malaysia, Philippines and Indonesia—followed in what an Indian diplomat called the age of 'pactomania'. Politics was not the only problem between India and South-east Asia. According to Fifield, '. . . the subsequent leadership role of Prime Minister Nehru and the attitudes of some of his followers were often resented by leaders in South-east Asia and contributed to the development of the (regional) concept there.'[11]

Prince Norodom Sihanouk gives an example of what Fifield may have meant by 'attitudes'. When he flew the Royal Cambodian Ballet, featuring his daughter Princess Bopha Devi, to Madras and Calcutta for performances, high-ranking Indian officials assumed the dancers were Indian and asked if he enjoyed their performance. 'They believed that at my reception it was an Indian troupe performing for them!' was His Serene Highness's outraged response. Worse followed. When Sihanouk explained that his two Dakotas had flown the dancers from Cambodia, astonished Indians added insult to injury by asking, 'You have a runway in Cambodia?'[12]

The resentment provoked by this 'generally superior attitude' (to quote the prince) did not escape Americans who disliked Nehru's 'neutralism', their term for what Krishna Menon called 'non-alignment', and opposed India's participation in the 1954 Geneva Conference on Indo-China. India was so much a presence behind the scenes (Krishna Menon installed himself in a hotel where he briefed delegates) that French Premier Pierre Mendès-France spoke of 'this ten-power conference—nine at the table—and India'.[13] But Nehru's efforts to make something of the International Commission of Supervision and Control for Indochina, which India chaired, were frustrated by a mix of criticism, ridicule and obstruction that reached its peak eight years after his death when South Vietnam in effect expelled the Indian delegation.

Bandung, which ushered in the 'century of the awakening of the coloured peoples' in Sukarno's flamboyant words, was the high point of India's Asian involvement. If it was triumph and disaster for Nehru, thanks to Nehru, it was unalloyed triumph for Zhou whose aircraft to Bandung strategically developed 'slight engine trouble' and had to land in Singapore where India's representative, R.K. Tandon, had booked the airport VIP lounge and arranged Zhou's first private meeting with a senior Western diplomat—Malcolm MacDonald, son of Britain's first Labour prime minister, high commissioner for Southeast Asia and later for India. MacDonald called the meeting 'the start of one of the most fascinating friendships of my life'.[14] At Bandung, as Lee said in his funeral oration, Nehru introduced Zhou 'to the non-Communist world and sponsored China's re-entry into the comity of Asian nations'. Zhou repaid the favour by instigating Pakistan's prime minister, Mohammed Ali Bogra, to make common cause against India.[15] Yet, Nehru 'regarded Zhou's success as his own personal triumph'.[16]

Asia was Nehru's ideal—he made Panikkar's *Asia and Western Dominance* compulsory reading for his diplomats—but the West represented reality. Tyabji, one of Nehru's advisers at Bandung, explains that the foreign office recognized 'that India's main interests lay in Asia, and the principal aim of our foreign policy was to establish a close relationship with our Asian neighbours.' But Europe, where many Indian diplomats had spent their impressionable years, was intellectually, culturally and materially more familiar. It was also more glamorous.[17] No wonder then that Abu Abraham, the cartoonist, told a parliamentary committee that even in the late 1970s Indian foreign policy resembled figures in Egyptian murals with the head pointing one way and the feet another. Tyabji himself went to Jakarta with a sense of doing his duty. When he advocated closer relations with the region at a meeting of ambassadors to South-east Asia, Nehru, who was in the chair, exploded, 'Do you gentlemen want India to become friendly with Coca-Cola governments?'[18]

The phrase has passed into mythology with Singapore diplomats unable to decide whether Indira Gandhi or Ceylon's Sirimavo Bandaranaike, the world's first woman prime minister, used it to deride South-east Asia. Indians regarded Coca-Cola as a guilty indulgence long before the company was thrown out for exchange control violations and refusing to divulge its secret formula. But Nehru was not referring to wild tales of intoxicants and aphrodisiacs. 'Coca-Colonialism', a phrase that the radical chic tabloid *Blitz* coined, meant that any Third World leader who bagged Coca-Cola's bottling and distribution franchise was assured of American patronage.

Tyabji wanted India to replicate the British model of 'a high-powered mission in Singapore with overall political responsibility for the whole of the South-east region.' It would save money and manpower if junior officials in the other capitals took instructions from 'a high-powered, well-equipped regional representative' in Singapore which would be India's regional hub. When New Delhi did not respond to his proposal, Tyabji assumed it had been 'consigned to the archives.'[19] It may never have reached Nehru. When another of his reports contained 'a critical remark about Nehru's neglect of Indonesia and Indonesian misperception of Indian foreign policy', his ICS colleague, Subimal Dutt, then foreign secretary, drew a line in the margin and wrote, 'This need not be shown to the prime minister.'[20] 'Need' meant 'must' just as 'may' meant 'shall' in the bureaucratese attributed to Lord Curzon.

Lee as Salesman for Malaysia

Lee Kuan Yew's first official visit to India in 1962 was a personal and political coup for the relatively inexperienced young premier of a not-yet-independent city-state. He had two recommendations in Nehru's eyes: first, Cambridge; second, the leader of 'Singapore's million turbulent Chinese' was the first overseas Chinese politician to visit India.[21] Singapore being a semi-colony, Britain's high commissioner was at New Delhi airport to receive Lee with Lakshmi N. Menon, a junior minister in India's external affairs ministry. The appurtenances of statehood were still a novelty, and Josey could not get over the ceremonial honours with Singapore flags fluttering along New Delhi's grand avenues. Not only were there more of them than in Singapore but they were bigger and of 'much better quality than Singapore-made flags'[22]—a rare admission!

Since expense mattered, Josey had explored the hotel market to report that the Imperial in New Delhi charged US$37.62 a night against the state-owned Ashok's US$22.58. In the event, Nehru saved them money and did Lee proud by putting him up in Rashtrapati Bhavan. Protocol pundits saw this as stretching a point. That was recalled many years later when Lee wrote disparagingly of the 'run-down' palace: 'The crockery and cutlery were dreadful—at dinner one knife literally snapped in my hand and bounced into my face. Air conditioners, which India had been manufacturing for many years, rumbled noisily and ineffectively. The servants, liveried in dingy white and red uniforms, removed hospitality liquor from the side tables in our rooms.'[23]

His criticism was vindicated early one morning in 2007 when A.P.J. Abdul Kalam, India's twelfth president, telephoned his secretary, P.M. Nair, to say that water had dripped into his bedroom all night. 'I know you will immediately set things right in my bedroom,' he said. 'What I am worried about are those houses on the President's Estate where they may not have a second bedroom to shift to when the only one that is available leaks.'[24]

There were already signs that India and Singapore worshipped different gods and detested different devils. They also nursed different geographic and cultural images of what constitutes Asia. While India's inclusive definition prized the refinements of Iranian and Arab civilization, Singaporeans were captivated by Sinic-Confucianist 'Chopsticks Asia'.[25] India did not feature in the pages the *Straits Times* devoted to Asian news. The educational and cultural links inherited from the British were wearing thin. Trade was minimal, investment and joint projects non-existent, and in 1950 a delegation led by a director of Tata Industries—a name that, as the seventh chapter shows, deserves greater recognition in Singapore—led nowhere. Whereas Rajaratnam told the United Nations in his maiden speech on 21 September 1965, 'Singapore is essentially a trading community', India's share of world trade dwindled over the years as she sought self-sufficiency through import substitution. Each country accorded higher priority to its immediate neighbourhood. Carrying the burden of eternity, her roots lost in the mists of time, India was happily colourful, chaotic and confused; Singapore strove manfully to live up to the Mandarin saying that an MP quoted in Parliament, '*Re re gen xin*' (One must be newer and newer day by day).[26] Upgrading was more than a word or a way of life. It was a national compulsion.

Nevertheless, Lee courted India. Foremost among his reasons for doing so was the need to win support for the Malaysian Federation. Subandrio was not the only obstacle. Pakistan followed Indonesia. China denounced Malaysia as an imperialist conspiracy. The Philippines claimed Sabah. The Afro-Asian secretariat in Cairo objected to Britain's continued military presence. At home, Barisan's Lee Siew Choh thundered for seven hours that Malaysia would prolong colonial domination.[27] Lee had promised a referendum on merger but Barisan quoted Lakshmi Menon as saying it did not allow respondents enough options, and Krishna Menon's caustic comment that merger would make Singapore an 'estate' not a 'state' of Malaysia. Only Nehru's benediction could convince non-aligned, Afro-Asian and Commonwealth nations that Lee was neither Chinese chauvinist nor colonial stooge but 'a reasonable nationalist, basically a neutralist'.[28] Security was another concern. It still is.

The focus on India illustrates Lee's ambivalence about China. He said in 1962 that India was the only country that could 'keep the other end of the see-saw'.[29] He repeats forty-five years later that 'India alone had the weight and girth to fill the vacuum'.[30] Lee welcomed China's rise as an Asian counter to Western dominance; the Americans would not otherwise have bothered with the region and that would have been disastrous for Singapore. But South-east Asia also feared it might be overwhelmed by the Communist heirs to an empire that had never dealt with foreign governments as equals. The Son of Heaven knew only tributaries. Some modern historians argue that the tributary system was a form of trade and that the visitors took back more than they brought.[31] But the ritual also established the Celestial Empire's higher status by reaffirming the Hokkien principle of '*boh tua, boh suay*, no big no small', used to rebuke someone who does not know his place.

Lee knew that given its power, actual and potential, China 'must be a part of any arrangement for peace and stability' and that the region's smaller countries would have to learn to live with it. But that did not mean they could be sanguine about China's 'peaceful attitude of correct non-interference in the internal affairs of other countries' or overlook Chinese support for revolution and insurgency. America's presence was 'reassuring' but even the United States was an outsider with a hegemonistic record. Japan—remembered for the 'cruelty, brutality, hunger and deprivation' during its wartime occupation—was an offshore archipelago and, for all its economic might, could not counter-balance China.

> Korea is too small. Vietnam is too small. South-east Asia is too disparate. You need another big player to hold the balance. Then we have all more room. Let me put it simply like this—I am motivated by wanting a stable South-east Asia that will thrive and prosper because the environment around is favourable both in security and in economic terms, and it is culturally vibrant within the region and between the regions, between the Asean region and China and India; between Japan and Asia; and Japan and the Western allies. I see that as the ideal for this region.[32]

China's economy was then 'in a total spin'. Its subsequent buoyancy has only increased the need for an Asian corrective. India alone can provide ballast for stability.

Mission India's second justification was systemic. 'India was in juxtaposition to China' and the world was waiting to see which model would succeed and could be emulated by other emerging nations. 'And we felt the Indian way was more suited for us.'[33] As he outlined in the Legislative Assembly a year before Malayan independence, the Congress Party's constitutional and political example would enable Malaya peacefully to take over a functioning administration as India had done. That was why India was better governed than Indonesia. Any attempt to copy China where Mao's revolutionaries swept away the past would plunge Malaya into race war.[34]

Indian economic planning was also still attractive. 'Mr Nehru will prove that India can be developed and industrialized by democratic socialist methods,' was Lee's optimistic prediction.³⁵ He spoke of India moving 'towards the machine age: Steel mills, giant hydroelectric projects have gone up by her third Five-Year Plan, and will take India, by her fifth Five-Year Plan, in another fourteen years, into the industrial age.' India was the only Asian country to demonstrate 'any appreciable progress towards the industrial society, with the erection of steel mills (and) hydroelectric dams as the infrastructure of the modern industrial state.'³⁶ Though Singapore engaged the Dutch economist, Albert Winsemius, in 1961 and was firmly set on the capitalist road, it took time for Lee to break completely with the ideology that Nehru symbolized.

Nehru's charisma was a potent factor. It represented for Lee a distillation of everything that he most admired in East and West. Natwar Singh's colleagues (some of whom called him 'Nitwit Singh') attribute Lee's liking for him to a similar mix of Anglophile (Mayo College, built originally to educate India's princes, and Cambridge) and Sinophile (he learnt Chinese at Peking University). Lee says he got on with Natwar Singh—'a very powerful supporter of the (Nehru–Gandhi) family through thick and thin' and 'an intellectual socialist who believed in what he said'—'because he is bright ... he is articulate.'³⁷ But there was no point trying to talk economic sense to him because Natwar 'would go whichever way they [the Nehru–Gandhis] thought was in India's national interest'. Indira Gandhi 'made use of him as an interlocutor and he used to come here bringing Indian silverware ... oil jars and things'.³⁸

The Priest and the Acolyte

There were two lengthy meetings at Teen Murti House, the imposing residence of British Indian military commanders where Nehru ('one of the great men of our generation') lived. The first was over lunch (Nehru 'was very dainty with his fingers' while, as Lee recounts in his autobiography, he and his wife fumbled and floundered), and lasted an hour and a half. Nehru asked him to return in the afternoon and they chatted for nearly three hours. Lee assured Nehru that Malaya's British bases existed under treaty and did not represent colonial control. Also, in spite of the emotional pull of Mao's republic which had been enormously successful 'in transforming China from a corrupt, decadent society into a disciplined, clean and dynamic if regimented one' and in installing instinctive pride in China's resurgence, Singaporeans knew their future lay in identifying with the region they lived in. An independent Chinese island would incur the enmity of the surrounding Muslims: 'I told Nehru that we do not want to be a Chinese entity in South-east Asia. He understood this very clearly, that we did not want to be isolated like Israel in a hostile environment.'[39]

Nehru 'was pleasantly surprised' to find a Chinese determined to reject Communist control and Beijing's influence.[40] That morning's *Malayan Times* reported Nehru's support for Singapore's merger with Malaya. To Lee's delight, India's 'journal of record' (the *Times of India*) also reported that 'Malaysia had evoked appreciation in official circles'. Gratitude was tempered by Lee's shrewd assessment that in befriending Singapore, India was serving her own national interest—Nehru considered Malaysia 'a sound development because it would help to keep China's influence out of South-east Asia'.

Did the meeting help Singapore? Politically, yes, was Lee's emphatic answer, but not economically. At least, not yet. 'But we are not isolated. The Communists can't use the Afro-Asian nations against us ... Mr Nehru was in full sympathy with our views.'[41] The journey was 'more than worthwhile', said Josey, adding that Lee felt 'he might now be considered a junior member of the Afro-Asian leadership' and spokesman for a couple of million Asians anxious to throw off the last remnants of colonialism. Josey thought Indians were impressed by Lee's interest in everything and 'his amazing ability' to outtalk them at the sight of a mike or a reporter: 'He now knows, I think, that he hasn't got to put on an act to be accepted as a leader. All he needs to do is act normally and he comes through by sheer weight of intelligence.'[42]

There is an endearing suggestion of manipulative skill. The difference in rank and age between host and guest and the informal nature of their discussions ruled out the joint statement Lee would have liked but 'frankly, was a bit shy about asking the old man'. So they requested socialist friends in India's Parliament to ask questions about the talks. Lee was confident Nehru would 'give very friendly answers'.[43] The visit led to India's Lok Sabha speaker Hukam Singh and Deputy Minister for External Affairs Dinesh Singh visiting Singapore the following year.

Singapore between India and China

Zhou's 10,000-word-note to twenty-five Afro-Asian governments in November 1962 called the Sino-Indian dispute 'a legacy of British imperialist aggression', but Nehru saw China's claims, demands and peremptory ultimatums as a reflection of its Middle Kingdom complex. Lee said nothing about the dispute but Thailand and the Philippines supported India, and the Tengku, who sailed to Madras with a twelve-man delegation in October 1962, did so vigorously.

Lee gave him a ceremonial send-off with the Singapore Infantry at the quayside and the Tengku threw a cocktail party on board the *Asia*.[44] The tour included Hyderabad, Poona, Ajmer and Jaipur—with the Tengku publicly and unambiguously condemning China at every halt—until he reached New Delhi where Nehru held a banquet in his honour and called him a 'friend in need.'[45] Mindful that more than 30 per cent of Malayans were Chinese, the Tengku argued that the Sino-Indian conflict had no bearing on race or country but was about ideology. Totalitarian China would not 'tolerate . . . a successful democracy which is giving leadership to Asia.' It sought 'to topple democratic governments . . . and replace them with Communist regimes completely subservient' to Peking.[46] Back in Malaya, he urged Chinese Malayans to set aside ethnic loyalty and support India: 'You are not true Malayans (if you don't), all your protestations of loyalty as Malayans are all false and nonsense.'[47] His Save Democracy Fund sent a million rupees for India's war effort. Lee attributes this vigorous campaigning to self-interest: 'Yes, he was very anti-China. He considered China a very dangerous Communist regime that was creating trouble in Malaya and South-east Asia. So did we. They were very antagonistic towards us because they knew that merger with Malaya would destroy the Communist front elements in Singapore. That was our intention!'[48]

Rajaratnam also attributed Malaysian support for India to the Tengku being 'anti-China.'[49] The Malaysian prime minister's outspokenness encouraged the MIC to collect money for India's defence but Indians in Singapore were hurt and baffled by the government's silence. Some sent private donations; an Indian Singaporean wrote to Nehru placing his understanding of the Chinese psyche at India's service. 'I remember the great unhappiness among Indians when Singapore maintained a neutral silence during the Chinese invasion of Tibet', Rajaratnam wrote, Tibet being an obvious slip for India. It strengthened his view that unassimilated immigrants judged Singapore's policies in terms of whether they 'had a favourable or adverse impact on India, Pakistan, China, Indonesia or Malaysia.'[50]

Lee gives two reasons for not following the Tengku. First, Singapore was not accustomed to handling international situations. The idea of making a pronouncement was unfamiliar because Singapore was not—and did not regard itself as—a global entity. The British had prepared India and Ceylon for gradual independence 'with municipal elections and representative government or partially representative government, state governments, and so on.' But the theory of 'gradualism' with so many years set for India or Ceylon to become independent did not apply to Singapore which only 'had nominated legislators and that was a very great concession.' Singapore accepted it was a backwater. 'We had no universities, no nothing!'[51] Second, Singapore was not sovereign, and Lee says he had burnt his fingers by responding on 30 November 1963 to Zhou's letter of 2 August that year calling for the 'complete and thorough destruction of all nuclear weapons'. He adds, 'Tengku said, "You mustn't do that." I should not intrude into his space because that's foreign affairs. So we steered clear of any foreign pronouncements.'[52]

The letter controversy was a full year after China invaded India. But Lee says he explained to Nehru even then that he had 'steered away from taking positions intentionally' because Singapore was deeply involved in merger discussions with Malaya and foreign affairs was a federal subject.[53] Lee says, 'The Tengku was very insistent that I should not make any pronouncements on foreign affairs because we were going to come under his wing.'[54]

Malaysia was obviously more rigid than Britain, which had not been able to prevent colonial Singapore from expressing itself vigorously on controversial global issues. Marshall sent unofficial delegates to Bandung, issued supportive statements and led a trade and goodwill mission to Indonesia. Lee expressed support for liberation movements in the Congo and Algeria and, ignoring British disapproval, organized a giant welcome rally outside City Hall for Algeria's Ferhat Abbas. Apparently, times had changed. Referring to the referendum a year earlier when 70 per cent of half-a-million voters gave what Lee called 'the seal of public and popular approval' for merger, Yusof bin Ishak, Goode's successor as head of state, confirmed on 29 November 1963, 'On first September 1962 we in Singapore decided to place our future together with Malaya. The centre of gravity of political power is the central government of Malaysia.

The latter acquired sole authority over defence, security and foreign affairs.

Singaporeans who think Lee Kuan Yew is not the man to be inhibited by 'legal niceties' or the Tengku's sensitivities offer another explanation—the domestic challenge from Third China nationalists. Mao's revolution had generated tremendous enthusiasm among the overseas Chinese. 'Many boys, seventeen- and eighteen-year-olds, went back to help build the new China,' says Dhanabalan. 'There were frequent pictures in the *Straits Times* of parents saying goodbye to their sons on the quayside.'[55] Many dedicated Maoists stayed back, and the Nanyang Chinese University to which Jumabhoy gave money was a product of that exuberance in which racial pride stiffened ideological zeal. Muscular Reds lurked under the Barisan bed, and Britain's high commissioner, the Earl of Selkirk, assured Barisan leaders they could form a government if they won the election. Lee Siew Choh warned in the Legislative Assembly when India absorbed Goa in December 1961 after 461 years of Portuguese control that the fate that had overcome 'the intransigence and obstinacy of Western colonialism' also awaited the PAP. Though Operation Cold Store imprisoned 107 leftist activists in February 1963, Barisan still attracted more than 33 per cent of the votes and won thirteen seats in the election seven months later.

Lee admits by implication that his hands were full battling opponents of merger. Chinese middle-school students were seen as dangerous agents of Communist China, 'creating big unrest and troubles, strikes, go-slows, endless problems.' He says he was considered very 'reckless' for being involved with them. But he 'knew full well that we were both competing for the same ground—the Chinese-educated who were then the majority—and that this arrangement to ease the British out was a prelude to a contest between them and us for who was to take over.'[56]

The foreign office in New Delhi's South Block, Edwin Lutyens's imposing pink sandstone secretariat that also houses the prime minister's office, may have misread the mix of race and ideology. 'There was a very strong feeling in New Delhi,' says an Indian diplomat, 'that Singapore being Chinese was in any case part of the enemy camp.' The PAP was seen as a party with Communist leanings. Ethnic passions ran high in Calcutta with its established Chinatown, and Japanese businessmen pasted 'JAPAN' stickers on the windscreens of their cars. Singapore's Indian residents attributed the undercurrent of hostility to the hard-headed Chinese respect for success which, they felt, compounded traditional racism. Some xenophobic Chinese celebrated India's military reverses. If Rajaratnam and Dhanabalan were examples to go by, with a few outstanding exceptions, English-educated ethnic Indians in high position were not much more sympathetic either. But the Third China danger did not arise, Lee says, until Singapore was 'kicked out of Malaysia in 1965 August'.[57] It would have been a starter only if Barisan had captured power though Singapore's Malays, Indians and English-educated Chinese 'wanted no truck with the Communists or Communist China'.[58]

Whatever the reason for his silence, Lee rejects the theory advanced by Neville Maxwell, the Australian-born India correspondent of the *Times*, in *India's China War*, that Nehru's 'forward policy'—the unilateral occupation of disputed territory—left China with no option but to hit back. Even if Nehru did give such orders, Lee does not think they constituted an attack. He feels Mao planned the invasion to make a political point that misfired. It 'was a considered incursion to demonstrate that they are capable of inflicting punishment or whatever', he says, echoing President Liu Shao-chi's remark that 'China was a great power and had to punish India once.'[59] However, Lee wonders 'whether they believe in retrospect it was wise to have antagonized India'.[60] He recognizes the importance to China of the Aksai Chin road, lopping off nearly 15,000 square miles of Ladakh to connect Tibet with Xinjiang, but sees no justification for aggression across the 550-mile McMahon Line between Tibet and the 32,000-square-mile north-east Indian state of Arunachal Pradesh: 'They lost a lot I think by that. They alienated the non-aligned nations that looked up to India.'[61]

Apparently, Zhou also believed that the 'invasion' which had happened only because China's 'generals had taken the bit between their teeth, and had gone too far' was 'counter-productive' and a 'mistake'.[62]

Asked to consider that on the contrary, the non-aligned nations respected demonstrated strength in a winner-takes-all contest, Lee reflects, 'I am not so sure,' without totally rejecting the possibility of might being seen as right. 'At the same time, nations, weak nations, have their interest in the rules of international laws being observed. Their survival depends on that.'[63]

It is clear that in upholding the rule of law, Lee is thinking not of India but of the Little Red Dot which feels under perpetual siege, sharing with Alice's Red Queen the certainty that 'it takes all the running you can do to keep in the same place'. Despite Singapore's booming success, Jaswant Singh found Lee 'troubled and apprehensive' about the future.

Gamble of 'Independence'

India's wounds from the border war were still raw in early 1963 when Tom Abraham, a burly Syrian Christian career diplomat from Kerala, was posted to self-governing Singapore as assistant commissioner with instructions from M.J. Desai, the foreign secretary, to become friendly with Lee because India needed to work through him in reconstructing her South-east Asian policy and regain lost ground. 'I got in there when we were at a very, very low ebb,' says Abraham, recalling 'brittle early encounters' with Lee. Differences between Lee and the Tengku made his task easier: 'We were able to get on to a much better wicket thanks to the quarrel between Singapore and Malaysia.'[64]

There might not have been a Singapore to befriend if it had not been for several Indian diplomats, including Natwar Singh whose book-lined study in New Delhi displays the two volumes of Lee's memoirs. Both are inscribed by the author. Lee has written 'My old friend' in one and 'In admiration' in the other. The inscriptions recall his speech at the farewell dinner for Dinesh Singh: Lee hesitated, according to Abraham and looked at him before going on to say that 'very few people know how much Singapore owes to India—and will, I think, continue to owe to India—for India's friendship and help'.[65] The debt has never been spelt out.

Natwar Singh and Abraham are two of the four Indian diplomats who played a crucial role in the untold Singapore story. The other two were senior ICS officers—Abraham's boss in Kuala Lumpur, High Commissioner Yogendra Krishna Puri, and Chander Sekhar Jha, India's permanent representative to the United Nations and chairman of the United Nations Committee of Seventeen (the decolonization committee; later the Committee of Twenty-four).[66] Natwar Singh was the committee's rapporteur. He and Jha played midwife during Malaysia's birth, while Puri and Abraham helped the Singaporean toddler find its feet in the diplomatic nursery. Lee calls Puri 'a very shrewd observer' who was sympathetic to Singapore. 'He was still of the older generation of Indian diplomats—highly educated, polished, secular. You had good people here who were very helpful to us.'[67]

They had a role because of local and international opposition to merger. As a British historian records, 'After they lost the debate on Singapore's referendum bill in July 1962, a group of Assemblymen led by the Barisan Socialis and David Marshall sent an appeal to the United Nations.'[68] Natwar Singh says that though Lee broke down and wept when he appeared before Jha's committee, he 'made an instant impression' on the members.[69] Lee himself resented having to appear a second time to rebut the anti-merger case. He blamed Jha for giving the Barisan leader, Lee Siew Choh, a hearing after agreeing 'there was no alternative to Malaysia' and 'that since Singapore had a freely elected government, its actions could not come under review by the committee'.[70] South Block explains that since Lee Siew Choh had flown all the way to New York, it would have been unfair not to hear him and that the procedure allowed Lee to demolish the anti-merger case in a second appearance. 'We also stopped a Syrian motion to take the Barisan and Labour Front memorandum on board,' says Natwar Singh. 'We were very grateful for that,' Lee acknowledges.[71] 'Once we survived the decolonization committee that was the end of it.'[72] Marshall called India's action 'the cruellest blow of all'.

Britain and Malaya had agreed in principle on 1 August 1962 that the Malaysian Federation would come into being at the end of the following August. They signed a formal agreement to this effect on 8 July 1963.[73] As Abraham records, 'When the merger did not happen on the scheduled date—I think there was some feudal problem between Malaysia and Brunei—LKY decided that deadline or no deadline, British or no British, he was going to become independent.'[74]

Hence a baffling ceremony on 31 August when Abraham and other invited diplomats heard Lee declare Singapore's independence 'within Malaysia' from the steps of City Hall. Neither the United Nations nor any foreign government was asked to recognize a gesture that did not amount in Abraham's opinion to de facto or de jure independence. Lee 'did it for tactical and strategic reasons' and India's representative did not take it seriously. But he was not surprised to learn that the British objected to the independence declaration. 'Very privately, they told him this was just not on.'[75] With the benefit of hindsight, however, it is clear that what looked like a constitutional sleight of hand or an attempt to pressure the Tengku, who showed signs of dragging his feet over merger, may have been a shrewd move that saved Singapore's future. That was not apparent till two years later.

Lakshmi Menon represented India in Kuala Lumpur on Lee's fortieth birthday when the federation was born. Abraham attended the City Hall ceremony where Tun Ismail Abdul Rahman, Malaysia's deputy prime minister and a friend of Lee's, represented the federal government. It is a measure of the climate of nervousness that Abraham comments that neither the Tengku nor Defence Minister Tun Abdul Razak bin Hussain, later Malaysia's second prime minister, (his son, Najib Tun Razak, became the sixth prime minister in April 2009) was present. It was not logical to expect either to miss the celebrations in the national capital but sensitivities were so heightened that their absence was noticed.

Damage Control after Debacle

The merger promoted Abraham from assistant commissioner to deputy high commissioner. His relationship with Lee also changed.

> We found there were certain things on which both of us, perhaps, gained from an exchange. You know, the world view, what the Soviet Union was up to. What was happening in South-east Asia? Which way would the Chinese go? Which way would the Americans move? These questions were not always directly related to Indian foreign policy. They were conversations in which he found, perhaps, that what I was saying made some sense and we had ideas that sort off bounced off each other. And he was interested. We became very close friends. And very often he would ask me to come and have lunch with him. Either have a Chinese lunch or a steak.[76]

The lunches were in Sri Temasek, a nineteenth-century bungalow in the Istana grounds that was originally the British chief secretary's residence but used after 1959 for official entertaining. Abraham was usually the only guest, Lee driving over from City Hall where he had taken over the mayoral chamber, so that the two men could have a beer and talk.

Unlike Puri, Abraham did not play golf but did not find that a hindrance in establishing ties that still endure though—and this is a measure of the Chinese sense of privacy—he has never crossed the threshold of Lee's home in Oxley Road. Diplomats are usually forgotten when they move on but 'Lee Kuan Yew has a lot of time for Tom Abraham,' says Dhanabalan. Chandra Das corroborates that the former envoy can always 'walk into the Istana'. Nathan calls him up in Tiruvananthapuram where he has retired. There is less enthusiasm in New Delhi. 'Tom was for all practical purposes a member of the PAP,' says a former colleague. 'He was so close to the system that he saw things from their side.'[77] Abraham's defence is that he was always realistic. He was just as friendly with Devan Nair, who had a spectacular fall-out with Lee, and the charismatic Lim Chin Siong who was elected to Parliament when he was only twenty-two and spent nine years in jail. 'I remember Devan Nair teaching Chin Siong English by reading out passages from *The Discovery of India*.'[78]

Abraham has no illusions about the PAP: 'I am quite aware of the beatings and the tortures and all of what happened there. But the fact remains that on balance I think the PAP has done a remarkable job. Remarkable job!'[79]

He had absolute faith that the little island would make good: 'For me it was a very simple thing. I am not an intellectual. I admired the very tough pragmatic way in which this group of Chinese immigrants went about basically to establish one thing—that we are Singaporeans. We are not immigrant Chinese who are going back. Singapore is our home and we have to give every Singaporean a Singaporean identity.' As Abraham emphasizes what a very different Singapore he first encountered, one can hear strong echoes of Lee's own description of his achievement.

> You must not assume that Singapore of 1950s and 1960s is the kind of Singapore you see today. I have converted that whole Chinese-educated generation's children into English-speaking people. Yes, they can speak Chinese at home, they read the Chinese press, not as comfortably as English, they watch television comfortably, but they are better off in English. It has changed over the last forty-plus years.[80]

Driving home the point, Abraham recalls he was received in a hut that passed for Paya Lebar airport's VIP lounge. Chinese hawkers used sticks to beat out a rhythm in Morse instead of street cries. Dhoby Ghaut was just that, *Va naan theruvu* in Tamil, where Indian washermen thrashed out the laundry in the Sungei Bras Basah and dried it in the surrounding empty land. Bugis was a steamy transsexual paradise.

Another envoy, Ceylon's Canagaratnam Gunasingham, who went to Singapore in 1954 and made it his home after retiring as high commissioner in 1983, spoke of pot-bellied Chinese spitting everywhere. For Natwar Singh who first stopped there in 1958, Singapore was 'a poor man's Madras.' En route to Hong Kong to learn Mandarin a few years later, B.M. Oza, a future high commissioner, found the city of seedy gambling dens dirtier and shabbier than Bombay. Goh Chok Tong did not discover the wonders of sanitation where 'you could just pull the flush and everything disappeared' until he was twenty-one in 1962.[81]

Abraham inherited a modest mission with a first secretary, two officials for consular and trade affairs, and two or three clerks. The first secretary lived in a small flat in the chancery. Trade was the principal objective and some of India's earliest overseas trade fairs were held in Singapore. But his political brief became urgent in December 1962 after Srimavo Bandaranaike hosted a conference of six non-aligned nations to discuss a Sino-Indian peace initiative. The Colombo meeting highlighted India's isolation in the club she had founded. This erosion of prestige was one of the three points discussed in May 1963 when the heads of all regional missions assembled in New Delhi. Regional developments and the implications of the Sino-Pakistani entente were the other items on the agenda.

The meeting decided to send out a number of goodwill missions. Friendly Malaysia naturally received special attention, and a fleet of Avro-748s and three warships, including the aircraft carrier *Vikrant*, were despatched to Penang. There were consignments of anti-cholera vaccines, gifts of lions, Royal Bengal tigers and other animals and birds for Malaysia's national zoo. A silver chair for Kuala Lumpur's main mosque and official participation in a Quran recital contest stressed the ecumenical nature of the relationship. But as disappointed Malaysians pointed out, India did not support them over Konfrontasi.

This seemed particularly reprehensible because Malaysia attributed Indonesia's hostility to its support for India in 1962. When he met Sukarno in Tokyo in 1963, the Tengku 'inquired whether it was true that Indonesia had changed her attitude towards Malaysia because of Malaysia's attitude towards China, when China attacked India.' We will never know what Sukarno might have replied because Subandrio cut in to say that 'the Indonesians were a proud people and could not be influenced by anyone.'[82] Sukarno's animosity against Nehru's India, simmering since Bandung, exploded at the opening of the 1962 Asian Games. The ostensible provocation was Asian Games Federation senior vice-president G.D. Sondhi's view that Israel and Taiwan, both federation members, should be invited. Twenty thousand uniformed, though unarmed, servicemen savaged the embassy before marching off to Sondhi's hotel.[83] The explanation that though an Indian citizen, Sondhi was an international sports official who had acted in that capacity without consulting New Delhi did not impress the crowd that booed India's flag and anthem at the inaugural.

Lakshmi Menon almost provoked another outburst by saying in Kuala Lumpur that Indonesia and the Philippines had gone back on their commitment to accept the United Nations secretary-general's finding that Sabah and Sarawak had, indeed, voted to join Malaysia. But the mercurial Sukarno surprised everyone by calling at Indian Ambassador Apa Sahib Pant's residence to participate in a Gandhi memorial ceremony specially arranged for him a day after the anniversary. India had reason to be placatory. Indonesia was the world's most populous Muslim nation and the only non-Communist country to side with China. It was strategically located across the Bay of Bengal. Pu Breush in north-west Sumatra being only ninety-two nautical miles from Indira Point, southernmost tip of the island of Great Nicobar. And so Indonesia, too, was treated to Avro demonstrations that proved immensely popular. But the Malaysians could have shot back at India Ambassador Pant's 1963 Republic Day message to Indonesians, 'If a friend does not help you when you are in danger, what is the worth of such a friendship?'[84]

First of the Afro-Asians

Lee received a shock when he flew in from Addis Ababa in February 1964 full of the success of his whirlwind African tour to counter Indonesian propaganda. It was largely because of India's intercession with African governments and the 'unstinting assistance' extended by Indian missions in every capital he visited that Lee could report 'there was no question of them not recognizing Malaysia.'[85]

He came to say 'Thank you' and found Nehru a broken man. 'He looked weary and had trouble concentrating.' A stroke had left him pale and weak. China's invasion 'had destroyed all that he had hoped and worked for. His dream of a new age of Afro-Asian solidarity had turned to ashes.' But though Nehru had 'lost his vitality and his optimism' he was still alert enough to ask about the Malaysia–Indonesia dispute during their twenty minutes together.[86] A saddened Lee says he did not want to continue the conversation because Nehru's mind was slipping, and his aide looked anxious: 'He kept repeating "over the Himalayas". It was a shock to him. I concluded that he never expected the Chinese to do this to him over the Himalayas.'[87]

Three months and a day later, Nehru was dead. Lee telephoned Abraham soon after Deputy Prime Minister Toh signed the mission's condolence book. 'By the way, Tom,' he asked, 'are you having a meeting or something?' When Abraham said he was thinking of a gathering in the Indian Association, Lee replied at once, 'Look, the Indian Association grounds are not good enough. I want this to be held in the Jalan Besar Stadium.'

Abraham telephoned him to say the stadium, Singapore's biggest open ground, was booked for a football match, but 'Lee said, "Hang on, I'll call you back." He called me back and said, "Jalan Besar is free." Then he rang up again and said, "I will be there."'[88]

The stadium where Nehru had addressed mammoth rallies was 'absolutely packed' that day. Schools, colleges and offices were closed as a mark of respect, and Lee delivered a memorable oration that was all the more outstanding because 'the first of the Afro-Asians' could no longer reciprocate.

> Perhaps the most grievous blow that ever struck him was when his foreign policy, based on positive neutrality and non-alignment, reeled under the pressures of conflict over the Himalayas. That conflict... marked the end of an era. But he lived on for a further two years. That he was able at his age to take this blow with considerable restraint and dignity and to adjust his policies without renouncing his basic tenets of non-alignment was a tribute to the greatness of the man...

While Western analysts asked, 'After Nehru, who?' Lee's question, 'After Nehru, what?' went to the heart of Asia's political challenge. He did not despair but did not minimize difficulties either: 'The weeks ahead will show what kind of new leadership the second biggest nation in the world will have, and where its leaders intend to take it. Its consequences to us in South-east Asia will be momentous . . .'

The question had engaged him even before the 1959 law conference in New Delhi that exposed some of the problems of adjusting Eastern practice to Western principle. Nehru made even the absurdities of democracy—Lee includes universal adult franchise—meaningful. 'At a time when you want harder work with less return and more capital investment, one-man–one-vote produces just the opposite,' he told the Royal Society of International Affairs in London twelve months before Nehru died. The offer of more return with less work normally led to bankruptcy but worked in India only because of 'the enormous prestige of Mr Nehru and the quality of the leadership at the very top around him'. Millions of Indians were more loyal to the man than to the institutions of democracy.[89] But Lee demurs when asked if the commitment was to the singer not the song. Things might have been different if Nehru 'had been of a more authoritarian bent' but he sowed the seeds of democracy in fertile ground: 'The Indians already had a certain culture of non-violent change. The whole passive resistance movement, Gandhi's movement, was one of casual pressure to bring about revolutionary change. So I think it was already in the Indian tradition, or culture if you like, to have a mechanism that allows for changes to take place without overthrowing the whole system.'[90]

Hindu and Muslim societies were different in this respect, explaining Pakistan's repeated lapses into military dictatorship though the British left both sides with similar constitutional fundamentals: 'True, they had to start a new country and a new bureaucracy and so on, but they already had many ICS men who were well honed in a neutral bureaucracy, a neutral civil service, that serves the political masters of the day.'[91]

The difference lay in Muslim and Hindu culture. Indians are patient and prepared to wait for what Lee calls 'the stir for change'. So they hold elections every few years and prepare for gradual change in states and the centre. Pakistanis are more impatient.

Looking ahead, Lee declared that when India 'emerged as a modern industrial nation free from the bonds of caste and privilege, it would be because Nehru laid the foundations of modern India in the last seventeen years of his life, which were the first seventeen years of the life of a new India.' Malaysia (he was still a federal citizen) had lost 'a staunch friend' in the death of India's 'most illustrious son'.[92]

It was a worrying thought—and a predicament Lee did not want Singapore to have to face—that the only candidates for succession were Nehru's daughter and an old man.[93] Lee knew when the Congress old guard chose the seemingly innocuous sixty-year-old Lal Bahadur Shastri to keep out a more serious and even older contender, Morarji Desai, that India's political culture would undergo 'a shift from Western-orientated leaders to local-orientated leaders.' Shastri represented 'a minor shift, but a shift nevertheless . . .' Other changes would come, bringing 'a train of problems', he told the University of Malaya's Historical Society in Kuala Lumpur. It was the passing of an age.

> In South-east Asia, the most spectacular thing about the period from 1945 to 1965, the Age of Nehru (because he set the pace, the idealism, the belief in great principles), was the absence of cynicism, to a point where vast numbers of otherwise cynical people were led to believe that because Asians have gone through a common tribulation and common humiliation at the hands of the European powers, therefore thereafter they would always be brothers in a common struggle.[94]

Ever the realist, Lee added, 'That is not true, unfortunately.'

Changes had begun even in Nehru's lifetime. Reports of the American Seventh Fleet extending operations from the China Seas to the Indian Ocean worried him though his cousin, B.K. Nehru, an ICS man who was ambassador in Washington, optimistically suggested the move could 'possibly be intended to match the presence of Chinese Communist forces in the Himalayas.'[95] The prime minister was not comforted. 'We do not like nuclear weapons anywhere near India,' he declared.[96] He had paid no heed to suggestions that India should pre-empt China's nuclear programme. According to a State Department memorandum, 'While we would like to limit the number of nuclear powers, so long as we lack the capability to do so, we ought to prefer that the first Asian one be India and not China.'[97]

The Americans approached Homi J. Bhabha, head of India's atomic establishment, who reportedly put up the proposal to Nehru.[98]

Only nine days before his death, Nehru declared in a television interview, 'We are determined not to use (nuclear) weapons for war purposes. We do not make atom bombs. I do not think we will.'

Bhabha's death in an Air India crash in the Swiss Alps in January 1966 generated many conspiracy theories about sabotage to impede India's nuclear programme. Long before that—only six months after Nehru's death—China had exploded its first atom bomb. Lee responded with caution. 'Well, it was coming and everybody knew it was bound to come; now it has come . . .' China had made 'a deliberate statement'. It was 'the first time an Asian power had emerged as a member of the nuclear club. We do not know whether it will be a force for world peace. We will have to wait and see.'[99] He vehemently denies an Indian account which has him saying, after the test, 'India should also explode a nuclear bomb, at least for the sake of Southeast Asia, even if she wanted to throw it into the sea later.'[100] Lee denies this and says, 'No I did not say that! But I was quite confident that India would have the bomb. It was a matter of time. They never signed the anti-proliferation treaty. They were determined to have the bomb.'[101]

Away with the Old Socialism

Lee flew to Bombay on Tagore's 104th birth anniversary, as the *Times of India* noted, to inaugurate the Conference of Young Asian Socialist Leaders in May 1965 and deliver the keynote address, the only prime minister among thirty-two leaders from eleven countries. Though he told the gathering he was 'an unrepentant socialist', and the breach with the Socialist International was still eleven years away, his was a practical, not philosophical, creed. Seeing socialism as 'one of the most effective ways of mobilizing human resources', Lee would unhesitatingly discard it—as he did—if he hit upon a more effective means of harnessing resources. Meanwhile, he attributed the failures of South Asia's democratic socialist governments to poor management and insufficient technical expertise. Individuals did not work hard enough; they lacked any sense of public duty or service to the community.

He took an even more unorthodox position on Vietnam. Others publicly condemned American policy but supported it in private. According to American Vice-president Hubert Humphrey, even Indira Gandhi admitted that though domestic politics obliged her to criticize the United States, she was concerned about Chinese support for Vietnam and was glad the Americans were there.[102] Lee had no qualms about going public on South Vietnam's right 'not to be pressured through armed might and organized terror and finally overwhelmed by Communism'. He believed that they must 'seek a formula that will make it possible for the South Vietnamese to recover their freedom of choice, which at the moment is limited to either Communist capture or perpetual American military operations.'[103]

He breakfasted with Krishna Menon who was also staying at Bombay's Ritz Hotel, held a press conference and drove into the countryside 'to see something of India's agricultural development'. Despite mounting disillusionment with socialism, he called the Aarey Milk Colony, where the Maharashtra state government looked after 16,000 water buffaloes and sold the milk for the owners, 'a spectacular piece of practical socialism'. He warned Indian port and dock workers that unless 'proper measures' were taken, 'the gap between the rich and the poor in newly independent countries' would widen. Though 'imperialists' had gone, 'native capitalists' still denied the poor 'economic equality and social justice.'[104]

He flew to New Delhi where Malaysia's high commissioner received him—mark of Singapore's still subordinate status—with India's deputy chief of protocol who took him, this being a private visit, to the Ashok. There were meetings with Shastri, external affairs minister Swaran Singh and Dinesh Singh, and also a call on Indira Gandhi, who held the information and broadcasting portfolio and whom he had not met since her father's death. Lee followed it up with an impromptu visit without escort to the shrine at Rajghat where Nehru had been cremated while Josey telephoned Reuters' Peter Jackson and messaged the foreign ministry to airfreight a dozen golf balls. There was always time for a game.

Aung San Suu Kyi's mother, Daw Khin Kyi, Burma's ambassador to India, saw Lee and his party off since they were going to Rangoon.

They stopped in Calcutta en route, again staying at the Grand Hotel, and Lee expressed his disappointment that both North and South Vietnam were 'unimaginative' enough to reject the proposal for an Afro-Asian peace force made by India's philosopher president, Sarvepalli Radhakrishnan, whom he had met in New Delhi. Such a force would have made it 'possible for South Vietnam to exercise a freedom of choice as to its future without being coerced either by armed Communist groups in the country or the presence of American military might.'[105] Insult was added to injury when a reporter told him at Calcutta airport of President Lyndon B. Johnson's offer of US$100 million for peace was obtained in Vietnam. 'Such a carrot and stick attitude should not be used even on a donkey and it should be remembered that men have more self-respect than donkeys,' Lee exploded.[106]

Singapore and India were both in for rude shocks the following year. Eviction from Malaysia was still three months down the road but war clouds were gathering over an 8400-square-mile tract of marsh and mudflats in Gujarat called the Rann of Kutch where Pakistani troops attacked an Indian post. Asked in Bombay for his views, Lee had answered diplomatically that 'it was one of 'several conflicts' in Asia which the conference was discussing.'[107]

{4}

'An Absolute Pariah in the Whole World'

Three months after returning from India, Lee was standing on the steps of City Hall to proclaim that Singapore would be 'forever a sovereign democratic and independent nation, founded upon the principles of liberty and justice and ever seeking the welfare and happiness of her people in a more just and equal society'. He mentioned India no fewer than three times on that momentous 9 August. Yet, for all Lee's goodwill and for all the burden of history, independent Singapore and India seemed to have very little in common just then. Their foreign and military policy aims were substantially different; their economic strategies could not have presented a greater contrast. Size, geography, demography and culture set them apart. However, being then 'an absolute pariah in the whole world,' as Abraham says,[1] Singapore needed India's helping hand for political survival. And so, India was the first name that came to Lee's lips when a reporter asked about independent Singapore's diplomatic representation: 'Off-hand I would say India, perhaps Pakistan. I am not sure whether we can afford to have two missions for India and Pakistan.'[2] The second instance when Lee spoke of India was in the context of the India–Pakistan war which had moved from Kutch to Kashmir. It was a 'delicate question' but his 'sympathies' were with India.

I do not know the rights and wrongs of it, although I have heard both sides and I know the Pakistanis are pressing very hard the United Nations Security Council resolution—the plebiscite and so on; it was promised eighteen years ago. But the Indians are my friends. They were the first non-European Commonwealth country to recognize Singapore. The Pakistanis, I am sorry to say, although President Ayub and his government have always been very friendly to me, and we have been friends to them, have not recognized us yet.[3]

Though some Indians may have thought he sounded a little guarded, AIR made great play of the statement.

The third mention was the most momentous. Immediately after proclaiming independence, Lee asked Abraham and the Egyptian consul to see him in his office upstairs, beyond the waiting room where Abraham noticed the large aquarium of exotic fish. What he may not have expected was a request for military help. Lee had been busy all through the previous night dictating 'very brief and succinct' messages that were then encoded and transmitted to about twenty heads of government, including Shastri. Lee says he thought out all his moves only 'in the last few days' because the British had no intention of allowing Singapore's separation which, they felt, would break up the federation: 'Not only that. An independent Singapore would be a menace because of the Communist threat, the Chinese Communist base here in South-east Asia. That would be a disaster for the Americans and for them. So they would not allow it to happen.'

But the Tengku had warned there would be bloodshed if Singapore did not leave the federation. 'So,' says Lee, 'we had to contrive this secretly and push it through. Until it happened, we did not know it was going to happen. Everything had to be planned upon the seat of our pants.'[4]

He asked Egypt only to set up a coastal defence system but the terse two-page letter he gave Abraham wanted India in effect to replace Britain as the protecting power. Shastri should send a 'message of support' and, since the Anglo-Malayan defence agreement would antagonize 'some Communist and pro-Communist countries in Afro-Asia', India should build up Singapore's military.

Our armed forces constitute only two infantry battalions. Even these two battalions are short of trained officers and we are borrowing from the Malaysian government. We cannot afford to build up forces sufficient to protect ourselves from aggression by our neighbours but in spite of financial commitments we have given an undertaking to the Malaysian government to raise five battalions, that is three more than the present two as soon as practicable.[5]

He ruled out help from Malaysia ostensibly because its 'resources were already stretched to the utmost' though facilities were available at the Officer Training College in Port Dickson. Inducting British officers would encourage people to 'attack' Singapore 'as neo-colonialist'. Shastri should therefore 'send a team as soon as is convenient' to help raise the additional battalions; meanwhile, at least one Indian officer 'specially experienced in raising new units' should take over at once as military adviser to the new defence ministry under Dr Goh. He could be incognito, 'But he must be one who will know how quietly and not blatantly to inculcate attitudes of democracy and non-Communism, that is, resistance and rejection of Communist doctrines.'

It still rankles with Lee that Shastri did not even acknowledge the letter. The Indian prime minister did write to Lee (Abraham incorporated his few bland lines of goodwill in his own letter on 11 August)[6] but this was in response to the message flashed during the night of 8 August and made no mention of Lee's letter or his specific requests. Shastri merely noted 'with satisfaction' that separation was the 'result of an agreement' with Malaysia, and sent his 'sincere good wishes for the happiness and prosperity of the people of Singapore'. India, he added, looked 'forward to the development of close and friendly relations and mutual cooperation in many fields' with Singapore.

Abraham says Lee's biggest immediate problem was with the British. Harry Lee—the envoy's sudden reversion to the discarded English nickname is suggestive—was a creature of the British, 'culturally, linguistically and educationally'. He was very much under the influence of Lord Selkirk and his deputy and successor, Philip Moore. 'He has become independent. The British have not recognized him. He is absolutely desperate to get their seal and stamp of approval.'

9th August, 1965.

My dear Prime Minister,

    I have asked for your Deputy High Commissioner, Singapore, to send this urgent message and to ask for your assistance. As from 0001 hours 9th August, 1965, by solemn compact and proclamation, which for security reasons was published at 1000 hours 9th August, 1965, both by the Tunku and by myself, Singapore is now an independent and sovereign nation.

    I have given the relevant documents which establish our legitimacy as an independent sovereign nation and as the lawfully constituted government thereof to your Commissioner. The Anglo Malaysian Defence Treaty will continue to apply between the Governments of Singapore, Malaysia and the United Kingdom. I fear that when this is known some Communist and pro-Communist countries in Afro-Asia may attack us as neo-colonialist.

    I would be grateful for your message of support. Our armed forces constitute only two infantry battalions. Even these two battalions are short of trained officers and we are borrowing from the Malaysian government. We cannot afford to build up forces sufficient to protect ourselves from aggression by our neighbours but in spite of financial commitments we have given an undertaking to the Malaysian government to raise five battalions, that is three more than the present two as soon as practicable. For my government to use British officers to help in this may be said to be tainted with neo-colonialism. I therefore seek your government's assistance to send a team as soon as is convenient to advise us in this. The government of Malaysia will also help with their Officer Training College in Port Dickson, Malaysia, but their resources are already stretched to the utmost.

    Could you immediately send at least one officer, specially experienced in raising new units, to be military adviser to my Ministry of Defence. He could come either with a public announcement or completely incognito. But he must be one who will know how quietly and not blatantly to inculcate attitudes of democracy and non-Communism i.e., resistance and rejection of Communist doctrines.

    With best wishes,

Yours sincerely,

Sri Lal Bahadur Shastri,
 Prime Minister,
 India.

भारतीय डिप्टी हाई कमीशन सिंगापुर
DEPUTY HIGH COMMISSION OF INDIA
31, GRANGE ROAD,
P. O. Box No. 836
SINGAPORE

No. DHC/TS/65-XIII   Dated: 11th August 1965

Dear Mr. Prime Minister,

    I am instructed by my Prime Minister to convey to you with immediate despatch the following message:

    "Our representative in Singapore has transmitted to us the gist of your communication to him on 9th August morning to the effect that Singapore has separated from Malaysia and was now independent State. We have also been informed of the proclamation which has been issued both in Singapore and Kuala Lumpur.

    "We note with satisfaction that this development has taken place as a result of an agreement and has been approved by the Parliament of Malaysia.

    "On behalf of the Government and People of India I send you, Mr. Prime Minister, our sincere good wishes for the happiness and prosperity of the people of Singapore.

    "We look forward to the development of close and friendly relations and mutual co-operation in many fields between Singapore and India.

    Warm regards and personal good wishes,

        Lal Bahadur Shastri".

    Please accept, Mr. Prime Minister, the renewed assurances of my highest consideration.

(Thomas Abraham)
Deputy High Commissioner for India

The Hon'ble
Mr. Lee Kuan Yew,
Prime Minister of Singapore
Singapore.

If Britain and India did not recognize Singapore, no one else would. British recognition would bring in the United States and Europe; India's would set the precedent for Afro-Asia. An Indian physical presence would have a salutary effect on Singapore's neighbours as well as on Lee's domestic opponents. He was very anxious, therefore, for an immediate message from India 'which would help a great deal in establishing the identity and independence of Singapore'.[7]

Lee saw Shastri's silence as 'a diplomatic way of saying "No, I cannot do it."'[8] He did not know the new prime minister well. His reply when asked if there was any personal rapport with him—'Not the same as Nehru'—was a huge understatement.

> He was nondescript. He wasn't physically impressive. He was smaller than the average Indian. His bearing was not impressive. He was not like Nehru. When Nehru came into a room there was a presence.[9]

Shastri struck Lee as someone who 'would have gone by the advice of his secretaries'. Though 'intelligent,' he was not 'a decisive, incisive person' and 'would consider all the options.' That assessment would not have surprised Indians who saw Shastri as a stopgap, though no one expected his tenure to be so precipitately cut short, or that a sudden war would transform a lacklustre, compromise candidate into a national hero. The assumption was that sooner or later someone—Nehru's daughter or politicians acting in her name or an independent aspirant—would make a bid for power. They and Lee would have been surprised to learn of Shastri's own self-appraisal:

> Perhaps due to my being small in size and soft of tongue, people are apt to believe that I am not able to be very firm. Though not physically strong, I think I am internally not so weak.[10]

Nor was Shastri without a sense of humour. When American businessmen asked about India's population explosion, he smiled and said, 'I hesitate to give advice because I have six children myself!'[11] Lee blamed South Block which must have said, 'Look, on the one hand you have this huge country Malaysia, on the other hand a small island. Why do you want to get involved? Where are our interests?'

They never imagined, or they could not have envisaged, that forty years or even thirty years later, Malaysia would go green in the Muslim way, and Singapore, the Little Red Dot, become so cosmopolitan and share many of the attributes of India. Could not have predicted that![12]

But if similar values make for diplomatic partnership, the world's greatest democracy would have been allied to the world's largest instead of playing benevolent patron to the theocratic military dictatorship next door.

India Attacked in Kutch and Kashmir

New Delhi had confirmed the day before Lee's independence proclamation that Pakistan had opened hostilities in Kashmir. Five days later, Shastri again announced that India faced 'a thinly disguised armed attack . . . organized by Pakistan'.[13] India was wracked with anxiety during those hectic months between August and January when the conflict moved from Gujarat to Kashmir to Punjab. No element of the armed forces—'not a bullet, not a rifle, not a man' as a South Block official puts it—could be spared for overseas duty even if New Delhi had a mind to do so.

The war in Kutch, which did not go well for India, ended with a ceasefire arranged by Britain's Harold Wilson on 30 June, allowing Pakistan to retain 350 square miles of the Rann. The concession only whetted Pakistan's appetite and encouraged its military ruler, Field Marshal Ayub Khan, and his foreign minister, Zulfiqar Ali Bhutto, to exploit India's post-Nehru uncertainty by launching an even more audacious attack. They assumed that, humiliated by China, with an unknown and inexperienced premier, and the defence review that had been started after the 1962 defeat not yet complete, India would be easy prey. An additional factor was the indignation of Muslims throughout the country following the disappearance of a relic from a Srinagar mosque in December 1963. It seemed the ideal time for Pakistan to strike.

Ayub's Operation Gibraltar entailed infiltrating armed soldiers disguised as tribesmen across the Line of Control to incite Kashmiri Muslims to rebel, a gambit General Pervez Musharraf repeated in 1999 when as Prime Minister Nawaz Sharif's army chief, he launched Operation Badr in Kargil. Some 6000 of the 40,000 soldiers Ayub had trained for the purpose had already pushed through the LoC before India got wind of what was afoot. But far from supporting the intruders, Kashmiris handed them over to the security forces.

Trying to staunch the flow of infiltrators, Indian troops occupied posts on the Pakistani side of the LoC. Ayub retaliated with Operation Grand Slam—an assault using the Patton tanks given by the United States for defence against the Soviet Union and China—against the Akhnoor bridge to cut Kashmir off from the rest of the country. This was more serious than any skirmish in the mountains and provoked the major Indian diversionary move of sending troops into Pakistani Punjab so that Lahore was under fire. Pakistan's publicity machine claimed that India was trying to suppress a revolt by Kashmiri freedom-fighters. But the *New York Times* reported on 12 August: 'Reporters who were in Kashmir at the time saw no evidence of an internal rebellion. The Kashmiris seemed more concerned with selling rugs and renting houseboats to the tourists than in taking up arms for freedom.'

The war ended on 23 September with a ceasefire sponsored by the United Nations. Though the outcome was indecisive, Pakistan suffered greater losses in men and materiel and Ayub failed in his purpose of instigating a rebellion. India's loss was Shastri himself: grappling with this ultimate challenge of his brief career, the prime minister succumbed to a heart attack after signing a declaration with Ayub at peace talks hosted by Soviet Premier Alexei Kosygin in the Uzbekistan capital of Tashkent. Back in India, the Congress bosses propelled Indira Gandhi into his seat, believing her to be a *goongi gudiya*, dumb doll, who would do as bid.

Ayub Khan made a joke of the war a year later when Rajaratnam and Nathan visited Karachi for an Ecafe (Economic Commission for Asia and the Far East) meeting. Syed Sharifuddin Pirzada, who succeeded Bhutto as foreign minister in July 1966, was away, and Ayub invited the Singaporeans to stay for dinner to meet him. Nathan found the Pakistani dictator very Prussian in bearing and manner as he chatted with Singapore's foreign minister:

> You know we fought a war, Raja? I would call my friend Gary (on the Indian side) and tell him, 'I am going to have a shower, will you stop the bombardment?' And Gary would stop the bombardment. And I would have my shower. And Gary or whoever it was would call me. 'Eh Ayub, do you remember our mutual friend so and so? His son has been shot over your territory, look after him.' I would go there and say, 'Do you have a boy by this name? He's my friend's son. Look after him, will you.'

The Prussian image vanished and was replaced by a bluff British soldier as Ayub Khan prattled on merrily, making the war sound like a game of cricket. 'Very British!' Nathan laughs, 'Very, very British!'[14]

Such personal connections did exist among the brass hats on both sides who had attended the same military courses and played games and war games together; that espirit de corps surfaced again at the end of the Bangladesh war to the irritation of Bangladeshis who felt the camaraderie between victor and vanquished excluded them. But in 1965 it was neither cricket nor chivalry for Indians. It was a question of survival, though that may not have been the only—or main— reason why Shastri turned a deaf ear to Lee.

The blunt demand without the customary periphrasis must have surprised South Block mandarins who knew that however dangerous 'some Communist and pro-Communist countries in Afro-Asia' might be, Lee had more to fear from Third China advocates at home. The excitement that the separation from Malaysia sparked in Singapore's Chinese circles—clan associations and chambers of commerce—was matched by editoral jubilation in China's *People's Daily*, encouraging speculation that Chinese-educated leftists might feel emboldened to challenge the PAP's English-educated leadership.

The political climate in New Delhi fostered misgivings about the new republic. The American presence was strong in India, and Shastri's ICS principal private secretary, Oxford-educated Lakshmi Kant Jha, of whom Henry Kissinger thought so highly when he was ambassador to the United States during the Bangladesh war, is still remembered as the most 'pro-American' (Natwar Singh's term) of Indian mandarins. Some of Lee's speeches sounded anti-American. Some officials believed he was using India to reach out to Yugoslavia and the Soviet Union. Others suspected him of fronting for China. To use a bad pun, New Delhi found Lee something of a Chinese puzzle. According to a South Block analyst, 'It took us a long time to realize that he is just like one of us. He speaks left and moves right.'

His request for military help placed India in a difficult position. References to Afro-Asia and neo-colonialism were in order but bald mention of the Anglo-Malaysian defence agreement made no allowance for Indian sensitivities. Perhaps Lee thought that since Nehru had acquiesced in the original arrangement, his successor would have no objection to supping discreetly with the devil if the spoon were long enough. But this contradicted the distinction Lee himself drew between the Indonesian and the Indian positions on foreign military bases. While the 'whole object' of Konfrontasi was 'to remove the Western presence in the region' (especially military bases in the Philippines and Malaysia) because Sukarno hankered to extend his own authority, Lee recognized that India had no ulterior motives. Her objection was founded in principle.

However, he had concluded that India's rulers wanted to move away from their commitment of more than seventeen years 'to a fixed posture against military foreign European bases on Asian or African territory.'[15] He probably knew of covert Indian cooperation with the United States, Taiwan and Israel, especially after 1962, but the conclusion that India faced 'an acute dilemma' as a result and was looking for a way out of non-alignment would have been disputed. Despite developments on the ground, India's nuanced attitude to Communism dismissed the American theory of falling dominoes as a gambit to drum up support in the struggle for world leadership. At home, Communism was seen as one of many creeds (like Subud or Scientology) that sprout from seeds blown in from abroad, flourish, wither, die and are reborn under the indifferent sun of India's tolerance. Notwithstanding the Tengku's table-thumping, India was careful to keep ideology out of the Himalayan dispute. Speaking to a group of American businessmen a few months before the Pakistani attack, when relations with China were 'as bad as they can be' Shastri again advocated Peking's admission to the United Nations. He also 'shrank from endorsing the United States position in Vietnam.'[16]

Indians preferred Communism to colonialism. Abraham told Rajaratnam at the following year's Ecafe meeting in Bangkok that 'India had a lot of sympathy for Ho Chi Minh' who had vanquished French colonialism and was now forced to defend his country against the Americans. The regard was mutual, and while in jail Ho had written a poem to Nehru titled 'Together in adversity, Together in Freedom' that M.R. Sivaramakrishnan, an enterprising China-watcher in the foreign service whom I had encountered in Kalimpong, Hong Kong and London, translated into English.[17] 'We knew nationalism to be a stronger force than Communism,' Abraham says. As a Malayali, he harboured kindly feelings towards Kerala's former chief minister, E.M.S. Namboodiripad, the first Communist, leader anywhere in the world to head a democratically elected government.

Understanding this, Lee drew 'a clear distinction' between non-Communist and anti-Communist states, and accepted that the latter label did not cover India.

> We were non-Communist but in fact we were very anti-Communist. We did not want them to take us over. India was then quite secure that the Communists in India would not take them over, and the Soviet Union would not either. But we were not confident about ourselves.[18]

Though Nehru's 'non-Communist' India 'wanted to have no anti-Communist stance', as Lee shrewdly told his Legislative Assembly, that did 'not mean that when the Communists twist his [Nehru's] left arm, he will allow them to twist his right arm also'.[19] Still, the request for a specifically anti-Communist army officer overlooked both India's non-aligned commitment and her pride in a professional and completely apolitical defence force. It was unorthodox to expect the military 'to inculcate attitudes of democracy and non-Communism'. Soldiers do not spread the gospel in a democracy; that is the politician's preserve.

Lee's letter gave no hint of his problems with Malaysia though it obviously would not have been written at all if relations had not been strained. Singaporeans assumed that Abraham, who had been present at the creation and was 'very much in the know about what was happening' and 'played a very important part' in the sequence, according to Nathan, had briefed New Delhi.

> You see, pre-independence, Tom Abraham was here, he was very much in with us. He helped us walk through the non-aligned movement, walk through the radical non-aligned organization and in fact he was the key for Devan Nair and Mr Lee. He provided many of the arguments and inputs—they used to argue with him about preserving our non-aligned image despite having a British base. Tom was very much involved in that. But he was only the assistant commissioner because we were part of Malaysia.
>
> Whether Tom told them why we needed help, I do not know. But Tom was very much in the thick of it, guiding us, putting us in touch with other non-aligned, Afro-Asian countries.[20]

Like Lee, Nathan felt India had opted for Malaysia. 'That's our surmise,' he says. 'We have no evidence to say that, but we assumed they didn't want to disappoint a Muslim country.' It was a reasonable conclusion, and one that was in accordance with Singaporean pragmatism. India may have had more in common with Lee's promise of a secular egalitarian society than with an Islamic monarchy like Malaysia which gave preferential treatment to Malay Muslims, but more than 13 per cent of India's population was Muslim, and the Muslim vote was not only decisive in a hundred Lok Sabha constituencies but was also especially important to the ruling Congress Party. India under attack from a Muslim neighbour looked for other Muslim friends, and Malaysia would have been attractive even if India's political investment in Indonesia had not turned sour. India had not forgotten the Tengku's support in 1962. He helped to bridge differences with other Muslim countries when India claimed membership of the newly-formed Organization of the Islamic Conference in 1969. Singaporeans did not make an issue of it, but that same year India was selling arms and ammunition to Malaysia while the Chinese were being murdered there.

Though India refused to give Singapore military assistance, Indian diplomats were willing to help in other ways, often informally or through personal contacts. India was the 'first non-European Commonwealth country' to recognize Singapore, as Lee says, (not the first country to extend recognition, as some Indians still believe). India also supported Singapore for membership of the United Nations, the Commonwealth and non-aligned nations movement. A NAM preparatory committee was about to meet in Algiers to discuss the next summit and Lee was very anxious for acceptance there. 'And he said to me, I still remember, "Look Tom, I need at least a flicker of respect. If India sponsors Singapore, at least that much will have been gained."'[21] Nathan, who had to explain the separation at Afro-Asian meetings and rebut charges of Singapore being allied to Communist China, confirms this isolation: 'You know we were without friends, and after Zhou En-Lai's remark that Africa was ripe for revolution, people might have thought this was a Chinese city breaking away.'[22]

It was also necessary for Lee to get rid of any taint of neo-colonialism because of the suspicion, fanned by his Barisan opponents, that he had worked closely with British intelligence in jailing leftists. The membership of NAM under Indian auspices would save his reputation. New Delhi kept its word. When some NAM members questioned Britain's continued military presence, India argued that the sun was setting on the residual fragments of empire and the arrangement reflected economic necessity and not ideological preference. Singapore was an independent Asian country that subscribed to the movement's ideals.

Singapore's new foreign minister may have thought this an unnecessary elaboration since non-alignment had little to do with ideals and abstractions for him. Rajaratnam saw it as 'the safest ideology for small nations' that might otherwise be sucked into superpower rivalry. If a strategically important Singapore aligned itself with one power bloc, it would invite a counter-reaction from the other, especially with the superpowers already at loggerheads in South-east Asia. 'It would have also meant jeopardizing our recently won independence.'[23] To be non-aligned was a question of pragmatism, not principle. NAM itself was so much 'hot air'.

Three months after separation, Toh, Rajaratnam and a junior minister, Inche Rahim bin Ishak, paying a four-day goodwill visit to India, asked for 'assistance to constitute Singapore's diplomatic service'.[24] As Michael Leifer, the London School of Economics political analyst, says and Nathan corroborates, the foreign office was then only 'a collection of information gatherers and messenger boys'. Swaran Singh readily promised help and some Singaporean diplomats attended the Indian School of International Studies in New Delhi while others were attached to India's external affairs ministry. Singapore again turned to India when a North Korean vice-president decided to pay a call, and following the advice received, laid out the red carpet with a gun salute and guard of honour. 'Later we discovered they have some thirty or forty vice-presidents!' Nathan says ruefully.

Indian guidance was more useful when self-made, China-born tycoon Ko Teck Kin ('He speaks better Malay than he does English,' said Rajaratnam) became Singapore's first emissary abroad. Abraham was at hand to remind the Singaporeans to seek *agrément* from Kuala Lumpur before their very first Excellency set off in tails and topper as high commissioner-designate to present his credentials to His Majesty the Yang di-Pertuan Agong. The external affairs ministry report for 1966–67 noted, 'India has been extending technical and economic assistance to Singapore under the Colombo Plan as well as bilaterally.'

Abraham did not conceal from his Singaporean friends that he did not see eye to eye with Mustapha Kamal Kidwai who succeeded Puri in Kuala Lumpur in 1964. The new high commissioner, who belonged to a prominent Muslim landowning clan in Uttar Pradesh, was politically well-connected in India and friendly with the Malay elite. Abraham grumbles that he 'was more interested in preserving the Malaysian relationship'. Kidwai's report that the Malaysians expected a drowning Singapore to seek re-merger on their terms encouraged South Block to wonder how long the 'self-contradiction' of a notionally independent Singapore, lacking a hinterland or any natural resources and dependent on Malaysia for even an essential commodity like water, could survive. Some Indians did not give the Little Red Dot more than a week. British and Indian recognition were part of the bulwark Lee was building up to prove these Jeremiahs wrong: 'If Harold Wilson decided not to recognize us, the world would have stood back because this, the Federation of Malaysia, was a British creation. The Communist side would have thought that this was one of those theoretical plays within the group.'

He and Wilson knew each other well, and the British premier was aware that Lee had put his heart and soul into the Malaysia project. He also knew the Tengku. 'So when the federation broke up Wilson decided it was not mendable. "Okay," he announced, "let it go."'[25]

War Games after the War

The connection between Lee's unproductive request to India and the military assistance received from Israel has never been properly explained. Leifer feels 'Singapore had almost certainly decided on Israel as its most suitable defence partner' after comparing the special challenge the two states faced. It justified the decision by citing the reluctance of non-aligned countries, such as India and Egypt, which Singapore had sought to cultivate, to offend Malaysia by becoming involved in the republic's military development.[26] An Israeli strategic writer, Amnon Barzilai, goes further to suggest that, while making a pro forma approach to India, Singapore was already negotiating with the Israelis: 'It's not clear whether Lee, in fact, believed India and Egypt were capable of, or interested in, building up Singapore's army. Many Israelis believe the two leaders were approached only for appearance's sake.'[27]

Lee says he 'half expected' India to refuse his request.[28] But he vehemently denies making simultaneous applications or using the approaches to India and Egypt as a cover for negotiating with Israel.

> No, no! Rubbish, absolute rubbish! The Israelis would not have known of our possible existence. But when it happened, and after a few weeks they found this man, Moshe Sharuk, I think [he meant Mordecai Kidron whom he and Dr Goh had met in 1962 and 1963] who was their ambassador in Bangkok, flew in and saw the newly appointed defence minister Goh Keng Swee, and said, 'Look, you need an army, we are prepared to help you.' So when Goh asked me I said, 'Let me think it over—do we want to get involved with the Israelis, and the Israeli-Arab conflict?' In the end, we said, 'Okay, let's go ahead. They know how to build a citizen's army,' and so we went ahead.[29]

The sequence is worth repeating. While Lee was expounding his hopes to Abraham in his City Hall office and giving him the letter for Shastri, Dr Goh, transformed into defence minister, sat alone in his office in the Fullerton Building, now a luxury hotel, pondering on the need to immediately build up 'a credible defence force'. Goh Keng Swee admired the structure and discipline of the Indian army but Joe Pillay, then in the defence ministry, who calls Dr Goh 'the creator of Singapore's progress and prosperity', says he also kept a close watch on Israel's military. GKS, as Dr Goh's daughter-in-law and biographer, Tan Siok Sun, calls him throughout her book, 'had earlier conversed with PM Lee over the phone' and come to a conclusion: 'Impressed by what the Israelis had accomplished in Israel in such a short space of time, GKS decided to contact Kidron (whom he had met in Tel Aviv in January 1959) to seek his advice.'[30]

Kidron had called on Dr Goh and Lee in 1962–63 and claimed—incorrectly as it turned out later—that Malaysia had agreed to host an Israeli consulate. That was reason enough, he argued, for Singapore to follow suit. Lee stalled, recognizing, as Nathan says, 'the sensitivities of the region'. Dr Goh's biographer does not give the precise date on which he approached Kidron. But she says, like Pillay, he had 'been impressed by [Israel's] defence system, discipline and resolve', and implies that he did so as soon as he assumed charge.

And so, Kidron, accompanied by his first secretary Hesi Carmel, arrived in Singapore a few days after accepting GKS's invitation, and they immediately called upon both GKS and PM Lee . . . when asked by GKS for assistance in helping Singapore set up a credible defence force, Kidron was only too glad to offer his country's expertise in military training.'[31]

Isolated in Asia, the Zionist state welcomed the opportunity to gain a foothold in a non-aligned nation in the heart of the Islamic ummah. Israel's Histradut already had links with Singapore's National Trades Union Congress but nothing could be more vital than defence. Lee asked Dr Goh 'to keep it from becoming public knowledge for as long as possible so as not to provoke grass roots antipathy from Malay Muslims in Malaysia and Singapore.' And so, it was an open secret that the 'Mexicans' about town were really Israeli army personnel. Lee was still waiting to hear from Shastri. Nathan thinks it significant that in spite of the military training programme, Lee did not visit Israel until the 1990s because 'he recognized that we lived here in a Muslim world and Israel would be a very sensitive matter. And while we had the defence relationship, it did not mean that we were tilting towards Israel.'

However, the Israelis were not people to let the grass grow under their feet. Foreign Minister Golda Meir personally took a hand in arrangements and sent Rehavam Ze'evi, deputy head of operations in the Israeli general staff, to Singapore 'in early August 1965'.[32] How early? Singaporeans are vague about the precise date: it was 'very soon after 9 August' or 'a few days after 9 August'. That was the day when the requests to India and Egypt were made.

Lee was 'disappointed' when Nasser, whom he had known a long time and had admired for his firm secular action in suppressing the Moslem Brotherhood, opted out. Josey records they were 'boisterously friendly' when Lee visited Egypt to argue the case for Malaysia; the relationship was naturally chummier than with the much older Nehru. Nathan who was present at Nasser's dinner for Lee in 1970—only a week before the Egyptian leader died—says they talked and talked, confirming the 'great fondness' between them.[33] But Nathan doesn't think Egyptian help was ever on the cards. 'Egypt, I think was not possible, but India, Lee wanted. India was always very much on the radar screen.' He thinks a bilateral military relationship would have been a way of involving India in South-east Asia. 'Right from Day One MM had been emphasizing, calling on India to play a role in the region. When there was a negative response to his request, I don't think he took umbrage. He felt the consideration must have been about not upsetting the Malaysians.'[34] Nathan had to inform the Egyptian ambassador when Singapore and Israel established full diplomatic ties on 13 May 1969, and 'Lo and behold! Race riots erupted in Malaysia!' The rioting was unrelated but fortuitous. It swamped the media and completely distracted attention from a connection that would otherwise have caused a furore.[35]

Far from seeing any inconsistency in simultaneous approaches, Abraham admires Singapore for being canny enough 'not to put all its eggs in one basket'.[36] The preferred basket was Indian but who knew how the Indians would respond? Dhanabalan thinks it was just as well they did not. Otherwise, Singapore might have been lumbered with an army 'in British-style uniforms so stiffly starched they can stand up on their own!' Israel gave Singapore 'the substance of defence'.[37] It was a 'citizen's army' as Lee put it. Pillay went to Israel in December 1965 and came back impressed and convinced that the Israelis, being in the same position as the Singaporeans, were the best choice. He also 'recognized their technological prowess' which led to Israel helping to set up defence industries in Singapore. In October 1969, Lee confirmed to the Socialist International why he chose Israel: 'In our situation, we think it might be necessary not only to train every boy but also every girl to be a disciplined and effective digit in defence of their own country.'[38]

As for suggestions of similar approaches to Yugoslavia and Switzerland, Lee says he 'didn't want the whites to come'. He 'wrote to Nasser, who was a good friend, and Shastri. Just the two of them.'[39]

Sukarno's 'Oldefo' and 'Nefo'

If any country acted as China's surrogate during the 1965 war, it was not Chinese Singapore but fraternal Indonesia. In Lee's view Sukarno fell out with Nehru 'because he was egotistical, that's all'. Reminded that Nehru had his fair share of ego, Lee replies, 'But Nehru didn't have that megalomaniac streak!'[40] Sukarno saw himself as Asia's paramount leader and a global power broker; he wanted to transform NAM into a militant, radical, anti-Western bloc unlike Nehru's sophisticated vision of a gently mediating force that would ultimately dissolve differences between the two Cold War contestants.

China, moving away from the Soviet Union, instigated Sukarno for its own ends so that each minor difference exploded dramatically. Paradoxically, so did the Soviet Union, and Anastas Mikoyan, the Soviet first deputy premier, told a public rally in Jakarta that his country would give Sukarno modern weapons that were 'far better than the British possess in this area' in order to 'crush Malaysia'.[41] Indonesian rent-a-crowd tactics burst out again in April 1964 during the preparatory meeting for the second Afro-Asian conference to be held in Jakarta the following March. Sukarno lumped India with 'non-Asian countries in Asia' like Israel, South Korea, South Vietnam, Formosa and the short-lived Arab Federation, as well as with Malaysia which did 'not exist legally'.[42] If Malaysia thought it had incurred Sukarno's wrath by supporting India, India knew that Indonesia had taken umbrage at Nehru's endorsement of the Commonwealth prime ministers' communiqué on forming Malaysia, and subsequent support for Malaysia's admission into the Afro-Asian conference in Cairo, and the celebrations to mark the Bandung conference's tenth anniversary.[43]

Singapore was also entitled to attend the anniversary celebrations (having sent unofficial envoys to Bandung) but the Indonesians managed to exclude its delegation from the third Afro-Asian People's Solidarity Conference at Moshi in Tanganyika in February 1963. Singapore's trade and cultural office, operating out of the British embassy in Jakarta, was closed down. The cessation of its traditional barter trade with Indonesia had already hit Singapore's economy; the city-state suffered further when Indonesian commandos attacked fishing boats and bombed a number of sites in the island. An explosion in MacDonald House in Orchard Road, next door to the Istana, killed three people and injured thirty-three.

Though China, Turkey and Iran (the last two bound to Pakistan by both religion and common military links with the United States) were also vocal in Ayub's defence, no one was as vociferous as Sukarno. 'Indonesia is positively standing behind Pakistan,' he thundered, threatening to seize the Nicobar Islands and send a submarine, two air force squadrons and a million 'volunteers' to fight India. Militant rhetoric was matched by a repeat performance of the mob tactics for which the Indonesian ruler was notorious. India's embassy was again ransacked; so were India's consulate and information centre and the Air India office in Jakarta. Air India and Garuda suspended flights to each other's country, and Indonesia closed down its Calcutta consulate.

The Tengku again supported India. Though he was less outspoken in public this time, Pakistan took 'serious exception' to a speech by Ramani, the lawyer Nehru had met in 1946 and who had since been appointed Malaysia's permanent representative at the United Nations. According to the *Far Eastern Economic Review*, Ramani's speech only 'interpreted some non-neutral ceasefire facts in an objective way'.[44] The eminent jurist, Mahommedali Currimbhoy Chagla, who had been Jinnah's secretary and became Indira Gandhi's external affairs minister, confirmed that Ramani's 'utterances were not partisan or partial to India but were an objective and impartial appraisal of the conflict and the causes that led' to it.[45] But Pakistan branded Ramani 'pro-Indian' and snapped diplomatic ties. Pakistani newspapers harped on his Indian ancestry. So did some Malaysian papers but the Tengku stood by his man.

A month later Lee described India and the smaller South-east Asian countries as 'nuts' in a nutcracker formed by Indonesia in the south, and Pakistan and a very big power (presumably China) to the north. 'I hope in the end that President Ayub will recognize that perhaps we are not as Oldefo (Old Dying Established Forces) as President Sukarno likes to believe.' He paid Sukarno a backhanded compliment on his turn of phrase. Oldefo was not the only evidence of the

Indonesian leader's verbal creativity: 'He is very good. He coins new words and slogans like Nefo, New Emerging Forces.'[46]

Why Is the British Flag Flying Here?

Speaking to a group of British correspondents at the end of August, Lee described his first meeting, after the federation broke up, with Selkirk's successor, Lord Head, an ex-brigadier and former secretary of state for defence.

> And I said to him: 'You know, of course, as far as I am concerned, I will prefer my first recognition from an Asian country such as India. And if I were you, I would get in touch with the British high commissioner in India, Mr John Freeman, of whom I happen to be a friend, and tell the Indian government that the British really cannot intervene. Once the British say that, the Indians will recognize me.' He did not do that. He whipped back to Kuala Lumpur. I do not know what signal he sent to London, but within seventeen hours I got recognition from the British government.[47]

Lee told Abraham that 'the British were unhappy; very, very unhappy' at the separation. There was a danger, at least in theory, of Britain trying to say that having been expelled from Malaysia, Singapore had reverted to its earlier colonial status. Could some prescience about that possibility have accounted for the unilateral declaration of independence a fortnight before the proposed merger? Lee also described watching Lord Head drive up in his Rolls Royce with the Union Jack flying, and asking himself what the British flag was doing in an independent Singapore that Britain had not recognized, and to which the envoy was not accredited. As Abraham saw it,

> Head was pointing out he was still high commissioner because the Queen still had not formally recognized the breakaway of Singapore, its independence. That was the whole business

of flying the British flag. It implied Singapore was still part of Malaysia.[48]

With his grasp of the niceties of protocol, Lee understood Head's subtle insistence on his continuing diplomatic jurisdiction. Abraham always found Lee very particular about details like that. 'He has an obsession about tidiness, neatness, temperature, heat, so many things.'[49]

Abraham flew to Kuala Lumpur the morning after these tumultuous events. He was Kidwai's junior until New Delhi's recognition of Singapore's independence meant promotion to the rank of India's acting high commissioner.

As Lee's letter to Shastri indicated, some—about 10,000, he says—federal troops were stationed in Singapore when it became independent. Normally, such a contingent would have been regarded as a leftover from the past, waiting to be tidied up. But Lee read sinister intent when Malaysia refused to move the troops even though Singapore's own two battalions were about to return from Sabah.[50] Worse, Nathan says that when Singapore's soldiers did come back, the Malaysians ordered them to go into tents in Farrer Park because federal troops would continue to occupy the barracks. Nathan believes that only the presence of Australian, New Zealand and British forces, and Indonesia's continuing Konfrontasi restrained Malaysia from attempting more. Ostensibly, the federal forces were there for Singapore's defence but Lee angrily mocks the suggestion: 'We were supposed to be independent and they were going to keep the troops here to look after us?'

He describes an incident that took place on the December day Parliament was to open as proof of Malaysian intentions. There was a lot to do, like amending the constitution, and Lee was just about to set out when the senior-most federal army officer in Singapore, Brigadier Syed Mohamed bin Syed Ahmad Alsagoff, turned up. The Brigadier, a Singapore Malay who was under Malaysian control, said, 'Sir, my instructions from the Tengku are to escort you to Parliament with outriders.'

Lee says he paused and with his appreciation of the politics of protocol, considered the implications. Though saying yes would show that the Tengku was in charge, the price of refusal could be high. 'I said "Okay, you drive, you escort me to Parliament."'⁵¹

Nathan, too, thinks Alsagoff's action was planned to demonstrate 'the Tengku's suzerainty over Singapore.' It was not a question of what the brigadier could or could not do. 'That was not the point. The symbol of him, the public perception, that's what mattered.'⁵² Such needling continued until 1969, the 150th anniversary of Raffles's landing, when Singapore pulled off a master stroke.

> We invited all our four defence partners here, Malaysia, Australia, New Zealand and Britain. And then we produced AMX-13 tanks at the parade. And Razak knew—he was Malaysia's defence minister then—that these 10,000 troops without tanks could not control us.⁵³

Nathan, too, saw the tanks as proof of Singapore's military competence and preparedness.

> We had to demonstrate to the world and to them that we were capable of taking care of our defence. And I think this display was part of that process, reminding them that, 'Look, we have capabilities which you have.'

In a burst of pettiness, Malaysia refused to allow the police band, a federal unit, to perform at Singapore's National Day rally. 'The refusal prompted the forming of any number of bands, school bands, people's association bands, and so many other bands so that we could say we can do without you!' Nathan says.⁵⁴ Asked if Malaysia intended to control Singapore even after ejecting it from the federation, Lee replies with a vigorous affirmative:

> Oh yes, absolutely! That was the whole idea. Through the control of water and their troops they would control us. They would do what they liked and in fact the Tengku told Anthony Head that 'if they act funny, we'll just cut the switch, cut off the water.' The evidence is all in Anthony Head's cables to London which we have dug up.⁵⁵

Malaysia 'wanted an independent Singapore just in name so that we would not be able to interfere in their politics. We were too much of a problem for them, this multiracial rainbow, before the phrase was formed.'[56]

The End of the Affair

Lee was 'very, very upset' when Abraham was transferred. 'You know why I was transferred?' the former envoy muses in his retirement in Trivandrum, and proceeds to supply the answer. 'Kidwai and I did not get on; because he was extremely pro-Malaysian to the extent of becoming anti-Singaporean. The relationship between Malaysia and Singapore was very, very bad, you know—1964, 1965, 1966—so he decided I must be got rid of from a certain foreign policy angle, and also from a personal angle.' Abraham had done the normal run of three years but wanted to stay on.

> The fact of my departure at that time—I am not flattering myself—left a tremendous void in Kuan Yew's group of personal gongs which he could sound, you know, like a wave sends out a signal and it rebounds and comes back. I was one of those things. He was very upset and he could not understand why I was transferred. And of course there was no one else with whom he could talk about so many things.[57]

As a Malayali Syrian Christian, Abraham felt an outsider in India's mainstream; an outsider, moreover, who did not take kindly to the north Indian aristocracy to which Kidwai and Dinesh Singh, titular Raja of Kalakankar, belonged. Abraham's successor, Surendra Singh, His Highness the Maharaja of Alirajpur, was an even grander personage before Indira Gandhi abolished titles and privileges. Alirajpur in Gujarat, more than three times Singapore's size, had been one of India's semi-independent princely states, and Surendra Singh, who used his lost kingdom as a surname, had attended Marlborough College in England before being inducted into the foreign service like other sprigs of royalty.

One of his earliest postings was in London under Nehru's sister, Vijaya Lakshmi Pandit, where, though only a junior aide, he succeeded in upstaging her—if South Block gossip be true—by arranging for the guns to boom in his honour as he escorted her to some formal British event. Alirajpur was entitled to a thirteen-gun salute unlike the high commissioner who enjoys no salute at all. Though not particularly prepossessing of appearance, he dashed around Singapore in a red Mustang and quickly gained a reputation for fast living. He had no respect for people which made his peccadilloes even more unbearable in a city-state with a small-town mentality and a strong puritanical streak. No one could present a greater contrast to the earnest church-going Abraham who tried to put off his departure, even, say some, to the extent of delaying the formalities for Alirajpur to take over as India's first full-fledged high commissioner. Abraham did not rise above the temporary rank in his first incarnation.

All this emerged later. Lee wanted Abraham to stay, not because he disliked the new man whom he did not know then, though he was instinctively wary of the aristocracy, but because he had come to rely on his friend. It was not Abraham's fault that his tenure did not yield much economic benefit for either country. India's first obligation of feeding and clothing her deprived millions meant looking inwards to the vastness within. Singapore, whose aircraft were in somebody else's air space within moments of take-off, had no option but to look outward. Both had preoccupations nearer home. The upheavals India underwent between 1964 and 1966 were matched in Singapore by the race animosity that flared up in two rounds of rioting in 1964, leaving twenty-one dead. Nathan reflects on those agonized months of disturbances: 'The bloodshed! The kind of people who came (from Malaysia) to start those riots. The partiality of the police and the army, of which people were conscious!'

Growth aggravated acrimony. 'We were developing Jurong to create jobs for ourselves,' Nathan says. But the Malaysians expected their policy of favouring *bumiputera*s to extend to Singapore after it became a federal state. 'When we went into Malaysia, the two areas where we wanted autonomy were education and labour but they argued that Malay rights should apply in Singapore too, that jobs should go to them first and so forth.'⁵⁸ Malaysian politicians insisted on extending *bumiputera* preference to Singapore because that was where the most development projects were going on and where there would be the juiciest plums for the picking.

> Since we were a part of Malaysia, they felt they had the right to come and go as they liked. Our transport system was threatened when they brought in all kinds of vehicles and ran pirate taxi services. Areas of Singapore were denuded of trees. Buildings mushroomed overnight. There was no control.⁵⁹

Kuala Lumpur also tried to hijack most of the country's joint quota of textile exports to Britain.⁶⁰ Asked if his first priority on 9 August was security or the economy, Lee replies at once, 'Both!' 'The economy came first because having just got rid of us, Malaysia was not going to take us back, were they?' he asks, referring to expectations of imminent economic collapse. 'But I knew that the moment we showed any signs of independence they would want to put us down. So we had to get some muscle, to be able to say, "No, you cannot treat us like this."'⁶¹

And so Singapore set out to prove, as ambassador-at-large Tommy Thong-Bee Koh puts it, 'Size is not destiny.'⁶² On the contrary, deploying Sun Tzu's strategic advice on turning weakness into strength, Singapore demonstrated that it could teach much bigger countries a thing or two in resilience, political dexterity and, above all, national reconstruction. Singapore's junior minister for foreign affairs, Inche Rahim bin Ishak, used the colourful analogy of a small but pungent *chili padi*—'a very important ingredient in a palatable arrangement we seek in the South-east Asia region.'⁶³ Lee likened Singapore to the less palatable 'poisoned shrimp' that would infect and destroy a bigger neighbour who tried to swallow it. He took a stern view of the future and noted, 'Quite a number of countries, after gaining independence, have failed economically and collapsed socially. They lacked one essential quality: self-discipline, either in their leaders, or more often in their leaders and their people.'

He repeated that the world did not owe Singapore a living, and that the begging bowl destroys a nation's pride and undermines its self-confidence: 'It is sad to see how in many countries, national heroes have let their country slide down the drain to filth and squalor, corruption and degradation, where the kick-back and the rake-off have become a way of life, and the whole country sinks in self-debasement and despair.'

He drew a colourful picture of Singapore being towed out to the middle of the South Pacific. Instead of two million active and vigorous Singaporeans, there would be Singaporean South Sea-islanders with flowers in their hair dancing to languorous tunes; instead of an enormous sea and air traffic and the stimulus of people bringing new ideas, these South Sea-islanders would lounge on the beach watching the occasional cargo ship drop anchor. To avoid that fate, Singapore reinvented itself and carved out a new niche in global affairs. So triumphantly did it succeed that the *Economist* wrote 'it is hard to avoid the suspicion that the little country's unforgivable offence is being richer and more successful than its neighbours, and not particularly apologetic about it.'[64] Lee says with satisfaction:

> It's different now because now the developments of the last forty years have made for a different configuration. Our potential was never envisaged. Our potential was created. We created this. Had we just remained what we were, there would have been nothing to talk about. But we decided, 'All right, let's go global' before the word was coined. The word was the economy. Let's link up with all the big economies of the world. That's our hinterland. That's what happened.[65]

Inevitably, a physical transformation of this order has a psychological coefficient. Himself a master of realpolitik, Kissinger calls Singapore leaders 'cold-blooded'. What is more significant is that the mild-mannered, soft-spoken, devoutly Roman Catholic George Yeo seizes on the term as a compliment. 'We have to be,' he says. 'Having to scratch out an existence within rather tight margins, we cannot afford to be too subjective or sentimental.'[66]

Forward with No Regrets

Independent Singapore's energies were entirely devoted to getting 'some muscle', as Lee put it, so that there was no danger of succumbing to Malaysian pressure. Israel helped to develop the military capability

India would not. But it was Winsemius, economic adviser since 1961, who reinforced a capitalist commitment that was far removed from India's autarky. The Dutchman was initially wary about accepting the assignment on account of Lee's radical rhetoric and the PAP's leftist reputation but changed his mind after a dinner party at the Istana that Lee and Dr Goh gave for him and Tang I-Fang, the ethnic Chinese deputy leader of the United Nations Mission, soon after they arrived. Winsemius remarked after the dinner, 'I don't smell any Communists in there. Indeed, they are the wisest leaders I have ever encountered.' Those were the days when the joke went that if a factory was put up in Jurong on Monday, banners screaming 'Exploitation of Workers' festooned it by Friday.

But if Lee and his finance minister were reassuring, the old fears came flooding back when the United Nations team visited the SIPB in the Fullerton Building. From his office window, Puthucheary, the SIPB chief, pointed to Raffles's statue overlooking the Singapore River. 'Look,' he said, 'That was left over by the colonialists. What would you think if we replaced it with a statue of Marx or Lenin?'[67] It was a troubling thought for the international economists, and Lee says Winsemius made it a condition of accepting the job that the statue was left undisturbed.[68] Raffles still strikes a heroic pose by the Singapore River, arms folded determinedly across his chest. It was felt that moving him would erode investor confidence.

India, of course, packed away all the ostentatious Raj statuary of king-emperors and queen-empresses, viceroys, governors and military commanders. The action was symbolic of a thinking that was the antithesis of Singapore's. India's Soviet-style Planning Commission, described as extra-parliamentary and extra-constitutional, became the supreme economic authority. The Food Corporation of India was set up in 1965 and together with the Agricultural Prices Commission consolidated the Public Distribution System. More drastic measures were to follow. Insurance, banking and coal mines were nationalized. The government ran everything from a bakery to Air India. It was not socialism but state capitalism with the bureaucracy vested with enormous power in what became notorious as India's licence-permit-quota Raj.

Yet, no matter how much Lee might lament decisions and developments that were so far removed from Singapore's, India lost none of her appeal for him. Indira Gandhi's radical fiats had as little effect as Shastri's rebuff. Singapore was always ready to write off yesterday's losses and work for tomorrow's profits. Lee must have realized even before Singapore became independent that, despite his respect and admiration for Nehru, and a certain idealistic yearning on his part for the cultural continuity and political dynamism that India represented, the two countries were too far apart in thinking, methods and objectives for close cooperation on the ground. But he never forgot that proper deployment of India's weight and girth would still make her a formidable force in world affairs.

Ignoring the ambiguity of parallel approaches to India and Israel, three questions must be asked. First, was Singapore seriously handicapped by India's inability or unwillingness to provide the military assistance Lee sought? Second, did India lose by not being more obliging? A more personal supplementary question could be: Would Abraham's staying on have made a difference to the relationship? The answer to all three questions is an emphatic No. Given objective circumstances, a single contract for military training would not have amounted to more than just that. If India had taken Israel's place, she would have been no more than a short-term service provider until more substantive reasons emerged for mutually profitable long-term interaction.

India's failure to meet the basic needs of her own people and defend her territory in 1962 was more relevant in shaping Singaporean opinion. Dr Goh acknowledged to Dhanabalan that though India might be 'self-centred and cut off from the world,' she was 'an industrial power of some substance'. Always innovative, he tried to benefit from that experience but the experts he imported from India were seldom conspicuously successful. 'Such a portly gentleman!' says Pillay, whose distinguished career also included being finance secretary, of a British-trained industrial development adviser from New Delhi with excellent theoretical qualifications but little hands-on experience. He found the Indian practice of Five-Year Plans, adapted from the Soviet Gosplan, equally unrewarding. Disappointed in India and Indians, Dr Goh, who had also initially thought of a close meshing of the two armed forces, looked more and more to other countries for inspiration. If he went to Israel for military training, Japan was his favourite economic model. Not sharing Lee's aversion to Japan for its wartime actions, he thought it significant that the all-time bestseller among Western books on the subject, *Japan as Number One*, by the Harvard professor Ezra F. Vogel, was also a bestseller among Singapore's top public officials and business executives.

Abraham, being Indian and emotional, repines and regrets. When India honoured Goh Chok Tong during her 1994 Republic Day celebrations, the long retired diplomat, who had left Singapore some thirty years before, grieved 'the folly and stupidity' that accounted for the 'absurd decisions' of the ministry he had served all his life. 'It is India that has rejected the hand of friendship offered by Singapore,' he lamented in the *Hindu*.

> In 1965 during the war with Pakistan, Mr Lee Kuan Yew said, and I quote from memory, 'The Indians are my friends and I stand by them.' This of course was jubilantly broadcast over All India Radio, but when Singapore wanted technical help in the training of its troops, in weaponry, or in the loan of defence personnel, we were so reluctant that Mr Lee thought it best to go to the Israelis.[69]

Despite Abraham's sentimental dirge, the setback did not prevent the unsentimental Lee from making another bid for India's support the very next year.

{5}

India's 'Monroe Doctrine for Asia'

Lee was not alone in seeking out Indira Gandhi in 1966. While he was paying his first call as independent Singapore's first full-fledged prime minister on India's 'young, energetic and optimistic' leader in September, Tengku Abdul Rahman also flew into Delhi, but unannounced, checked into the Ashok Hotel and insisted on seeing Indira Gandhi at once. Fearing that India might accede to Lee's appeal either for bilateral military help or to make her presence felt in some way in South-east Asia, the Malaysian leader pleaded with Indira Gandhi 'not to have anything to do' with Singapore's prime minister.[1]

It was a time of tectonic global shifts. United Nations membership had exploded because of decolonization. Fissures rent the Communist monolith, and Soviet unwillingness to help China's nuclear programme compounded the great schism that forced dutiful Indian Communists also to take sides. China accused revisionist Russia of racial arrogance and—ironical in view of what was to come—of conspiring with the Western barbarians. Not having tumbled as yet to the opportunities offered by the quarrel, the Americans annoyed China by courting war-torn North Vietnam through the Paris peace talks. Britain was packing its Asian bags, and South-east Asia seeking a viable and more inclusive alternative to Maphilindo, possibly unaware that American strategists were also thinking out their future for them. Lee hoped to interest Indira Gandhi in the region until disillusionment set in and he became convinced that despite the spectacular achievements abroad, including in Singapore, of so many Indians, psychological and political factors would prevent India from realizing her potential to take the lead in Asia. Even Nehru's genius, he concluded, would not have been able to goad the Indian elephant into a stampede.

There was also a housekeeping angle to his efforts to draw in India. British spending on the base with 30,000 civilian employees and 10,000 female domestic workers was roughly 20 per cent of Singapore's gross domestic product and he feared that 20,000 people would 'be out of jobs by 1971, adding to our already large pool of unemployed.'

The *Straits Times* reported that Lee would 'sketch out [to Indira Gandhi] a possible future role for India as guardian of South-east Asia ... in ten years, time when the British "policeman role" came to an end'.[2] Obviously, he had no idea when exactly the British would pull out; nor that sterling's devaluation by more than 14 per cent in November 1967 would hasten matters. Even his fear that a power vacuum might 'eventually threaten smaller countries in the region with erosion of their independence' suggested a long time frame. He looked to India for rescue and told journalists that 'India would be the power to enforce a "Monroe Doctrine for Asia" because she had been conducting her foreign policy "on a basis of equality and not on a basis of power relations."'[3] She was 'the only possible Asian power that had the potential to stabilize the region against China and the Communists'. Looking back, Lee now believes that India could have done so in conjunction, albeit indirectly, with some of the Seato powers.[4] Since India, apparently, 'scorned' (Lee's word) Seato, that seems as extraordinary as his expectation of a politicized Indian military battling Communism, but Lee thought that India's leaders were 'becoming extremely conscious that if these bases were removed prematurely, then their national interests might well be in jeopardy'.[5]

He told the *New York Times* it would be a 'disaster if the British ... were replaced by the Americans'. Today, he argues that Singapore had established an easy equilibrium with the British over 150 years. Americans, in contrast, were 'very bossy ... a different civilization ... a power on the ascendant that behaves like one'. Vietnam was one warning. Now he adds the Philippines and Iraq. 'We did not want to get ourselves into that position. We still don't.' So, when the United States sought an alternative to Subic Bay, Lee said, 'We are too small to take you. But you can use our facilities and logistics as a transit point.'[6] He is astonished when reminded that he spoke of offering base facilities to the Soviets.[7] 'No, I never said that! How can I say that? I would never offer it to the Soviet Union!'[8] It was obviously only a bargaining gambit. But Singapore–Soviet relations were far from frosty. When Rajaratnam went to Moscow in 1976— taking Kishore Mahbubani, a bright young Sindhi diplomat whose parents had moved to Singapore when he was a child and who headed the Ministry of Foreign Affairs (MFA) from 1994 to 1998—he told Andrei Gromyko that Singapore was only pro-Singapore. Being 'brutally into realpolitik', Singapore continued to welcome Soviet ships at its repairing docks, allowed Aeroflot, Tass, Novosti and the Moscow Narodny Bank to operate in the island, and even had a joint fishing venture with the Soviets whose fleet trawled the Pacific and the Indian oceans.

> We canned the fish and repaired their trawlers. Their sailors would pass through and there were a few shops with Russian language signs.[9]

They were hostages to fortune. 'We were not pro-Soviet but never anti-Soviet,' says Mahbubani. 'We never became a formal ally of the United States for that reason.'[10] However, the United States and Japan pumped money into Singapore, trained managers and provided expertise. Though Moscow sent an ambassador in January 1969, the Soviets did not help economically. Lee recalls an American industrialist telling him in the 1970s why the Soviets would never beat the West.

> Look at the motor cars they make. They order two windscreen wipers for each car but windscreen wipers are stolen, so you have cars with no windscreen wipers. They don't respond to demand and supply. This is all part of the Gosplan or whatever they call it. You pinch the side mirror, you pinch the windscreen wipers![11]

Lee found the explanation simple and profound. Learning from it, Singapore geared production to demand. 'Everything is on the market, everything can be replaced. Finally it isn't worth stealing.'[12] If demand for some item falls, it is withdrawn at once. Lee cannot understand why India did not do the same. 'Maybe it is because we have to be pragmatic, we are not in a position to try out theories,' he muses. 'Our options are limited. If we make a wrong choice we will starve. So we have to make pragmatic choices. And we found that works. That's how we got here.' In the process Singapore built up a brand name. He adds, 'Was it planned from the beginning? No! It was a process of learning, adjusting, refining and passing it on to the next generation so that they don't have to relearn the process.'[13]

Lee claims he did not mention any specific plan to Indira Gandhi. But specific or not, it was hardly the time for bold initiatives abroad by an inexperienced prime minister who had been in the saddle only eight months and already faced a bitter leadership struggle as her Congress Party headed for a major electoral setback. Her left turn was a ploy to rally support: though the conservative Jha remained her secretary, Indira Gandhi's court attracted many radicals, including people she had been friendly with as a student in England. P.N. Haksar, a Kashmiri Brahmin like herself, who succeeded Jha in May 1967, was the most prominent. As a law student in London he was influenced by the doyen of British Communism, Rajani Palme Dutt, half-Indian, half-Swede, but wholly upper-class English. 'Left-leaning' (his self-description) Natwar Singh was already the first career diplomat in the prime minister's secretariat.

This Moscow Mafia, as some called the group, denounced the Vietnam war as imperialism's last stand and regarded most Southeast Asian governments as American or Japanese puppets. Thailand (America's 'one staunch, cheerleading, on-the-field friend' according to *Time* magazine) and the Philippines ('the backside of America' in Krishna Menon's colourful words) were political outcasts for 'progressive' Indians. Haksar's disapproval of Lee and Singapore was obvious at a meeting he chaired at the India International Centre, watering hole of New Delhi intellectuals, when someone began a question with 'Countries like Singapore . . .' Haksar's sneering 'You call that a country?' provoked a protesting voice from the audience,

'Please, please! You are speaking about my country!' It was Singapore's high commissioner.[14]

Lee thought the realignment of global forces important, and commented in his Blausten Lecture several years later that 'foes have seemingly become friends', and the United States was 'more friendly to China, a Leninist-Maoist state, than to India, a democratic state with a free representative system of government'. Similarly, China was more cordial to capitalist America and Japan 'than towards Communist Russia'.[15] Observing the shifts from India's Peking embassy, Jagat Mehta said only half jokingly that the Soviet Union was the only 'ally' the Americans had in Vietnam.[16] His comment was prompted by the dusty answer Kosygin received when he stopped in Peking en route to Hanoi in February 1965, hoping to undo the damage of Nikita Khruschev's angry suspension of aid when Vietnam refused, at China's instigation, to sign the Partial Test Ban Treaty. Mao wanted no Soviet meddling in his backyard. Jagat Mehta was the only foreign diplomat at Peking airport when a rebuffed Kosygin left.

Indira Gandhi's domestic compulsions determined her foreign policy. When the rains failed, food grain production dropped by 17 per cent and the shade of Malthus stalked the parched fields of Bihar and Uttar Pradesh. Only the Americans sent wheat in history's largest food rescue operation but Lyndon B. Johnson's 'short tether' policy meant the begging bowl had to be permanently extended, with every grain of wheat that fell into it counted, listed and proclaimed. American academics warned that the high-yielding Mexican dwarf wheat on which India had pinned her hopes would not succeed without 'educated, alert farmers, capital, and a commercial system of agriculture'. Inevitably, American admonitions were remembered and generosity forgotten as the Washington–Peking entente supported Pakistan against India over Bangladesh.

Lee says his interest in India in the 1960s was not economic. It was strategic. Singapore's investments came from Taiwan, Hong Kong, Japan and, later, America.

India didn't have the manufacturing capabilities to give us jobs. It was only trade. But what we wanted was an Indian interest, because we saw the gradual pull-out by the British and we were not sure what would happen in the Vietnam war. That would leave a vacuum in this region—vacuum means instability.[17]

B.M. Oza, desk officer during the visit, recalls Lee asking for military and civilian experts. Indira Gandhi agreed to Singapore air force personnel being trained in India and to lending a dozen air force officers to pilot Skyhawks and Hunters, but not civil servants or diplomats.[18] She did not think Britain's withdrawal endangered Singapore or that a military pact would be any solution if it did. She and Swaran Singh laughed that it could be said the British exit from South Asia also created a vacuum. Lee held his peace. He pointed out instead that India could start small in South-east Asia, and the stake would grow with the commitment so long as she accepted that cooperation with the region was in her long-term interest. He sought a statement of intent, 'This was in principle and in principle it was a no-go. India was too preoccupied with the subcontinent—with Pakistan.'[19]

Mandarin with a Hakka Accent

The Tengku, however, feared progress on Lee's requests. Natwar Singh, present at one of his meetings with Indira Gandhi in 1966, recalls her disclaiming any intention of taking over from Britain; she had problems enough at home with 500 million Indians. He could well understand, the Malaysian leader replied laughing, having a million Indians in his country. Apart from banter, the Tengku expressed surprise at her inviting Lee who was not to be trusted. 'You are Nehru's daughter,' he pleaded, 'you can't do anything to hurt Malaysia.'[20]

Lee was taken aback in 2007 to be told of the intervention, then burst into a guffaw. He did not think the Tengku could have influenced Indira Gandhi. 'She would come to her own conclusions.' But he understood the alarm.

In 1966 he [the Tengku] wanted to keep us as a satellite. He kept his one battalion here, and with a battalion and control of our water he thought we would have to do what he told us although he told us to get out and be independent! That was his thinking. If India had come in when the British left, that would have spoilt his plans.[21]

He told Indian journalists that Singapore sought a multilateral bulwark against imperialism or expansionism, 'The only reason why anybody suffers somebody's force is basic mistrust of the intention of other people of the region. If neighbours are peace-loving, I have no need for a burly Englishman to guard me with sturdy Gurkhas.'[22] Which neighbours? Malaysia? Indonesia? 'The menace of mainland China?' Coy about names, Lee prevaricated. 'Mainland China? What other China is there?' He talked of tribes and nations fighting each other since time immemorial and the necessity of preserving Southeast Asia's integrity 'from whatever sources trouble may come'.[23] Listeners assumed he meant Indonesia. To an extent he did, seeking guarantees that 'Indonesia would not go berserk and just move troops in'. China, Vietnam and the PKI (Partai Komunis Indonesia, the world's largest Communist party outside the Soviet Union and China) were 'the three claws of Russian influence'. Sukarno 'was gung-ho with China which was supplying arms to the PKI, operating as an extension of the Soviet Union in this part of the world'. He had taken Indonesia out of the United Nations. Sukarno was displaced in March 1966 when Subandrio was jailed for life, but Konfrontasi continued.

The full extent of American backing for Suharto, who became president a year later, was not yet evident.[24] But Lee always had his suspicions of the 'Foreign Hand', Indira Gandhi's shorthand for the American Central Intelligence Agency, and in 1988 Lee Hsien Loong disclosed Singapore's belief that the CIA had 'channelled S$700,000' to a minister in Lim Yew Hock's government in the 1950s. The revelation was prompted by Lee's demand that Washington withdraw a senior diplomat and 'put a stop' to interference.[25] But as with the Communists earlier, Lee thought he could work with the Americans who alone were prepared to oppose Communists wherever they threatened and whatever the cost: 'Because Americans were resolutely anti-Communist and prepared to confront them, Nehru, Nasser and Sukarno could afford to be non-aligned. This was a comfortable posture and one I had adopted without at first realizing that it was a luxury paid for by Americans.'

The Third World greats were losing their allure. Lee thinks Southeast Asia enjoyed stability only because Sukarno was displaced and the Americans enjoyed a free run.

> Otherwise this place would be another broken-down region. Whatever you say about Suharto, he put down the PKI. It was brutal; half a million people were killed, including many Chinese. He then embarked on a path of construction, on growth instead of aggrandizement which was Sukarno's policy, so they had thirty-plus years of Suharto and the whole region grew.[26]

Indira Gandhi could hardly agree with her guest's calculations. But they disagreed with savoir faire. As the flashlights popped, Lee turned to ask if so many cameramen always accompanied her. 'No,' she smiled. 'They are specially for you!' He was not discomfited when he didn't know the answer to her question about the subject of the wrapped painting he had brought as a present. An aide whispered it was a *kampong* scene. He exuded charm. India 'was a very special friend'. Indira Gandhi and he operated a system 'which requires a great deal of tolerance, patience and effort in political guidance'. She must have chuckled to hear him describe them both as 'socialist by conviction and pragmatic in practice'—Peter Hazelhurst, Maxwell's successor as the *Times* correspondent, dubbed her politics 'slightly left of self-interest'.

Disappointment did not keep Lee away from Rashtrapati Bhavan's nine-hole golf course where he noticed how avidly highly placed Indians grabbed the golf balls he gave them. Oza, a Sinologist and proud of his Mandarin, spoke to Lee in Chinese. Replying likewise, Lee wanted to know how his Mandarin sounded. 'Sir,' Oza replied diplomatically, 'your vocabulary and composition are better than your accent and intonation!' It was the nearest he could venture to saying that Lee's Mandarin was strongly influenced by his native Hakka. Probably as a result of this exchange, Radio Singapore interviewed Oza for its Chinese service.[27]

India spurned or India spurns?

Though Alirajpur tried to compensate for Indira Gandhi's refusal to be drawn into South-east Asia by attending a conference of regional leaders in Malaysia's Cameron Highlands in 1966, India was left out when five regional leaders gathered in the Thai beach resort of Bangsaen the following August 'to play golf and tell stories and jokes' and settle the more serious business of founding Asean.[28] 'The fact that Asean was formed without India so much as being consulted was a stunning blow to India's ego,' says a Thai academic.[29] India was not only excluded; she was also outflanked. She had emphasized in Baguio in 1950 that South-east Asians should cooperate in an economics-oriented Asia-for-Asians organization in which Americans or anti-Communism played no part. Sixteen years later she boycotted the nine-nation Asia and Pacific Council set up in Seoul and hailed by Washington as a bulwark against Communism. Indira Gandhi explained that 'as a non-aligned country we do not go to any such meetings'.[30] The Asean that emerged represented everything India claimed to abhor.

Thanat who was Thailand's foreign minister, from 1959 to 1971, and a key player, told A.N. Ram, India's ambassador to Thailand that Asean's purpose was to checkmate China. Though Nathan, who led Singapore's delegation, pushed hard for 'a strong declaration on economic cooperation . . . [he] couldn't get anything substantive,' says Dhanabalan who was a member of the team. Dhanabalan thinks the founding meeting would have been better sited in Jakarta than Bangkok.[31] It is not clear at what stage the resentment of India Fifield spoke of hardened into a decision on exclusion but the 'geographical footprint [of] peninsular South-east Asia, from Burma to Vietnam to Singapore to Indonesia' (Nathan's phrase) rationalized a Cold War position. Ironically, it also defined the Further India of lore and legend. In fact, the eventual ten-nation grouping was French orientalist George Coedes's 'Indianized States of South-east Asia' in modern garb. Asean enshrines the traditions of Temasek, Champa, Funan, Kataaha, Mataram and all the other lost kingdoms of the Sri Vijaya and the Majapahit empires that ancient Indians knew collectively as Suvarnabhumi.

Some South-east Asian governments were uncomfortable with reminders of that age of Hindu influence. Others discounted modern India as a serious player, sharing the dismissiveness that Congress Party president S. Nijalingappa encountered 'wherever he went' in Europe. The Europeans he met thought of India as a starving country of quarrelling people without a stable government.[32] Indira Gandhi, too, admitted that India was seen as a large but poor nation whose population lived in abject poverty and whose leaders were idealists with a philosophy that bore little relevance to current realities.[33] India's ties with the Soviet Union and prickly relations with the United States—Asean's patron—were powerful deterrents for South-east Asia's anti-Communist regimes. Nor had they any wish to be dragged into endless Indo-Pakistani bickering.

Yet, J.N. (Mani) Dixit, perhaps the best remembered of Indian foreign secretaries, who died shortly after Manmohan Singh appointed him national security adviser, writes that India was invited 'to be a full member of Asean' at the inception but refused because of the Cold War, Vietnam, and suspicions of American sponsorship.[34] Others claim that Deputy Prime Minister Morarji Desai was sounded out. It is in this context that Singaporeans accuse Indira Gandhi of sneering at the region's 'Coca-Cola governments'. But the public record and recollections of people in key positions at the time only show that, intrigued by the rumours floating around and by the reticence of South-east Asian leaders, Indira Gandhi's government decided to do some probing of its own.

Though India's relations with Suharto's Indonesia were returning to normal, Foreign Minister Adam Malik breathed not a word about a regional organization when he visited New Delhi in late 1966. Nor did he mention it the following January when, unlike previous external affairs ministers whose first official trip was to the West, Chagla made Jakarta his first halt, taking with him T.N. (Tikki) Kaul, another Kashmiri Brahmin who became secretary-general in the foreign office. Far from rejecting any offers, Chagla 'put forward a tentative proposal for an Asian common market or an Asian development council on the lines of the one established in Europe'.[35] Though Thanat, too, had derived inspiration from Europe, Chagla's proposal fell on stony ground. Visiting Singapore some months later, he admitted that being kept in the dark about Asean was 'a matter agitating the minds' in India.[36] He repeated that India would participate in any form of regional cooperation if asked. No one asked. His hosts remained incurious even when he gave a lofty name—Council of Asia—to the organization he proposed.

Chagla also promised Singapore economic help and offered eighty Ladakh horses for a cavalry regiment. Both Lee and Dr. Goh were fascinated by India's presidential trappings, and the prospect of horses prompted about a hundred military officers to take up riding at Singapore's Turf Club. India sent a four-man delegation led by a defence ministry official in 1967 and proposed seconding a major, a junior commissioned officer and four non-commissioned officers from the 61st Cavalry Division for a horse regiment. 'It could have been the beginning of military cooperation,' says Brigadier-General Kirpa Ram Vij, Director General (Staff) of the Singapore Armed Forces and the first de facto army chief. Vij blames Alirajpur for 'messing things up'. There was confusion over whether the horses should be Ladakhi or Australian; then over numbers; and, finally, whether India would give or sell them. It was suggested at various stages that some horses should be Ladakhi and some Australian, some should be given and others sold. Eventually, the idea petered out.

The Bangkok Declaration founding Asean was signed on August 8. Dining with Abraham, then chargé d'affaires in Thailand, the night before, Rajaratnam wondered if India was interested in joining. Thai diplomats also mentioned it when Abraham met them socially. These casual remarks hardly amounted to a serious invitation but diplomatic veterans say the biggest balls are set rolling with a throwaway comment that can be taken up or ignored.

Doubts About Asean's Paternity

Canagaratnam Gunasingham also asked if India had been approached. Ceylon had—he said, explaining the last-minute hitch after Anwar Sani, a Dutch-trained diplomat who was director of political affairs in Indonesia's foreign ministry and 'Adam Malik's righthand man'—done the rounds with various drafts and obtained agreement in the *mushawara* and *mufakat* (consultation and consensus) process that became Asean's hallmark. Nathan explains the delay:

> What happened at the last moment was that the Tengku insisted on inviting Ceylon. And so Razak appealed to the other ministers and they waited. As you know, the Thais are focussed on astrology. We reached a certain time and nothing happened, so we went ahead without Ceylon.[37]

Ceylon's prime minister, Dudley Senanayake, whose conservative United National Party headed an uneasy coalition, was keen on an anti-Communist alliance. As chargé d'affaires in Bangkok, Gunasingham recommended an approach and receiving Colombo's coded approval, got in touch with Thanat who 'was obviously happy' to include Ceylon as a founding member. So were the other Asean leaders with the solitary exception of Ceylon-born (Tamil) Rajaratnam who objected 'vehemently', say his Singaporean colleagues. According to Thanat's aide, Sompong Sucharitkul, Rajaratnam 'argued the country's domestic situation was unstable and there would be trouble'. Ceylon would hamper the new organization.[38]

South and South-east Asia were still flexible and overlapping terms and entities. Romulo included India in his plans in 1949 and Nehru spoke of India as a South-east Asian country at a United Nations seminar ten years later. In 1968 Lee called Singapore the 'cleanest and greenest city of South Asia' adding, 'No other community in South Asia offers its people these standards.'[39] Cartographically, Ceylon was a moveable feast. As the fifteenth century exporter of Theravada Buddhism to Thailand, it had retained stronger Suvarnabhumi links than India. That unity survives with many Tamils in the Malaysian peninsula backing the Liberation Tigers of Tamil Eelam. On one occasion, each empty gas cylinder in a consignment from Singapore to Colombo was found to have neatly inscribed under the cap, 'Long live Tamil Eeelam!' The Sri Lankan navy's operations against LTTE ships off the coast of Sumatra in September 2007 confirmed the overlap.

But Gunasingham's masters developed cold feet about sending the formal application without which Ceylon could not join Asean. Having waited beyond the last moment, and with the stars fading out, Gunasingham had no option but to ask for Ceylon's case to be put on hold. It was scuttled, he thinks, by domestic politics when Srimavo Bandaranaike's Sri Lanka Freedom Party staged protests and derided Asean members as 'the errand boys and running dogs of the United States in Asia'.[40] That's when she is said to have used the 'Coca-Cola' phrase, warning that a SLFP government would tear up any agreement.[41] Foreign pressure 'brought home the complexities of the international environment,' says Gunasingham. 'India was the unhappiest. It saw its sphere of influence and its claim to hegemony being eroded.'[42]

Senanayake echoed that charge in Malaysia two months later. Other reports suggested Soviet and NAM pressure. The deciding factor may have been China's threat to abrogate its rubber-rice barter pact with Ceylon.[43]

The saga demonstrated that Asian nations were not fully masters in their own house in those Cold War years. Seafet aroused uncomfortable memories of Seato. American coolness obliged the Philippines to abandon the Pacific Union. Ceylon could not join Asean because other nations disapproved. Lee, who wanted India in, asks, 'How could we on our own invite India?' Singapore, incidentally, came in almost as an outsider after the other four had decided to act. Lee suspects—without evidence he is quick to add—an American hand in forming an anti-Communist bloc. 'I believe the Americans, the British and other Western powers must have egged the Thais, Filipinos, Malaysians and Indonesians to form this.'[44]

Moscow was equally suspicious. A Soviet diplomat told Nathan at the reception to celebrate the signing that Asean was 'an American tool'. Singapore's future president asked for his reasons, and the Russian mentioned one of Fifield's books, even down to the page number: 'I looked and sure enough, there's a reference to Asean in his *South-east Asia in United States Policy*. You see they were dismantling Seato and proposed some kind of organization and gave it this name.'[45]

Fifield proposed a collective security treaty for the entire region from Burma to the Philippines to Indonesia. 'In view of national sensitivities, the alliance might be termed an Association of Southeast Asian Nations (Asean).' The acronym in brackets was Fifield's but Dhanabalan is convinced Malik 'suggested "Asean"' when Thanat asked him to propose a name. 'It was absolutely so appropriate and superior to anything we had in mind that no one had the temerity to put up any other name.'[46] Thanat corroborates this. 'Asean owes its name to Adam Malik, master in coining acronyms.'[47] Fifield's book, also recommending that India and Japan cooperate with Asean as a counterweight to China, was published four years *before* the Bangkok Declaration. Talk of Asian politics imitating American political analysts or, for that matter, American strategy!

No wonder 'Asean was linked in the Indian perception with the by then defunct Seato in the belief that it was a pro-Western creation to bring colonialism by the back door'.[48] The United States 'acted like a midwife in the birth of Asean.'[49]

The Fifield connection poses an intriguing question. If the United States did plot out South-east Asia's plan of action before any Southeast Asian was aware of it, and if Dixit is right about overtures to India, it means the Americans were not seriously put off by Indira Gandhi's barbs about the Foreign Hand. Other evidence also suggests that relations were not always as bad as public rhetoric implied. India was always assigned a part—at least in theory—in the Western security map of the world, and Sir Olaf Caroe's vision of the original Baghdad Pact (later the American-led Central Treaty Organization) envisaged India in the lead role.[50] State Department records show that Dulles personally asked Nehru to join Seato. So did Henderson. When both invitations were rejected, did the United States try to inveigle India into an alliance via Asean? If so, Lee's supposition of India acting in concert with some of the Seato powers may not have been so far-fetched after all.

Unaware of Fifield's uncannily accurate predictions and projections and Lee's own surmise, Abraham fulminated twenty-seven years later, 'We expect Asean to look with favour on us. And yet, why do we forget our own attitude to Asean when it was formed in Bangkok in 1966 [sic]? When did we come round to saying one good word about Asean? We were convinced that Asean was an American plot.'[51]

Go Back to Your Poor Country!

Lee asked Harold Wilson to convert the naval base to commercial use so that people were not suddenly thrown out of a job. The British premier's refusal created a problem for India though not as acute as the one for Singapore where unemployment was already more than 9 per cent. The 45,000 work permits at stake were 'more or less evenly divided between Malaysian and Indian citizens', and the latter would not be allowed to remain in Singapore without a job.

Chagla assured the Lok Sabha that Lee had told him he would not 'discriminate' against Indians. There would be no forcible deportation. But Singapore's first obligation was to its own citizens, and non-Singaporeans would be given work permits only if they found alternative employment. Rumours flourished, and even some Indians who had Singapore nationality feared they might lose their citizenship or be deported if they were unemployed. The high commission was inundated with panic-stricken queries when another incident added to the alarm.

A Hong Kong-based journalist turned up at the high commission one day offering what he called top secret information in return for two bottles of expensive single malt whisky. He refused to divulge details but when the liquor was produced, handed over a tape supposed to have been secretly recorded at a closed-door PAP meeting where Lee allegedly ordered Indians who didn't like his policies to pack their bags and return to India. 'We make very good suitcases in Singapore,' he is said to have added. There was no proof the tape was genuine but it says something for the climate of uncertainty that Indian diplomats were—and still are—convinced of its authenticity. Though particularly addressed to British base workers, the warning was to all Indian Singaporeans. 'They used to call Little India an area of darkness!' recalls the official who handled the tape.[52] South Block hadn't forgotten it four decades later.

The high commission decided to clarify matters by reminding Singapore that local Indians could not fall back on India. Hence, a somewhat alarmist five-column annoucement in the *Sunday Times* which read under the heading WARNING in bold capitals, 'Indian citizenship is not a commodity that can be bartered or cast off like a worn-out coat and then pulled out of mothballs for the convenience of the individual.'[53]

It warned 'Singapore citizens of Indian origin . . . [they] are liable to be declared stateless if they renounced their citizenship.' They would not even be allowed to enter India without a visa.

A thinly veiled threat the very next day by Singapore Labour Minister Jek Yuen Thong appeared to justify the warning. Jek was a Chinese-educated former reporter on *Sin Pao* newspaper who wrote Lee's first Mandarin speech and later went to London as high commissioner. He announced, while opening a new wing of the Army Civil Service Union, that Singapore's Immigration (Prohibition of Entry) Order of 1966 authorized the government not to allow a citizen's wife who had been living abroad separately for five years to enter the country. Invoking the law, Jek advised Singaporeans who faced unemployment to rejoin their families abroad. They would be allowed to withdraw their full retirement benefits even if they had not reached the mandatory age of fifty-five provided they were to 'leave Singapore with no intention of coming back'. Their provident fund money would 'go a long way . . . since their country of origin enjoys a lower standard of living than Singapore.'[54]

He did not mention Indians but the *Straits Times* assumed the slighting 'standard of living' reference could have had no other target. The suspicion that a prominent government leader was trying to get rid of a chunk of the minority population prompted the fear that similar tactics could be extended against the entire ethnic Indian community. Jek's speech reached Chagla who summoned High Commissioner Baker to the external affairs ministry. Baker calls this the only serious problem he had to tackle during his time in New Delhi.

A Goat in Maharani Bagh

Singapore almost didn't have a representative in India at this critical time, partly because of the problem of choosing the right man from a small resource pool. India's crowded bazaars, poor hygiene, pollution, beggars and inadequate facilities—'the biggest shop in Delhi was the size of an average Seven-Eleven here'[55]—upset many Singaporeans.

A *bustee* (shantytown) still sprawls near the high commission compound in the diplomatic enclave of Chanakyapuri. A young Singaporean wife was reduced to tears and wanted to fly out at once when she saw the butcher in the Sarojini Nagar wet market urinating by his stall. Peter Chan and his wife were outstanding exceptions. They enjoyed Bollywood films, shopped at the INA Market and became friendly with two Calcutta Chinese, Wong and Leong, who worked for AIR until they migrated to Canada. Their first child was born in Delhi's Holy Infant Hospital. 'I used to tell my MFA colleagues to keep an eye on India.'

All three Singapore races presented problems when it came to choosing an envoy. Ethnic Chinese were not keen on living abroad. Nor did Singapore want to be thought of as Chinese. Harry Chan Keng Howe, the first Chinese to be sent as high commissioner and that, too, as late as 1984, suggests a third reason: 'Following a disastrous war in 1962 with China, Singapore was hard put to disabuse India of any thought of our being China's fifth column and that was why no Singaporean Chinese had been sent till my time.'[56]

If an ethnic Chinese recalled Communist China, a Malay might project a Muslim image. Paradoxically, Indians were the most problematic. Anxiety about not being treated with proper deference seemed substantiated when security stopped a senior Singapore minister, an ethnic Indian, from following his prime minister into South Block. Punch (Punchardsheram) Coomaraswamy, a Jaffna Tamil who had been parliamentary speaker since 1966 and succeeded Baker in January 1970—the only Indian to hold the job—confided to a friend that his Chinese first secretary received better treatment at New Delhi airport. George Abraham, secretary of the Singapore Indian Chamber of Commerce, felt that Indian Singaporeans were actually at a disadvantage in India 'because Indian businessmen may prefer foreigners rather than another Indian'.[57] This perception of race awareness may have been one reason for Pillay to turn down the posting when Mahbubani offered it to him in the 1990s, though his asthma, New Delhi's pollution and family obligations possibly also explained his preference for London.

As an Anglo-Indian academic, Baker seemed inoffensive but was inexplicably tardy about taking up the post. Though appointed in

November 1966 he kept delaying going until Rajaratnam introduced him to Chagla at a party in the latter's honour in May 1967 with the comment, 'You know, Mr Baker has a record now of being high commissioner-designate for the longest time in history!' He added wryly that Baker might even retire as high commissioner-designate.[58] There was no dawdling after that. Though Alirajpur, who threw a farewell party for him, warned that New Delhi would be a furnace until September, Baker took the BOAC flight in June. It was his second visit. Rajaratnam had sent him to a cultural conference where R.K. Narayan, the novelist, praised his paper on Singapore's multicultural future and regretted the stilted English of Indian academics.

With President Zakir Hussain away in Canada, Baker had to wait three weeks to present his credentials. When the time came, he rode to Rashtrapati Bhavan in an open Cadillac which, 'though of ancient vintage, was impressive enough in a procession of black limousines which drove through the city', to be met by twenty-four splendidly uniformed and turbaned horsemen who split into two groups, a dozen before and a dozen behind the car. Baker 'was strangely moved by the impressive rendering of Majulah Singapura' by the president's band and says, 'it is only in a foreign country that one's national anthem makes such an emotional impact.'

Indians who thought of Singapore as Chinatown frequently mistook the sharp-featured Baker for India's representative there. His pretty wife, also Eurasian, added to the confusion by appearing sometimes in Western frocks, sometimes in the fitting Chinese *cheongsam* with side slits, and sometimes in a Malay *sarong kebaya* (a blouse and long sheath skirt), three of the four dresses favoured by Singaporean women. She regrets she could not find anyone to teach her to drape a sari, the fourth. Mrs Chester Bowles, the American ambassador's wife, wore nothing else, but reputedly embarrassed her Indian friends by wearing it extremely badly.

Baker spent seven months in the Ashok Hotel inspecting a number of properties with Oza. Eventually, they found a place in Maharani Bagh next door to the Saudi ambassador who promptly sent over a large black goat as a housewarming gift. When Baker tried to decline the present, the ambassador apologized that if they had been in Saudi Arabia he would have sent a camel. 'That ended my protests.' There were more serious discomforts. Baker's salary remained the same as at university though a thirty-nine dollar (then under ninety-eight rupees) entertainment allowance was eventually sanctioned. His three-man mission was housed in a small building on Ring Road where the workmanship was shoddy and the electricity erratic. When he asked for an air cooler-cum-heater (Delhi winters being as bitingly cold as the summers are blazing hot), the MFA told him to make up his mind whether he wanted a cooler or a heater. The continuous flow of heavy traffic outside added to discomfort. A municipal demolition squad tore down the gates and fences of nearly seventy properties along a mile-long stretch because they encroached on public land and the road was being widened, prompting him to write, 'If the road should be completed, the traffic would be passing practically under our windows.'[59] His Chinese assistant fell in love with the Punjabi receptionist and took an overdose of pills when her alarmed family hastily arranged a marriage for her.

There are happier memories. His elder son Edmond played cricket for the local St. Columbus's school. And the Indonesian ambassador became a friend even during Konfrontasi tensions. Though he lowered the embassy flag to half-mast when Singapore hanged two Indonesian marines for the MacDonald House bombing, the ambassador stopped students from demonstrating outside Baker's office. The two envoys always conversed in Bahasa at the unending round of diplomatic parties to show Whites they were not estranged. He met Dr Goh's request for birds for Singapore's bird park, and arranged Indira Gandhi's visit to Singapore when Natwar Singh asked him round for coffee and explained that she planned to visit South-east Asia and Australia. It would be an Indian prime minister's first visit to independent Singapore. But Baker was disconcerted to find Indira Gandhi 'doodling all the time' when he went to her office with the formal invitation.[60]

The many speeches he made in New Delhi reiterated Lee's case (repeating Panikkar's point about security) that India cannot afford to neglect South-east Asia. Baker told an audience of 200 at Delhi University's political science department that the American military intervention in Vietnam gave 'a chance to non-Communist governments of South-east Asia to establish themselves'. A Communist victory in

Vietnam and a precipitate American withdrawal would encourage subversion and revolt in countries that faced economic difficulties and racial tensions. Also echoing Lee, he told the National Defence College that Sukarno's attempts to change the Indian Ocean to Indonesian Ocean impinged on India's space. An Indian military presence would be 'an indirect incentive for investment'. India's participation in underwriting South-east Asia's security would 'be a great contribution to world peace' though it was 'merely wishful thinking to expect it.'[61]

A questioner wanted to know if India had 'as capable a high commissioner in Singapore as Mr Baker.'[62] Alirajpur had a rough time. Even if Abraham had been welcoming, he would have suffered by comparison with a diplomat of whom Singapore's leaders thought so highly. But against the many negative tales of his tenure is one that redounds to his credit. Apparently, Lee vented his feelings about the high commissioner to a reporter who promptly showed his notes—as he was probably meant to—to the subject. Alirajpur immediately forwarded them to Kaul with the comment that he might wish to send a more acceptable envoy. Already irritated by reports of Singapore seeking Alirajpur's recall, Kaul retorted that India 'didn't take this kind of crap from anyone, especially small countries'.[63] Baker felt Alirajpur might have been more comfortable among the Malay sultans. Before his tenure ended, he drove down to the Singapore General Hospital to donate a pint of blood. This fourth donation was his farewell gesture.[64]

Baker's own tenure drew to an end when Rajaratnam telephoned him in May 1969 to say that Malaysia's communal riots had prompted fears of a Chinese exodus and even a military takeover in Kuala Lumpur. The foreign minister ordered him to go there at once as high commissioner. Like many Singaporeans of his generation, he was originally from Malaya, having been born in Alor Star. The Tengku called him an 'accidental Singaporean' because separation found him 'on the wrong side of the fence'. Defence Minister Razak and he were even closer. 'Once a Malay regards you as a friend,' Baker says, leaning on a walking stick the Tengku gave him, saying it would come in handy one day, 'you're always a friend'. He bears Malaysia's Tun Sri title.

Baker tried to delay his departure to pay another visit to Nepal. When he had presented his credentials to King Mahendra (after persuading a Singapore tailor to stitch a morning suit in half the usual time), the monarch said, 'You chaps in New Delhi, you rarely come to see us. You only come when you present credentials and when you leave.' Baker explained that Singapore was a small country with limited resources but wanted to develop friendly relations with everybody. He would visit Kathmandu 'much more often than that'. Rajaratnam brushed that aside. 'Never mind. Your successor will go.'

Saying goodbye to Morarji Desai, who had fallen out with Indira Gandhi, was a saddening political lesson. 'I was determined to see him,' says Baker, 'because I respected him.' Desai had attended Singapore's National Day reception and no alcohol was served while he was there. On previous visits Baker had found a crowd of supporters and admirers thronging the bungalow. This time, there was only a secretary who ushered him to where the former deputy prime minister sat alone spinning. He looked forty but was actually seventy. 'I was very impressed,' says Baker. Morarji was bitter about 'this woman' whom he had helped to become prime minister: 'I think she's a Communist.'[65]

It would have been a feather in Baker's cap and a watershed in bilateral relations if Swaran Singh, then defence minister, had gone through with his initial willingness to let land-strapped Singapore use one of the twenty-two sparsely populated Nicobar Islands for military training. But the minister later pleaded India's proposed naval base in Car Nicobar. Singapore went on to station its forces in Australia, New Zealand, Taiwan, France and even the United States. Lee's hope of defence cooperation with India was an idea before its time.

Culture Is Destiny, Culture Is History

A cartoon in the *Hindustan Times* newspaper showed a tiny Lee perched on a recumbent giant, bearing a striking resemblance to Nehru (who had been dead two years by then), prodding him with a pencil and yelling, 'Stand up!' Shown the drawing over forty years later, Lee stares at it for a long time before admitting he 'became worried, not worried, resigned' to India ever getting out of the rut of a statist economy.⁶⁶ India needed an economic system that promised hardworking Indians the same reward at home as abroad, an efficient and impartial civil service and a unifying language. 'I gave up,' he says. 'I got resigned. India was not going to break through. I mean it was so obvious what the problems were. It was not that Indians couldn't perform. It was their system that was wrong!'⁶⁷

The outlook seemed bleak after the false dawn of liberalization in 1966 involving Asoka Mehta, Indira Gandhi's planning minister, whom he and Josey knew through the Socialist International. Lee worried that the emerging Concert of Asia would lack balance and symmetry if one of the two principal architects did not pull her weight. 'We are going to have an emerged China,' he warned, 'and either there is also an emerged India, or there will be a submerged Asia.'⁶⁸ He feared that 'unless India changes course, China will become the dominant power in Asia.'⁶⁹ He admits now that not having the measure of India at the time, he might have demanded too much too soon.

> As a young student and later as a young prime minister in my thirties, in the 1950s and 1960s, I did not know all that so well. I had read about India but I had not visited it often. I had seen Indians here, not in India. So I did not understand that there was a certain cultural tempo that will not go at a speed that it is not comfortable with. That is something I have learnt in the last sixty years.⁷⁰

It was unrealistic to expect India to forge ahead like Singapore. Apart from size and population, India's ebullient media, civil society and political pluralism rule out comparison though Lee refuses to see democracy as an impediment to growth, citing Japan's post-war reconstruction. But, yes, excessive political activism is a deterrent. When growth is assured, 'you can oil the frictions' and it's all right now for Tokyo to indulge the farm lobby's objection to more runways at Narita airport. But India did not have growth, or very little growth, and the frictions mounted up. He did not blame democracy so much as temperament, the devolved system of government—central, state, municipal—and fissiparous pressures. He now knows that India will move more slowly than he had imagined. There will be periodic adjustments at the Centre and the states, and the speed will not be maintained at a high revolution all the time: 'I think it is part of the constitutional system which has been accepted by the people and is established now. There will be a constant tinkering around with state boundaries, linguistic affinities, caste quotas . . . All those adjustments detract from a dynamic meritocracy and prevent India from maximizing its potential.'[71]

Looking back, he feels that even Nehru, given the best support he could have had, would not have been able to make India go at the pace he desired because that is not India's culture: 'India is not in favour of sudden and rapid change.'[72] George Yeo agrees. 'Culture is destiny,' he says. 'Culture is history.'[73] Lee had thought otherwise to start with. The Indians he met, officials and ministers, 'were all men of great education and quality'. He found them most impressive.[74] Disappointment with their actions accounted for the censoriousness that Kamal Nath had noted, as mentioned in the Introduction. But Lee and his views were never known widely enough in India to provoke any rancour. His visits did not arouse excitement in a capital where the flags changed so often along Rajpath and Vijay Chowk, the main promenades, that few Indians knew whether their president was entertaining the queen of Tonga or the president of Venezuela. Nobody knew that Singapore had 'put very high hopes on India as a major achiever' when framing its foreign policy, as Lee confessed to JRD.[75] Lee had become a global figure, beyond bilateral contention, by 2005 when he reiterated the view in his Jawaharlal Nehru Memorial Lecture: 'I have always taken a keen interest in both China and India. Like all democratic socialists of the 1950s, I tried to forecast which giant would make the higher grade. I had rather hoped it would be democratic India.'

Indian perceptions of Singapore were a mix of half-truth, wishful thinking and myth. Ignorance distorted images, and when a Calcutta chartered accountant asked me in the late 1990s whether Singapore had 'a metro like us', I was sorely tempted to reply, 'No, not like us!' thinking of Singapore's glittering trains and burnished stations, with air conditioning, smooth escalators, electronic signs, clockwork efficiency and courteous, smartly uniformed staff. There was always some discrepancy between claims of help given and admissions of help received. Some credited Bangalore with inspiring Singapore's parks and gardens and blamed New Delhi for rejecting a host of Singaporean offers in the 1960s and 1970s. They ranged from developing special economic zones to manufacturing light combat aircraft and using vacated British defence buildings as a depot for South-east Asian trade. According to one academic, Lee hoped India would convert the former base into a shipbuilding and repairing yard.[76] Air India is said to have both helped to set up Singapore Airlines and turned up its nose at the request to do so. Nathan and George Yeo think SIA might well have sought the assistance of what was then a leading airline but Lee strongly denies it, 'No, No, No! SIA grew out of Malayan Airways, which had Dakotas and Fokker Friendships. The British ran Malayan Airways. When we joined Malaysia, it became Malaysia Singapore Airlines.'[77]

Pillay bears him out. During the twenty-four years he was SIA chairman, Pillay 'took the carrier from a small-town operator with just twelve aircraft to an industry leader admired as much for its profits as for its service, reliability and modern fleet (eighty-one planes, including advanced "megatop" B747–400s, flying a network spanning forty-one countries)'.[78] He adds that so many Indian pilots were drawn by SIA's higher wages that India complained of poaching to the highest level. High Commissioner Chandrasekhar Dasgupta, a staid man not likely to indulge in patriotic excess, is certain help was both requested and given. 'You can take it as confirmed,' he declares.[79] He recalls the seventy-eight-year-old JRD on his way back from skiing in Switzerland—he was infuriated by Dasgupta's anxiety about his ability to negotiate the Grange Road stairs—having a lot to discuss with Pillay.[80] JRD also met Singapore's director-general of civil aviation, Lim Hock San, on that visit.

Though Lee was not well known in India, the few who met him were disarmed. They would have been astonished at his self-description of a tough who puts on knuckle-dusters to waylay enemies in a cul-de-sac because 'there is no other way you can govern a Chinese society.'[81] Kissinger feels fate was cruel to confine Lee's genius to the small stage of a city-state. Chagla 'could not resist his obvious charm' and thought Lee 'exuded brilliance, had a most alert mind, and was a most vivacious personality.'82 Jayaprakash Narayan—JP—the apostle of non-violence whom Indira Gandhi sent to Singapore on the eve of the Bangladesh war, thought him 'a deep humanitarian, and [a] sincere and pragmatic politician, concerned with moral values.' JP regarded it as 'a rare combination.'83 Lee appreciated better than any other leader that India had no imperial design in East Pakistan and did not covet territory. The attraction was mutual. Lee told Prem Bhatia, a journalist he had met at dinner during his 1962 visit and who succeeded the hapless Alirajpur as high commissioner, that JP had the 'look of a good man earnest in the pursuit of a good cause.'84 Singapore did not support the American-sponsored United Nations resolution condemning India over Bangladesh. 'We thought it too extreme and imbalanced,' says Deputy Prime Minister Shunmugam Jayakumar.

Lee's elitist views and genetic theories did not single out any particular society for, as his Raffles College associates confirm, he has always been impatient with the less gifted irrespective of race. Visiting the Changi Tamil School—not a high-profile constituency, so, what he said there did not earn publicity—in December 1966, Lee declared himself 'a friend not only of the Indians here but of the Indian people, and a great admirer of their civilization and their culture.'85 That was why he could afford to complain that the local Indian 'does not work as hard as the Indian who is domiciled in India' (meaning visiting labourers from India) who does two overtime shifts, day and night. 'They eat frugally, they save their money with which they are able to buy land in India,' whereas Singapore Indians have 'become like the local gentry' craving 'style'. Lee had to force them to work harder and earn more.86

In general, he believed as time went on that though Indian Singaporeans were not intellectually superior to their caste/class brethren in India, they were doing better because of Singapore's more open and competitive atmosphere, 'political stability, honest bureaucracy and an economy based on incentives'.87 He would have agreed with JRD's vice-president, Nani A. Palkhivala, a brilliant jurist whom Morarji Desai sent to the United States as ambassador, that the overseas Indian can buy from a Scotsman, sell to a Jew and still make a profit once he is freed from India's bureaucratic stranglehold.

Lee says that if Indians can do it in Singapore, they can do it in India. He told JRD that talented young Indians were emigrating on a large scale for lack of 'an economic environment which permits them to give their best to their country'.[88] Though India had 'enormous problems' she also had 'enormous potentialities' and was not doing justice to her young by not rewarding their talents.[89]

Rajaratnam, too, thought it sad that 10,000 Indian PhDs should work abroad 'because the economic and political climate [at home] was not particularly conducive to the development of fruitful and satisfying careers'.[90] He called this brain drain a new refugee problem and welcomed reports of 'plans to establish a high-technology township to lure back the country's scientists'. They would be needed, Indira Gandhi had declared, for India to enjoy her share of industries like atomic energy, space science and technology, environment, electronics and ocean development.

Lee's interest was not only philanthropic. There could be no meaningful linkages with Singapore unless India developed her economic capability. The so-called Hindu rate of growth of about 3.5 per cent mired millions of people in poverty for three decades while the population soared. 'Every time you saw a new moon, there were another million people,' Senator Daniel Patrick Moynihan, United States ambassador to India, told a Congressional committee. Taking time off from his embassy to spend a week with Lee in Singapore, Moynihan 'said he couldn't understand why Calcutta (which he dubbed a 'necropolis') could not move on while Singapore, which it used to govern, had done so!'[91] Lee warned that swelling numbers year after year cancelled out even the fruit of painfully low growth: 'At this rate, while so many countries of South-east Asia have doubled their per capita income in nine to twelve years, you will require almost thirty-five to forty years only to do that.'[92]

Lee continued the argument with Indira Gandhi when she visited Singapore in 1968, leaving listeners to wonder how she reacted to his implicit criticism. 'You may find Singapore Indians look like Indians, speak like Indians,' he said, 'but those who have been born and educated here, as you get to know them, are no longer Indians.'[93] Under competitive pressure from other races, all aspiring to modernity, they had discarded many taboos of caste and custom. Chandra Das—

though Lee did not name him—illustrated the melting pot. His grandfather was born in Borneo, his father in Malaya. Tamil was his first language. But the Naidu in his name indicated Telugu roots. His wife's mother was Chinese and one of his wife's sisters married a Pakistani Muslim. Another sister's daughter married a Muslim of Sri Lankan origin. It was the same with the Chinese: 'If a man from China speaks to a Singapore Chinese, he will discover that the Singaporean is already a distinct and different type.'[94]

Lee claimed that local Indians were less conscious of caste and community than Indians in India. 'You may have noticed they have also married Chinese wives. And some Chinese have married Indian wives. All that would have been unthinkable in the old days.'[95] Yet, in Indian Singaporean circles a Chinese spouse is still sometimes seen as a short-cut to acceptance. But his claim of Indian achievement in Singapore sounded convincing enough.

> Look, we have eighteen or nineteen (Indians) in the Cabinet. The Indians are 7 or 8 per cent. So that should be only about two Indians in the Cabinet, right? You see how many Indians there are; several times the number. Is it by affirmative action? No! On merit, on their ability to get things done.[96]

A popular joke had a European dignitary wondering if he had taken the wrong flight and landed in India instead of Singapore when he was received at Changi airport by President Devan Nair and introduced to Foreign Minister Dhanabalan.

{6}

'India Alone Can Look
China in the Eye'

Air India, of which Lee once thought so highly, represented all that was wrong with India. There was much that he still admired—India's public schools, for instance, and the values that the ICS embodied—but he thought Indian other-worldliness, reserved quotas, the three-language formula and the media's obsession with trivia to the exclusion of fundamental issues like economics were some of the serious obstacles to growth. He still wanted India in South-east Asia as a counter to both China and Japan but expectations from the visit by Indira Gandhi, with whom he had an enigmatic relationship, led nowhere. More and more, his thoughts turned to the progress that ancestral China was making. Though Lee says, 'I am no more a Chinese than President Kennedy was an Irishman,' there is no denying his immense pride in China's achievements. 'We are all ethnic Chinese; we share certain characteristics through a common ancestry and culture.' But ethnic pride does not obscure political judgement. Pride may also be tinged with a complex for, as he told Deng Xiaoping, the Chinese (in China) are 'the progeny of the scholars, mandarins and literati who had stayed at home' while Singaporeans are 'descendants of illiterate, landless peasants from Fujian and Guangdong'.[1] Eu Mun Hoo Calvin, who became high commissioner to India in 2006, is an exception, counting a long line of Ch'ng dynasty notables among his forebears.[2]

China is a touchy subject in India. Japan can be a model for Indians but not China. The 'competitive cooperation' Jaswant Singh speaks of may apply at the highest levels where Manmohan Singh's gentle conciliation sets the tone, but Singaporeans are acutely aware that most Indians do not relish the comparison. Mukherjee recalls how his father, a veteran nationalist, grieved in 1962 that the freedom he had fought for was in jeopardy within only fifteen years of independence.[3] Singaporean offers to mediate—Toh Chin Chye suggested a facilitator's role when visiting New Delhi in 1975—were as unproductive as Lee's efforts to goad India by citing Chinese achievements. Yeo found that a 'very bullish' speech about China he gave in Bombay quoting a prominent Dubai businessman's claim that Chinese workmen are much more productive than Indians was not well received.[4] He misses in India the 'sense of raw vitality' that characterizes China and Vietnam. He has often woken up in the middle of the night in Ho Chi Minh City to find the din of traffic like daytime. 'They don't sleep. They are working all the time. They are attending classes on Saturday.' China exudes the same feeling with people doing taichee at four or five o'clock in the morning. 'You go to India you don't sense the same intensity,' says George Yeo, 'so LKY has always been very honest, very analytical, in this, even if it's not politically correct to say so.'[5]

Recalling his first visit to China in 1979 when Mao's Four Modernizations had just started, Dhanabalan, who is a more severe observer of the Indian scene than any Chinese, says that the new India is only evident in Bangalore's Whitefields and in the Wipro and Infosys offices. India's airports and roads make him shudder. There's no infrastructure and the system doesn't move, 'The Indians are always talking, quarrelling, modifying. The Chinese are always doing, though, of course, there were some stupidities during the Cultural Revolution like claiming chickens laid bigger eggs if the Little Red Book was read to them.'[6]

But Yeo endorses Lee's view that the upper reaches of Hindu society, the 'Varna' castes, perform with the same intensity, whether it's writing, research or investment banking, as the Chinese or anyone else. It's different, he says, when it comes to broad numbers though no one mentions it in polite society.

This matters to Lee whose strategic thinking has not changed since he told Auckland University students that South-east Asia's future hinges on two factors. First, the leadership's ability to identify common interests and act in concert; and secondly, 'on the intentions and policies of the two big potential industrial powers in Asia: China and India.'[7] He still sees India as a counter—or, preferably, balance—to China's rising power. Asean cannot look China in the eye, he told a distinguished Indian visitor, but India can. Asean plus India add up to a considerable weight. The combination can be the saving of a Singapore that is nervous of China's economic might. 'We don't want to be overwhelmed,' he exclaims. 'We don't want Singapore to become like Laos or Cambodia!'[8] The surrounding Asean countries are similarly uncomfortable though the 'relationship is growing by the day, well by the month, definitely by the year.' Trade and investment will spiral even more when the China-Asean free trade agreement is in operation. However, 'There is an underlying, I won't say discomfort, but there is an underlying unease with China's rapid growth.'

No one has forgotten Mao Zedong's famous declaration, 'We must have South-east Asia, including South Vietnam, Thailand, Burma, Malaya and Singapore... After we get that region, the wind from the East will prevail over the wind from the West.'[9]

George Yeo also addresses the additional responsibility that China's rise places on India.

> As India integrates its economy into East Asia, India can also help to stabilize the region by counterbalancing the other political heavyweights. Because the fear of China will grow with the growth of the Chinese economy, Japan and Asean will always value the strategic presence of India.[10]

Not that South-east Asians want to sever a connection that brings obvious benefits. 'China has overtaken America as Japan's most important partner.'[11] Lee anticipated this runaway success even when China's growth was a 'pitifully poor' 2.5 per cent. Speaking with what he called 'some insight into the psychology of the Chinese people,' he told JRD that the Chinese, like Indians, are 'a strange mixture of Puritanism and materialism' but the materialism would prevail when Mao retired or died. His successors would 'quietly dismantle his quest for bringing Communism into every Chinese home'.[12] Being a very pragmatic and intelligent people capable of immense hard work, they would 'show the world they can rival not merely small city-states like Singapore and Hong Kong, but even Japan, in achieving a very much higher rate of economic growth' once they had shaken off the debris of ideology.[13] The Chinese did not need the crutches of the state to achieve great things. They needed only—perhaps he was conveying a message to India—'political stability, a solid bureaucracy and a system of socially oriented free enterprise'.[14]

India had political stability. As for a 'solid bureaucracy', Lee never ceases to regret the passing of the ICS which, adapting Voltaire on the Holy Roman Empire, might have been neither Indian nor civil nor a service, but which he sees as the epitome of meritocracy. He repeats that the British based the ICS on China's Mandarinate which ensured administrative stability through the turbulence of Mongol and Manchu dynasties. Lee always enjoyed hobnobbing with ICS officials, inviting them to breakfast in his suite at Rashtrapati Bhavan and predictably finding them 'impressive'. He believes that Nehru would have left a lasting legacy by preserving the service. He would have been surprised to learn that Nehru felt he had retained too much—and not too little—of the ICS, to India's disadvantage. Asked three years before he died to identify his greatest failure, Nehru reflected for a long time before saying gently, 'I failed to change this administration. It is still a colonial administration.'[15] Varindra Tarzie Vittachi, his Sri Lankan interlocutor, felt that for Nehru, the successor Indian Administrative Service was too much like the ICS.

Lee's romantic vision draws on writers like Philip Woodruff—Philip Mason of the ICS in real life—who immortalized 'the men who ruled India' as the Founders and Guardians. Modern writers mock that classical idyll:

> Much nonsense has been written about the romantic, glamorous notion of a single ICS officer riding around his district, dispensing even-handed justice to a grateful and submissive peasantry. Settling law cases before breakfast, such a paragon apparently corrected land records before lunch, shot a tiger or two before dinner and wrote some Latin verse before taking a cold bath and retiring to a camp bed.[16]

Nevertheless, it riles Lee that Nehru did not try to recast society in his own enlightened secular image.

> He had the strength then—his political position was so towering, he could have forced India to go in a different direction. He could have made concessions at lower levels—but at the top level, the top echelons of the civil service, the judiciary, the military and the police, he should have kept it on merit.[17]

Lee is not alone in that judgement. Sharing his assessment, James Cameron, the distinguished British journalist who adored Nehru, thought Nehru 'made India and lost it'. Nehru 'could have done with India anything he wished, but he let it wither . . .'[18]

Despite his dissatisfactions, Lee continued to look to India for models so that no one was surprised when he commended to Singapore school principals an Indian version (presumably produced in schools like Doon) of the ideal of the hardy British public schoolboy who can flourish in the bush. He added the caveat that there was 'this slight difference' from the original—'the Indians have never placed emphasis on the physical side. They have always placed it on the spiritual side.' His educational ideal would probably be Haileybury, the East India Company College till 1858, whose purpose was to produce proconsuls to lord it over palm and pine.

Lee saw the British Indian bureaucracy as one of India's strongest assets, providing the efficient governance that enables politicians to adhere to democratic principles and depriving the military of any excuse to intervene. Three countries 'in South-east Asia' (Pakistan, Indonesia and Burma), he told Singapore civil servants at the opening of the Political Study Centre in 1959, had failed to create democratic states whereas two others in the same region (India and Ceylon) had succeeded because they 'had the administrators to run the machine of the democratic system'.[19] South and South-east Asia remained interchangeable terms. More to the point, only good administration guarantees stability in a political democracy.

His point is that administrators who take and implement decisions affecting the lives of hundreds of millions of people must be nurtured with care. He fears that ICS values might languish in the IAS whose members cannot afford to maintain the bungalows that go with their jobs, being paid 'less than a *cha-wallah*' as Dhanabalan puts it. Singapore abolished expatriate perks like housing but raised salaries to guarantee a comfortable lifestyle, attract the best talent and reduce temptation. 'You need an elite administration to run a vast country like India in an effective way,' Lee says, regretting the concessions to caste and language that 'the democratic process' demands.

> You redrew your state boundaries, you gave quotas for jobs, you gave quotas to universities. All that kept India together but at the cost of quality. And that is one reason why I say India cannot go as fast as China, because the Chinese run completely on merit. You go to university, you get there by merit. No quotas![20]

In spite of harping on the harm reservations have done to administrative efficiency, Lee was not at all put out when my son, who had been studying the foreign service for his DPhil thesis, told him that some of the reserved category entrants scored the highest marks. 'Naturally,' he at once agreed with Deep Kisor. 'They are the ones who are highly motivated because they want to climb up, but it doesn't mean they are the top performers.' Whether your car wins or the next car wins depends on your horse power. Another analogy he chose was of a cricket team: 'Can you have quotas for a winning first eleven?'[21]

Quotas might be politically expedient but 'are an impediment to effective governance.' Favoured entrants will not be up to the mark. 'They won't do you justice.' He adds philosophically that there's no point crying over spilt milk. Only another revolution can change the system.

Too Little, Too Late

China's per capita income was already two-and-a-half times higher than India's by the time India changed course under Narasimha Rao and Manmohan Singh, and Lee does not think India will be able to close the gap for a very long time unless the Chinese falter: 'Mind you, the gap may not widen. Over the next twenty to thirty years if this goes on, I think the gap will not be so stark because India would have got past the infrastructure stage, and would be on a better platform to compete. At the moment you can't really compete because your infrastructure is not in place.'[22]

China's roads, bridges, canals, the Three Gorges dam, all prove how quickly the system responds to central government directives. Watching a Discovery Channel programme on the Three Gorges, Lee was impressed at the speed and efficiency with which a city of a million people that would be submerged was evacuated. 'Three-quarters of the people had already been decanted to the other side of the river.' Asked if there was resistance, he breaks into chortles at the very idea of such a thing in China and says, 'Of course, no resistance!' The resistance the media plays up is confined to cities 'along the coastal provinces where local governments in league with developers are getting rid of farmers because they want the land to build power stations and so on at low cost.' But the Shanghai relocation was a government project, and alternative jobs and housing were assured.

> That's the difference. Let me put it simply this way . . . and it's not that I don't want India to succeed, but if they had a city like Bombay—and I saw how they created a new Shanghai—I think in five to ten years you would have a spanking new Bombay![23]

But Bombay's squatters 'get back the day after tomorrow' every time they are cleared. That's because the local authorities don't have the power or the will 'to give them an alternative site to build homes and provide them with adequate alternative jobs'. In Shanghai the planners have created a new livelihood for the displaced.

Shanghai was a 'dilapidated, broken-down city' when Lee first went there in 1976. He was put up in the best hotel but was horrified when he, his wife and their security officers ventured out at night and saw 'the crammed humanity, the unbelievable pavements and roads in semi-darkness with poor, dirty, scruffy street lights, the shops in darkness . . .' The reconstruction plan designated Shanghai the Dragon's Head, the Dragon's Body being the Yangtse River going right up to Tibet. The Dragon's Head led the development of the entire Yangtse basin with roads, bridges, railways and other urban amenities. Lee had not expected them to move so quickly. But progress has been dramatic, clean and green. People were moved to a new city called East of the River, Pudong, and streets and buildings were knocked down. He is sure there was 'some pain and suffering' but people have adjusted to new homes and jobs and a better life. He adds, 'India can do that, but, I mean, to do that you will need a civil service. This is at state level you know. Delhi can't order Maharashtra—Bombay is [in] Maharashtra?—to do that. The state government hasn't got the apparatus; hasn't got the army. It's only got a police force.'[24]

China works smoothly like a dentist or surgeon with all his instruments at hand. 'That makes a big difference to the speed of implementation. It's all done according to plan with the bridges and tunnels in place. The whole resources of the nation of a thousand million people went into Shanghai.' Initially, there was misallocation of funds, and the huge high-rise buildings remained empty. That could have been avoided, Lee thinks, by using market forces to develop Pudong and saving the government's capital for more productive purposes. But he sees the end product as a triumph of central planning and the ability to execute.

It is action that Lee admires, not argument. The discursiveness he deplores as an Indian characteristic owes something, according to Leifer, to 'the deeply irritating presence for a time in Parliament of J.B. Jeyaretnam—depicted by Lee as a fly-by-night politician'.[25] (Jeyaretnam, who died on 30 September 2008, was Singapore's best-known and most tenacious opposition leader, and novelist Philip Jeyaretnam's father. He and Lee were at loggerheads for many years.) Lee blames India's media for not living up to its responsibility to point out what was wrong with the system and suggest correctives. Josey quotes the *Far Eastern Economic Review* as writing, 'It could be argued (and Lee Kuan Yew would probably argue) that one of the factors in India's bitter years of agonizingly slow progress has been the amount of dissent voiced by its free newspapers.'[26] If India's newspapers had really cared, Lee thinks, they would have analysed the reasons for backwardness and outlined solutions. His hackles rise at the suggestion that the media is exciting in its outspokenness.

> Exciting in what sense? Exciting in the sense of A versus B versus C? But it's not exciting in the sense of a vision, of a new India and how to get there. There wasn't any of that. The newspapers were quite happy as far as I could make out with the status quo, with what India was achieving, and not concerned with what was not there.[27]

They were immersed in trivial politicking instead of questioning and examining the fundamental reasons for under-achievement: 'I saw India in the nineteen-fifties and sixties. Dozens of newspapers in New Delhi. I did not see enlightenment. I saw confusion. That's only the English press. The contrariness was greater in the Indian language press.'[28]

Josey thinks he had Indian and Ceylonese journalists in mind when he invoked a Chinese allegorical saying, '*Chu pa Chieh*, pig-faced scoundrel, look in the mirror: have you no shame?'[29] It was a contemptuous reference to migrants to the West who pontificate from there on Asian matters. 'Their advice is worse than useless. They have no sense of shame or they would stay and help their own countries' progress and their fellow countrymen live less wretched lives. Instead, they flee to greener pastures and give us advice.'

He has never regarded press freedom per se as the answer to development problems. It is a Western myth that Asians should resist. Free newspapers do not bring 'light and reason' to public affairs, whether in India, the United States, Britain or the Philippines.[30] Another myth is that a free press curbs corruption. 'The media itself is corrupted,' he says, pointing to Taiwan, the Philippines and South Korea.[31] 'Some are naïve enough to believe that freedom of the press is sacrosanct and unlimited,' he told the International Press Institute in Helsinki. 'Freedom of the press really means the freedom of the owner, the man who owns the newspaper, who hires and fires the journalists.'

Josey and Rajaratnam, both former journalists and office-bearers of the Singapore Union of Journalists, did not disagree with Lee's views. But having worked both sides of the fence, Rajaratnam recognized the 'love–hate' relationship between journalists and politicians. They were 'both in the same business of influencing public opinion'.

English Should Be India's Language

China scores yet again in achieving linguistic unity. Ninety per cent of the Chinese already speak the same language (though pronunciations vary) as a result of China's efforts since 1911 to banish dialects. Thanks to television and the Internet, Lee thinks complete success is now within reach. Japan, too, did away with its dialects and imposed standard Japanese. 'But in India you are not going to get ever, I think, one language which is going to be universal!'[32] Lee knows that India has distinctly separate languages and not dialects to contend with, but is concerned that this diversity inhibits integration, political authority, effective administration and educational uniformity.

It is virtually impossible for a nation to be strong, united and informed without linguistic unity, Lee says. Language, for him, serves two purposes. It must be the means of acquiring knowledge. How can knowledge be disseminated in so many tongues? It must also be a vehicle for political mobilization. How can people be inspired and mobilized without a common language? Fascinated by the mechanics of crowd manipulation, and seeing language as the principal instrument, he accompanied Abraham to a public rally when C.N. Annadurai, the charismatic DMK politician from Madras, visited Singapore. Anna—elder brother—spoke in chaste Tamil of which Lee understood not a word. But he was entranced by the crowd's delirium and the knowledge that forty million people in Tamil Nadu (and more in Ceylon) were similarly captivated. Elder Brother had cast his spell over both Sparta and Athens, he exclaimed in wonder. But whether the Tengku spoke in English or Malay, not more than 40 per cent of listeners followed what he said. That was true of Nehru too, but he had 'the charisma of the leader' and that was compensation enough. 'Thousands flocked to hear him, not understanding what he said, it is true. But they thought to be in his presence was to have been blessed. And so when Nehru passed, an age passed in India,'[33] said Lee a few months after Nehru's death, when Lee feared Shastri would 'face immense problems without the same charismatic touch, the legend of the leader'.[34]

The following year Lee had direct experience of how volatile the language question can be. After speaking in English for half an hour in the Malaysian parliament (Singapore was still in the federation) he switched to Malay. The atmosphere which had been desultory until then at once became electric. 'I think if they could have cheered, they would have,' said E.W. (Eddie) Barker, Singapore's future law and national development minister, who was one of the 500 people in the chamber. Barker believes that was when the Tengku 'felt it was better to have Singapore and Mr Lee out (of Malaysia)'.[35] Lee has not forgotten. Hindi, English, Tamil or Tagalog reaches only a section of the populace. De Gaulle and Winston Churchill could galvanize the nation in a time of crisis because they spoke the people's language. 'To move people you have to speak directly to them.'[36]

Every nation needs a common language. India's should be an Indianized English since English will not be dislodged as the global repository of knowledge in medicine, science and engineering, especially now with the Internet. Language is only a tool, he says. English doesn't belong to the British just as Chinese doesn't belong to China. 'We use it!' Americans are no longer beholden to the Oxford dictionary, their standard is Webster. He thinks 'India could have done likewise. An Indianized version of English which would be understood throughout India and also by English-speaking people abroad would be the answer. Of course, you must keep within certain rules so that you can get a wide audience.'[37]

He concedes the strength of nationalist feeling but with Indian writing in English winning worldwide acclaim, India should make more of its mastery of the language. Nehru could have seen to that. 'The Indian leaders don't lack intelligence. I feel they should have had in mind the long-term higher objectives of an effectively governed and administered India, and not given way so much to sentiment on the ground' because 'once you start fiddling around with two languages or three languages or five, or thirty-two languages, everything becomes very difficult.'

He told a gathering in the university's Bukit Timah Campus that after Prime Minister Desai explained India's three-language formula (Hindi, the mother tongue, and English) to him, Lee discussed it with a south Indian who said it was all right for Desai since his native 'Gujarati was very close to Hindi', which made the three-language formula a kind of 'bilingualism' for Northerners. When Lee mentioned this to a north Indian, the man replied, 'We are prepared to learn Tamil or a southern Dravidian language to make it fair.' But Lee is 'quite confident, knowing the history of the whole of the south' that Hindi will never displace Tamil or Malayali. 'It is unthinkable! It is not possible!'

He told Oza that 'the human mind has limited capacity and would find three languages too much to grapple with. People should not have to learn more than two.' Oza argued that two languages would be restrictive in India's vastness and variety. An Indian has to communicate with family and friends in his mother tongue, with various levels of officialdom in English, and with people in other parts of the country in a common Indian language. Lee was not convinced.[38] He cites the case of Quebec where linguistic duality hampers governance even though French and English are cognate languages. 'You have to have one master language. Your laws must be in that language and everybody must operate within that context.' He rejects my mention of romanized Hindustani because language must lead to data. 'You can have everybody using romanized Hindustani, but where is your store of new knowledge? Are you going to translate all the latest discoveries in medicine—diagrams, everything—from American into romanized Hindustani? No!'[39]

It is bad enough in Singapore with only four languages but it was right, Lee thinks, not to succumb to the majority which wanted Chinese.[40] Lee feared that Malay and Indian resentment would lead to riots as in Ceylon. 'I was determined not to go that road.' English was the only way of keeping together even a tiny country such as his, and opening up the treasure house of global knowledge for future generations without cumbersome translation. This was not an

Anglophile prime minister's unilateral imposition. Lee's colleagues—Dr Goh, Rajaratnam and Toh—felt the same way. As he tells it, he was no more than primus inter pares.

English may not have been internalized as yet, but about 65 per cent of Singaporeans speak it and the remaining 35 per cent are older people. He is confident English will be the working language in another twenty years. Many young members of Parliament who were urged to speak in their mother tongue had to prepare their scripts in English and then translate them. It took hours. Not that Singaporeans have surrendered the mother tongue, but they have 'relegated it to another position.'

Learning two languages (leave alone three as in India) is still 'a huge burden for children, especially for Chinese children because Mandarin is so difficult.'[41] The problem arouses painful memories of the prime minister's mammoth National Day Rally oration that could go on for up to three hours and was delivered in English, Chinese and Malay. It was 'very exhausting—physical energy required' and Lee would have to lie down on the studio floor between the different language broadcasts: 'The radio reporters thought I'd collapsed, seeing me lying on the floor because I was exhausted.'[42]

'Mehta the Central Planner'

Though his comments on the 'spiritual side' of Indian education sounded neutral, Lee blames India's 'next-worldly' approach to life for economic stagnation. The concept of 'If you do good, then in the next world you'll get rewarded' kills incentive. Speaking on 'Indian mysticism' and 'self-negation' at Singapore's Ramakrishna Mission, he confessed to being torn between spiritual values and 'hard material facts.'[43] One gets the feeling he was being polite to his hosts who had renounced worldly pleasures but that he himself was unable to appreciate either their commitment or the 'saintliness' of Gandhi and his disciple, Vinoba Bhave, who started the *Bhoodan*, land-gift, movement to persuade landowners to donate land for the landless.

India with her 'sadhus, holy men, people who abjure the world, who go around giving land away or begging from the rich to give to the poor' was a 'totally different culture' from China. The Chinese 'were very intense types, hard-driving, hard-striving people' who had no time for saints and savants. 'In China, the model is . . . the kind of hero who forms a robber band and kills off wealthy people. You don't go begging from the wealthy to give to the poor. You just kill the wealthy and take from them. The Indians have a more tolerant and forgiving approach to life. More next-worldly.'[44]

Those were the years when the mix of Gandhian piety and English snobbishness made money a taboo subject in India. Even the richest entrepreneur could not bring himself to acknowledge merit in wealth generation. 'Who wrote about the free market in the 1960s?' asks Arun Shourie, quick-witted and intellectual, international banker, journalist and fierce free marketer, who served in Atal Behari Vajpayee's Bharatiya Janata Party government as disinvestment minister, and was Singapore's twenty-third Lee Kuan Yew Exchange Fellow. 'There were only a few of us—Jagdish Bhagwati, Padma Desai and I. Everybody was a socialist then!' Shourie's doctoral thesis at Syracuse argued vigorously against government controls. 'We were called World Bank stooges!'[45] Even JRD, high priest of the private sector, would not deny the public sector its due. The government had to play an active role in promoting development in a mixed economy. 'None of us believes that the less the government the better; but we do believe that government must get its priorities right. We have an over-taxed, over-regulated economy with government too spread out to be effective.'[46]

Lee recalls Asoka Mehta as the apotheosis of India's blend of Fabian socialism and Gandhian austerity. 'Mehta the Central Planner' is lodged so firmly in his mind that mention of Jagat Mehta at once brings the other Mehta to mind. Lee says, 'I said to him, "Why don't you have more private enterprise?" And he said to me, "We don't have the capital. Only the state can create the capital to go into big industry." At that time I believed the way to go was to have a mixed economy. Have both state and private enterprise, and let them compete.'

Lee 'had not yet come to the conclusion that private enterprise was superior'. That came only in the late 1970s or 1980s when he compared Britain with Japan and the United States.[47] The frustration wells up again and his voice rises in querulous perplexity as he asks forty-five years later. 'And that's the part I don't understand about India. Its leaders were well read. They knew what was happening in the world. Why didn't they read the signs? Why did they stick to this?'[48]

His conversation with Asoka Mehta took place against the background of the wars and drought of 1965 that had emptied the exchequer, forcing India to accept a World Bank devaluation package amidst intense anguish and argument. Mehta told Parliament in February there was 'no question' of devaluing the rupee but agreed three months later—under Jha's influence, says Natwar Singh—with World Bank President George Woods to do so as part of a reform programme to encourage foreign aid and investment, and boost trade. The actual announcement in June by Finance Minister Sachin Chaudhuri, a wealthy and stylish barrister whose prized possessions included his Daimler car and collection of Elizabethan pewter, was part of an 'aggressively pro-trade budget speech'. But Chaudhuri was a political outsider and the reforms were dumped. So was he. Asked about the liberalization-cum-devaluation package many years later, Jha 'laughed merrily' and said, 'Oh that! That was what George Woods told us we had to do to get aid.'[49]

Indira Gandhi's instinct was against liberalization. The Moscow Mafia thought India was being mortgaged to the Foreign Hand. The political right, the Jana Sangh, progenitor of the BJP, which supported the free market, joined the left on a xenophobic bandwagon. Political India loves accusations of a sell-out, and Indira Gandhi happily stoked fears to mobilize radical support for the coming showdown with the Congress old guard and conservatives like Morarji Desai. The media spoke luridly of opening India's womb to foreign entrepreneurs.

Asoka Mehta was not of the ultra-left. Josey quotes him telling the founding conference of the Asian Socialist Conference in Rangoon in 1953 that he was a socialist because he knew that meeting a person's 'animal wants'—'hunger, shelter, a piece of cloth to cover the body's nakedness'—should be the first task of any government. He was 'fully aware that government-owned factories have proved to be far less efficient than private enterprise'.[50] Nor was he a fanatical fellow traveller. He quit the government over its ambivalence when Soviet tanks rolled into Prague in the ill-fated spring of 1968. But he would have been aghast at the remedies that Lee, who thought India was too easygoing for her own good, recommended at an international forum in Tokyo organized by the German socialist foundation, the Friedrich-Ebert Stiftung. Lee attributed India's stagnant economy to 'the abstinence from the use of the spur or the whip on the working class in the public sector, plus the checks on outright exploitation of the working class in the private sector'. But he also praised 'the absence of jingoism which has marked the policies of rational democratic government in India'.

Lee did not think developing countries could expect more than 'some assistance in the basic training of personnel, managers, administrators, professionals, technologists and also capital equipment on favourable terms for simple manufactures'. The outcome depended on the recipient's capacity to make use of assistance. He faulted India's economic practice even in terms of her own theology. Her bureaucracy held India to ransom not because it was steeped in ideology but because government controls brought it handsome benefits. India's mixed economy was not 'based on incentives but on controls'. The narrow self-interest of politicians and bureaucrats held business at their mercy: 'It is a socialism in which the principal goal is to ensure that the state commands the dominating heights of the economy; it is not a socialism in which the creation of the right economic environment is the first priority.'[51]

There's No Air about India

Recalling the time when Lee 'used to ask to be booked on Air India flights', Nathan laments the deterioration after JRD was eased out. 'Tata's!' he reminisces admiringly. 'Once it [Air India] became government then you had all this. It's sad.' Decline was inevitable. 'I ask you, how do you run an airline when every chairman when he retires—he's got a new job—still travels free? It's an entitlement! Like that, every Tom, Dick and Harry has his share. Are you a commercial airline or are you not? And then, of course, service has deteriorated.'[52]

Nathan recalls flying with his wife as ordinary fare-paying passengers. 'The crew, the staff, the stewards and stewardesses, they couldn't be bothered with us. Lolling away behind, drinking, chatting, having *tamasha*. No discipline at all!' Lee's prescription is predictably drastic. He would 'let Air India die naturally' instead of breaking heads and making life miserable trying to revitalize it.⁵³ It would be 'better [to] start a new airline' and cater separately to VIPs.

> You can have Indian Air Force One, Air Force Two, Air Force Three for the President, Prime Minister and ministers and officials. No problem! The difference is that a dynamic airline also helps the economy. You have to take into account the number of tourists it will bring, the businessmen, the connections it will create.'⁵⁴

A senior member of the Prime Minister's Office in New Delhi says diplomacy will improve the day Air India is abolished. He also points out that business class passengers no longer fly Air India.⁵⁵ Shourie would agree. He talks of the airline's huge losses and undisclosed debts, adding that when privatization was on the cards a Congress MP told Parliament that the Cabinet secretary, India's senior-most bureaucrat, opposed it. In Singapore, Chandra Das feels that New Delhi will sooner or later have to decide between Air India and tourism.

Lee thinks India and Indonesia suffer from similar inhibitions. He says he once advised Indonesians that if they allowed low-cost flying all over the country, all the hawkers, garment-sellers, toymakers and everybody would have coins jingling in their pockets because of improved travel and trade. They ignored his advice. 'It's a mental block you know. So I am waiting to see which moves faster, India or Indonesia. Sukarno and Nehru were of the same generation, about the same age. Both were anti-colonial and both turned that way . . .'⁵⁶ It was a challenge for 'genuine socialists' to 'strive for economic equality and social justice'.⁵⁷ Not for him the satisfaction of Nguyen Co Thach, Vietnam's urbane foreign minister, fluent in English and French, whose infamous boast was, 'We are not without accomplishment. We have managed to distribute poverty equally.' Socialism for Lee meant raising the poor to the level of the rich.

Amiable but Little Substance

Well might India's external affairs ministry hail Indira Gandhi's two-day visit to Singapore as 'a resounding success' for there were cheering crowds everywhere—mainly local Indians—and an orange-red orchid was named Holttumara Indira Gandhi in her honour. It was a measure of Lee's anxiety to make the event a success that he was heard to remark while personally supervising arrangements for his guest's comfort, 'If that woman falls down and breaks her head, all hell will break loose!' People noted their easy camaraderie. Finding the road to the Istana jammed because of the Thaipusam festival, Indira Gandhi suggested that public mortification of the flesh should be discouraged. 'We don't have it in India, Harry,' she said, a claim Yeo with his south Indian connections disputes. 'You know, Indira,' Lee replied, 'if I touched it I'd have a riot on my hands! People have brought this with them; they have celebrated it from the time of their ancestors and they want to preserve it. It's also a tourist attraction, so I let it go on and see it is properly managed.'[58]

Still hoping for a defence relationship, he expressed the hope that the arrival of an Indian navy flotilla (the *INS Mysore*, *Rajput* and *Ranjit*) would be 'the first of many visits': 'Our harbour will always be a friendly haven for Indian naval units. Placed as we are, with one avenue looking westwards into the Indian Ocean and the other eastwards into the Pacific, not unnaturally we feel more relaxed and comfortable when there is no oppressive and overpowering hegemony by any single power.'

His guest was sublimely above such concerns as she advised her host that economic cooperation was the best guarantee of security and assured South-east Asians, with a touch of complacence, that she accepted them as 'friends and equals'. Her reiteration that India had no intention of taking Britain's place was expected but the rider that India would not like another power to do so militarily may have sounded a trifle presumptuous. Somewhat surprisingly, and a portent of things to come, she welcomed the entry of Australia and New Zealand into regional affairs, telling a questioner that she had always thought the two white dominions 'should be in Asia' and welcomed signs of them 'veering to what we thought'.[59]

Alastair Buchan of the Institute of Strategic Studies in London recommended 'a treaty of mutual cooperation between India, Australia and Japan' that 'need not be too specific on the subject of cooperation'.[60] Two Australian ministers, Paul Hasluck (foreign affairs) and Allan Fairhall (defence), suggested similar alignments. Morarji Desai, regarded as closer to American thinking than most Indian politicians, thought India, South-east Asia, Japan and Australia should close ranks against the Chinese threat.[61] Strangely—or, perhaps, not so strangely—the notion also excited the Americans and Fifield who said, 'Neither India nor Japan, acting alone, is likely to become an effective counterweight to China but acting together they could have an important role in creating a stable pattern of power among Asian states.'[62]

It could have been Lee thinking aloud. It might have been an early blueprint for Malabar-07, the five-power—Australia, India, Japan, Singapore and the United States—naval exercise in the Bay of Bengal in the first week of September 2007.

Indira Gandhi's meetings with all the Indian envoys in Southeast Asia, first in Kuala Lumpur and then in New Delhi, and recurrent references to Asean and the phantom Council of Asia, implied she shared the region's concern even if she was not prepared to admit it or commit herself. Her self-perception would not allow India to be an appendage to someone else's security pact; at the same time, domestic and external politics prevented India from taking the lead Lee wanted. Indira Gandhi did once suggest that the big powers should guarantee the neutrality and independence of aspiring nations and help them develop their nationalism through popular governments but baulked at spelling out her ideas. Questioned, she pleaded she had only been indulging in 'loud thinking'.[63]

For Lee, this was another instance of India's disregard of ground reality and of the power of the United States. He knew that whatever India or Singapore might think, the Americans would do 'whatever they think is in their long-term interest.' Similarly, the North Vietnamese would not change their position and the war would go on for a long time.[64] He found it incredible that a huge nation with vast potentials and an educated leadership should allow herself to think the world would believe in world order, that the rule of law would prevail, that international rights would be respected, and that force would be eschewed as a means of settling international disagreements and disputes. This was yet another of Nehru's idealistic legacies.

I think one of the most tragic personal events was when Mr Nehru faced the agony of disillusionment in his basic, fundamental belief. That, in fact, power politics in Asia is as old as the first tribes that emerged, and that, whether we like it or not, if we are to survive and maintain our separate identities, it is necessary that we should learn what is in the joint interest at any single time of a group of nations . . .[65]

Lee complained that though a big tree, India gave no protective shade to smaller states.[66] His avowed aim was to end that isolation and persuade India's leaders that they needed South-east Asia for the reasons Panikkar had set out so succinctly. India's political right was at one with him and accused the government of neglecting its own Council of Asia proposal. B.R. Bhagat, the minister of state for external affairs, tried to refute the charge in tortuous prose that nevertheless indicated that India objected to American influence in the region and was anxious not to do anything that might provoke China or offend the Soviets. She favoured 'a broad-based economic organization' that 'no single country or group of countries from Asia or outside can dominate.' Bhagat went on to deny any wish 'to *gatecrash* into any regional organization that may be there' (emphasis added), which confirmed that Asean had not invited India.[67] In fact, regional leaders took no notice of the hints Chagla and Indira Gandhi continued to drop, not even when she told the Lok Sabha that a Council of Asia would promote 'economic, technical and other ties with neighbouring South-east Asian countries' and that India had 'a vital interest' in the relationship. As noted, Malik passed by several opportunities to engage India.

Some Indian diplomats say Chagla's proposal was no more than 'an ad hoc response to please his local hosts.'[68] Some South-east Asians say Chagla was not taken seriously. There was no sign of a structured Indian plan and no follow-up. The Tengku was promised details; when the promise was not kept, he dismissed Chagla's council as 'an empty suggestion'.[69] Even Lee's colleagues lacked his enthusiasm for bringing India into the region. Defence Minister Lim Kim San ruled out any single successor to Britain: the vacuum could 'only be filled either by a major power (read the United States) or by all the nations in South-east Asia, extending as far as Australia and New Zealand working together in concert for the security of the region.'[70] India was not mentioned.

But Indira Gandhi still chased the hare she had raised, mentioning an alternative to Asean even when visiting Kuala Lumpur in late 1968. The Asian Council of Ministers for Economic Development of Asia 'for the promotion of regional economic cooperation in South-east Asia' affiliated to Ecafe, whose name was changed to Escap (United Nations Economic Commission for Asia and the Pacific), was India's consolation prize.

Buoyant economic ties might have bridged the gap in perception but India was not a trading nation. Apart from one year—1964—when India–Singapore trade touched the glorious high of a whole 2 per cent, bilateral trade hovered at a little over 1 per cent of Singapore's total. Though Indira Gandhi asked for more trade delegations, trade with the region as a whole declined. She also stressed the 'great scope for joint ventures' as 'industrialization gathers greater momentum' but ideas were not translated into practice, as G. Ramachandran, chairman of the joint standing committee of Singapore's chambers of commerce, told her. His father, P. Govindasamy Pillai, had been a prop of Singapore's original Indian community and a hallowed but now vanished name in the retail efflorescence of Little India; he was the only Indian to feature on a Singapore stamp. Ramachandran pointed out to Indira Gandhi that though India had joint ventures in sixteen countries, high taxes and tortuous laws made it difficult to make and save enough money legitimately for foreign investment without the additional hassle of transferring it abroad legally.

Ramachandran suggested several areas of cooperation. Singapore was the world's fourth-busiest port (having pushed London down to fifth place) and was equipped to take containerized ships, while the airport was being expanded to receive Jumbo jets. Defence was another likely area and a civilian official from India's defence ministry who led a four-man mission on a twelve-day visit discussed training facilities for officers, artillery courses, a Pushpak trainer aircraft and mechanics as well as Chagla's by now somewhat shopworn offer of cavalry horses. A team of experts from India's state-owned Hindustan

Steel carried out a feasibility study under Ecafe auspices for a steel mill. India–Singapore relations held a great capacity for promises that came to nothing.

Indira Gandhi charmed Singaporeans but the discerning among them thought Kaul, who accompanied her, was 'blatantly pro-Malaysia'. They also noted her sharp tongue. Seeing the ever-faithful Brahmin Sankaran in constant attendance, she asked if he was the secretary for the occasion, suggesting that Lee had dredged up an Indian to impress her with his catholicity. She could be gracious too, and another Singaporean admired the way she put at ease the nervous waiter who spilt a drink on her sari at the official reception in the Conference Hall in Shenton Way. Her entourage noted that Lee was playing golf with Josey, both men in shorts, in the Istana grounds when her motorcade passed by. Lee smiled and waved. A smiling Indira Gandhi waved back but one of her aides thought Lee's greeting too casual for respect and says that though she said nothing, she probably did not forgive or forget the supposed 'slight'.[71] Indira Gandhi, like Lee, invited contrary opinions on almost every aspect of her being.

Conflicting perceptions of their relationship compound the complexity of bilateral ties and, even more, the task of recording them. Many stories were told of alleged spats. Journalists (Indian and Singaporean) covering international events formed one impression, Nathan another. 'Not cordial' is a senior Indian politician's verdict on the relationship. At our first encounter (unrecorded) at the 1983 Commonwealth summit in New Delhi, Lee declared that he was attending 'only because of Madam Gandhi', for whom he 'had the highest respect.' Dixit told Ong—who called the former foreign secretary his guru—that Lee greatly admired Indira Gandhi.[72] Gujral told Jayakumar that Indira Gandhi 'treasured' her 'personal relationship' with Lee. 'There was mutual respect and a lot of admiration.'[73] See Chak Mun, high commissioner to India (2002–06), noted during an earlier stint at the United Nations how impressed Lee was by the rank and number of notables who flocked round her. His regard was reciprocated. When Abraham told Indira Gandhi in 1973 that Lee would be fifty on 16 September, 'she immediately sent him a very warm letter on his birthday.' Another Indian diplomat who observed them at close quarters was reminded of Margaret Thatcher's famous question, 'Is he one of us?' With them, the People-Like-Us syndrome meant they had the same ways and small talk and knew similar, if not the same, people internationally. That does not stop talk of a clash of egos.

Lee, who has recorded his impressions of Indira Gandhi in some detail, has only contempt for stories of the two being at it hammer and tongs at every conference. 'Rubbish, rubbish! Absolute rubbish! They probably didn't know of the personal relationship.'[74]

As for all those tales of snubs and sarcasm doing the rounds of the press gallery and anterooms, 'No no, they never took place. Personally we never clashed.'[75] He couldn't with 'Nehru's daughter' who was his hostess in her father's time. Perhaps the 'Nehru's daughter' tag holds a clue. Chester Bowles was highly successful during his first ambassadorial stint (1951–53) when Nehru was prime minister but less effective during his second term (1963–69) after the woman he thought of as his old friend's daughter took over. Indira Gandhi was not for patronizing. She was four years older than Lee though he became prime minister seven years before her. They were family, but contrary members of it, highly talented, extremely complex, and neither predictable nor likely to take a one-dimensional view of each other. It is also possible that her sycophantic entourage regarded anything other than abject deference an affront to 'Madam'.

The visit highlighted the contrast between personal and political relationships. There is no doubt that Indira Gandhi and Lee got on well socially, far better, perhaps, then he did with any other Indian politician. It is equally certain that their politics were far apart. Morarji Desai, on the other hand, was closer to Lee in his ideology, but could not have been farther removed in personal terms. The deputy prime minister, who also visited Singapore during Baker's tenure when a goat had to be tethered in the Istana to cater to his inflexible dietary requirements, was not an easy guest. Of his eccentricities, Baker writes, 'He was noted for drinking his own urine every morning. I suppose it was very pure because of his vegetarian diet.'

Whatever his foibles, unpunctuality was not one of them. Desai arrived on the dot for his appointment with Lee and did not like having to wait. Nor did he relish Lee's opening remark when he did make a belated appearance: 'I understand you live on nuts!' Bridling, he retorted tartly, 'Yes, I do live on nuts but so did our ancient ancestors.' Desai held forth on India's world view and the morality (or absence of it) in contemporary politics during their long meeting so that Lee could barely get a word in. In the car on the way back, Desai boasted to High Commissioner Bhatia in Hindi, *'Tum ne dekha, mainey usey baat nahin karne di?'* (Did you see I did not let him talk at all?)[76]

Indira Gandhi's visit left a far more amiable impression but it is doubtful if it left anything else.

'Japan Versus the Rest'

Lee's 'instinct' led him, when other plans fizzled out, to involve India in countering an initiative that many condemned as Japan's 'bid for regional leadership'.[77] This was the third ministerial meeting—the first and second were in Tokyo and Manila—of the Conference for Economic Development of South-east Asia or Seamced that the Japanese set up in 1966. Acting President Coomaraswamy opened the conference of about a hundred delegates and observers, and Jagat Mehta and Manu Ratilal Shroff from the finance ministry went as observers.[78]

Instinct is seldom without logic, and Jagat Mehta, who saw the conference as coterminous with the wartime Greater East Asia Co-prosperity Sphere, thinks Lee sought to balance Japan's economic strength with India's political maturity. Lee had good reason to wish to broaden the focus for he remained uncomfortable with Japan's past. As he says, 'I was nineteen—or was it twenty?—when I first realized what it was all about. It was the Japanese who did it. They came down and slapped me about, beat me up, shoved me around. It was pretty educational.'[79]

Some suspected Japan of trying to upstage the infant Asean with Seamced. Some resented Japanese plans for a permanent Seamced secretariat. Japan's thirty-man team under Foreign Minister Takeo Miki objected to observers from outside the region, but Rajaratnam told them 'it was for the host country to invite' whomever it liked. Jagat Mehta and Shroff watched in silence. 'We could not intervene but our presence itself was noted as proof of India's interest,' says Jagat Mehta. As for the conference, 'It was Japan versus The Rest to the very end,' as the local media reported.[80] It moved to Bangkok, Jakarta and Saigon and was due to return to Singapore in 1975 but uncertainties in Indochina killed it. Lee thinks the time was not right—'We had to wait until now when we had the East Asian Summit'—for very prosaic reasons.

> There wasn't the same understanding of what linking up can do because the technology was not there. Yes, there were aircraft, there were steamships. But there wasn't the computer, the Internet, and there was not the ease and security with which people and goods can move which exists today and which makes sense if we link up.[81]

The instinct that prompted the invitation to India 'is still there', Lee says, reinforced by the larger civilizational rationale that underlies his strategic sense. Jagat Mehta and Shroff spent an hour with him. Lee was convinced that with Asean in its infancy, India's participation in the region was necessary for both sides. But Mehta knew India was unprepared. 'I am afraid, we were then looking too much to the superpowers positively and negatively. India neglected South-east Asia because most of it was deemed to be pro-West and Seato-inclined.'[82] When she did move closer, it was, in Mehta's words, 'alas thirty-five years too late. Meanwhile, Asean has galloped (ahead) economically.'[83]

Not that the Cheshire Cat's grin of cordiality was entirely disembodied. Bilateral trade went up by 50 per cent during Bhatia's tenure. India was Singapore's nineteenth trading partner in 1973 with a turnover of just under S$170 million. Singapore–China trade was in excess of S$700 million[84] but Chandra Das acknowledges that relations with India were always more open than with China, whose economy was more closed than India's and governance entirely authoritarian. Singapore, the Beirut of the East, was Asia's centre for spies and commodities, encouraging suspicion that some of

China's earnings from rice exports were being diverted to Communist insurgents in Indochina. Many foreign, including Indian, companies set up shop in Singapore to trade with China; determined not to lose a slice of the cake, Singapore, which has always lucratively worked the margins, launched Intraco in 1968 as the equivalent of India's State Trading Corporation, to bring the trade under control with permits and levies.

Some of the problems the Bhatias faced at the personal and domestic level were similar to those of Maurice Baker in New Delhi. When the high commissioner asked for air conditioners, South Block countered that Singapore enjoyed a 'salubrious climate'. When he persisted, the ministry demanded temperature charts for several months.[85] Bhatia played golf with Lee and Toh, and though a heavy smoker, refrained on the golf course out of deference to a prime minister who, having once been an addict, was now as pernickety about tobacco as Morarji Desai was about alcohol. High Commissioner Dasgupta says he had to keep the doors and windows of the room, where Lee would be entertained, open for half an hour before his arrival because he was 'extremely sensitive to smoke'.[86] Lee made an exception only for Deng, placing a blue-and-white porcelain spittoon and ashtray 'ostentatiously for him alone' in the Cabinet room for their formal talks and even 'urging him to smoke' at dinner.[87]

It was a fulfilling time for Bhatia's wife, Shakuntala, who founded the Asian Women's Welfare Association in Serangoon Road with the wives of the Indonesian, Malaysian and Ceylonese envoys. She took lessons in Chinese cooking from Lee's mother who had written a treatise on Peranakan (the Chinese community long settled in the Straits Settlements, to which she belonged) cuisine, and charged S$30 for a course of six classes in her modest but comfortable house. The lessons were a talking point, while the Nehru–Gandhis were deferred to as India's first family, for the strict Lee would not allow his relatives to bask in the glory of his position. His father served behind the counter of a well-known Ceylonese jeweller's shop, and well-to-do Indian visitors still talk of buying silver salvers and teapots from him. 'People used to tell me,' Lee recalls, '"Your father is selling watches at B.P. de Silva."'[88]

It had been four years since Lee's last trip to India, the longest gap since the ritual began in 1959. South-east Asia had settled down since then but India seemed to be veering left. Lee decided to return Indira Gandhi's visit at the end of August 1970. Equally meticulous in her hospitality, she demanded minute details of the likes and dislikes of her guests. Bhatia reported that Lee drank only Chivas Regal or Johnnie Walker Black Label whisky and perhaps a little white wine. Certain vegetables that the Chinese believe cause wind were taboo.

{7}

Goh's Folly to
Goh's Glory with Tata

Indira Gandhi was not at the airport when the Lees landed in Delhi in 1970; she was in the Lok Sabha moving a bill to strip 500 Indian princes of their privileges. This genuflection at the altar of socialism marked the start of a momentous decade during which India cut Pakistan down to size, liberated Bangladesh, invited American sanctions that are in place to this day by exploding her first nuclear bomb, and provoked further recrimination from China by annexing the Himalayan kingdom of Sikkim. Banks and coal mines were nationalized and a ceiling clamped on how much town land an Indian could own. At the same time, a pioneering Tata venture set Singapore's industrial ball rolling.

Those years also saw the only serious political disagreement between the two countries. Lee viewed Vietnam's invasion of Cambodia as expansionism by the Soviet Union with which India signed a twenty-year peace and friendship treaty in August 1971. Pranab Mukherjee claims that the treaty pre-empted an American strike from Diego Garcia during the Bangladesh war; but it also gave rise to so many misgivings abroad that Swaran Singh felt obliged hastily to break journey in Singapore and assure Lee at a brief late evening meeting after the National Day rally that the treaty did not provide for Soviet troops. The two men had met last in January 1971 when Swaran Singh led India's delegation to the Singapore Commonwealth Summit and Lee asked Bhatia if the Sikh wore an ice cap under his turban—he was always so cool and composed![1]

Despite Cambodia, Lee's personal relations with Indira Gandhi remained quixotically cordial. Feeling that Morarji Desai and Charan Singh treated her badly during her months out of power, he even justified her Soviet links in terms of national interests, which were 'the most reliable guide for the actions and policies of governments'.[2] Jha would have been delighted to hear him argue in the second Blausten Lecture that while the Soviet Union's standing in India had never been higher, 'it does not follow that, because the Russians have given considerable economic and military aid to India, therefore India will necessarily be in bond.'[3] Jha himself assured Kissinger that 'India was not going to be anybody's diplomatic satellite.'[4] Tactfully omitting United States help for Pakistan, he added, 'India was looking for a counterweight to Pakistan's boasting that in a new war China would be on its side.'[5]

The decade's coup de grace was the Emergency Indira Gandhi imposed in August 1975. Six weeks later she sent the tourism and civil aviation minister, Raj Bahadur, to explain to Lee her reasons for inviting international opprobrium. He was one world leader who needed no convincing. Lee says India would have been transformed much faster if 'Mrs Gandhi had continued the declaration of Emergency for ten, twenty years after making the trains run on time.'[6] Asked why he did not say so publicly, he laughs, 'How could I? They would all squat on me! I am already thought to be authoritarian. Here I am supporting a democrat who is turning into a dictator!'[7]

He didn't have 'the audacity' to follow British Labour Party leader, Michael Foot, who welcomed the Emergency as providing 'a smack of firm government', though Foot later denied the remark: 'I thought she was trying to do the right thing for India. I didn't think she was trying to do India in, trying to do it for her glory or her wealth.'[8]

Lee's fastidious attention to protocol averted an awkward situation during his dinner for Indira Gandhi during the 1970 visit. It was just as well that a copy of the printed seating plan was handed to him by mistake as he arrived for pre-prandial drinks, for he asked at once, 'Why is Mrs Gandhi on my left?' The printer had bungled the typesetting. High Commissioner Coomaraswamy and his first secretary, Low Choon Ming, destroyed the seating plan, quickly switched place cards, and, helped by India's chief of protocol, personally escorted the sixty guests to their changed places. Heads might have rolled otherwise, 'starting with mine,' says a much-relieved Low.[9]

The visit broke with precedent by starting in Madras (now Chennai) because Lee wanted to see for himself the part of India with which Singapore has the strongest demographic links. As George Yeo remarked two decades later, 'It is south India, and Madras in particular, that Singapore can twin itself with, given the region's geographical and cultural proximity to the republic.'[10]

Many ethnic Chinese use 'Indian' and 'Tamil' interchangeably, as they do 'Singaporean' and 'Chinese'. Tamil is Singapore's official Indian language, and the education ministry official, who demanded to know why my son sought exemption from learning it as a schoolboy at Raffles Institution, was bewildered when my wife and I explained that Hindi is India's national language. Local Tamils did not like it either when some of Little India's Diwali banners were in Hindi. This was Lee's first visit to south India and Nathan had commissioned the MFA's Kemal (Tony) Siddique, a tropicalized Lenin with his goatee, to write a paper on the DMK which had created so much excitement in Singapore's Parliament only a couple of years earlier. Muthuvel Karunanidhi, Tamil Nadu's DMK chief minister and a former film scriptwriter, told Nathan that his cinematic fantasies vividly presented a slice of life (landlord, employer, policeman, bandit, etc.) for peasant audiences. Dhanabalan, also Tamil, complained that the films were 'vulgar' and had a damaging effect on Singaporean morals.[11]

An Indian air force TU-124 VIP jet took the Lees to Bangalore where the Raj Bhavan's ground-floor suite had been specially redecorated with a deep-red carpet and two dressing rooms. Governor Dharma Vira, also of the ICS, introduced Lee to tandoori chicken which became such a favourite that it was served at breakfast too. Lee scoffs at the watches—a novelty in 1970 but now available in Singapore's Mustafa Centre—he and his wife were presented at the Hindustan Machine Tools factory set up in 1953 with technical collaboration from Mademoiselle Oerlikon of Switzerland and later Japan's Citizen Watches. The technology was all right to start with but soon became obsolete. 'Why didn't you open up the competition?' he asks. India 'would then have Casio, the whole lot would have come in.' Possibly thinking of the ubiquitous Ambassador car, he contrasts India's strategy of entering into an arrangement with one technology provider and mastering its skill with China's competitive approach: 'All the car manufacturers are there in numbers. Some are privately owned, some are joint ventures. And people are working and learning. They have learnt the latest expertise because no automobile maker brings in his best models. They are not so stupid!'[12]

Yeo more indulgently describes the products of India's 'fossilized phase' as 'charming but anachronistic'. Manufacturing has moved on since then. The Titan watch he was given when Jamshedpur Tata's company town near Calcutta (now Kolkata), celebrated a century in 2007 was 'the thinnest in the world'![13]

Lee also thought Indian tape recorders too big and expensive for Singapore's 'sophisticated market' and doubted if Indian cosmetics would catch on globally. Sushil Dubey, acting high commissioner, found that Singapore importers did not have confidence even in India's sophisticated manufacturing.[14] Despite inherent strengths and significant innovative abilities, Indian industry's competitive skills had been weakened by the emphasis on import substitution and a huge captive domestic market. The Lees were more impressed by the Lalbagh Botanical Gardens, one of the most diverse in Asia, 240 acres of parkland laid out in 1740 by Haider Ali, ruler of Mysore, and expanded by his son Tipu Sultan. The British had further developed the park with rare plants from Kew Gardens. Its Glass House was modelled on London's Crystal Palace, and HMT built a surreal floral clock, surrounded by Snow White and the Seven Dwarfs. Two hibiscus plants were named after Lee and his wife. The Singaporeans sent back saplings of the flowering Ashoka tree (*Saraca indica* or *Jonesia ashok*) to be planted along roads but the shallow roots could not withstand South-east Asia's heavy rains.

Lee put searching questions to the foreign-trained curator and concluded that his expertise was inadequately rewarded. Nathan remembers Lee bringing this up with Indira Gandhi as they chatted informally in New Delhi: 'Why do you allow your bureaucrats to dictate terms to a man who has a world market value?' he asked. 'There must be many like that whom India needs more than your administrative staff!' Her reply was, 'Well, Harry, you know I have enough problems on my hands, I don't want to take that one on also.'[15]

Lee again brought up the British withdrawal from South-east Asia. It would prompt the Soviet Union, Japan, China and the United States to increase their naval presence, which Singapore welcomed for the more the players, the greater the balance. To quote Rajaratnam, 'When there is a multiplicity of suns, the gravitational pull of each is not only weakened but also, by a judicious use of the pulls and counter-pulls of gravitational forces, the minor planets have a greater freedom of navigation.'[16] But the mosaic was incomplete without India, which could best guarantee Singapore's security. 'Why is India holding back?' Lee asked. He spoke of non-alignment trying to 'find new relevance in the vastly changed world' as Sino-American détente, Sino-Japanese rapprochement and the prospect of peace in Vietnam altered Asia's strategic landscape. All the more reason for working for stability which alone could permit the economic development India and Singapore sought.

A blistering editorial in the *Statesman* on the last day of the tour saying it 'might as well not have been made' and that Lee's only achievement was to have 'created a society of soulless conformists'[17] was a jarring note that the next day's *Singapore Herald* picked up. Packing his bags for the NAM summit in Lusaka, Lee was surprised and hurt by the virulence of the only open criticism he ever encountered in India. It was not clear whether the article sought to impugn his domestic operations or value as an ally. The strictures were also out of character for the last of India's British-owned and edited dailies to pass into Indian hands, and probably reflected the personal predilections of the writer who had spent some—apparently unhappy—professional years in Singapore.

After this tirade, Lee might have found some comfort in reading in the 10 September issue of the *Eastern Sun*, a Singapore paper that was not necessarily supportive of his government which eventually closed it down, that 'in India . . . he would have had an object lesson in what not to do'. The *Sun* listed corruption, inefficiency, chaotic politics and Indira Gandhi's pro-Russian stance. But neither he nor Rajaratnam would have agreed with the claim that 'a tendency is clearly evident in India to dismiss Singapore's views as unimportant because it is a small country'. Rajaratnam toasted Chagla with the compliment that India was 'one of those countries which does not make a small country feel small'. But the *Sun* struck a familiar chord a month later when it said, 'India is building her navy, manufacturing sophisticated aircraft and may even develop nuclear arms. But India has always taken little interest in South-east Asian affairs and her defence problems appear to relate only to Pakistan and China.'[18]

Still Only Talking about Defence and Economics

President V.V. Giri's arrival to the boom of ceremonial guns in September 1971 offered another opportunity to try to involve India in the region. The Istana was being renovated and the first Indian head of state to visit Singapore was put up at the Hilton Hotel with his extended entourage, including a son, son-in-law and two daughters, whose ladies-in-waiting status created problems of protocol, precedence and presents.[19] They did not lack foreign exchange for the mounds of saris they bought.[20] Rejecting the hotel's offer of a special cook, Mrs Giri, a strict and fussy vegetarian, converted one of the rooms in their suite into a kitchen with a *sigri,* an Indian-style portable oven, on which she did the cooking herself.

Calling on the President, Lee stressed that India should invest in the Asean countries. 'India should be able to play her role from within the expanded Asean', Rajaratnam reiterated.[21] At the state banquet later that evening Singapore's President Benjamin Sheares, a leading surgeon, dwelt on the need for a contemporary coefficient of ancient ties so that history matched eternity: 'It would be a pity if the close links between our two countries, which in modern times were forged as components of a now vanished empire, were allowed to rust away into the passage of years.'[22]

Giri asked for 'a greater role' for the Asian Council of Ministers (India's baby) under Ecafe auspices. He also referred to the looming crisis in what was still East Pakistan and the 'recent influx of over eight million refugees across our eastern border . . .' The President was told that twenty out of the PSA's eighty pilots were Indian nationals, some of whom were paid by the high commission under a modest technical and economic cooperation programme. More than 300 Indian vessels, belonging mainly to the Shipping Corporation of India, visited Singapore each year, and Ameer Jumabhoy, Rajabali's son and SCI agent, ensured the crew gave Giri a rousing send-off, raising their caps to a 'Hurrah!', as he toured the harbour in a launch. Giri invited him to New Delhi for the 1972 Republic Day celebrations. There was a car on the tarmac and hospitality at the Ashok. 'I sat in the President's box looking down on Punch (High Commissioner Coomaraswamy) below!' Ameer Jumabhoy recollects delightedly.[23] Ignoring protocol, Giri warmly embraced Lee who saw him off at Paya Lebar airport and spoke of 'three unforgettable days'.

It was a time of burgeoning hope as contacts multiplied. A ten-member parliamentary delegation from India announced a chair of Indian studies at Nanyang Chinese University. Several commercial missions came and went. There were trade fairs, engineering exhibitions and constant talk of more joint ventures in petrochemicals, fertilizer, diesel engines, engineering and steel. Special economic zones were mentioned. Singapore was especially keen on commercial links when the oil embargo following the Yom Kippur War threatened its refining operations. Indian Finance Minister C. Subramaniam hoped for downstream projects in which India could participate. Pranab Mukherjee discussed Colombo Plan assistance and measures to curb smuggling when he visited Singapore as commerce minister. But very little emerged. The inertia Lee mentions could be one reason. But trade and investment may also have been casualties of the same Singaporean preference that had earlier eased out Indian teachers and textbooks. Singaporeans complained of India's bureaucratic bottlenecks. Indians complained of not being able to transfer funds. Their contribution to joint ventures abroad was in the form of second-hand machinery imported tortuously from Europe because Indian machinery was not acceptable.

Deputy Minister for External Affairs Bipinlal Das unwittingly hit on a fundamental difference in thinking when he urged developing countries to 'cooperate to achieve self-reliance and build a new world order'. South-east Asia was not interested in either self-reliance or a new world order. It was keener on catering to Japanese and multinational corporations looking for low-cost Asian sites. India was caught between two stools. Indian industry was not developed enough for relocation, and concessional facilities for multinationals were out of the question politically. Singapore, for instance, guaranteed Texas Instruments freedom from union trouble which would have been unthinkable in India.

New Delhi was not conspicuously supportive even when Asean declared the region a Zone of Peace, Friendship and Neutrality (Zopfan) in 1971. Oxford-educated High Commissioner Venkata Siddharthachary, fluent in Mandarin, French, English, German and Latin, and almost a local since he had attended the English School in Johor Baru, and Raffles Institution in Singapore before going to Magdalen College, Oxford, where he gained a Rowing Blue, sounded sceptical: 'Peace is indivisible. If there is no peace in the subcontinent, there will be no peace in South-east Asia. Peace has no boundaries.'[24]

Singapore's security problem had been solved by the time Lee returned to India at the end of 1971 after touring Europe. Failing to persuade the British to stay on, drawing a blank with Indira Gandhi, uneasy about the United States and Japan, and still suspicious of China and the Soviet Union (to say nothing of closer neighbours), Lee had ensured the Anglo-Malayan defence agreement's extension and expansion as the Five-Power Defence Agreement. Mountbatten recorded, 'This Force known as ANZUK (Australia, New Zealand, United Kingdom) took over on November 1, 1971 when our Far East Command Organization was dismantled.'[25]

Singapore and Malaysia were the two Asian members of an arrangement that Singaporeans believe saved their country. As late as 1998 Tony Tan claimed that the FPDA ensured that Malaysia, Britain, Australia and New Zealand remained committed to Singapore's security.[26] Some South Block officials suspect that, like the approach to Israel, the FPDA had been agreed on (or, at least, discussed) either before or at the same time as Lee approached Shastri. Negotiations must have started early for Pathma Selvadurai, a PAP MP, to ask in January 1968, 'How real are the possibilities of establishing a five-nation defence system?'[27] Lee says that 'the moment after separation, talks began about a new tri-power union because Britain's defence agreement with Malaysia lapsed.' Britain preferred a new agreement to 'an automatic commitment.' He still hoped for military relations with India, and told Parliament that Singapore would 'have developed a sufficient defence capability' by the end of

1971 to make it 'a dependable and a desirable partner in any defence arrangement.'[28] But an Indian diplomat was quoted as saying that while India might provide military help, equipment and even troops in an emergency, a pact like Seato or Nato was out of the question.[29]

Victory in Bangladesh transformed India's military profile. It was in this new climate that Vij led a delegation of eight Singapore Armed Forces (SAF) officers to study India's successful tank warfare in swampy terrain. They spent two weeks touring military training institutions as the guest of Field Marshal S.H.F.J. (Sam) Manekshaw, the army chief who masterminded one of the quickest victories in recent military history. A major outcome of the Vij mission was Singapore's decision to send cadets to the National Defence Academy at Khadakvasla near Poona. There was no formal agreement, only an exchange of letters, but the NDA followed up in 1973 by sending a team of cadets, including visiting foreigners, on a goodwill visit to Singapore. Dr Goh, who followed Vij two weeks later, also met Manekshaw, ordered regimental colours for the SAF and arranged for Singaporeans to attend the School of Artillery in Deolali. Rajaratnam went next. Nathan, as director of intelligence, then brought Manekshaw to Singapore though ostensibly on a private visit to his daughter and son-in-law who lived there. Another outcome was that Singapore officers would attend courses at the Defence Services Staff College in Wellington and the National Defence College in New Delhi.

Lee Hsien Loong explains these arrangements as the background to the more inclusive military agreements under his auspices. The prime minister's first army posting was at the School of Artillery, and his commanding officer there had just returned from a year at Deolali. He said, 'We have kept on sending people because these are very professional institutions and we learnt much from them, says the prime minister. 'Also, we operate different types of equipment, so we exchanged valuable notes with each other.'[30]

The arrangements could have blossomed into a full military relationship as exists between the United States and many friendly countries. General Colin Powell describes how some of the top leaders of the world's armed forces rub shoulders with each other as well as with the cream of the American military, eating, studying and playing together at the United States Air Command and General Staff College at Fort Leavenworth. 'Thus are old-boy networks born.'[31] But hopes of similar camaraderie faded, Vij says, when the first National Servicemen—Singapore introduced compulsory military service on the Israeli model in 1967—came out of uniform and looking for jobs, found that an Indian imprimatur did not help. Comparable courses at the British Defence Academy at Shrivenham or the Officers Cadet School at Portsea in Australia were far more attractive, especially for Chinese Singaporeans who were reluctant to go to India anyway. To repeat Lin Yu-tang, the Moon looks more beautiful when viewed from the West.

Tatas' Pioneering Role

Lee's face is wreathed in smiles, when he is told thirty-six years later that Indira Gandhi summoned Abraham to her office in 1972 and said, 'Your friend Lee Kuan Yew wants you back. I would have liked you to go to Indonesia.' Saying she had known Lee too long to be able to refuse him, she asked if Abraham was happy with the posting. Concealing his delight, the diplomat replied tactfully, 'If you think I'll be useful there,' adding, 'I think I will be.' Her response was, 'All right, go!' Bhatia left at the end of 1972. When he died twenty-three years later, Lee sent flowers and a letter of condolence to Shakuntala.

Abraham cites the exchange to substantiate Josey's claim, 'Mrs Indira Gandhi and Lee Kuan Yew get on well.' The high point of this second stint, this time as full-fledged high commissioner, was the establishment in Singapore of Tata Precision Industries Pte Limited and Tata Government Training Centre. That was entirely because of 'a very clever fellow called Syamal Gupta,' Abraham says. 'Syamal got Naval Tata to come over and his son, Ratan,' a graduate in architecture and structural engineering from the United States who eventually inherited and expanded JRD's empire.[32] Gupta, one of the company's youngest superintending engineers, had graduated in mechanical engineering from Calcutta's Jadavpur University before further training at the Imperial College of Science and Technology in London and in Düsseldorf. He had been apprenticed to Tisco (Tata Iron and Steel Company) in Jamshedpur and was an early product of the Harvard Business School's advanced management course.

Dr Goh told Ambassador V.K. Rajan, Singapore's acting high commissioner to Australia, how JRD had called on him in the Fullerton Building towards the end of his second stint as finance minister (1967–70) with plans to invest in Singapore. The Indian industrialist was stumped when Dr Goh said he wanted Tatas to make as much money as possible. 'No, I'm not joking,' explained the finance minister who 'could not stand frivolity' according to Rajan. 'I am serious. We are starting from zero at Jurong. The place is a swamp. The more profit you make, the more the government's share, and the more the workers get as bonus.'[33]

An astonished JRD explained there was no response when he had submitted the same proposal in New Delhi. When he inquired a year later, it was to discover the papers were lost. He was told to submit the proposal again in duplicate. A senior member of the Cabinet, Jagjivan Ram, who later quit the Congress Party and became Desai's deputy prime minister, asked why a rich man like JRD wanted to make more money. 'Let others do it!'[34] JRD should take up some other project. 'India's loss was our gain,' said Dr Goh, who did not want low-wage industry. His visit to Tisco's sister company, Telco (Tata Engineering and Locomotive Company, now Tata Motors), marked a milestone.

Gupta and three other Tata officials also toured Singapore, Malaysia, Thailand and Indonesia in 1970, and acknowledged that India 'had a lot to learn from globalization (a new concept then) and exposure to new technology'. The dialogue continued when JRD, Sumant Moolgaokar, vice-chairman of Tisco and Telco, and Dr Goh's LSE friend, Freddie Mehta, stopped in Singapore on their way back from Australia in 1971. According to the Tata group's official chronicler, Singapore was known then for fishing and garments but Lee wanted industrialization and asked Tata, who were only in heavy engineering, to start a precision engineering industry plus a training institute for young people. 'It was a tall order, for India was also a closed economy short of foreign exchange. But they took up the challenge to manufacture semi-conductors and computer peripherals. The Tatas had to train themselves first. They chose Syamal to start the project.'

'In those days, there were no websites to refer to,' Syamal adds, 'but Siemens did help.' Not long after, GE, Siemens and other international giants became customers.[35]

Ng Pock Too, who had just joined the EDB, recalls it was not all plain sailing. Nothing had been clinched by 1970 when Dr Goh handed the finance portfolio to Hon Sui Sen. Tang I-Fang, the EDB chairman, and Ng tried very hard to close the Tata deal over a long dinner with Moolgaokar at the Malaysia Hotel (later the Marco Polo and now an apartment block), but it was still wide open at midnight when the meal ended. Since Moolgaokar, who succeeded JRD as chairman of Tata and Sons, was leaving early the next afternoon, Tang told Ng to prepare a letter as quickly as possible setting out all that Singapore was offering by way of tax incentives, land and other facilities. Ng worked till three in the morning, went to the office early, collared a secretary, got her to type out his draft and had it on Tang's desk by nine. After the EDB chairman's 'vetting' and Hon's 'approval', Ng 'rushed' to the Imperial Hotel at the end of River Valley Road, now also a block of flats, where Moolgaokar was staying, to catch him before his flight. Singapore's ability to produce such an attractive concrete offer at such short notice clinched the deal. Ng Pock Too confirmed this sequence to the author though Edgar H. Schein replaces Sumant Moolgaokar with JRD in his very similar account that does not, however, name either hotel.[36]

Tata Motors, Tata International AG and DBS (Development Bank of Singapore, Dhanabalan was chairman) promoted Tata Precision Industries in February 1972. It was probably the first Indian company in Singapore and for many years the only one. Godrej set up a factory but soon moved to Johor. Usha fans were imported. Even Tata trucks came from Pahang in Malaysia. Truck manufacture was mooted but Singapore roads were not then meant for heavy traffic. Lee's long recorded conversation with JRD began with him thanking Tata 'for establishing the first technical training institute in Singapore.'[37] He told Derek Davies, editor of the *Far Eastern Economic Review*, that Tatas ran one of Singapore's 'several specialist industrial training centres'.[38]

Lee knew that India's private sector was 'superior to China's'. If it was not the equal of the best in America and Japan, that was only 'because of India's semi-closed market'. As he acknowledged in 2005, when 'Indian multinationals [were] acquiring Western companies in their home markets', India had 'several near world-class companies, like Tata Consultancy Services, Infosys and Wipro'. Indian companies followed international rules of corporate governance and offered higher return-on-equity than their Chinese counterparts. India also boasted transparent and functioning capital markets.[39] Gupta, who spearheaded operations as the first managing director, 'vividly remembers Singapore's transformation from a more or less semi-urban entity to a great metropolitan city with a hi-tech modern economy.' The development of various institutes greatly enhanced the economy.' He credits the EDB with the achievement.[40]

A small foothold but a path-breaking one that still evokes wonder. Though closely associated with the project, Dhanabalan could not understand why JRD took the risk when 'all kinds of acrobatics were needed for Indians to travel, leave alone set up overseas operations'. Precision tools and dies were a difficult field. 'Most other companies would have folded up and gone home. But Tata was unique for India's private sector. It had stamina. It kept ambition realistic.'[41]

Dhanabalan thinks Tata may have 'stashed away' some of the income from its New York operation to make this venture possible. It showed a way out of India's closed economy and foreign exchange restrictions, and established India's reputation for training in highly specialized fields. He was greatly impressed by the Tata Training Institute 'which was the only private one', the two others being Japanese and German government ventures.

It was a personal success story for Gupta who was the only Indian to live in Singapore's exclusive Goodwood Hill area where he occupied a two-bedroom flat in a 'black and white' bungalow, as mock-Elizabethan colonial houses are called. Despite comfortable quarters, life was trying. Paya Lebar was 'only an airstrip with sheds'. Singapore 'buzzed with mosquitoes' and was worse than Calcutta. Gupta uses a Bengali colloquialism—'*teem teem*'—for its flickering electricity supply.[42] He had a 'tough time' setting up the two operations but the assignment was an 'interesting and exciting' challenge:

> I bought land in Jurong and engaged an architect. It took an hour and a half to get there. The land was marshy. They called the reclamation project Goh's Folly. Then, when it was a success, it became Goh's Glory.[43]

Gupta's Goh was, of course, Dr Goh Keng Swee. Gupta also brought fifty or sixty technicians and a supervisor from India. Tata Precision, with its own building in Jurong, was a joint venture with DBS and Sime Darby to start with, but Tatas bought out Sime Darby. Ng recalls, 'People here knew nothing about Tata. India was not known for precision instruments either. It's impossible, some thought. But we knew. EDB's chairman Chan Chin Bock knew. So did Finance Minister Hon.'[44]

Many others who did not know asked why they should buy from an unknown seller. Gupta's standard reply was that import substitution was India's culture. Indians were constantly innovating. Tata Precision made semi-conductors and sophisticated tools and precision components in Singapore that it did not in India. He goes on to say that 'We developed the technology here. That's the name of the game. We had the world's fifth wire cut park erosion machine in the world. Two German companies had the other four. This was possible only in Singapore. It gave us exposure to people, technology and markets.'[45]

Tata sold its products from Singapore to top international companies like Fairchilds, Nat SemiConductor, Motorola and Texas Instruments. It was a mark of high confidence when Lee invited Gupta, a foreigner, to join the EDB team he led to Atlanta in 1976 at Jimmy Carter's invitation to attract American investors to Singapore. Reluctant to see him go when he was transferred back to India in 1982—the year when *Euromoney* named Hon 'Economic Minister of the Year'—Singapore officials wanted to plead with JRD himself to let him continue.

Asked why, after such a glorious beginning, Tata faded out, Ng replies, 'The quality of people who came afterwards was not the same as Syamal!' Others confirm that only a bunch of clerks held the Tata office indifferently in the new millennium. They did not even replace the equipment when it became old and dated. (Ratan Tata's acquisition of NatSteel in 2005 was a separate operation though it may not have been possible without Gupta and that early beginning.) Dhanabalan concurs with Ng's view of Gupta who is remembered with affection and admiration. The best compliment came from a distinguished public servant, Ngiam Tong Dow, EDB chairman from 1975 to 1981, and later DBS chief. He called Gupta 'India's man in Singapore and Singapore's man in India'.

Many years later Freddie Mehta mused in *Heart Work*, a collection of 'stories of how EDB steered the Singapore economy from 1961 into the twenty-first century', on how 'with no market of its own, with no raw materials to supply to the world and with no specialized technical skills', Singapore astounded the world by 'lifting its per capita income from US$500 in the 1960s to the current level of US$20,900.'[46] He attributed the miracle to three factors. First, the EDB served as a public relations agency 'if only to let would-be investors know where Singapore was situated.' Second, it identified new projects, evaluated them and targeted potential foreign investors. 'Third, EDB resolved to establish training institutes—and we can say with pride that the Tatas established the first Technical Training Institute in collaboration with the government of Singapore.'

Neither this foreword nor Ratan Tata's congratulatory preface appears in the main edition of *Heart Work* which is the only one Singapore readers see. Both encomia are tucked away in the Indian edition with the result that the part Tata played in Singapore's growth remains unknown, even more of a grey area than Air India's connection with SIA or Bangalore's example as the archetypal garden city. Yet, the EDB approached Gupta when, recognizing that India was about to make an economic breakthrough, it planned an office in Bombay. Even if Singaporeans are not aware of it, a modest graduate of Jadavpur University in Calcutta's southern suburbs can claim some part in the transformation of Goh's Folly into Goh's Glory, and thereby making the Singapore miracle happen.

Ratan Tata's foreword to *Heart Work* congratulates Singapore on its overall achievement, while Freddie Mehta refers to his own experience: 'It was the privilege of my colleague, Mr Syamal Gupta, and of myself to have worked with EDB in the late 1960s and early 1970s, earn the friendship, particularly of such emerging giants like Mr Dhanabalan and Mr Philip Yeo—a friendship that both of us value very highly.'[47]

Singapore acknowledged the debt on 29 August 2008 by bestowing the signal distinction of honorary citizenship on Ratan Tata for, to quote from the citation, helping Singapore 'tap into higher value-added growth sectors'. President Nathan presented the award at a solemn ceremony at the Istana. Speaking on the occasion, Deputy Prime Minister Wong Kan Seng said Singapore 'welcomed global talent who can add value to Singapore' and described Tata as an 'exemplary business leader' who had made extensive contributions to the city-state's development. 'The award is a reflection of Singapore's gratitude,' he said.[48] It was also a reflection of Singapore's gratitude to Gupta, to which Nathan paid handsome, if less public, tribute at the same event with the gift of a book on Indian culture in which he had inscribed:

> With much appreciation for your abiding interest in Singapore and all that you have done over the years to promote Singapore as a place of business opportunity beyond the Tata family.[49]

Balancing China's Bomb

Freddie Mehta records that when an aide passed Lee a slip of paper during his dialogue with JRD, Lee's face 'registered a definite sense of surprise, if not shock.' He turned to Tata and said, 'Your country has this morning exploded an atom bomb. This will now trigger off a whole chain of imitations, with the smaller countries surrounding India getting more frightened.'[50]

As a member of the Atomic Energy Commission, JRD was even more surprised. India's premier industrialist had such a poor opinion of his government that he could not believe it had been able to keep such a tremendous secret. As Freddie Mehta's note concluded, 'Mr Lee once again thanked Mr Tata for his contribution to the technical development of Singapore, but it was obvious that the prime minister was rather eager to have more details of India's atomic implosion, as quickly as he could.'[51]

Curiously, Dhanabalan also recalls the day of the explosion but at a dinner party that a local politician hosted at the Pine Court restaurant in Singapore's Mandarin Hotel in honour of JRD, Freddie Mehta and Syamal Gupta. Someone—Dhanabalan can't remember who—whispered in JRD's ear and he broke the news of the explosion to the company.[52] Lee thinks Freddie Mehta's account must be the correct one since 'he sat there taking notes.'[53]

Asked if he felt an Indian bomb would balance China's, he replied at once, 'Oh yes, I think so! Oh yes, I think so!' So he was not averse to the idea?

No, why should we be averse? I think we need the balance. I believe the reason why South-east Asia survived is because there is a balance of forces that kept it like this. If supposing there was no Communist threat, I think American and Japanese dominance would have been overwhelming. But because there was a Communist threat their influence became benign.[54]

Prem Singh, a pleasant blustery former army officer who was high commissioner in the mid-1990s, recalls that Bilahari Kausikan at the MFA called him in after the 1998 tests for 'only a pro forma protest'. Though mindful of the niceties of international arrangements, Lee was not to be deflected from his long-term vision of a Concert of Asia that could compete with the European Union or the United States, and whose leading members were not hamstrung by restrictions imposed by the West. To that end, he had told the CHOGM in Ottawa that the United States and the Soviet Union ought to allow China to reach nuclear parity if they really wanted a global peace agreement that limited strategic arms.[55]

Though Singapore shied away from admitting it officially, relations with China were moving steadily towards a predetermined cordiality. Eager backbenchers in Singapore's Parliament—more Indians than Chinese—zealously pressed for what they called 'a more realistic reappraisal of relations', meaning official ties. Rajaratnam rejected such calls, saying in 1970 that Beijing did not regard Singapore as an independent state but as 'part of what the Chinese government refers to as Malaya'.[56] Though the Sino-American entente made China politically respectable, Lee was still anxious to avoid rekindling Third China suspicions. Four years later, Rajaratnam announced that Singapore would establish diplomatic relations with China after all its neighbours had done so. The seventeen-member delegation he led in 1975 flew to Hong Kong to catch a train to Guangzhou before boarding an aircraft for Beijing.

In contrast with the stagnation in ties with India, the number of sporting, professional and commercial exchanges with China exploded after 1971. 'Extensive trade ties exist with China,' Law and National Development Minister Barker told Parliament. 'In fact, China is our twelfth largest trading partner.'[57] Understandably, Chinese-educated officials and politicians worked for closer connections at all levels but the PAP's loyal Indians were even more vociferous on this count: P. Govindaswamy archly accused the government of 'neglecting a country that is too large to be neglected'.[58] It was left to Lee to champion India with Dhanabalan wondering whether 'he knew exactly what Indira Gandhi's policies were'. The former foreign minister thinks the combination of India's 'blinkered politics' and 'lack of ability to get things done' had 'almost ruined the country'.[59] Prominent Indian Singaporeans did not appear to be over-fond of India.

Nathan was the exception long before he became president. Indian diplomats always found him friendly and helpful in his various positions in the foreign, home and defence ministries and, jumping ahead, in Kuala Lumpur and Washington. It was Nathan who disclosed at a dinner to celebrate Lee's seventy-fifth birthday in 1998, when the first volume of his memoirs was launched, how Lee demonstrated his impartiality during his first visit to China in 1976. Prem Singh was among the guests and remembers Nathan, who had accompanied Lee from the MFA, describing how the prime minister snubbed Premier Hua Guo Feng at their first official meeting. As Nathan recalls, Hua gave Lee a copy of Maxwell's contentious book, *India's China War*, saying it was the 'correct version' of the events of 1962. But 'after a cursory look at the front and back covers, despite the propriety expected of him,' Lee returned the book, politely saying, 'This is China's version of the war. There is another—the Indian version. Singapore is in South-east Asia. We have people of Chinese, Malay and Indian origins. Singapore has no direct interest in such wars.'[60]

Leaving aside the expectations of common ethnicity, this was a grave rebuff by a tiny city-state to a formidable power, known to be touchy about protocol and prestige. Hua took the insult in his stride 'but the foreign minister—the late Qiao Guanhua—was taken aback by this response.' Nathan stresses that Singapore 'did not wish to take sides'.[61]

The watershed year for Sino-Singapore relations was 1978. It was a time for plainspeaking, for telling Deng that Chinese Singaporeans do not regard themselves as 'overseas Chinese'.[62] Lee 'gave a firm warning to Beijing to keep Singapore Chinese out of any future planning by the PRC.'[63] In Lee's own words, the thaw came only after Deng visited Singapore in November 1978 seeking to mobilize a united front against Vietnam's invasion of Cambodia: 'And that's when I said, "If you want that you've got to stop all this. You are the troublemaker, not the Russians!" So they stopped and they wanted to woo us to support the anti-Vietnamese resistance in Cambodia, which we did together with the Thais and the Malaysians.'[64]

All Janata Chiefs and No Indians

India had gone through major cataclysms since Lee's visit in November 1971. The Emergency and the parliamentary election that followed it, throwing out the Congress Party for the first time since independence, were defining experiences. With Indira Gandhi in the political wilderness, rightist politicians who favoured free enterprise, close ties with the United States and rejection of all things Soviet, were prominent under eighty-one-year-old Desai, chosen by JP from among several contestants, as the first non-Congress prime minister. Lee decided it was time to make another trip in December 1978, his first in seven years, the longest gap so far. Asked why he had neglected India, he says, 'You were not relevant to our future,' and repeats 'our future' before going on, 'we were looking for partners who could improve our lives and our economy. And our stability and security. Now you have become relevant. But if I had kept going there then, we'd have had nothing to discuss!'[65]

Abraham's second stint had ended. His successor, Siddharthachary, was summoned to the MFA just before he, too, left Singapore and told that two junior Indian health ministers who had visited some months earlier had molested their Singaporean women escorts. The incident might have been hushed up but the editor of the *Illustrated Weekly of India*, M.V. Kamath, wrote a blistering column stressing that VIPs should know what is permissible when travelling abroad. 'We should expect some behavioural norms from our ministers.'[66]

Oza succeeded Siddharthachary in August 1978. The linguistic bond forged between him and Lee in New Delhi twelve years earlier had strengthened and the two men lunched together once a month. The high commissioner played squash with Dhanabalan and Mahbubani. Lee continued to take a special interest in matters Indian, suggesting to Oza during one lunch meeting that, with high-rise buildings going up all along Grange Road, the property should be profitably developed. It could take a building of at least twelve storeys to accommodate the five Indian banks in Singapore, tourism offices and diplomats' flats. Banks would gladly lend money for the project.

New Delhi ignored his detailed report. 'It was a grave, grave mistake,' Oza says, thinking of the millions of dollars India lost. Yogesh Mohan Tiwari, who presented his credentials as high commissioner exactly a decade later, was roundly told when he made similar suggestions regarding both the mission and the Peirce Road residence, that the Government of India was not a rentier. Another diplomat recalls South Block saying snootily it was not 'a Dalda salesman', Dalda being the brand name of a popular cooking medium. Meanwhile, Loke Wan Tho's old wooden house had not had any anti-termite treatment for forty years. 'You cut one tree and another threatened to fall into the balcony!' says Tiwari. Prem Singh abandoned the bungalow when a tree did fall in, and the house was left slowly to sink into ruin until 2007 when New Delhi sent a new high commissioner, Subramanyam Jaishankar, with instructions to take up reconstruction.

Pillay saw the neglect of three substantial properties—Peirce Road, Grange Road and staff quarters in Stevens Road—as telltale evidence of Indian mismanagement. 'A delegation of three permanent secretaries came to look at them and we thought New Delhi was at last serious about development,' Pillay says. 'But nothing happened. The properties remained exactly the same.' The many inspection teams that came and went encouraged the suspicion that they were really on shopping and sightseeing sprees. Other evidence contributed to this adverse impression. When the *Straits Times* foreign editor, Seah Chiang Nee, wrote about his visit to India, an Indian engineer, R.C. Cooper, commented on the deterioration of education in thirty-two years, and wrote about 700,000 graduates among India's twenty-one million unemployed. His point was that New Delhi had sat for years on a major water management plan that would have revived the economy by bringing a huge area under the plough, created jobs, generated hydroelectricity, increased agricultural revenue and promoted highways and waterways.[67] A Singapore diplomat tells of the lights going off while Lee was addressing India's Cabinet in New Delhi. Apparently, it was raining, and the Cabinet Room roof leaked so that people had to rush around with pans to collect the water. True or not, such anecdotes compounded a picture of incompetence.

Unusual responsibility for a foreign diplomat, Oza was made a member of Singapore's school textbook committee when he complained that his seven-year-old daughter found the Chinese stream at Raffles Girls School tough going. 'It might be all right for ethnic Chinese,' he said, 'but not for Indians and Malays.' Lee sent for him several times before going to India in 1978. Not that Desai was a stranger. They had met many times, and See Chak Mun believes that 'in spite of Morarji's idiosyncrasies, his habits, etc., he and LKY got along well'. In theory, this visit promised much since Desai was politically closer to Lee than to Indira Gandhi, and being committed to 'genuine' non-alignment, was expected to dilute, if not sever, the Soviet connection. Lee detected encouraging signs of change: India had recently lifted foreign exchange regulations and permitted investments overseas. This opened up more possibilities for further Indian investments and joint industrial ventures in Singapore.[68]

That could explain his high-powered twenty-one member team (including Hon Sui Sen, Lim Kim San, Dhanabalan who was then a junior minister, and Lim Chee Onn, political secretary for science and technology), apart from his wife and daughter. While some Singaporeans suggest the prime minister had matters unconnected with India to discuss with heavyweights like Hon, others believe that since Singapore was opening up to China, Lee hoped to induce a similar thaw in Sino-Indian relations and sponsor long-term coordination in energy security, developing technological skills and global trade. Lee's own explanation for the delegation is that with the Emergency behind them, he hoped Indians would realize the futility of going back to the old ways. 'After that experience and seeing how the world had changed and how the old system had failed, I thought India would open up.' He expected change. 'But it did not happen, so that's that! So what do you do?' The flat statement masks another disappointment. 'India was not ready!' There was a certain unalterable drumbeat. 'Desai was an old man and was so used to the old system that all he could do was make some incremental changes. India needed what the IMF forced Manmohan Singh to do in 1991.'[69]

Lee also knows that if Desai had broken away from the Soviets, India would have had nowhere to go for military supplies. The West would only transfer medium-grade technology and on very high market terms at that.

> You had no special relationship with the Americans or British or anybody else. They would not sell you advanced equipment. Certainly not what the Russians supplied you, because they were not sure whose side you were on. Remember you were supporting the Russians in Vietnam and supporting the Vietnamese attack on Cambodia. So, a military relationship with the West was not possible.'[70]

It is possible now, he says, because of the Soviet collapse. Though India maintains links with Russia she knows the Russians cannot deliver the economic benefits that only the West can. 'And the West knows a strong India will balance China.'

Unable to change course in mid-stream, Desai blew hot and cold on new initiatives, as is evident from the infructuous clandestine visit by Israel's Moshe Dayan. The Janata prime minister was also hamstrung by a fractious coalition with more chiefs than Indians, and every chief a prime ministerial aspirant. Home Minister Charan Singh was the prickliest of them, Jagjivan Ram not much better. External Affairs Minister Atal Behari Vajpayee, who played a key role in Dayan's visit, was lukewarm about Desai's grand strategy of building up ties with neighbouring countries and pleaded a last-minute 'stomach ache' to get out of going to China in October 1978.

After much goading by the prime minister, he did go in February 1979, 'but had to come scurrying back home because China had—as Deng Xiaoping had vowed to do—militarily intervened in Vietnam while Vajpayee was in China.'[71] Vajpayee confided in Brajesh Mishra,

India's ambassador to Indonesia who was in New Delhi for consultations, that he 'had made up his mind even before he went to China to give a rebuff to the Chinese if they were belligerent'.[72] Mishra, a career diplomat whose father had been a Congress stalwart, was himself close to the Janata leadership. Vajpayee appointed him his principal secretary when he formed the second BJP government in 1998 and national security adviser in the aftermath of the May 1998 nuclear tests.

Desai treated Lee and Dhanabalan to a two-hour account of his adventure the previous day when he had walked ten kilometres—quite a feat for an octogenarian—after escaping a car accident near the north-eastern town of Jorhat. Then he talked about Pakistan. Once again, Lee had little chance of coming to grips with economic liberalization or India's role in South-east Asia. But Desai did extend support for Zopfan and 'indicated India's desire to establish closer relations with Asean'.[73] The Singaporeans were again put up in Rashtrapati Bhavan whose huge rooms 'were in very bad shape', says Mahbubani. 'I remember the state banquet, it was enormous, there were fifty to a hundred waiters on each side, one waiter per chair. Quite a stunning sight!' Dhanabalan noticed that Desai did indeed munch only nuts at table.

Lee's meeting with Indira Gandhi who had boasted in defeat that the three sights of India for foreign visitors were the Taj Mahal, the Qutb Minar (a thirteenth century tower near Delhi) and Indira Gandhi, caused some flutters. Indians had written her off. Singaporeans were surprised at his graciousness to a defeated opposition politician. While Indira Gandhi had called on Prime Minister James Callaghan at Rashtrapati Bhavan, Lee took the trouble of visiting her bungalow. He has a practical explanation for the gesture—a turn of the electoral wheel would return her to power not necessarily because of any inherent virtue in her or any weakness in Desai but because of what is nowadays called the anti-incumbency factor: 'In your system the electorate would soon get dissatisfied and would bring her back. Must do! You can never get what you really want. No government can deliver. So after a while, it says, okay change again.'[74]

The rest of the time was spent sightseeing and coping with such problems as the monkey that sneaked into the Lees' suite in Bangalore's

Lalit Mahal Palace Hotel, a stomach bug in Hyderabad and a cold that prevented him from going to Mysore. His aim in 1978 was no different from what it had been in 1962. Asked whether India had the capacity to compete with the United States, the Soviet Union, China and Japan in South-east Asia, he replied, 'India, as a major power in South Asia, and in the Indian Ocean, can influence the attitudes and policies of the US, the USSR and China. Further, three of the countries of South-east Asia are washed by the waters of the Indian Ocean.'[75]

Picking up the Asean Thread

The wheels of an India-Asean connection had been turning, albeit slowly, even after the initial burst of activity spent itself. Indira Gandhi sent a feeler to Asean in December 1976 and the external affairs ministry's report for 1979–80 noted India 'took [the] initiative to seek [a] dialogue with the Asean for cooperation in various fields'. This was in the form of a Janata government memorandum indicating possible areas of cooperation that an Asean experts committee was reportedly studying in depth. The process did not encourage optimisim because, judging by Dhanabalan's comments, regional leaders looked on India as a backward country with little to contribute. Dhanabalan says 'Asean-India relations hardly featured [in discussions: because India was not an economic power. She was never a factor in Asean meetings.'[76] Lee alone thought otherwise: 'India is more advanced industrially than any Asean country. She can invest in industries in the Asean countries.'[77]

Singapore was trying to encourage entrepreneurs, especially in labour-intensive industries, to move to low-cost countries like Bangladesh and Sri Lanka. There were signs of a new era of economic inter-dependence and, given the Janata government's thinking, Lee hoped that the head start India enjoyed in economic planning, heavy industries, engineering skills, multipurpose projects and technical education, would enable her to give a lead to the process.

Before retiring to his native Mysore—Singapore was his last posting—Siddharthachary announced that India was ready for a formal dialogue with Asean. He, too, recognized the strategic value of the Nicobar Islands as a stepping stone to the region. 'Unless we develop the islands we will not be able to exert our influence on Southeast Asia,' he told a local reporter, Gerry de Silva.[78] When Asean foreign ministers met in Pattaya to consider relations with non-Asean nations like Japan, he assumed that a decision in principle would also apply to India. 'The ball is in Asean's court.'[79]

Asean secretary-general, Ali bin Abdullah, did visit New Delhi soon afterwards (November 1978) for exploratory talks but, quoting Lee, 'talks remained talks so long as India didn't open up'. Economics was (and is) for him the sine qua non of a political relationship and he stresses that Asean admitted countries like Laos, Cambodia and Myanmar only because of future promise: 'We believe they will open. How long can the generals last in Burma? Another fifty years? Ten years? I don't think so. Already there is trouble between Number One and Number Two.'[80]

Vietnam, seen as the agent of Soviet expansionism, was Asean's—especially Singapore's—immediate concern in the late 1970s. Worried about the Hanoi-oriented United Front for National Salvation that had been set up in Cambodia to overthrow the murderous Pol Pot regime, Lee sought Desai's help in persuading Moscow to pressure Vietnam to exercise restraint. His fears were well founded for Vietnam did invade Cambodia and replace Pol Pot with its own nominee, Heng Samrin, at the head of the People's Republic of Kampuchea, though whether for humanitarian reasons or to push Moscow's influence is another matter. Lee found it difficult to believe that 'one Communist government had set out deliberately to subvert and overthrow another'. He did not see this as only intra-Communist strife. It was evidence of Vietnam's historic hegemonic ambition.

Lee draws a distinction between the Vietnamese who had been transformed from 'good guys who fought bullying imperialists into the guys who became bullies in their turn' and Indians who 'never became bad guys because they moved out' after 'the Indian army was forced to go into East Pakistan'. He excitedly rejects any comparison:

> No no no! Not at all! India had no intention of staying in Bangladesh. But the Vietnamese had every intention of becoming overlord in Cambodia. Heng Samrin was going to be their man.

I have no doubts about it. They believe they are the successors of French Indo-China. That includes Laos and Cambodia!

Desai's government fell in July. Charan Singh, who became prime minister with Indira Gandhi's support, did not attend the sixth NAM summit conference in Havana, capital of Cuba, which could hardly be called non-aligned, in September. External Affairs Minister Shyam Nandan Mishra whom he sent alarmed Rajaratnam and Dhanabalan, by then senior minister of state for foreign affairs, by demanding that Cambodia's seat be kept vacant. The Khmer Rouge's Democratic Kampuchea was the official representative but, says Mahbubani, who was a member of Singapore's delegation, the Cubans 'kept them in a remote hotel fifty miles away so that there was no contact with other delegations.'[81] The Havana communiqué then declared the seat empty (as Mishra had proposed) which, says Dhanabalan, was 'unilateral and illegal'. There was no consensus on unseating the DK, and Rajaratnam had flaming rows with Mishra and the Vietnamese minister. Havana resounded with the grinding of knives for fiercer battles to come.

Sharing the scepticism of Olaf Ihlau of *Suddeutsche Zeitung* who referred to Soviet Trojan horses bringing the NAM 'to the verge of collapse', Lee said that the process of subversion had been going on for several years. Yugoslav 'Communists were assets to the movement' but not Moscow's proxies. Was India also at the back of his mind? 'Two members have special treaties aligning them with the Soviet Union. If, with the help of other members who, although without special treaty obligations, are nevertheless indebted to the Soviets, they can subvert the movement and turn it to their purposes, then the non-aligned movement will splinter and break up.' He praised the Yugoslavs for trying to avoid this but was not sure 'whether the movement is worth preserving.'[82]

Meanwhile, fresh elections in India brought Indira Gandhi back to power in January 1980. Such was the personal bonding, irrespective of political differences, that Lee's message of congratulations on her 'redoubtable achievement' in overcoming the 'formidable obstacles and pressures' she had faced 'in the past thirty-three months' implicitly criticized Desai and Charan Singh.[83] But he knew that her Congress Party manifesto had promised to extend diplomatic recognition to Heng Samrin. Rajaratnam told the University of Singapore Political Association in November 1979 that since India had derecognized the DK and since diplomacy abhors a vacuum, it was only a matter of time before she recognized the puppet regime that had been foisted on Cambodia with the twofold intention of establishing Vietnam's control over Indochina and extending Soviet hegemony to South-east Asia. India–Singapore relations were heading for an acrimonious spell that was never, however, quite as bad as it looked.

{8}

'The Lowest Point in
Bilateral Relations'

Asean linked the Vietnam–Cambodia controversy to its perceptions of Soviet aims in Asia. India saw it in terms of China which supported an increasingly Islamized and unstable Pakistan with, in Lee's view, a 'visceral' hatred of India. He does not think China will ever give up on Pakistan just as he does not think Pakistanis need Chinese encouragement to mount terrorist attacks against India. India–Singapore relations were further bedevilled by reports of clandestine traffic in men and merchandise but Cambodia remained the major headache, with Lee's philosophical understanding of Indira Gandhi's motives not affecting sharp exchanges at lower levels.

No other South-east Asian government was as strident as Singapore in lobbying against Vietnam and the People's Republic of Kampuchea. Singapore's superior debating skill and command of English was one reason, but Singapore was also staunchly pro-Western. Malaysia was less anti-Soviet, and Brajesh Mishra does not think Indonesia, which was deeply suspicious of China, joined the campaign at all. But Singapore was relieved when Indira Gandhi seemed in no hurry to redeem her promise to recognize Heng Samrin, and took the lead in acting on India's pending memorandum to Asean. The result was a meeting of officials—the first of its kind—four months after Indira Gandhi's return to power when Asean Secretary-General Ali bin Abdullah and the five regional representatives met with a senior Indian diplomat, Eric Gonsalves, in Kuala Lumpur in May. The calm did not last long, and Rajaratnam's high-pitched rhetoric and the fervent advocacy of an MFA booklet, *From Phnom Penh to Kabul*, were continued in another Singapore publication denouncing the Havana summit as the 'lowest point of degradation', and melodramatically asking India to rescue NAM 'from the brothel area into which it had wandered.'[1]

Then followed the fiasco of Asean's thirteenth ministerial meeting in Kuala Lumpur on 25–26 June, to which India was invited. A patronizing press release 'noted with satisfaction that Asean has expanded its dialogue to include developing countries as evidenced in the start of the Asean-India Dialogue'.[2] Indonesian Foreign Minister Mochtar Kusumaatmadja also announced that Asean was engaging in its first dialogue with a developing country. Oblivious of Lee's tribute to India's higher level of industrialization, Asean members presented themselves as developed First World nations!

Both communiqués were premature, for Narasimha Rao decided at the last moment not to go to Kuala Lumpur. The explanation that Malaysia's high commissioner to India warned him to expect a grilling seems plausible in view of Dhanabalan's announcement that the meeting's primary task would be to persuade India not to recognize Heng Samrin.[3] Others suggest Narasimha Rao was anxious not to miss out on the political fall-out when Sanjay Gandhi was killed in a flying accident on 23 June. Though Indira Gandhi's younger son held no official position, he exercised such tremendous influence that his death was expected to produce significant changes. Incidentally, Rajiv Gandhi's assassination eleven years later catapulted Narasimha Rao to the prime minister's chair. His personal reason for not attending the Kuala Lumpur meeting in 1980 was that he had to be at the bedside of his ageing and ailing mother who died not long afterwards. Dasgupta says Narasimha Rao was outraged at suggestions that he had used her as an excuse. 'How dare they insinuate that?' he fumed. 'I wouldn't have brought my mother into it!' For a long time, he refused to stop over if he had to fly anywhere via Singapore.[4]

Oza telephoned Dhanabalan at around five in the evening—two-thirty in the afternoon in India—on 7 July after receiving a secret coded message to say Indira Gandhi was about to do the unthinkable. The foreign minister was in the shower but called back, heard the news and thanked Oza for the warning of Narasimha Rao's Lok Sabha announcement the following day. He was 'sad and disappointed' at a 'regrettable' decision that was 'contrary to Asean's interest'.[5] Devan Nair went further: Indian officials believe he wanted Singapore to break diplomatic relations with India.

Mahbubani describes this as the 'lowest point' in bilateral relations. It seemed like that to Oza when someone scrawled on the high commission wall, 'If you see a snake and an Indian, kill the Indian first.'[6] Rajaratnam pointedly warned of the grave consequences of recognizing the PRK.[7] Gonsalves had earlier promised India would 'give weight to the region's views'[8] and had asssured Dhanabalan, who took over from Rajaratnam in June, that Singapore would be given advance notice of India's decision.[9]

'How could India do this?' Lee asked bitterly.[10] But as always, he was more understanding than others. Oza thought India-Asean ties were set back 'by many, many years', and Abraham saw recognition of the PRK as 'a fatal blunder' that was typical of India's insensitivity towards South-east Asia and that 'still rankles in Singapore'. Lee pragmatically compares Indira Gandhi's action with Singapore's over Iraq: 'That was the price you paid. This is the price we pay by going to Iraq. Do we agree with the policy? No! Do we have to go? Yes! We have no say in the policy. We knew from the day they announced they were going to democratize Iraq that it was an unattainable goal.'[11]

Richard Perle (one of President George W. Bush's most militant neo-conservatives) had admitted that the biggest mistake when Baghdad fell was not to have handed over authority to the Iraqis. The British also told Lee that the Americans should have got hold of the strongest general, put him in charge and got out. 'You cannot do more. This was a more complicated bundle of problems than the Balkans. And you untie this bundle? Boy, to go nation-building in one American election term!'[12] But Singapore had no choice. It was like a football match where you cheer the team whose colours you wear.[13] India was not a 'great promoter' of Soviet expansionism in South-east Asia or Afghanistan, any more than Singapore was of American intervention in the Middle East. Both countries had to go along. He says, 'You were caught up, these were the obligations that you had to honour because of your close ties, military and economic, with the Soviet Union.'[14]

Though Indira Gandhi told Andrei Gromyko that India sought an early Soviet withdrawal from Afghanistan,[15] she could not publicly criticize the only nation that could contain China. She called Southeast Asia 'an arena of battle' where 'the interests of the great powers are in conflict'. Deputy Prime Minister Jayakumar agrees that 'there was a little bit of a Cold War going on over Cambodia'.[16]

Like Konfrontasi, Cambodia, where history and eternity merged in legends of the nation's founder, an Indian prince called Kambu, placed India in a quandary. Recalling Kambu, Prince Norodom Sihanouk declared, when Nehru visited Phnom Penh in 1954, 'We are cousins. The Khmer civilization is a child of the Indian civilization and we are very proud of that.'[17]

He reiterates that apart from Cambodia's first king, India also provided its religion, philosophy, script, art and architecture. Invoking the '2000-year-old ties which unite us with India' when dedicating a boulevard in Phnom Penh to Nehru in 1965, the prince noted that 'the first navigators, Indian merchants and Brahmins brought to our ancestors their gods, their techniques, their organization. Briefly, India was for us what Greece was to the Latin Occident.' In contrast, 'The Chinese began sending immigrants later on, but we got only blood from the Chinese: they brought in the merchants and bankers—no culture.' But culturally consanguineous Cambodia failed to arouse the emotional response with Indians that politically fraternal Vietnam did. One reason could be Prince Sihanouk's own admission that 'while Cambodians are cognizant of their Indian heritage they are much closer sentimentally to China'.[18] Cambodia had paid tribute to the Celestial Empire, and the prince, the nominal head of state of Democratic Kampuchea, was Mao's protégé.

By the time Vietnam invaded, India saw Cambodia as a Chinese pawn that had to be rescued. The detestable Pol Pot regime was the perpetrator with China's backing of the unspeakable horrors of the Killing Fields. Lee's accusation that Vietnam, 'Cuba of the East'[19] and a Comecon member, was planning to use its stockpile of abandoned American weapons to realize the 'fond dream for many years of the Indochina federation' to which even Ho Chi Minh subscribed, cut no ice in New Delhi. Far from being expansionist, the Vietnamese had survived Chinese, French and American imperialism. A Calcutta street jingle '*Aamar naam, tomar naam, Vietnam, Vietnam!*' (My name, your name, it's Vietnam, Vietnam!), drew on John F. Kennedy's '*Ich bin ein Berliner*'. Vietnam was also a strategic partner. Though Indira Gandhi rejected Leonid Brezhnev's proposal for an Asian Collective Security System, analysts thought the Indo-Soviet treaty achieved the same effect through an interlocking series of agreements linking India, Bangladesh, Laos and Vietnam. Vietnam allowed the Soviet navy to use its Cam Ranh Bay facilities under the peace and friendship treaty signed in November 1978, and extended similar privileges to the Soviet air force in respect of Danang airfield.

If Asean and the United States viewed Vietnam as the spearhead of Soviet hegemony, India feared that China, which had comfortably bedded down with the Americans, was exploiting the crisis to extend its own influence in South-east Asia by restoring a murderous regime. Following Lee's warning to Deng, senior Chinese policymakers secretly met Thai Prime Minister Kriangsak Chomanand at Thailand's Utapao air base in January 1979. Soon afterwards, China stopped supporting the Communist Party of Thailand and established a conduit through Thai territory to supply arms to the ousted DK forces.[20]

Lee's credit was high with the Americans who were equally determined to help China to, as they saw it, contain the Soviets. That meant punishing Vietnam, China's historic adversary. Sino-Vietnamese disputes included an unsettled land border, the Spratly and Paracel Islands, the exodus of a 160,000 ethnic Chinese (Hoa), and aid termination. Eloquent as ever, Nguyen Co Thach warned of the peril of 'a billion Chinese ... at our doorstep for eternity.'[21] Lee's mention of 'proximity and geopolitical necessity' and of 'the bas relief at Angkor Wat depicting elephants with Chinese on them coming to town' bore that out.[22] But China's 1979 invasion of Vietnam was not a conspicuous success, enabling Prime Minister Vo Van Kiet to gloat that, though China had dominated Vietnam for more than a thousand years, the Vietnamese gave 'more than 500,000 [Chinese] troops' a bloody nose not because of military superiority but because they were defending their own country.[23]

Asked what he thought of New Delhi's calculation that, whether or not backed by Moscow, Vietnam had intervened in Cambodia to check Chinese penetration of Indochina, Lee replies, 'We never contemplated that one. Our intention was to prevent the Vietnamese from installing a puppet government and running it as a satellite. It's as simple as that. We were not interested whether China was going to be blocked or not.'[24]

And so, while Singapore's Washington embassy lobbied American policymakers, Singaporean diplomats engaged India, Vietnam's only non-Communist friend, in a series of global debates to ensure the DK was not done out of its representation rights.

Singapore's Three Musketeers

Lee appointed a three-man team (Barry Desker, Mahbubani and Siddique) for the purpose under the veteran Tommy Koh, who speaks with affection of Brajesh Mishra, leader of India's United Nations delegation. Their friendship went back to 1968 when the thirty-year-old Koh, young, innocent, ignorant and without any diplomatic experience, became Singapore's United Nations ambassador. Three Indians, G. Parthasarathi, Brajesh Mishra and Alfred Gonsalves, 'mentored' him. 'This is why I have always called Brajesh my guru,' says Koh.[25]

There was a certain poignancy in this confession made after fierce and unforgotten battles over Cambodia. Mishra's intense campaigning and lobbying led some Singaporeans to suspect him of taking instructions from the pro-Soviet Indira Gandhi rather than the anti-Communist Prime Minister Charan Singh. Others, like Nathan, plead 'he was only doing his job', while Lee counters that if Mishra exceeded his brief, it was because diplomats often suffer from 'localitis' which convinces them they know best how to serve the national interest. Mahbubani and Siddique contrast the aggressiveness with which Mishra pushed the so-called Soviet line with his colleagues' laid-back attitude but boast he could not stop two United Nations resolutions.[26]

The General Assembly voted on 21 September that the DK was entitled to represent Cambodia, rejecting India's amendment to keep the seat vacant. Then on 14 November it adopted Singapore's resolution 'deeply regretting the armed intervention by outside forces in the internal affairs of Kampuchea' and calling for 'the immediate withdrawal of all foreign forces'. Predictably, Pakistan and Bangladesh supported Singapore, as did several African nations whose votes China's president, Zhou Ziyang, had canvassed while touring the continent. 'We got a stunning victory,' Mahbubani says, claiming ingenuously that his only weapons were reason, logic and charm. Everybody was 'shocked' when more and more countries voted for the resolution every year. 'The tide was going against Vietnam.'[27]

Mahbubani mentions three surprises. First, no other Indian diplomat 'was so very active on the Cambodian issue as Mishra, and after he left, the others just didn't get involved.' Siddique adds that the others privately criticized their leader's militancy. Second, Mahbubani 'was stunned' when he visited India in the 1990s to find Mishra, a dyed-in-the-wool leftist in New York, a key player in Vajpayee's right-of-centre BJP government. 'It was astonishing!' he exclaims and continues, 'Then he seemed very pro-Soviet, the most pro-Soviet among the Indian diplomats. Very outspoken in defence of Soviet policies.'[28]

The third surprise was that Mishra 'had completely forgotten all about those hectic tussles in New York'.[29] Singapore could not because a small country had been overrun by a bigger power, a concern that Mahbubani does not expect India to share. 'Being vulnerable, we ferociously defended the principle that the independence of small countries is inviolate.' Echoing Lee's belief that unlike India in Bangladesh or Tanzania in Idi Amin's Uganda, Vietnam was out to grab territory, Mahbubani claims Nguyen Co Thach confessed 'in a moment of candour' that Cambodia was 'within Vietnam's natural sphere of influence' and the Vietnamese went not to liberate but to stay. 'He was very honest in private conversation,' Mahbubani says, 'he admitted that the Khmer Rouge only provided an excuse for the invasion and occupation.' The Vietnamese emphasized 'that their presence in Cambodia was irreversible. They loved the word "irreversible"!' Nguyen Co Thach supposedly 'made the mistake of privately confessing' to United States Congressman Stephen Solarz that 'Vietnam did *not* [Mahbubani's emphasis] invade Cambodia to save the Cambodian people from Pol Pot, even though this was the official propaganda line'.[30]

The battle sometimes took a bizarre turn. Late one night during a NAM meeting in New Delhi, Mahbubani decided 'to teach these guys a lesson' because the larger and more vocal pro-Soviet delegations were all 'singing from the same song sheet' on Cambodia and Afghanistan.

So at two in the morning, having been at committee all night, I gave a very passionate one-hour long speech on why the Soviet occupation in Afghanistan had failed. It was from two to three in the morning, and then a young Afghan delegate put up his hand and responded in the spirit of whatever-you-can-do-I-can-do-better for another two hours, from three to five! By then the Africans were saying enough is enough, let's get some sleep.[31]

Mahbubani sees the crisis in Cold War terms. Concerned about American and Chinese support for Pakistan, 'India wants a balancing supporter, so it develops a strong alliance with the Soviet Union, and goes along with Soviet policy'. He does not think 'the merit of the case decided India's stand'.[32] It was 'the Soviet Union, Vietnam and India on one side, China, Pakistan and the United States on the other'.

No other differences separated India and Singapore. Nor did the dispute spill into other areas. For all the excitement, neither side lost sight of long-term imperatives. Mahbubani's friendship with his Indian bridge partners when he was chargé d'affaires in Phnom Penh survived. From New York, Kamlesh Sharma, later Commonwealth secretary-general, and his wife, Babli, introduced Mahbubani's American wife and daughter to India. Unlike many Indian Singaporeans in high position, he retains strong Sindhi links, collects Mohamed Rafi CDs and argues that Hindi should be a United Nations language.

Four years later with the dispute still unresolved, Natwar Singh, then a foreign office secretary, announced, after spending ninety minutes in the MFA, that Cambodia was not an obstacle to bilateral ties.[33] Visiting New Delhi around the same time, Peter Chan, by then second permanent secretary, compiled a euphoric note on relations despite sticking points. When Tommy Koh was invited to deliver the seventh India-Asean Eminent Persons Lecture in New Delhi, he wanted Mishra to chair the meeting. Delighted when the invitation was accepted, he said he would like to 'offer a special garland' to his 'good friend and guru, Brajesh Mishra'.[34]

For all his understanding of India's position, Lee warns that things might have turned out differently. 'We factored in the fact that, however good our bilateral relations, if it came to the crunch, if the Vietnamese were a problem to us, you would be on their side.' He saw India as going along with the Soviets if they were on the winning side, and if Vietnam went on 'to invade Thailand and influence the rest of South-east Asia'.[35]

Despite New Delhi's stand, no Indian diplomat was anxious to serve in war-torn Vietnam-occupied Cambodia. New Delhi sent a chargé d'affaires, Nigam Prakash, to Phnom Penh via Hanoi while the fighting was still on. He had no staff and was cloistered in a hotel room where he could hear sounds of fighting and feared for his life. Oza received frantic appeals for rescue and, worried that Prakash would suffer a breakdown, sent his deputy, B.M.C. Nair (who went on to become high commissioner to Singapore in the early 1990s), to bring him out. 'He said people were after his blood. He couldn't sleep.'[36] The evacuated diplomat spent a week recuperating in the Peirce Road house. 'Where was the need to try to open an embassy in Cambodia in such a hurry?' Oza asks. At the time, he loyally defended his government. India could not overlook Pol Pot's butchery under China's patronage. It was not a question of supporting invasion. Humanitarian considerations apart, the 'realistic consideration' was that Heng Samrin was in control, Pol Pot was not.[37]

'Smiles That Did Not Last' in New Delhi

Lee took a thirty-six-strong entourage (including Trade and Industry Minister Goh Chok Tong and Dhanabalan) to New Delhi for the sixteen-nation Asian and Pacific Regional Commonwealth Conference or CHOGRM in September 1980. Dhanabalan also attended the NAM foreign ministers' meeting the following February, and represented Singapore at the seventh NAM summit in March 1983 which Lee refused to attend. Seven months later he accompanied Lee and his wife to the full Commonwealth summit (CHOGM) which was held in India for the first time in September 1983. South-east Asia featured on the agenda on all four occasions.

Singapore's *New Nation* published a picture of the Lees and their hostess at the CHOGRM under the heading 'Two short-lived smiles' and the caption, 'The smiles exchanged between Indian Prime Minister Indira Gandhi and Premier Lee Kuan Yew, with Mrs Lee beside him, were not to last beyond this greeting just before the opening session of the Commonwealth meeting.' But Indian diplomats dispute this, saying that Indira Gandhi was positively bubbling with cordiality for 'Harry' compared to her frostiness with Ceylon's Jayewardene. She walked all the way down with Lee at the end of his call on her in South Block while Jayewardene was despatched with a handshake in her room. But, yes, the *Indian Express* agreed that India was 'isolated' as the only CHOGRM member to recognize Heng Samrin.

Lee's fifteen-minute speech demanded condemnation of Soviet aggression in Afghanistan and Cambodia, and criticized the new 'doctrine of justifiable intervention outside the framework of the United Nations'. Though he says Indira Gandhi did not try to rebut him with any 'vehemence', she did point out that Heng Samrin was in effective territorial control while Pol Pot was supported by outside 'groupings', meaning the Asean-China-United States alliance. Her friends were more strident offstage. Communist MP Bhupesh Gupta found Lee's speech 'outrageous' and accused him of 'misuse of the occasion and of India's hospitality'. The newspaper, the *Patriot*, reflecting the Moscow Mafia's views, thought Lee was only 'parroting' the American line with his 'outbursts of anti-Communist hysteria'. Indians noticed that while Lee denounced the Soviet invasion of Afghanistan and Vietnam's of Cambodia, there was nary a word about China's aggression against Vietnam. But the *Statesman* found virtue in the points Lee made: he was 'obviously voicing the majority view' and his speech was 'notable for its bluntness and the transparent honesty with which it was delivered'. Kamal Nath, then three years into his first term in Parliament, heard him and told friends, 'Here is a man who speaks his mind.'

New Delhi followed the Havana precedent and kept Cambodia's seat vacant. Dith Munty, the PRK ambassador, who had presented his credentials four days earlier, was spotted driving to the inaugural in a Japanese car with a temporary 'CD [corps diplomatique] registration applied for' plate. Prince Norodom Sihanouk must have been grievously wounded since he had sought an invitation and been fobbed off with the excuse that India had no mandate and it would be up to the conference to invite him if it wished. 'There was no question of allowing Sihanouk even to come to Delhi, let alone speak,' according to Natwar Singh, the conference secretary-general. If the prince did arrive, 'he would be flown out by the next available flight.'[38] Norodom Sihanouk responded with a pained letter saying this was no way 'to treat an old friend'. Brushing aside Singaporean complaints of bias and Rajaratnam's impassioned speech about Soviet proxy wars and countries living 'in fear of Third World neighbours with military ambitions', NAM's thirteen-point New Delhi Message contented itself with platitudes.

CHOGM opened under the shadow of the American invasion of the Caribbean island of Grenada and the Turkish revolt in Cyprus. The *Straits Times* reported that South-east Asia had been 'conspicuously omitted' from the draft agenda though Singapore specifically asked for a discussion. This was Indira Gandhi's last major international event. She was conference chairman, India's spokesman and NAM leader. 'To roll up the three roles into one person and still be impartial would require the sense of justice of a Solomon,' said Lee drily. But 'Mrs Gandhi as chairman was fair and scrupulous in allowing all participants to put their views across and did not try to steer the course of discussion in particular directions'.[39] He was the star of the show and the Commonwealth secretariat was flooded with requests for interviews.

Here, too, Lee demonstrated his ability to separate public and private positions. Australia had refused to co-sponsor an Asean resolution supporting a Cambodian coalition that would include the DK which Prime Minister Bob Hawke thought a 'murderous regime'. Malaysian Foreign Minister Ghazali Shafie showed his displeasure by walking out while his Australian counterpart, Bill Hayden, was speaking. Nevertheless, Lee and Hawke spent most of the time together in New Delhi, and Hawke took a ride with him when an SIA flight was diverted from Dubai because suddenly bleeding piles forced Lee to leave two days before CHOGRM ended. Dhanabalan, who stayed on, says Lee was very concerned that his apologies and reason for disappearing should be explained to Indira Gandhi. Apart from his ailment, Lee enjoyed the retreat in Goa, driving to Fort Aguada, a sixteenth-century Portuguese citadel, in a white Mercedes, and jogging on the beach while the others wandered among the ruins.

CHOGRM was his first meeting with Indira Gandhi since her return to power nine months earlier. It was no surprise that they found time to chat amidst the arguments. Her confession that India's 'three Marxist states (West Bengal, Kerala and Tripura) gave the central government immense trouble and little joy to the people they were in charge of' prompted Lee's conclusion that she 'was supremely confident that no matter what foreign policy India adopted, there would never be a Marxist government in New Delhi'.[40] They also had what he calls a 'memorable one-to-one discussion'.

> I said to her—her son Sanjay had just died—so I said to her, you must continue. She had been displaced, she had come back. 'Take this chance, open up India, change the policy, you look at Indians overseas, see how well they are doing in England, in Singapore, all over the world. You are confining and conscripting them by your policies, [by] your bureaucracy.'[41]

Whatever Indira Gandhi thought—and her aides claim she did not relish criticism or even advice—she played along, telling Lee she had given up. The entrepreneurs she approached would say that the industry was not theirs to open up. Or they would ask her to liberalize some other sector first. 'So they tell me one thing but when I want to do it they tell me another. I cannot do it. This is this. That's the way India is. I gave up!' Lee responded with despair.

> I said, 'Oh Gosh!' because I did not see anybody else. She had the gumption to declare a state of Emergency, and by the time you got the guts to do that, you should have the guts to change the system and let Indian enterprise break out. So that was when I became resigned that India was going to go the slow path. And at that time I saw China rising . . . breaking away from

Communism. So I knew that the race would not be an equal one. I gave up, I was losing heart then.'[42]

His disillusionment was to last two decades, partly explaining the perception that he favours China. 'I went to China because I was young and active but another reason (for the perception) could be that, when I wrote my memoirs, which was in 1998, and the second volume was published in 2000, India had not yet settled on this (reforms) course. It was still iffy. I wasn't convinced. So I concentrated on China because I knew China was going to grow and I did not think India was going to grow because the policy was still iffy. But now I am convinced.' Lee remained doubtful 'until Atal Behari Vajpayee changed course.'[43]

Indira Gandhi's response at the 1980 CHOGRM confirmed his scepticism. But it is possible she gave him the answer he expected and, perhaps, even liked hearing. For it is difficult to think of 'the only man in a Cabinet of old women' as a helpless damsel in distress at the mercy of unruly industrial barons. 'Indira Gandhi was the toughest woman prime minister I have met,' Lee says in his memoirs, describing her as being consciously 'feminine' but not 'soft'; as 'more determined and ruthless' than Margaret Thatcher. 'She affected some feminine ways, smiling coquettishly at men during social conversation; but once into the flow of an argument, there was that steel in her that would match any Kremlin leader'.[44] Many who worked with her would agree. If she ignored Lee's recommendations, it was because she did not think them in India's—or, more likely, her—interest.

India Can't Be Like Singapore

Dasgupta was told before he left for Singapore in June 1981 that Indira Gandhi would spare him five minutes for a routine farewell call. He walked past an intimidating line of distinguished persons waiting to be ushered into her presence to find her at her desk reading and signing papers. She continued to do so without looking up, though inviting him to take a chair. As she read and wrote, she also spoke for thirty-five minutes almost without a break. The theme was that Lee had done wonders for Singapore. She had great admiration for his achievement. Having first visited Singapore in the late 1960s, when Nathan, a foreign office director, entertained him to lunch, and found the island 'worse' than provincial Nagpur, Dasgupta did not disagree. However, Indira Gandhi did not think the Singapore miracle relevant to India. Whereas most reservations centred on abstruse social factors, hers were pragmatic:

> This model of development holds no lessons for large countries like India and China. It's driven by foreign investment. That is possible in a small place but can you imagine what a massive capital flow would be needed to make it work here? Where would so much money come from? It's impossible![45]

Dasgupta was impressed at the time. Today, with India leading global remittances (US$27 billion in 2007), and her cumulative foreign direct investment between August 1991 and July 2008 standing at US$91,534 million, he is not so sure. Indira Gandhi also rejected Lee's strategic theories. Singapore and Saudi Arabia were the closest friends the United States had in Asia; but though Lee believed the American presence contributed to regional security and stability, it was inimical to India's interest. She preferred the Soviet Union not out of romantic or ideological attachment—Indira Gandhi was as hard-headed as Singapore which had continued brisk trading with Vietnam all through those months of crisis—but for practical reasons: 'It's not that the Soviet Union loves us. But it's the weaker of the two superpowers and needs us more than we need them.'

That might explain Lee's feeling that she went perfunctorily through the motions of supporting Vietnam. 'When I met her one-to-one, I knew that she knew that what I was saying was right.' But she would not go along with him. 'She calculated that India's national interest required her to stay on the other side. That's all.'[46]

Indira Gandhi had a high regard for Lee's ability. But she spoke of him with respect, not warmth. 'He is not with us,' she told Maharajkrishna Rasgotra, head of the foreign office in the 1980s. Dasgupta says that though Indira Gandhi spent most of her time on domestic problems she had a highly developed strategic sense and a masterful grasp of foreign affairs.[47] The greatest achievement of her prime ministership was abroad. She assessed foreign issues in the light of the security and other challenges India faced. China threatened India's western flank through Pakistan. China stretched along her entire northern border. China's influence was manifest in three neighbouring countries—Nepal, Bangladesh and Sri Lanka. China was also an increasing presence in the surrounding seas. Rasgotra wrote in the introduction to *The New Asian Power Dynamic*, which he edited, that though no Chinese territory bordered the Indian Ocean, 'it is now being described in Chinese circles as "China's next frontier"'.

She had sought to improve relations with China in 1969 by sending Brajesh Mishra. 'I am in a box so far as relations with China are concerned, and I want us to get out of that box,' she told him.[48] But she was prepared to backtrack when she feared that, tacitly helped by Asean and the United States, China was becoming the dominant force in South-east Asia.

Lee's earlier misgivings about China had changed since his meeting with Deng. He believed that, devastated by twelve years of the Cultural Revolution, China did not have the industrial or military capacity to threaten South-east Asia 'other than by aiding guerrilla insurgencies and through sabotage'. The purpose of this indirect intervention was not to take over countries so much as to create 'a strong enough domestic factor to influence the government's attitude towards China'. But the strategy backfired, turning regional governments against China. 'So there was no chance of the Chinese getting any influence until they stopped supporting the guerrillas and stopped instigating them which they did at my behest after the Vietnamese invasion.'[49]

A Vietnam-controlled Cambodia would hardly be an obstacle, Lee argues, if China were seriously bent on infiltrating South-east Asia. Chinese influence could spread through adjoining Laos, Thailand and Burma. 'There is no border between Cambodia and China.' Admittedly, a more powerful Vietnam could be a brake, but he does not think Indian support for the invasion, which did India a great deal of harm and turned non-alignment into fiction, strengthened Vietnam. Admitting he does not know all aspects of

India's motivations, Lee thinks it was a quid pro quo: 'If you wanted Russian help with your armaments, and your steel, etc., this was the price. You were banking on a world in which Russia was a major power indefinitely. We, too, expected Russia to be a major power indefinitely. And we didn't want it to come down here, this way.'[50]

It does not occur to Singaporeans that if supporting Vietnam meant aligning with one Cold War contestant, then opposing it meant aligning with the other.

Prgamatic China, 'Visceral' Muslims

Asked if India is paranoiac about encirclement, Lee replies pensively:

> No I wouldn't say it is paranoia. You have to look at all the possibilities. The situation might change, and then China may become an aggressive big power. But I don't see them wanting to dominate India. They may want to prevent you from thwarting their influence over South-east Asia or Pakistan or Burma, or even Bangladesh.[51]

There is no profit—a favourite phrase—for China in an open clash with India which cannot be occupied even if the Chinese could defeat the Indian army. It would mean crossing the Himalayas and lead to world war, which India's nuclear weapons rule out. Lee does not overlook China's long-term ambitions, but thinks all it seeks now is to have friends all round, including India, and not to provoke anything that might obstruct growth. To ensure that, 'they would like to have on their periphery nations which are friendly to them and support them on critical issues.'[52] The Chinese are 'convinced that if they have peace and stability year by year, decade by decade, the gap between them and advanced countries will close'.

Having studied how Taiwan, Hong Kong and Singapore became rich, they wonder why they did not think of it earlier instead of remaining isolated without access to American technology, markets, investments and education. Now, scrambling to make up for lost time, China has joined the WTO. Half a million Chinese are studying all over the world, including one or two hundred thousand in America.

China wants American investments. 'They don't want any trouble with America though they don't want to be ordered to upvalue their yuan.'[53] But Lee thinks the Goldman Sachs prediction that China's GDP will be as big as America's 'by 2030 or five-ten years after that' too optimistic. 'It is more likely to be in Japan's range.'

His analysis indicates that even if China does not seek to dominate India, it will try to box her into a national straitjacket, smaller than geographical South Asia. Surrounded by states that are in some way beholden to China, India would find her diplomatic options and economic scope automatically restricted. Chinese resistance to Indian membership of the Security Council and her civilian nuclear deal with the United States suggests as much. That is where Pakistan, which has never got over the loss of Bangladesh, comes in: 'They [the Chinese] will want to have influence. They want to have governments that are friendly to them. Pakistan is on their side and they are not going to give up on that long-standing tie. It will survive even if Musharraf is displaced. [This was said several months before President Pervez Musharraf announced his resignation on 18 August 2008.] Whoever becomes Pakistan's leader will be useful to them.'[54]

But in Lee's view Pakistan does not need to be instigated by China to be anti-India. Pakistanis are anti-India because 'there is something visceral in them . . . that is completely independent of China'.[55] India would have trouble with Pakistan even without Chinese support because 'it's inherent in their Muslim fundamentalism'. Speaking nearly twelve months before the Bombay attack of November 2008, Lee saw low-intensity terrorism and sabotage as endemic in their culture.

Nevertheless, like Jagat Mehta, Lee thinks preoccupation with Pakistan holds India back. Though things began changing under Vajpayee, the bogey should have been exorcised in 1971. 'I mean after Bangladesh, Pakistan was no threat to India!' he exclaims. 'The weightage was so unequal!' he told Lehigh University students fifteen months after the 1971 war that the South Asian equation had changed and that India was now 'the dominant power in the sub-continent'. It might 'take some time for the dust to settle, and for Pakistan to adjust to the changed circumstances' but Pakistan could not equal or rival an India that has liberalized her economy, carried out social reform and mended fences with the United States and China.[56] 'How can they compete?' he asks. 'They are not educating their people in the way you are. How can they win?'[57]

Even the Americans are not so daft any longer as to equate India and Pakistan. 'They still need Pakistan for different reasons... Muslim fundamentalism... the Taliban threat...' but they cannot insist on parity between 160 million Pakistanis and a billion much better educated Indians. 'How can they be on par? It's impossible!' The United States may have believed during the Cold War that India might try to dominate or dismember Pakistan, but 'the Cold War's over and they have switched'. Yet, everything still turned on Pakistan even when Goh and Narasimha Rao were discussing turning over a new leaf.[58]

The Americans know, Lee says, that it's not India but Pakistan that now threatens the subcontinent.

> If Pakistan breaks up and becomes a Taliban country, you will have a real problem on your western border. How are you going to break up Pakistan? It's already nearly breaking up by itself! If I were a member of India's defence and security team, I would say, 'We've got a problem here! The problem has been transmuted from the danger they could be to us to the danger they could be to themselves and to the world and to us.'[59]

The nuclear stand-off meant there could be no all-out war. 'All there can be are these border incursions, terrorism, that do Pakistan no good, add no value. They are not going to get Kashmir. The LoC is the de facto border. I believe the generals recognize that. Their feeding of these extremists has created a deep problem for themselves; they have generated such a momentum that they are unable to reverse the trend. It's now a problem for them.'[60] And a bigger one for India. Lee fears that conditions in Pakistan will worsen. He was certain in 2007 that Musharraf, whom he called the 'only' Pakistani general 'who is totally secular in his approach' and India's best friend there, would not last: 'And then what? You are going to have a Taliban state with nuclear weapons! It is a very big problem. I think it is a major distraction for India.'[61]

For a committed secularist like Lee, the monster Pakistan has created and which threatens to devour it is a feature of the global menace evident even in tiny Singapore with its 14 per cent Muslim population and militant Jemaah Islamiya organization. It prompts him to ponder on the nature of Islam and to say that, whatever reasons might have been formally cited for awarding V.S. Naipaul the Nobel Prize, he is sure it was really for trying to come to grips with Islam in *Among the Believers: An Islamic Journey*. 'I read it. I think he was perceptive. They are like that.' Naipaul 'saw through the problem, saw through the religion.' He reflects, 'But it is very strange you know, he never fitted in with the British. He said he went to Oxford where he was very unhappy. He is the very opposite of Natwar Singh!' It's an intriguing comparison that deserves perhaps to be followed up.

Naipaul is sui generis, Lee says. 'But many other Indians are cast in that mould, Indian in their basic culture though their high culture is Western.'[62] This aspect of Lee's interest surfaced when Vice-President Mohammad Hidayatullah, India's first Muslim chief justice, visited Singapore in 1981. Hidayatullah had won a first in English Literature at Cambridge and that was what most interested Lee. Conversation was about Cambridge and legal studies.[63] Chagla, another Westernized liberal Muslim, had to make excuses to get out of accompanying the Tengku to the mosque. There were not many like them in Lee's Asia, making him wonder about the equation between Muslims and non-Muslims: 'Is there a modus vivendi between Singapore and Malaysia? Yes! But can there be real warmth? Difficult. Because they are Muslim Malays and they want to dominate the Chinese and the Indians in Malaysia. That affects their attitude towards Chinese, Indians and others in Singapore.'[64]

He demurs when it is suggested that there is no historical animosity between the Muslims and the Chinese. 'I wouldn't say that,' he says, mentioning Kublai Khan's Yuan dynasty (1279–1368). There are still mosques in Beijing and Yunnan—'Not out in Xinjian, Uighur country, this is China itself'—because the Chinese were conquered by the Muslims. The Ma surname is a relic of that past. 'Now there are many Mas who are not Muslims because the Chinese have a way of assimilating them. But Ma originally was a Muslim surname.'[65]

The furore over Salman Rushdie's knighthood prompts him to ask what it has to do with Pakistanis and Iranians. 'It makes no sense. Now the Malaysians have barricaded the British high commission! What business is it of theirs, a British knighthood for a British subject? There is something visceral in them,' and Lee refers to 'this global jihad business'.[66]

Smuggling of Goods and Humans

Singapore is a shoppers' paradise for Indians. It is also a place for attractive jobs. The two combined to make it a destination of special attention in those austere years when a Naipaul character in Delhi said she was 'craze for *phoren*' (meaning scarce imported luxury goods), and even men and women with tertiary degrees were unemployed, as Cooper pointed out in the *Straits Times*. The clandestine movement of men and material became a major problem in the 1980s. But while the contraband trade in electronics, watches, synthetic materials and other consumer goods was worrisome for India, illicit immigration threatened Singapore with demographic and economic consequences.

Both forms of clandestine traffic were rooted in India's shortages and controls. Both, especially manpower movement, were also features of a worldwide phenomenon that had created the world's oldest democracy and greatest trading nation of the modern age. Singapore, too, is peopled only by immigrants who have become rich on commerce. But it is difficult to focus on the global when the local is so overwhelming, and despite Lee's ruminations on the mobile world, especially after a trip to Australia, the two crises were handled summarily on a strictly short-term basis. Stringent checks and harsh punishment, which placed some strain on bilateral ties, overlooked the mix of culture, politics and economics that created the Suvarnabhumi that lives on for simpler Indians in the more accessible entity conveyed by 'Singapur'.

Since shopping underpinned tourism, it was unbelievable that an increase of more than 40 per cent in the number of Indian visitors in 1982–83 did not yield proportionately higher Customs revenue. The reason was smuggling, as Conrad Raj explained in the *Sunday Times*. Singapore 'accounted for a significant proportion of the estimated S$6 billion worth of goods smuggled' into India that year. Though each day's flight from Singapore to Madras ('We call it the Smugglers Route, long queues, people carrying all kinds of things,' George Yeo says) yielded duty of between S$150,000 and S$250,000, 'at least an equal amount was lost through smuggling.' The report went on to say, 'The Indian smugglers range from individuals avoiding tax on a television set and a few garments to well-organized groups bringing in container loads of television sets and video recorders. Tourists from Singapore find they can pay for their return air ticket from the profits on a fifty-centimetre Sony television set, even after paying the duty.'[67]

The perfumes, cigarettes, alcohol, synthetics and electronic gadgets were bought perfectly legally mainly from ethnic Indian shopkeepers in High Street and Serangoon Road, clandestinely taken to India and resold in the Madras bazaar known appropriately enough as Singapore Market. Sony TV sets and video recorders were status symbols in a Hindu dowry.[68] Taxes on them ranged from 170 per cent to 240 per cent, and the loss of millions of rupees prompted India's finance ministry to 'regularly send its officials on hush hush missions' to Singapore 'without even the high commission being aware of them'.[69] There was no means of knowing how many of these 'hush hush' trips actually investigated offences or were excuses for free jaunts. Or how much shopping the investigators themselves did, using their official position to sail through customs. To repeat Juvenal's classic question, *'Quis custodiet ipsos custodes?'* (Who will guard the guardians?)

India was not starved of just consumer goods. Indians were also subject to rigorous travel and foreign exchange restrictions. A passport was a privilege. Then there were 'P Form' complexities. The Foreign Travel Scheme allowed travellers to distant countries to take US$500 with them. Singapore, originally 'distant', was reclassified in August 1989 as a 'neighbourhood' country which halved the allowance. It was a sore point that Bangkok, which was en route to Singapore from New Delhi, qualified for the FTS as did Middle Eastern destinations that were no farther from Bombay than Singapore is from Madras or Calcutta.

Illegal migration was a more complex form of smuggling that also thrived on deprivation, controls and venality. There had been warnings galore but matters came to a head one April day in 1982 when the SCI vessel, the *Chidambaram*, which regularly plied the

Penang–Singapore–Madras–Singapore–Penang route, docked with 685 passengers. Only sixty-five of them, being either Singaporean or Indians with valid papers or sufficient funds, were allowed ashore. The rest 'were either found to be short of money to last them till their date of departure, or were without return tickets or confirmed onward bookings'.[70]

Singapore's practice was to allow passengers to disembark providing they had a daily supply of S$10. But the immigration authorities informed the SCI's agents two months before the *Chidambaram* arrived that the benchmark would be raised to a daily S$30 from 26 April. While many passengers claimed to be unaware of the hike, the SCI's regional director argued belatedly that the old rate sufficed. 'These people don't stay in hotels.' They 'could share reasonably rented rooms at Serangoon,' buy a meal for S$1.50 and 'spend no more than S$10 a day.'[71] He also disclaimed any responsibility for the passengers. 'As long as they have been cleared by immigration authorities before they board the ship and have bought a valid ticket, it is none of our concern.' The high commission pleaded total ignorance. Nobody knew, nobody cared, though Singapore's immigration department disclosed that the agent had confirmed having notified his principals in India of the new rate. There were angry scenes on board with frustrated passengers throwing furniture about.

This particular source of misery came to an end three years later when a fire broke out on board the *Chidambaram* while the ship was 300 miles from Madras. The end of one tradition did not, however, end the older tradition of migration to the Land of Gold. The controversy was repeated on a much bigger scale as the next chapter will show, prompting Singapore to crack down hard on illegal immigrants.

Indians Versus Indians

The demographic challenge calls for an explanation of the complexities of Singapore's Indian community, not one community really but three and each divided by chasms of language, religion, education and income. Tharoor writes that 'people of other ethnic groups in Singapore lump them all together as one undifferentiated group of

"Indians"'.⁷² They themselves know better, as shown by the locals versus expats controversy that erupted in 2007.

Most Indian Singaporeans are descendants of the early settlers, ranging from convicts and the 'half-naked' labourers whom the Indian Association refused admission, to merchants, minor civil servants, teachers, doctors and lawyers. They came under the protection of the Raj and now know no other home. Traditionally, they comprised about 7 per cent of the population, and as was evident from the education ministry's question about my son's second language, the overwhelming majority is Tamil. But the community is not monolithic. The president of Singapore at the time of writing is Tamil; so is the humble server in what is locally called a *mama* shop, usually a little room tucked away in one corner of a modest housing estate selling basic groceries, stationery and toiletries. Some of Singapore's most distinguished ministers, diplomats, civil servants and academics are of this race, as are the security guards in hundreds of condominiums. However 'Indian' these Singaporeans might appear in their cultural orientation, they identify with Singapore and, as mentioned before, have a complex attitude to ancestral India. They are Indians who are not Indians, as Lee told Indira Gandhi.

When the Indian share of the population jumped from 7.1 per cent to 8.7 per cent between 2000 and 2005 it was not because these Singaporeans had suddenly become uncontrollably fecund. Nor did the accompanying increase in education and income indicate a dramatic overnight transformation of the core group's profile. The answer to the riddle lies in the influx of professionals with Indian passports—90,000 according to one report—not only from India but also her diaspora. Some came from as far as the United States because Singapore wages are as good, working conditions more congenial, living is absolutely safe and they are nearer India with easier access to Indian culture. The racial mix is also more comfortable. These Indians may be on short assignments or on employment passes for anything from a year to a decade. An increasing number is applying for Permanent Resident status. A small handful commutes between Bombay, Delhi, Singapore, Hong Kong and Jakarta. Or even further afield to Europe and North America. Tharoor says these upmarket migrants prefer to call themselves 'Global Indians'.

It is a trend Lee understands. 'This a mobile world,' he says. 'It's a very mobile, fluid situation for the highly educated throughout the world.' A million out of five million New Zealanders have gone abroad. So have a million out of twenty-three million Australians. Why? Because at that level Australia doesn't give them the stage they want.[73] So Rupert Murdoch went to Britian. When Britain proved not big enough, he moved to America. So did another Australian, James D. Wolfensohn, the World Bank's ninth president. 'He is also into culture, he plays the cello . . . Australia did not offer him the stage to maximize his capabilities.'

Lee compliments Australia, an immigrant nation whose past insularity threatened to reduce it to the level of 'white trash', on now joining the world. 'It knows it can never fill up the empty spaces with whites, and the whites who come do not make the same contribution as Asians who are brighter, drawn from a higher socio-economic class, and will link them up with Asia's growing economies.' Australia already has 50,000 Singaporeans and wants to attract more, especially for its security forces. Singapore policemen retire at forty-five or fifty. Being English-educated, well-trained and honest, they are much in demand. 'It's not the push factor, it's the pull factor.'[74]

Some families he met in Perth keep their Singapore passports and send their sons back to do National Service. 'If there is a down-turn there, they will come back here.' He saw settlers from other Asian countries, including many Indians working at the Sheraton Hotel where he stayed. Asians have an easier life in Australia with a bigger house and two cars. They don't have to strive so hard. But Lee feels too many Indians stay on in America. 'How many do you get back?' he asks. 'Maybe a thousand. I went to Bangalore where I met Indian returnees. I asked, "Have you got a home here?" They said not yet. I asked, "Where's your home?" And they replied California!'[75]

That's where their children were. Lee asked what made them go there, and was told the economy and the quality of life. He believes India will provide all those creature comforts in ten years at the most. China already does. Not long ago the Chinese, too, used to think in terms of doctrine, philosophy, the pure society, but China has caught up with the global zeitgeist, and knows that what matters is providing a better life so that people with ability and qualifications can pick and choose.

Though there was always a trickle of middle-class Indian settlers to Singapore, serious migration at this level is a recent phenomenon reflecting a conjunction of conditions in Singapore and India. Unable to afford its brain drain but unable to stop it either, Singapore set up Imac—the Immigration Affairs Committee—in 1989 to woo professionals and skilled workers, with two special task forces to attract talented Malays and Indians. Lee says Indian immigrants are highly educated. Singapore tempts them, particularly engineers, with the prospect of walk-in job interviews and the promise of PR. Students are offered scholarships that lead to employment and citizenship.

The real spurt came after India's economic reforms when 3000 Indian companies opened branches in Singapore. The newcomers were generally between the ages of twenty-five and forty-five, upwardly mobile, middle class and above, and tertiary-educated. They raised the Indian community's share of university graduates from 20 per cent to 31 per cent between 2000 and 2005. While all monthly household incomes increased, the rise was highest among Indians, from S$4560 to S$5170.[76] These expatriates, 'articulate, bright and extremely confident of themselves and what they can bring to the table', are making their presence felt in Singapore's 'upmarket shops, restaurants, condos, movie theatres and tourism destinations like Sentosa and the Night Safari, all of which are on a charm offensive to get a slice of their business.' A local woman was 'pleasantly surprised by the royal attention she got from a salesgirl at Tangs' (a large department store) until the girl asked, 'Are you an expat?'[77]

Global Indians pay high rents for luxurious flats in fashionable condominiums or snap up property in prime districts. Their lifestyle is defined by the expensive elegance of a shop like Mumbai Se in Orchard Road or Skybaba antiques in Scotts Road. The Song of India restaurant provides an expensive contrast to traditional Little India eating houses. The boom has also given birth to the India Club, a glossy magazine for NRIs, fashion shows, displays of Indian jewellery, entertainment extravaganzas and several schools that offer the Indian curriculum from kindergarten to junior college level. Even the *Straits Times* makes up handsomely for past snootiness with a new free weekly, *Tabla*, for Indians.

A Singaporean journalist described the new breed he encountered at a reception: 'There was the macro-economist from J.P. Morgan, another from Morgan Stanley, and yet another from BNP Paribas. But the most memorable introduction was to this entrepreneur who owns four banks in India and has a stake in a sovereign wealth fund-linked company.'[78]

The contrast with locals is highlighted in plush condominiums where new residents may be global Indians or worldly NRIs of Punjabi or Bengali extraction while the security and maintenance staff are Singaporean Tamils. English is the only means of communication between these two groups of Indians. Tharoor writes that the new arrivals have 'been slow to identify themselves with the local Indians, especially if they do not relate to the Tamil language and customs.' Of the many differences, he mentions two. Many expats throw away fish-heads which are a delicacy for locals; locals devotedly celebrate Thaipusam of which many expats have never heard. Lee adds that 'new Indians' don't marry Chinese or even across caste lines, though their children might. 'I believe they are more socially a part of India. Their social values are more part of the Indian contemporary scene.'[79]

As a result, expats might be bringing back a disappearing caste system, George Yeo fears. 'It ceased to be a major problem for a long time. But now new Indians come in with their dietary requirements, and they bring their values here. It is felt among the local Indians.'

Two PAP MPs, Indranee Rajah and Inderjit Singh, complained in Parliament of the gulf between, old and, new Indians, with the former feeling that new citizens and PRs don't mix with them. 'They stay apart and in some cases consider themselves superior to the local Indians', said Rajah. According to Inderjit Singh, 'Singaporeans by birth' feel threatened by 'the better educated and wealthier newer arrivals' who keep their own company.[80] Both are feathered friends, laughs Tony Siddique, ducks and chickens who squawk differently and hence the disconnect. The controversy sparked lively exchanges in the media, with an expatriate's unashamed if foolish justification of aloofness bearing out local grumbling: '. . . the new Indians are better educated and wealthier, on average, than Indian-Singaporeans. So our lifestyle is better, totally different and even enviable.'[81]

There is a timelessness about such arguments that may have raged even in the palaces and temples of Sri Vijaya and Majapahit. But the debate is too rarefied to affect attitudes at the grass roots. Chinese Singaporean heartlanders in public housing estates know nothing of India's booming bourses or sophisticated society. The only Indians from India they are exposed to are thousands of foreign workers— euphemism for unskilled labourers—crammed into insanitary dormitories. Technically, they are not migrants. The law allows them only short-term contracts, but they come and go in an unending streams and it makes little difference to the host community whether names and faces change or not. For simpler Chinese, it's the face of unchanging India. Even Lee is scornful of such people driven by obvious want.'At the bottom end who wants them? Nobody wants anybody in the lower 50 or 60 per cent. You only take them in the lower 30 to 40 per cent. In the upper 30 to 40 per cent, surely!'[82]

Their labour is needed, they are not.

{9}

'Scent of the S'pore Dollar'

False signals, both optimistic and pessimistic, continued to bedevil the relationship. Rajiv Gandhi's accession prompted Singaporean hopes of a new era of liberal economics. Goh Chok Tong's succession encouraged Indian fears of a touchy and suspicious Singapore. In the event, neither hopes nor fears were realized, and business continued much the same though race attitudes threatened for a time to complicate the controversy over illegal immigration.

If foreign workers had been provided with comfortable quarters and a congenial clubhouse, Mandarin-speaking PAP backbencher Choo Wee Khiang would not have had occasion to grumble that Little India—where Indian and Bangladeshi labourers congregate massively on Sunday afternoons—is in 'complete darkness (*hei qi qi*) not because there is no light but because there are too many Indians around.'[1] The warning some years later by another ruling party politician, Tan Cheng Bock, that Singaporeans felt 'threatened' by Lee's proposal to relax immigration rules to attract more foreigners touched a raw nerve amidst unemployment fears in the wake of the 1997 economic crisis.[2] That the Chinese MP had his finger on the public pulse was proved two years later when he won by the largest margin in the 2001 elections. At another level, there was a furore over the 'racially insensitive' podcast of two Chinese customers asking for pork in an Indian-Muslim restaurant.[3]

These undercurrents of race tension did not explode only because of Lee's iron discipline. But they should have enabled Harry Chan, the

MFA's permanent secretary and thus the seniormost career diplomat to be sent as high commissioner, to appreciate India's ethnic nuances. He had been a civil servant in British Singapore when there were no computers or air conditioning, when fans had to be switched off to conserve energy, envelopes and carbon paper were re-used and—most significant—there was no socializing with British colleagues outside the office. Asians were not allowed into sanctuaries like the Tanglin Club. 'It was a different world.'[4]

Conditioned by that past, High Commissioner Chan went round to his host's office the morning after a small sit-down dinner in an Indian home to point out that, though he had been given the place of honour on the hostess's right, the liveried bearers borrowed for the occasion from an exclusive colonial-era club had served a much junior British diplomat, seated next to the host, first. Refusing to be mollified by the explanation that patriarchal Indians assume that whoever sits nearest the host is the most important, he argued that since the club was originally whites-only, like the Tanglin, the bearers preferred a sahib. He also confided in a Singaporean friend that Indian bureaucrats combined the deviousness of British Indian civil servants with the Brahmanic tradition (as he thought) of talking about everything and doing nothing.[5]

Harry Chan took a lively interest in India. He rummaged among East India Company records in Calcutta, warned his masters that Bangalore was blossoming into an IT hub, and ensured that SIA was the only international airline to fly to all four major Indian cities. Sri Lanka's President Jayewardene was so grateful when SIA flights to Colombo were resumed, overriding local vested interests, that he lent Harry Chan the presidential helicopter to visit Trincomalee, where Asia's second-biggest flour mill was still intact despite the raging civil war with the Tamil Tigers. It was a matter of considerable satisfaction that Britain's high commissioner, though resident in Colombo, had to wait longer for a ride. Another *angmo* envoy (Australia's) was trumped when Bhutan's King Jigme Singye Wangchuck received Harry Chan in his Himalayan capital before any other Commonwealth diplomat.

Like Baker, he enjoyed the viceregal panoply of presenting credentials, though with a tinge of regret that Rashtrapati Bhavan sent an open sedan car instead of a horse and carriage. But he was gratified by the protocol escort's colourful uniforms and the guard of honour by the President's Bodyguard which he called (in British mimicry) 'Bengal Lancers' and 'Horse Guards'. Everything was spick and span and—a Singaporean's ultimate accolade—Rashtrapati Bhavan's solemn grandeur recalled the White House.[6]

The ceremony was delayed because, as Chan says ruefully, he was 'a Jonah among diplomats', followed by death and deposition wherever he went. His advent spelt doom for Norodom Sihanouk, New Zealand's Prime Minister Norman Kirk, and Egypt's President Anwar Sadat.[7] The biggest upheaval was in India where Indira Gandhi's Sikh bodyguards gunned her down shortly after he landed in Bombay. It was revenge for Operation Blue Star four months earlier when the Indian army stormed the Golden Temple in Amritsar, holiest of Sikh shrines, to flush out a messianic priest and his armed rebels. President Zail Singh, himself a Sikh, swore in Rajiv Gandhi as prime minister within hours of his mother's murder.

Sikhs also plunged Singapore in turmoil. In the 1950s Lee had thought that the tussle over the Corbusier-designed town of Chandigarh 'generated tension among Sikhs in Singapore' only because nearly 60 per cent of them had been born in Punjab and had migrated 'after their cultural values were settled'. He expected the second generation of Sikh Singaporeans to be immune to events in India. But the *Mungkali kwai* (Bengali devils)—as the Chinese called the first batch of about 200 Sikhs in 1879—continued to react to whatever happened to co-religionists in the old country.

The incongruous *Mungkali kwai* description has prompted many speculative theories. Some attribute it to Singapore's early link with the Bengal Presidency. After the Chinese and the Tamils were counted, the residual population had to be Bengali. Others say the first Sikhs arrived by boat from Calcutta in Bengal. This is not their only nickname. These burly, bearded and turbaned Punjabis are also called *Jaga* (awake) because many were employed as night watchmen. An Assemblyman, John Mammen, touched on yet another distinction when he told members that if a Sikh friend dropped in, the neighbours would jump to the conclusion he had been borrowing money. 'Whenever we hear the word "moneylender", two communities are associated with it, even if they are good—the Chettiars and the Sikhs.' Moneylenders were notorious for saying in Malay, '*Kalau tuan tidak ada wang, ta'apa. Baya bunga dahulu*' (If you have no money, it does not matter. Paying interest will do).[8] The extra large 'Bengali glass', almost a pint measure, for beer in some bars acknowledged another kind of prowess.

Lee calls Sikhs 'a remarkable people'. Though anthropologists dismiss the concepts of warrior and non-warrior castes, watching a passing out parade of officer cadets one 'might think that Singapore comprised about 15 to 20 per cent of Sikhs'. At under 15,000, they are one of the island's smallest communities but 'seem to jump, run and charge better' than others. Even *Jaga*s have 'educated their children to be high court judges, surgeons and to fill the other professions'.

A Sikh friend of Lee's who went overboard trying to be Western may have shaped his ideas regarding the politics of cultural ballast and his commitment to what became famous as Asian Values. Lee said at the Guru Gobind Singh celebrations in January 1967, and repeated at a Tamil festival a month later, that he would never forget this Sikh trying to break 'away from his past too fast and too quickly', and finding himself 'betwixt and between' as a result.

> He threw off his turban, and threw off his beard—but not quite, not quite . . . He never really had a haircut like I have. And, in the end, under emotional pressures, he cracked. Because he got himself caught between two worlds—a world he was leaving behind and a world, a modern world, with modern moralistic values he was trying to achieve, but too quickly.[9]

The episode left Lee with the abiding conviction that it was 'best to make haste slowly' when modernizing.

The response of Singapore Sikhs to Operation Blue Star emphasized how close they remain to their roots. About 500 Sikh shops and restaurants downed shutters at once and more than 4000 men, women and children assembled at the Khalsa Dharmak Sabha in Niven Street to don black turbans and armbands.[10] When the police refused to allow militant Sikhs (a Singapore air force pilot among them) to demonstrate outside the Indian high commission, they downsized the protest to a low-key walk past and a vigil, and left a note at the mission.[11] The Criminal Investigation Department summoned local Sikh leaders to its Robinson Street headquarters the same day to administer a warning, while the two priests at the Khalsa Dharmak Sabha, being Indian citizens, were expelled.

Indira Gandhi's assassination threatened more upsurges. Some Sikhs celebrated by distributing sweets in High Street, others complained of threatening phone calls, physical assault and attacks on their properties. Tamils sent grief-stricken messages to the *Tamil Murasu* and Indian community leaders planned a condolence meeting which the police scotched. There was another outburst in January 1989 when one of Indira Gandhi's two assassins (the other was killed on the spot by the other guards) and an accomplice were hanged. The Khalsa Dharmak Sabha announced a requiem for the two 'martyrs'.

Despite his regard for Sikh valour, Lee was not going to allow communal unrest. And so, acting Deputy Commissioner of Police Jagjit Singh, himself a clean-shaven Sikh, warned the Sikh Advisory Board not to 'import foreign politics into Singapore', as the local formula has it. Simultaneously, Reggie da Silva, the Eurasian Deputy Commissioner of Police (Operations), told the Hindu Advisory Board that Singapore should not be dragged into Indian disputes. Sikhs would have to decide whether they were Singaporean or Indian. Da Silva had been instructed to tell those who felt their loyalty was with India that they were free to go back. 'We will not hesitate to come down hard on anyone who chooses to act irresponsibly on matters affecting the interests and security of Singapore.'[12] Sikhs might curb their feelings but no one could compel them to attend Indian high commission functions.

India responded to the problem by introducing visas instead of the twenty-eight day permit issued on arrival. It was supposed to be a temporary security measure, forced by 'evidence that unwanted foreign elements' were 'creating problems in Amritsar'.[13] The move drove another nail into the coffin of free travel within the Commonwealth and warned of the future closure of one of the last countries Indians could visit with relative ease.

The Implications of Immigration

When Singapore's home affairs ministry announced in September 1986 that Indian nationals would need visas in another twelve months, it was not retaliation but to deter illegal immigrants drawn by 'The Scent of the S'pore dollar', to quote a *Straits Times* headline. The decision followed another eruption in April 1985 when the high commission baulked at guaranteeing that 139 Indian nationals, who had been refused entry at Changi airport, would return home within two weeks if they were allowed in. Singapore suspected them of being 'disguised tourists' seeking employment.[14]

Dasgupta had left. Rajaratnam, who did not usually go to diplomatic parties, attended his farewell, explaining this departure from routine to a fellow Singaporean by saying 'the man has merit'. The foreign minister appreciated the high commissioner's quiet efficiency. His successor, A.N. Gopalakrishna Pillai, a Kerala politician whom New Delhi preferred outside Kerala, enterprisingly suggested that just as Singapore could be India's gateway to the Asia-Pacific, India could be Singapore's springboard to Eastern Europe. The focus being on illegal immigration, he also asked the external affairs ministry to ensure that travellers had a confirmed return ticket and US$500.[15] An editorial in the *Straits Times*, appropriately titled 'Screen with Sensitivity', and a reader's letter went to the heart of the matter. The editorial noted that India was 'a valuable source of tourist revenue, being our fifth most important source of arrivals', that many of Singapore's 'most highly-trained professionals' were Indian citizens, and that many Singaporeans were 'of Indian origin'. The controversy touched on human feelings and dignity as the report in the *Straits Times* indicates: 'In so delicate a matter as the control of immigration, when some countries produce certain skills and others large pools of unskilled labour seeking work overseas, it is only human that associations will be made with race and nationality.'[16]

Only clear, uniform conditions of entry could dispel suspicion of anti-Indian prejudice. Warning of the danger of stereotyping, the paper advised Singaporeans (meaning the Chinese) not to look down on tourists from countries that supply unskilled labour. It was a public duty 'to prevent a culture of discrimination against foreign workers or low-income tourists'.[17] The *Business Times* recalled that 'charges of xenophobia [and] outright racialism were thrown at the Thatcher government' when Britain regulated the entry of West Africans and South Asians. Singapore had also laid itself open to such accusations but restrictions were unavoidable for 'a swelling tide of illegal immigrants would put intolerable pressure on any country's economic and social balance'.[18]

A letter to the editor by an Indian professional married to 'a locally employed Singapore citizen' indicated that fears were well grounded. Evidently, he lived in India, travelling to Singapore from time to time, and was always allowed to stay up to two months. After the overstayers/illegals controversy, his pass was extended for only two weeks, and that, too, only after he produced a confirmed return ticket.[19] It seemed as if every Indian national was viewed as a potential immigrant until proved otherwise.

The storm burst in September 1986 when Controller of Immigration Lim Ek Hong announced on television that nearly 9000 Indian men in their early twenties had been arrested for working illegally. 'We Came for the Money: Overstayers' read another *Straits Times* headline. There were even more Malaysian illegals but Malaysia was next door. Indians stayed longer than Thais, Indonesians and Filipinos; and distance made repatriation more costly. Some had no money for a return ticket; others refused to leave jail after serving their sentence, finding life behind bars easier than the struggle outside. Some threw away their passports and tried to pass off as Singaporean.[20] Other races could be identified by accent and appearance but south Indians easily merged with locals.

A third explosion took place in 1989 after Singapore's Immigration Act was amended to provide for three strokes of the cane and jail of up to two years for overstaying more than ninety days. Harry Chan had left New Delhi, and since his successor had not arrived, South Block summoned Edward Tang Yew Chan, the first secretary, and told him of India's concern over nine workers being sentenced to caning and imprisonment. India expected to be informed if her citizens were arrested.[21] Though there was no formal protest, Narasimha Rao warned of 'severe repercussions on bilateral ties'. Stopping in Singapore on his way back from Indonesia, Natwar Singh added fuel to fire by calling caning 'barbaric'. Apparently, 'Singapore got very angry' and 'the relationship moved a few notches down.'[22] Two decades later an unrepentant Kunwar repeats, 'I still think it's outrageous.'[23] The comment also disturbed Singapore's otherwise tranquil parliamentary waters with Chiam See Tong, one of two opposition members, asking about bilateral ties. Foreign Minister Wong Kan Seng replied that it was an established diplomatic principle to base friendly ties on mutual respect for each other's laws and non-interference in internal affairs.

The Thais quickly repatriated nearly a thousand illegals but did not conceal their chagrin. 'Instead of sending ships, we should send warships to Singapore,' said Prime Minister Chatichai Choonhavan, while a black wreath was left at Singapore's embassy in Bangkok.[24] High Commisioner Yogesh Mohan Tiwari, who had taken over from Gopalakrishna Pillai, pleaded ignorance of any illegals, prompting an immediate rebuttal from the immigration department which had sent no fewer than eighty-eight letters to his office. There had been no response. The high commission did not seek details or consular access even when informed of jailed overstayers/illegals. Later, the first secretary, Mohan Menon, admitted to being aware of overstayers and 'barefooted tourists' with little or no baggage but the mandatory US$500 to ensure they were allowed in but not of the numbers.[25]

This prevarication did not pass unnoticed in India. The *Statesman* accused the high commission of making 'lame excuses' and that, too, only 'after the horse had bolted'.[26] The *Indian Express* criticized 'shockingly inept handling'.[27] Both mentioned 'loss of face'. In Singapore, Chandra Das, chairman of the parliamentary committee for defence and foreign affairs, urged the government to grant a 'final amnesty' to all illegals, while also calling on foreign governments to ensure their nationals surrendered and were repatriated. The Thai ambassador, Asda Jaynama, personally appeared on television to appeal to his countrymen but only an impersonal message was read in English and voiced over in Tamil on behalf of India's high commission.

The mission did not start registering Indian workers until five months after the new law was enacted. One thousand five hundred and eight-five illegals surrendered, earning the right to go home without punishment. Another 166 released from jail brought the total to more than 1750. They had no money, no jobs and nowhere to go while awaiting repatriation. This was one of those rare occasions when the entire Indian community, expatriates and locals, rallied to what it saw as a national cause. Volunteers donated money and material, helped to set up tents in the Grange Road compound, served food and attended to inmates' needs. A former Singapore armed forces regular, K. Johann, called a 'one-man show' because of the twelve to fourteen hours he spent every day in the tent city, ordered food at his own expense from a Serangoon Road restaurant and also paid the airport tax for some of those flying back. Grievances forgotten, Sikhs from the Sri Guru Nanak Sat Sangh Sabha sent rice, dal, curry and yoghurt every day. Ultimately, complaints from nearby condominiums, and hygiene and sanitation considerations prompted the government to remove the illegals to the civil defence camp in Jalan Besar. Presidential clemency spared the nine convicts the cane.

Neither the crisis nor its amicable resolution changed fundamentals. Indians still constitute a substantial portion of Singapore's 756,000 foreign workers, modifying to a great extent the impression of worldly affluence described in the previous chapter. It stands to reason they would not so eagerly have sought menial jobs and a lowly position on the fringes of society in another land if their own country had assured them an adequate livelihood. A perspicacious young Indian Singaporean girl asked me if this could have been Lee's reason for keeping so quiet about his courtship of India. 'The Chinese were bound to ask, "What can poverty-stricken India give us?" if they had known of MM's Mission India!' she said.

So many foreigners can create adjustment problems in a small host community. Few workers even have a smattering of English; their already austere lifestyle is further constrained by the need to save. The lacuna that prompted Choo Wee Khiang's comment led to the Battle of the Void Deck. With nowhere to spend their spare time, workers used the void deck—ground floor patio—of public housing estates to sit around chatting, eating, drinking beer and playing cards. Some flat owners fenced in their void decks to prevent this; others mounted regular patrols to keep out foreign workers. A twenty-eight-year-old construction foreman from Tamil Nadu who had worked in Singapore for more than eight years was predictably bitter about being evicted from tenements he had toiled to build in Jurong West.[28]

Driven out of that meeting place the men could only wander the streets in the few hours they had to themselves at weekends and invite more serious charges.

The responsibility for ensuring that these semi-literate men in an unfamiliar environment are neither exploited nor allowed to become a social nuisance rests largely with employers who are usually their only local contact. They alone can mediate between foreign workers on one side and the host government and mainstream society on the other. But the benign paternalism that the task calls for is often subordinated to the profit motive. Seventy-four employers who hired or re-hired illegals to avoid paying standard wages or dodged the mandatory levy employers have to pay were fined S$360,000 in the first four months of 1989.[29] Similar problems a decade later suggested that some employers felt the risk worth the gain.

Complaints of wages being docked to pay the government levy, of workers being tricked out of their passports, or of being made to slave twelve hours a day on substandard pay persisted. Another accusation was that illegals were reported only when they demanded their dues. There were whispers, too, of a blind eye being turned to illegals so long as their labour was essential. Many worked at Changi airport and at industrial sites in Jurong and Tuas, and their expulsion reportedly delayed major construction projects. Changi airport's S$650-million Terminal Two project was said to be two months behind schedule because of manpower problems. Construction of the central expressway was also affected.[30]

Voyaging to Modern Suvarnabhumi

While the CID was investigating the Singapore end of the scam, Indian newspapers urged New Delhi to identify and punish middlemen who exploited gullible labourers.[31] So did the *Straits Times*.[32] New Delhi could not have chosen a more quietly competent man for the job than Shashank, a future foreign secretary who then headed the ministry's consular division. As ambassador to South Korea, he arranged the Daewoo and Hyundai investments of US$3 billion; as ambassador to Libya, he ensured the return of a US$45 million loan to Colonel Muammar Gaddafi; and as economics secretary he helped to organize the India–Brazil–South Africa alliance and the Asean-India summit.[33] He and a colleague found that negligence was the least of the problems in Tamil Nadu from where most illegal migrants originated. Collusion between officials and syndicates masterminding the traffic meant doctored passports and forged work permits. Shashank persuaded the Tamil Nadu government to put up notices at all bus stands and railway stations stressing the need for valid passports and Singapore visas, and warning of the dangers of working without permission or of staying on after permission had expired.

Eternity dies hard, and Shashank found that 'a lot of simple Tamils still believed you just had to go to the bus stand or railway station, pick up a ticket and go to one of the ports and sit in a ship bound for Singapore!'[34] They might have been voyaging to Suvarnabhumi. Or to Singapur. 'The intermediaries who ran the labour rackets took advantage of this innocence.' After Tamil Nadu, the investigators went to Singapore where their mandate was to ensure that the problem did not damage bilateral relations. It did not. The hope expressed by the *Business Times* that controls would not affect the S$40 million business that Indian visitors generated every month was realized.[35] More, Singapore's Kim Tah Holdings tendered for a billion-dollar contract for 400,000 housing units on 800 hectares of reclaimed salt land near Bombay. And Minister of State for Trade and Industry Mah Bow Tan led a seventy-man business delegation to India in November 1988. It is another matter that nothing came of these initiatives.

Shashank pointed out that these simple folk 'had helped greatly in constructing a first-rate country but instead of being praised, were being punished whereas the recruiting agents and the contractors who got cheap illegal labour that remained totally under their control got the benefit and the money'.[36] He also reminded the Singapore government of the grievance that violations were condoned until a labourer stood up for his rights.

So we said the problem needed a more sympathetic approach and they [the Singapore authorities] agreed. But they also complained that the Indian consular department should be in much closer contact with them.[37]

Shashank cites a typically bureaucratic conundrum for official callousness. Manual workers abroad swell India's foreign exchange reserves (US$27 billion in 2007) but barely eke out an existence beyond the pale of the social world of ambassadors and high commissioners. New Delhi's labour ministry was responsible for them until the ministry of overseas Indian affairs took over. External affairs ministry diplomats who run embassies, high commissions and consulates see themselves as a cut above both.

The fears of race prejudice that troubled both the *Straits Times* and *Business Times* highlighted Singaporean contrariness. 'Like you, I am a migrant. I have left my past behind me,' Lee, who sometimes refers to Chinese Singaporeans as descendants of 'riff-raff', told Sikhs.[38] But at some stage migrants become natives, acquire all the characteristics of a long-entrenched elite and pull up the drawbridge against those who would follow in their footsteps. Add to that the Chinese cultural and historical complex that Tregonning mentioned. A respected Australian journalist, Michael Richardson, noted the paradox of the 'latent xenophobia' of a city built by immigrants.[39] Though many well-placed, English-educated Indian Singaporeans would have it that Chinese Singaporeans are as colour-blind as Lady Mountbatten, Lee, who has written about the colour bar he encountered as a student in England, has no need for self-delusion. As he told an interviewer,

> Let's not pretend that there isn't colour prejudice deep down in the middle strata of every population. I am not going to absolve myself or my population from this. We have a multiracial community and we still suffer from this difficulty of getting overseas Chinese and the Indian migrants and the Malays to accept each other completely and without reservation. I think it's going to take a very long time.[40]

It will take longer if India is seen as a country whose poverty-stricken citizens must earn a living abroad by hook or by crook, especially crook. The rationale for short-term workers is that Singapore needs labour and Indians need jobs. But a complementary relationship that is perfectly sound for goods and services is not always apposite when it comes to flesh and blood. It's not like China flooding India with cheap plaster images of Hindu gods and goddesses; it's more like Filipino domestic workers fanning out across the globe and feeling they are regarded as a demeaning national symbol. Movement at this level and of this magnitude exposes harsh inequalities in an India that has produced some of the world's richest tycoons and most brilliant thinkers and scientists, but also accounts for the world's poorest peasantry.

Choo Wee Khiang apologized for his 'pitch dark' jibe. His warning that if 'foreign workers with different skin colours start a rebellion' it could create 'unrest' among Singapore's other communities may be dismissed as hyperbole.[41] But the comment that 'too many foreign labourers' can affect Singapore's 'social security and stability' merits attention. One report says the construction sector needs 50,000 more workers. Ng Eng Hen, then the manpower minister, announced at the end of 2007 that the resident labour force (including foreigners who enjoy PR status) cannot exceed two per cent, especially with unemployment at a ten-year low.[42] Complaints will multiply if workers are imported without adequate housing and recreational facilities; if employment conditions are not supervised; and if Singaporeans are not educated to take a more sympathetic view of these strangers in their midst whose labours help to build the Singapore of the future. Excessive strain on the receiving society's social equilibrium will bring to the fore tensions that are normally kept under wraps. But whatever the measures taken, migration, even temporary or seasonal, dims the lustre of what propagandists call Shining India, that is now Incredible India.

Shades of Third China

Harry Chan thought India was in a permanently anti-Chinese mode ever since 'Hindi-Chini *bhai-bhai* (Indians and Chinese are brothers, slogan of the halcyon Nehru–Zhou 1950s) became Hindi-Chini bye-bye.'[43] He avoided the company of diplomats from China lest he be mistaken for one of them and upbraided Edward Tang at the end of his term for preferring a party at the Chinese embassy to one of his own farewell receptions. The first secretary was not certain whether the reprimand was on account of the gathering he missed or the one he attended.[44]

The high commissioner possibly overlooked changes in the twenty years since the Sino-Indian war. India, under a dynamic young leader whose interest in international affairs went hand in hand with a sound appreciation of maritime security, did not lack confidence, Shashank says. Determined to normalize relations, Rajiv Gandhi visited China—the first visit by an Indian prime minister in thirty-four years—in December 1988 with his Italian-born wife Sonia. Rajiv also made path-breaking trips to Vietnam and Thailand, and was so impressed by the changes in Bangkok that, according to an aide, he showed 'the first flicker of serious interest' in South-east Asia. A visit to Singapore was discussed but did not happen. However, a five-year stalemate in high-level contacts with Asean was broken in August 1985 when a three-man delegation of Malaysian, Singaporean and Bruneian diplomats arrived in New Delhi. Three years later, Foreign Minister Wong predicted during the run-up to the Jakarta Informal Meeting on Cambodia: 'For Singapore, the global changes and the settlement of regional disputes such as Afghanistan and Cambodia has opened up the prospects for a closer relationship with India.'[45]

The breakthrough with China was Rajiv's real achievement. It started a process that led to Hand-in-Hand 2007, a joint anti-terrorism exercise near Kunming, and to the 2010 trade target of US$40 billion being achieved two years earlier.

If China was suspect in the 1980s, that was not a hangover from the past but a spin-off of contemporary politics, says Shashank. America's strategy of courting the enemy's enemy seemed like supporting Chinese aims in South-east Asia, regardless of the impact on India's security. Asean, especially anti-Soviet Singapore, and China 'were normally on the same side in Indochina'.[46]

> India always felt the Vietnamese stood for their own and Asian nationalism, whereas the Chinese were trying to promote the Americans in the region to curb Vietnam for their own reasons. Many of the South-east Asian countries were going along with that and making common cause with Pol Pot![47]

However, Shashank also feels that despite this Cold War game, India was beginning then to revise her assessment of China's aims in the subcontinent. The Chinese had stopped exporting ideology, arms or military training to Indian insurgent groups, he says. New Delhi also had the distinct impression that the Chinese were advising Pakistan to sort out the Kashmir question bilaterally. 'They told us that once India and Pakistan had resolved the Kashmir issue, the territory Pakistan gave China could be discussed and a final solution decided.'[48] This was a 2000 sq. mile slice of the part of Kashmir that Pakistan occupied and which it ceded to China in 1963. Shashank felt the Chinese were trying to behave like a mature status quo power rather than subvert regional politics to their advantage. However, as Rasgotra's comment quoted in the previous chapter showed, not everyone in South Block shared his assessment, and the increasing Chinese activism in southern Asia revived and fuelled old suspicions.

When Peter Chan visited New Delhi in 1984, he was accompanied by the unassuming chairman of the citizens consultative committee in Goh's Marine Parade constituency who was also honorary consul in Singapore for Bhutan. As an Intraco employee, Lam Peck Heng had accompanied Chandra Das on an earlier visit to the Indian capital, but little did he know he would spend three and a half years (1993–96) there as high commissioner during the most dynamic period in India–Singapore relations. Lam was a victim of accident and happenstance. 'One can't swim against the current of life,' he says. 'I believe in fate.'[49]

Young Man in a Hurry

Lee felt sorry for Rajiv Gandhi who had been forced by his brother's death into a job he did not want. 'I thought he was ill prepared for it.'[50] He was 'a political innocent who found himself in the middle of a minefield.'[51] Some of that concern is evident today in his attitude and advice to Rahul Gandhi. He had met Rajiv, most notably at the latter's first CHOGM at Nassau in the Bahamas in 1985. Natwar Singh, who accompanied India's new young prime minister, records, 'On the opening day he [Rajiv Gandhi] was the second speaker after Mrs Thatcher, who was at her combative best. Rajiv excelled her. He had not a piece of paper with him and spoke off the cuff.'[52] Going up to congratulate him later, Lee said, 'You remind me of your grandfather.'[53]

Even without visiting the new India, Lee had a good idea of the challenges Rajiv faced. He indicated that in Parliament when speaking of corruption—'vast' in Russia, 'unprecedented' in China.

> We know that the Indian prime minister has a herculean task. He is cleaning up the Augean stables. It is no secret. It is a fact of life. To be an Indian MP you will have to spend a few million rupees. Having got in, you must get back those few million rupees. And amongst the perks, which is one of the sad things I discovered when we had to withdraw recognition of Indian medical degrees is his right to nominate at least six candidates to all the medical schools in his constituency. It is a right of patronage, not whether the boy qualifies or not.'[54]

New Delhi denied the charge but there was no argument because Singapore was more interested in Rajiv Gandhi's new Exim policy. Ordinarily, this is an annual event; this time, it was made known that subject to modifications and amendments, the significantly liberal rules would remain valid for three years. 'Everybody called Rajiv the new John F. Kennedy!' recalls Ang Sing Hock, a perky economics graduate of Australia's University of New England who had also done his masters in commerce in Australia before joining the Trade Development Board's export development unit.

'Before 1985 nobody went to India,' Ang says. But Chandra Das with his Indian business links decided amid the excitement over the new Exim policy to open a TDB centre in Bombay. Claiming that just 1 per cent of India's market would suffice for Singapore companies, he sent a ten-day fact-finding mission—the first ever—in April. Ang's team, the Oil and Gas Mission because it focussed on India's Oil and Natural Gas Commission, followed in September, and met everyone from the chairman, Colonel Satyapal Wahi, down. The ONGC was a natural target because Singapore was a major oil refining centre, and had built the world's largest oil rigs since colonial times and towed them to destinations worldwide. Keppel and Sembawang were famous names in the industry.

There were other stirrings. An Indian Investment Centre opened in Singapore; the high commission promoted a series of dialogue sessions with senior Indian officials; and the TDB planned a number of other missions to investigate possibilities in the electronics, car components and accessories, and packaging industries. Singapore promised greater participation in Indian trade fairs.[55] Trade had grown eightfold from US$236 million in 1975 to US$1.95 billion in 1984, and more companies were interested in joint ventures. Though Tan Chin Tuan's wartime bank in Bombay had vanished, the OCBC was nosing around for fresh opportunities. So were DBS and OUB. But the difficulty Neptune Orient Lines faced in trying to repatriate a large sum of money earned in India—senior executive Lim Boong Heng flew out in an attempt to sort things out—was cited as a typical deterrent.

Not everyone in India welcomed Singapore's quest for stronger economic ties. A prominent New Delhi academic wrote in a semi-official yearbook that 'hitherto neglected countries like India began to appear "attractive" at least as a stop-gap arrangement' only because 1985 was Singapore's first year of negative growth since 1963. He cited the Pan-Electric Company's collapse which had 'severely eroded the credibility of Singapore's financial institutions', and bankrupted companies and individuals, forcing a three-day stock market closure for 'for the first and only time in its history'.[56]

Dissonances in the political field were conveniently overlooked by the Singapore spokesmen when they broached the topic of techno-economic collaboration with India.[57]

There was nothing 'convenient' about it however. As noted earlier, Singapore continued to do business with a Soviet Union that it regarded as the enemy and traded with Vietnam while vehemently opposing Vietnamese foreign policy. Similarly, it saw no reason to allow general political differences or the Cambodia dispute to stand in the way of ties with India. Responding with matching pragmatism, New Delhi lifted the ban on importing vegetable oil from Singapore that had been imposed three years earlier when it was found to be adulterated with beef tallow—a serious offence for Hindus who revere the cow as sacred—and promised to resume tea auctions in Singapore.

Five months after his recce, Ang landed in a Bombay paralysed by a *bandh* against a rise in the price of petrol, to set up the TDB's first Indian centre. His office in Maker Tower IV was modest with just an Indian secretary, but the site was reckoned to be the world's most expensive on a per square foot valuation and Ang advised his bosses to buy it. The residential flat he rented in Cuff Parade was luxurious by any standard. 'I lived like a maharaja,' he chuckles back in Singapore. 'Here they are all coolies!' Three years later he moved to New Delhi with diplomatic rank and the additional designation of first secretary in charge of trade. His jurisdiction extended to the Middle East.

The TDB was not alone in reading the tea leaves. Lee, who had not been to India since the 1983 CHOGRM, thought the signs propitious to revive Mission India. As he says, 'Our divergent policies on Cambodia kept me away from India until March 1988, when I tried to establish contact with ... Rajiv Gandhi.'[58] Lee felt Rajiv was someone with whom he could connect. He was 'bringing India into the age of the computer, the satellite, the space shuttle and the space station,' he told AIR's Mukhopadhyay. He 'was trying to feel his way forward in a very complex situation, learning so many things all at the same time, the electoral politics of India, the intricacies of the Congress Party, the personalities involved'. Everybody wanted to use him and his name to get votes.

Singapore had sent ten trade missions to India in the previous two years. Alan Yeo, Businessman of the Year in 1987, succeeded Chandra Das as TDB chairman and led another delegation of seventeen top executives from fifteen companies to Bombay even as Palaniappan Chidambaram, minister of state for home affairs, was receiving the Lees and their party at New Delhi airport. Lee recapitulates Rajiv's dilemma.

> It was tough. How can you move from a job as airline pilot, keeping fit, flying from A to B, resting a few days, then flying back, you've got to check this and that ... Suddenly you are confronted with this enormous jigsaw puzzle. This is one that is one—you've got ten jigsaw puzzles, and you can't mix them up. Must be terrifying.[59]

No wonder he leant on advisers. Echoing Indira Gandhi's comment on Richard Nixon's visible dependence on Kissinger, Lee noted that during their discussions, Rajiv 'often turned to Natwar Singh'.[60] He must have approved for he thought the Kunwar had 'a sharp mind and (was) a good presenter of difficult Indian positions'. Natwar Singh says Rahul Gandhi ('a voracious reader') showed him the passage in Lee's memoirs. 'I told Rahul, you and I are the only two people in Delhi to have read the book!'[61]

The new government's partiality for imported colour TV sets was one indication of its impatience with the austerities of the past. People were also travelling more. A twenty-six per cent rise in the number of Indians visiting Singapore annually raised the figure to 244,000. The number of Singapore residents returning from India went up 5 per cent to 21,400. Rajiv stressed the importance of competition and efficiency. He welcomed foreign investors, especially in economic zones for 100 per cent exports. He encouraged joint ventures with minority foreign equity. He reduced some Customs and import duties and streamlined procedures. Pepsi's return just before Harry Chan left prompted the question, 'Can Coke be far behind?' These measures—modest by the standards of Singapore or what Narasimha Rao attempted later—encouraged Lee to hope for more trade, tourism and investment. He had been hoping for years.

Trade did go up by 15 per cent, and Lee saw scope not only for a further increase but for joint marketing and industrial ventures. He wanted to import more manufactures from India, and offered Singapore's experience in low-cost housing, oil and gas exploration services, and port and telecommunications infrastructure development. 'Our industrialists and businessmen should be encouraged and supported to exploit this potential for more trade, investments and technology transfer' he told reporters.

> You've got a tremendous industrial output which should find its way into the South-east Asian and Singapore markets.[62]

Lee's innovative proposal for an industrial estate and free trade zone in Tamil Nadu where the Jumabhoys were committed to investing heavily in joint ventures for exports to third countries was dubbed the Madras Corridor. It became the Holy Grail of bilateral cooperation, the shining ideal always tantalizingly beyond reach. Lee wanted to reduce Singapore's dependence on Japan and the United States. Western Europe was one area of diversification, India another: 'There's no reason why, if India looks outward in her economic policies and grows, we should not find India as one of our major, one of our first ten, trading partners. I hope this can be the case.'[63]

India's US$200 billion economy—with manufacturing accounting for 41 per cent—made her one of the world's ten most industrialized nations, 'a fact not well known because poverty remains a huge and intractable problem for any Indian government,' Patrick Daniel, who covered Lee's tour for the *Straits Times*, reported.[64] The opening that had begun after Indira Gandhi's second coming in 1980 had been lost in the ensuing communal turmoil. The infamous Hindu rate of growth was more memorable for the Western media than the achievements of business houses like Tata, Birla, Goenka and Kirloskar, catering to 800 million people. Lee adds that India put her bets on the wrong horse. 'We put our bets on the winner.' He is amused to be told that Singapore put its bets on both—or all—horses, and replies, 'No, but we put our bets on NAM and the rest. You put your bet on the Soviet bloc and the NAM. You never left the non-aligned group. We never chose the Soviet bloc. We were already convinced that the Soviet system was not going to get us there.'[65]

India's psychological orientation was a stronger impediment to the commercial ties Lee sought than the unresolved Cambodian problem with which both sides could live. He thought India could 'help to work out an acceptable formula for Vietnamese withdrawal, which does not result in the restoration of the Khmer Rouge.' The solution would have to be 'acceptable to the non-Communist resistance and to all the other countries in the region.'[66]

The two prime ministers, one old and experienced, the other new but eager to learn, had a great deal to discuss. Ameer Jumabhoy, again one of the party, recalls waiting for them at a TDB reception to be followed by a press conference. There was no sign of either leader. The reception and press conference were cancelled. Rajiv's appointment with a visiting Sri Lankan minister was postponed. The tête-à-tête went on for nearly three hours, after which they went straight to the state banquet at Hyderabad House.

Lee denies giving Rajiv any advice, even in avuncular fashion. 'I can't!' he protests. 'I don't go around giving advice. People won't want to see me if I do. I mean, that's not my job!'[67] But he admits he had something to say about how a big country should deal with touchy smaller neighbours, especially since South Block hoped the South Asian Association for Regional Cooperation, launched in Dhaka in December 1985, would emulate Asean: 'I did mention how Asean began to succeed only because Suharto set out by letting it be known that he was not going to be the big boss.'[68]

Unlike his grandiloquent predecessor, Suharto accommodated the point of view of the region's smallest countries and was deferential to their leaders almost to the point of anonymity, Lee adds. Indonesia was South-east Asia's leading nation in terms of size, population and capacity: all the more reason why it had to be the least assertive and demanding. Saarc's problems were more acute because of India's size and because it abutted all the other countries, each with its own agenda. They had less to do with each other than with India. Bangladesh sought to internationalize water-sharing. Nepal tried to play off China against India. Sri Lanka wanted British and Israeli military help and third country involvement in its ethnic crisis. Pakistan was a permanent headache. Listing each challenge, Lee says that India, which feared they would gang up on her, would have to play a crucial role in inducing cooperation.

He may have known that Jayewardene made precisely this point at Saarc's launch when he claimed that, being larger than all the other Saarc members combined, India could 'by deeds and words create the confidence among us so necessary to make a beginning'. Though no longer the power behind the throne, Haksar correctly interpreted the Sri Lankan leader to mean that 'India, as a big brother, must be at all times accommodating and tolerant towards the propensity for mischief-making of the younger brothers.'[69] This was later codified in the five principles of the Gujral Doctrine whose first point argued that 'India does not ask for reciprocity but gives all that it can in good faith and trust'.[70]

Anticipating Gujral, Lee, too, stressed the need for planned asymmetry in dealing with smaller neighbours. He says he has no idea how Rajiv received his views or 'whether he would take that as a hint that India should take a similar (to Suharto's) course vis-à-vis Pakistan.'[71] They must have been received well for Rajiv continued the exchange at a private lunch where he and Sonia entertained only the Lees and the ever-faithful Natwar Singh. Lee also described how Singapore had privatized public enterprises to enable top-level manpower to break new ground. Rajiv Gandhi 'found that interesting because that's the kind of terrain he was likely to travel in the next few years'.[72] India's prime minister must have been especially interested when Lee mentioned Joe Pillay as one of the three men (with Goh Keng Swee and Hon Sui Sen) who had helped to bring about the Singapore miracle. Sonia continued the link, looking on Lee as a friend and as her son's mentor two decades later.

Did Goh Really See India As Regional Bully?

Meanwhile, grumbles, muted and not so muted, about Rajiv Gandhi's naval build-up could be heard from Bangladesh, Malaysia, Indonesia, Japan, Australia and even Singapore. Though Lee had always sought India's protection for South-east Asia, his successor sounded nervous about the blue water navy on which Rajiv had set his heart. India's acquisition of a Soviet-built nuclear-powered submarine and aircraft carrier prompted Indonesian accusations of letting the Soviets use Indian naval bases, while 'Prime Minister Goh Chok Tong worried about the United States's withdrawal from its bases in the Philippines in light of India's rising naval power'.[73]

Australia's defence minister, Kim Beazley, was one of the first to voice concern, claiming to speak for his Malaysian colleague in the FPDA, Tengku Ahmad Rithauddeen. He may have had others, too, in mind when he said that though Australia's good relations with India appeared to rule out a clash of interests, 'this is a view which is not necessarily shared elsewhere in the region.'[74] Beazley's domestic critics accused him of crying wolf to develop a case for a two-ocean Australian navy, while Indians dismissed him as proxy for the Americans who imagined a challenge to their Diego Garcia base.

But it was Goh, then first deputy prime minister, who surprised everyone by warning at a PAP convention that any reduction of the American presence would lead to an Indian bid for hegemony.

> I always thought that India was only interested in the Indian Ocean, the countries round India—Sri Lanka, Maldives, Mauritius and some other neighbouring countries. But recently I read an article in the Australian *Age*, a Melbourne newspaper, quoting a former deputy chief of army of the Indian army ... as saying that India wants to be the dominant power between the Suez Canal and Singapore. When I met a foreign minister from a country in the Indian Ocean recently, I asked why India wants to be the dominant power up to Singapore. He explained that India regards all Indians as her nationals, even overseas Indians. She is trying to build up her power to be able to project herself up to Fiji, because in Fiji about 50 per cent of the population are Indian. If she can project herself up to Fiji then I think she can also become a dominant regional power.[75]

Was there some nervousness about protection being extended to Indian Singaporeans? Surprisingly, or, perhaps, not so surprisingly, Goh's only public support again exposed the psychological quirks of some overseas Indians. Jaswant Singh Gill, a Punjabi from the name and very likely a Sikh, wrote to the *Straits Times* applauding Goh for his 'timely' warning on 'India's regional ambitions'. He was shrill in scolding India for squandering money on the military and police while doing nothing to 'alleviate the lot of its impoverished millions'. India had 'been building up its army, navy and air force'; she crushed dissent, bullied neighbours and was a potential threat to all small nations between Suez and Singapore. Her military power was 'far beyond' what she 'legitimately' needed to protect borders and trade routes.[76]

There was no change, however, in Lee's standing welcome for an Indian regional leadership role. He calls Rajiv's accord with Jayewardene on curbing the Tamil Tigers 'an act of high statesmanship ... [that] deserves the international acclaim it has received'. However, while praising Rajiv's courage and enterprise, Lee also wonders if the forty-three-year-old prime minister took the risks fully into account before committing his army to what has been called India's Vietnam. 'I am not sure if he knew how courageous it was to send troops to Sri Lanka.' Putting himself in Rajiv's place, Lee says that despite Jayewardene's invitation, he would not have sent soldiers. He would have sent only trainers and commandos to show what could be done, because 'to go there as a dominant power and try to quell this rebellion was a very heavy political signal.' Lee is indignant to think of 'the opposition of Jayewardene's successor', Ranasinghe Premadasa, who did not appreciate that 'there was no profit in it for' India: 'The Indians would have done them a favour if the Indian army could have put down, or at least weakened, the Tamil Tigers. But he (Premadasa) thought Sri Lanka's sovereignity was being violated!'[77]

Rajiv paid with his life because he was 'dealing with a very determined, ruthless lot of people'.[78] The ruthlessness also took toll of 1,200 Indian soldiers before Gujral brought the last Indian units home in March 1990. Lee approved again five months later when, responding to an appeal from President Abdul Gayoom of the Maldives who was threatened by a gang of armed Jaffna Tamils, Rajiv Gandhi promptly airlifted a battalion of troops a thousand miles across the Indian Ocean. Lee thought Operation Cactus, as the Maldives rescue was codenamed, another necessary peacekeeping exercise such as the Americans undertake globally, and the Australians in the South Pacific.[79]

But the Cold War continued. Rajiv's liberal economics could not be equated with political alignment with the United States. Nor reconciliation with China with acquiescence in Chinese penetration of South-east Asia. Rajiv Gandhi wanted modern tools of growth and sophisticated instruments of defence—hence his unprecedented four visits to the United States—but his first foreign trip as prime minister was to the Soviet Union, and despite quiet contacts with Israel, he never abandoned formal NAM positions. He disapproved of Sri Lanka's plans to host a powerful Voice of America transmitter and was concerned at reports of American military facilities in Singapore, though, unlike Malaysia and Indonesia, India did not protest.[80] He also vehemently opposed Narasimha Rao's decision to allow American warplanes to land and refuel in India during the first Iraq war.

The economic revolution he dreamt of did not materialize. Rajiv may have endorsed Lee's comment that 'when the private sector takes an interest, given official support, the prospects are good', but India's political and administrative establishments thought differently. Liberalization threatened small entrepreneurs and bureaucrats. Industrial tycoons clung to the cozy cash-for-favours arrangement they had always enjoyed with the government. Politicians insisted on populist programmes with mass appeal. Lacking the experience and acumen to control wheeler-dealer Congress managers who mobilized votes and funds, Rajiv further weakened his own power base by encouraging apolitical hangers-on who were more interested in gadgets, gizmos and gimmicks. India could not afford many of his dreams. A report in *Time* magazine claimed that 'New Delhi's defence budget has doubled in real terms during the '80s and has in fact outstripped the government's ability to fund it.'[81]

None of this boded well for Ang and the TDB. But the immediate fallout showed what even a modestly open economy could achieve. India–Singapore trade rose by 23 per cent between 1986 and 1987; nineteen joint ventures were set up in Singapore; and SIA and India's tourism department agreed to sell India in the Asia-Pacific. A Singaporean consortium drew up plans for a US$15 million golf resort and hotel in India, and arrangements were made for the two foreign secretaries (A.P. Venkateswaran and Peter Chan) to meet regularly. But India was still grudging about SIA's request for additional flights, an Intraco-Godrej joint venture made little headway and the improvement in Singapore's trade with India was not as spectacular as with Brazil. Ang says there was little point in courting the ONGC which had the capacity and contacts to shop wherever it chose. Other business was handled by multinationals and Singapore's government-linked companies. Rajiv Gandhi's reforms facilitated domestic rather than external business. But as Lee implied at a Lunar New Year reception, the appearance of a stalemate may have been deceptive: 'Our growing links with India are not so obvious because, unlike China, an Indian private sector already exists and they are accustomed to dealing direct with our private sector.'[82]

Ang looks back on thirteen and a half personally fulfilling years. He shook hands with Rajiv Gandhi, enjoyed a vegetarian lunch off

English bone china with the Birlas on the top floor of their Calcutta mansion, took formula milk and diapers from Singapore for Keppel's Indian agent who did not trust local products for his baby, met the Goenkas in New Delhi, did business with the Tatas, and called on West Bengal's Marxist chief minister, Jyoti Basu, whose niece was director of the IIC in Singapore and had spoken fondly of him. He grew roses, kept dogs, sent his daughters to the American School, and indulged his fondness for collecting objets d'art. He could have passed off as Indian and, as he laughs, was often mistaken for 'one of those insurgents from the north-east'. His smattering of Hindi confused insular Indians who already found it hard to believe that a Chinese should speak fluent English.

Rajiv Gandhi's technocratically innovative regime ended when the Congress Party lost the 1989 election amidst a cloud of corruption charges. Lee's 1988 visit was his last as prime minister. He was familiar with India's politicians and civil servants and had studied the country's culture and customs. He had paid more visits to India than any other foreign leader. His Mission India had become Singapore's policy. Goh, who took over in November 1990 when Lee stepped aside—not down—to become Senior Minister, was known in India only for his remarks on India as a potential menace to the region. But he had an unbeatable personal advantage. Where the intellectual and analytical Lee could sound abrasive, Goh made it a point always to be consciously soothing: 'By contrast with his predecessor, he had declared his intention to introduce more "participation, accommodation and consensus" in a "kinder, gentler society".'[83]

His studiedly softer and, indeed, flattering style won over Indians. When an Indian journalist questioned Singapore's democratic credentials at one of Goh's New Delhi meetings, another journalist jumped up to say that while both countries were democracies, Singapore's was 'guided' whereas India's was 'misguided'.[84] The tactful Goh charmed everyone at the Nomura Asia Equity Forum in Singapore's Fullerton Hotel in July 2007 by quoting India's billboard at the previous year's Davos meeting: 'Fifteen years, Six Governments, Five Prime Ministers, ONE DIRECTION'. The clear message was that reform and liberalization were irreversible. He was even able to package the China comparison more acceptably. 'China serves both as an example of what a large country can do and a compelling reason for India to grow faster to keep up.'

In essentials, however, Singapore bore out Jean-Baptiste Alphonse Karr's nineteenth-century epigram, *'plus ça change, plus c'est la même chose'* (the more things change, the more they stay the same). Witty and incisive, a taxi driver spelt it out for me. Singapore Inc. continued as before, he said, except that the boss, the chairman, now had a new title. Who's that? I asked, and he replied in some surprise, 'SM of course!' that being Lee's designation at the time. What then was Prime Minister Goh? 'General manager,' the driver replied, paused, then added, 'Okay, you can call him managing director, CEO.' And the Cabinet ministers? 'They are departmental heads.' Mission India was still Lee's strategy but sustained by Goh's stamina and flavoured by his conscious charm.

{10}

Singapore's
'Mild India Fever'

Responding to the guidelines he had inherited, Goh made history. He abandoned his fear of Indian hegemony, sponsored India for membership of various Asian forums and made a major breakthrough with the Bangalore Information Technology Park. A grateful India invited him to be the first Singaporean guest of honour at New Delhi's Republic Day parade. But the first post-Lee high-level visit was by Lee's son, future prime minister Lee Hsien Loong while George Yeo was credited with carrying out the most exhaustive practical survey of the prospects for India–Singapore relations. There were disappointments, too, as several ambitious Singaporean proposals foundered on the rock of India's traditional suspicion of foreigners. But movement was forward and that was largely because Narasimha Rao also made history by opening India to the world, meaning the United States with which he sought economic and strategic ties after decades of frosty neglect. He also made history by being the first Indian prime minister to be invited to deliver the Singapore Lecture when Lee compared him with China's Deng Xiaoping.

Narasimha Rao inherited a bankrupt exchequer when Rajiv Gandhi's assassination pushed him centre stage as he was packing his bags to retire to his native Hyderabad. Few took him seriously. 'When in doubt pout' was one of the less impolite gags about the new prime minister. Rajiv's drive for modernization had boomeranged. Lavish imports of capital goods had created a huge balance of payments deficit compounded by the high cost of fuel and fertilizer, the end of rupee trade with the Soviet Union, the first Iraq war and suspension of workers' remittances from the Gulf. Foreign exchange reserves dwindled to US$1.1 billion, while foreign debts soared to US$70 billion. India was in crisis but the new premier lived up to the Chinese spelling of the word with two ideograms meaning danger and opportunity. He combined an acute strategic sense with a disarming turn of phrase. 'I will follow the Nehru line,' he told this writer after taking over, pre-empting charges of jettisoning cherished Nehruvian principles by adding, 'Manu the lawgiver gave the law but it was up to each Brahmin to interpret it.'

His precept was as mind-boggling as Deng's 'socialism with Chinese characteristics'. Determined that India should not wallow in a poverty-stricken neighbourhood bogged down in squabbles, yet careful not to offend political orthodoxy, he continued to swear by continuity while quietly turning foreign, military and economic policies inside out and nudging India closer to the United States which alone could provide the necessary funding and technological expertise. He sent a senior army general to the American-organized Pacific Armies Management Seminar in Seoul which India had always shunned and picked up and pushed one of Rajiv's discreet initiatives: Lalit Mansingh, deputy chief of mission in India's Washington embassy, was instructed to court the influential leaders of American Jewry as a bridge to Israel.[1] Singapore was also singled out because of its booming prosperity, access to eastern Asia and close economic and political ties with the United States.

He had not always been enthusiastic about South-east Asia and had warned Tiwari he would 'be wasting (his) time there' when the diplomat asked for Singapore because it was half-way to Tokyo, his heaven.[2] But Narasimha Rao was Rajiv's external affairs minister then and operating in an altogether different situation. As prime minister, he sought a relationship with the Asian country that had always been most friendly to India and could also provide an entrée to the Pacific, the ocean of the future. Lee had become a familiar figure in Indian government circles and Singapore's Indian links made it easily accessible. Moreover, the south Indian in Narasimha Rao, versed in Sanskrit and history, could not remain immune to the allure of Suvarnabhumi. He began to repeat, sometimes to the point of boring listeners, that the 'simha' in his name replicated Singapore's 'singa', and that the lost Telugu lullabies crooned over his cradle were still sung in Malaysia. He also commissioned non-papers on alliances with the United States, Israel, Mahathir's East Asia Economic Caucus (dubbed 'Caucus without Caucasians'), the Asia Pacific Economic Cooperation forum and, above all, Asean, and presided over brainstorming sessions at his 9 Motilal Nehru Marg bungalow.

If Narasimha Rao cultivated Singapore to court the United States, he also shrewdly countered South-east Asia's reservations about India with overtures to the United States. It was a dexterous dual process. His acceptance of a long-standing American invitation to hold joint naval exercises was one such overture. But, first, he allayed domestic misgivings about a sudden lurch into the Foreign Hand by holding exercises with the less contentious Royal Australian Navy. Then in 1992 came the epochal India–United States exercise codenamed 'Malabar' in the Arabian Sea. Finally, India reinforced her regional credentials with exercises with the Singapore, Malaysian and Indonesian navies.

Watching the new government at work from Singapore, Lee told Goh, 'This is your chance. Push it. Let's get them into Asean.'[3] Krishnan Srinivasan, alumnus of Bedford College in England and an Oxford Blue in boxing, who succeeded Dixit as foreign secretary, says, 'Singapore was the first and at that time, only, Asean country to take India seriously.' Looking back, he admits that the projects discussed 'sound old hat now but at that time it was pretty revolutionary'.[4]

The wheels were turning. K. Kesavapany, the MFA's director in charge of Asean affairs, suggested to High Commissioner Tiwari one day as they teed off at the Singapore Island Country Club that he should signal New Delhi that it was time for a fresh approach to Asean. Tiwari responded enthusiatically. 'Pany and I worked out a time schedule for India to begin with sectoral dialogue, graduate to full partnership in two years, and aim at the Asean Regional Forum in another year and a half.'[5] He then sent a seven-page note with annexures to the external affairs ministry. It was not acknowledged but the foreign secretary sent a formal letter to the Asean secretariat.[6] The new prime minister sent his external affairs minister, Madhavsinh Solanki, to the Paris peace conference on Cambodia where an agreement was signed in October 1991. The following January,

Asean's Singapore summit accepted India's application for sectoral partnership, and an Asean-India Joint Sectoral Cooperation Committee was set up, initially to discuss trade, investment and tourism but later also science and technology. India was admitted as a sectoral dialogue partner in March 1993.

Narasimha Rao's principal secretary, A.N. Verma, was keen on South-east Asia. So were Ambassador Ram with his Thai experience and High Commissioner Preet Malik who was familiar with both Singapore and Malaysia. The new finance minister, Manmohan Singh, a sixty-one-year-old apolitical economist trained at Oxford and Cambridge, and a favourite of the World Bank and International Monetary Fund, was especially qualified to take India West via the East, having 'always viewed India's destiny as being interlinked with that of Asia and more so South-east Asia'.[7] Manmohan Singh explains, 'We thought that if we had to market 'New India', we would have to begin in Singapore.'[8] It was an acknowledgement of the wider market opportunities available in and through Singapore and of Lee's persistent advocacy. As Lee says, he 'had been urging India for years to open up'.[9] His Mission India at last seemed likely to yield dividend.

But there were still hitches to overcome. If Narasimha Rao was passively negative about Singapore to start with, Goh continued to be actively so about India. His comment in a newspaper interview that 'India has the capability to project its navy way beyond its shores' was not an innocuous statement of fact but another expression of his suspicions. To the bafflement of Indians, he seemed to think India was poised to take over Asia: 'Countries in the region have a vital interest in ensuring that no power dominates the sea lanes and upsets the equilibrium in South-east Asia. India urges the world to understand its security needs. Similarly, I hope that India will also appreciate the security concerns of its neighbours.'[10]

Goh saw no danger of disequilibrium in American domination of Asia's sea lanes. Happily, no one else shared his misgivings. Not the two Singaporean foreign ministers, Wong and Yeo, and certainly not Lee who admits ruefully that he had tried 'since the 1960s to engage India in South-east Asia for economic and political reasons'. He laughs at his successor's fears. 'No, no, no!' he exclaims. 'You don't want to colonize us! It doesn't make sense.'[11] His explanation is that Goh was speaking for Indonesia which had taken fright at reports of Russia using India's Great Nicobar naval base though it was the end of history for Moscow.

Asked if he feels threatened by India, Lee Hsien Loong with his military background—he was an army brigadier-general and known locally as 'BG Lee'—replies, 'No, I don't think so. Why should we?' He is as emphatic as his father that India doesn't want 'to establish an exclusive sphere of influence'. Goh Chok Tong's successor knows that India will not operate 'aircraft carriers like the Seventh Fleet for a very long time to come'. She couldn't even if she wanted to 'because the Americans remain here and the countries in the region are not without resources to look after themselves.' Again like his father, he welcomes India's naval presence. 'I think it's good that you have a presence there and it will contribute to the security of the Straits of Malacca. You are an important user.'

India has 'a vested interest in free, safe passage', and Singapore draws reassurance from the Indian navy's regular port calls, journeys to the Pacific and exercises with countries like South Korea. 'We are very happy to see this. I mentioned this at the Shangri-La Dialogue the year before.'

Happily, Goh's misgivings about India did not last long. Benignity swept over him as suspicion had done, and he admitted that his 'perception' had changed. He had been worried 'reading reports of India's acquisition of a blue-water fleet' and by the *Age* article: 'Maybe this was just rhetoric of generals. But when these remarks appeared in cold print, you ask yourself, "What for?", "Why does India have to stretch her power from Singapore to Africa?"'[12]

As he 'got to understand India better', he appreciated that India needs 'a good navy to be able to defend its long coastline.' He saw, too, that India was opening up and 'not spending more on defence'.[13] Tiwari may have helped by explaining India's geopolitical compulsions and that China and Pakistan spent a much higher proportion of GDP on the military. Indian Defence Minister Sharad Pawar took time off from Asian Aerospace '92 to reassure Singaporeans that India's military expenditure was minimal and her interest in the region 'purely one of friendship'. Singapore was India's 'window on the world'.[14] The prospect of doing business with India was probably the most decisive factor. Narasimha Rao also changed his mind about Singapore to the extent that it became a corny Indian joke to call him the 'Goh-getter'![15]

Recognizing that the India-Asean relationship was 'the sum total of bilateral interaction' Narasimha Rao directed that special attention 'be paid to strengthening and deepening bilateral relations.'[16] Thailand took a long time to forgive India for Cambodia, but visiting Bangkok, Narasimha Rao struck a rapport with King Bhumibol Adulyadej by discussing Thai and Indian scripts and the scope for introducing them to the computer keyboard. Scheduled to last thirty minutes, the audience went on for two hours. India waived visa fees for Thai monks on pilgrimage, and after years of aloofness, the two countries agreed on scholastic programmes, an ambitious trade target and a political dialogue. Relations with Singapore were both simpler and more complex. They were simpler because of the legacy of eternity and history, overlapping interests and the human link. They were complex because Singapore demanded sweeping domestic action far more than token diplomatic initiatives from India. As Lee repeated ad nauseam, India could promote the relationship only by making trade and investment more attractive for Singaporeans.

The marketing of 'New India' that Manmohan Singh mentioned began when, barely two months after forming a government, Narasimha Rao sent Solanki to Goh and Wong with a request for investment and the assurance of opportunities for economic ties 'in a big way'.[17] Solanki was India's first external affairs minister to visit Singapore in a decade. Wong, who went to India in December, was Singapore's first foreign minister to do so in two decades. The governor of India's Reserve Bank followed Solanki. Then came Manmohan Singh and Chidambaram. They called on Lee, explained the reform programme and said India wanted to work with Asia's dynamic economies. Lee recalls the meeting and says, 'Both ministers were clear on how to improve India's economic growth and knew what had to be done. The problem was how to get it done with an opposition that was xenophobic on free enterprise, free markets, foreign trade and investments.'[18]

Actually, there were more economic xenophobes in the Congress and the Communist ranks than in the main opposition—the BJP—

which had always espoused free enterprise. Narasimha Rao astutely consulted party leader Lal Krishna Advani when drawing up his reform package, thereby ensuring that Manmohan Singh's announcement in Parliament was received with acclaim. The finance minister assured Lee that India would link up 'in a much more integrated way' to the world trading community. 'India has a new mindset. There will be no backsliding.'

B.G. Lee initiated the continuing series of high-level exchanges between India and Singapore in March 1992 by taking a nineteen-member delegation of senior TDB and EDB officials, as well as businessmen like the ubiquitous Ameer Jumabhoy, to India. The younger Lee finds it difficult to believe he started the ball rolling. 'Surely Goh Chok Tong was already there?' But, no, Goh didn't go until nearly two years later. Nonplussed by the BG prefix (India knows only brigadiers) newspapers wrote of 'Mr B.G. Lee Hsien Loong'. He and his hosts discussed the Madras Corridor as well as Ameer Jumabhoy's proposals for a 'strategic partnership' to manufacture for third countries and for Singapore to facilitate India's entry into the Asean market.[19]

B.G. Lee 'had a good meeting with Manmohan Singh' and also met JRD's designated heir, Ratan Tata, who showed him around 'and explained that they had to start to move overseas.' To his pleasant surprise, a man in the audience at one of his meetings turned out to have been at Cambridge with him. But though BG Lee acknowledged that Narasimha Rao had initiated 'a courageous set of policies', he did not think it was possible to 'make radical changes overnight'.[20] In his view, as in his father's, 'the political consensus actually did not develop until much later, around 2000 after the BJP came in.' But his report ('We have a systematic way to write up these trip outcomes') set the tone for Goh's meeting with Narasimha Rao in Jakarta where an uncertain NAM was holding its first summit conference since the Soviet collapse.

Goh asked Tiwari how Narasimha Rao would react if he invited Indian Institute of Technology graduates to Singapore. 'How many prime ministers would have the humility to check his ideas?' the high commissioner exclaims.[21] In Jakarta, Goh had separate meetings on the same day with nine Afro-Asian leaders. The topics discussed with

Narasimha Rao included the Madras Corridor, an industrial park in Bangalore, a permanent exhibition in Singapore of Indian art and artefacts, importing professionals, and—this would become a major Singaporean interest—real estate.[22] Narasimha Rao wanted Singapore to recruit Indian graduates to work in third countries. Ong Keng Yong says they liked each other because, while Narasimha Rao was not 'patriarchal', Goh was not a towering figure like Lee. He was 'disarming', 'sensitive' and 'understanding', and came across 'as a very simple earthly guy, quite sincere' who never interrupted a presentation by his counterpart. 'So he has the ability to put the other guy at his ease. I suppose the most important thing is that he follows up whatever he says he will do and always writes back to the leaders concerned. Mr Rao didn't come across as the grand old man either. They talked as friends.'[23]

It All Happened on Lam's Watch

Jayakumar thinks Jakarta was the 'turning point in relations.' It was also the beginning of a personal relationship. Goh referred to Narasimha Rao 'very fondly' in his correspondence. Lam Peck Heng, ensconced in New Delhi as high commissioner, noticed the 'good chemistry' between them. After Narasimha Rao was defeated, Ong accompanied Goh to the Motilal Nehru Marg bungalow where the former prime minister had retreated, ostracized by the political establishment, and again noted their 'very good body language'.[24]

Lam had studied at the Lawrence University in Kansas, Berkeley, and Rutgers, and yearned to teach mathematics at university. 'All my life I wanted to be a professor of mathematics, believing I would make some shattering discovery like Einstein.' But the government scholarship that sent him to the United States compelled him to teach at Raffles Institution. He quit the day his bond ended and held a succession of jobs when Goh invited him to join the Marine Parade citizens consultative committee. 'I couldn't speak a word of Mandarin and had never set foot in a community centre,' he says but is proud of planting the Jin Long Si temple's Bodhi tree (*Ficus religiosa*).

Lam owed the consular honour to Chandra Das whom Dhanabalan had introduced to Bhutan's foreign minister, Dawa Tsering. A simple man, he thought it a grammatical error when he received a letter from King Jigme using the royal we. Another linguistic surprise awaited him when a former student in the MFA telephoned to ask if Lam would go to Rangoon as chargé d'affaires: he was as baffled by the French term as by the royal we. Arriving in Rangoon, he was initiated into more diplomatic arcana. Preet Malik, India's ambassador, telephoned to say he would call, but did not when he learnt Lam's rank. 'I was chargé, he was ambassador!' Malik and he became good friends afterwards, Lam admiring the Sikh's skill at golf and bridge and his wife's talented dancing. After four and a half depressing years in Burma, Lam jumped at the offer of becoming high commissioner to India. His wife, a trained beautician, went first and, unlike some diplomatic wives, liked India. They were undemanding folk.

Barring B.G. Lee's visit, everything else happened on Lam's watch. It started with the other BG, George Yeo, then minister for information and the arts and second minister for foreign affairs, who has come to occupy a special place in the India–Singapore discourse, almost rivalling Lee in the breadth and depth of his knowledge and commitment. Like Lee (but unlike Goh) Yeo makes no secret of his impatience with many of the infelicities of Indian life. His understanding of both India and China enables him to see the bigger picture.

Like Lee, he also vests Brahmins with an aura that seems dated outside the time warp in which many Singaporeans are trapped. His first visit in 1986 was for the marriage in Madurai of a 'Tamil Brahmin' friend from Harvard. Another Harvard friend, 'a Brahmin from Patna', was an usher at the ceremony. Visiting Tipu Sultan's palace in Seringapatam, Yeo discovered Brahmins 'of a particularly high caste'.[25] While he may have inherited this awareness of Brahmins from Singapore's British rulers, Harvard taught him that Chinese Singaporeans are 'much more Indianized' than Chinese from China, Hong Kong and Taiwan, and that they and Indians mix more easily.

Yeo flew to Madras where a punctilious immigration officer gave him his first taste of India's bureaucracy by checking every item without missing a thing and making all his notes in green ink. His host's aunt's insistence on boiling drinking water reinforced the prudence that had prompted him to take along his own water heater. ('The water is very hard, so when you boil it, it becomes very cloudy.') For someone with a delicate stomach, Yeo turned out to be a glutton for India, flying there not only on work but also for private engagements like Kamal Nath's son's wedding.

He was back in 1988 as the defence ministry's director-general for planning. Singapore was building a new defence academy, and having studied Sandhurst and its American and Australian counterparts, he wanted to see Khadakvasla. The ethnic diversity of the cadets astonished him. 'You had people looking Chinese, Pathan, wiry Tamils, the whole range!' He was given a very warm welcome and invited to address the cadets by the superintendent who used to be defence attaché in India's Singapore mission. Yeo admits with gentle self-deprecation that he was flattered by the cadets' thunderous applause until he realized they were under orders to greet every visitor with thunderous applause.

His third visit in February 1993 as the guest of Human Resources Minister Arjun Singh is often said to have marked a turning point at least as significant as Jakarta. But it is incorrect to claim, as official records do, that the delegation of twenty-two politicians, bureaucrats and businessmen was 'probably the largest and most varied official Singapore delegation sent to India.' It was smaller than some of the teams Lee took and one-third the size of Mah Bow Tan's massive group. Trade and culture were the main objectives but there was a political agenda too: Singapore's request for government records for the years it was administered from Calcutta included documents relating to Pedra Branca (Pulao Batu Puteh) islet, where the Horsburgh Lighthouse stands, which Malaysia claimed. Lam had no advance notice of the visit and was not asked for any background papers.

The mission's 'surprisingly positive impression' prompted both Lee and Joe Pillay to advise caution. But the delegates were adamant that, though Narasimha Rao might have been forced to initiate reforms, the process had become irreversible. Goh supported them. Yeo reported that Manmohan Singh, who enjoyed 'almost total freedom to push the deregulation and liberalization process,' told them, 'The [reform] train had left the station.' Foreign Secretary Srinivasan explained that the only way Congress could be sure of re-election was 'success in the economic reforms programme.' Businessmen claimed that output and sales had gone up but they no longer faced prosecution and fines for exceeding quotas. 'All this nonsense had disappeared' the mission reported, and Indian businessmen were busy competing with the world.

India's red-tape was still daunting but 'battling the bureaucracy' took between 10 and 20 per cent of a businessman's time instead of the earlier 50 to 75 per cent. Yeo 'almost got a standing ovation' when he said the role of government was to provide law and order and get out of the way of businessmen. As he told the *Business Times*, businessmen were still 'not convinced that the political go-ahead will be translated down to the bureaucracy'. Apart from making some obvious comments about India not being about to break up and the administrative service being 'strong, confident and cohesive', he noted that even officials had begun to speak the language of business. A presentation by N. Vittal, secretary in the electronics department, was a 'tour de force in candour, clarity and conviction.' The team thought 'the proliferation of satellite discs all around India, including villages, must also be generating a mental revolution.'

Bangalore, India's Silicon Valley, which Karnataka Chief Minister M. Veerappa Moily wanted to be the 'Singapore of India', impressed them 'more than any other city'. They liked its salubrious climate, 'yuppie culture', leading universities and research institutions. The Indian Institute of Science was trying to persuade Indians to return from the United States, and Texas Instruments hoped to increase the number of software engineers it employed from 200 to 500 in the next two years. Yeo suggested direct Bangalore–Singapore air links. Karnataka also produced a surprise in the portly person of Srikanta Datta Narasimharaja Wadiyar, titular Maharajah of Mysore, who served tea in steel cups that were so hot as to burn fingers and lips in his ornate palace hung with portraits and mirrors and festooned with chandeliers.[26]

Ratan Tata flew back from an IBM Asia Pacific board meeting in Singapore to host a breakfast for Yeo. Arjun Singh gave a lunch party in his honour. The prime minister's willingness to receive a foreign minister was a departure from protocol: an informal chat in the garden was even more a 'significant symbolic gesture.' Being a little hard of hearing, Lam asked Mahbubani to take notes of the conversation. He thought Mahbubani also had difficulty with the whispering 'but he took down copiously!'[27] To everyone's surprised amusement, Narasimha Rao left out Mahbubani when shaking hands with the visitors. They assumed he mistook the Sindhi Singaporean for one of his own officials.

Narasimha Rao reiterated his personal commitment to reform, and Manmohan Singh and Pranab Mukherjee promised to visit Singapore for another seminar on investing in India. Yeo and Arjun Singh signed a cultural cooperation MOU. Direct communication links were promised between the EDB and the chief secretaries of Maharashtra, Karnataka and Tamil Nadu, as well as the prime minister's office in New Delhi. India's museums responded enthusiastically to the proposal for joint exhibitions in Singapore. After a renewed commitment to the Madras Corridor, the team visited the proposed site—sleepy little Shollinganallur village fifteen kilometres from Madras airport, where the World Bank would fund the draining and filling of 800 hectares of swampy land. They discussed a fifty-year lease and a circular railway, and received a 'relatively professional briefing on the project' pending a detailed report by a private team of consultants.

Ameer Jumabhoy says Singapore felt like a bride being wooed. But not everything went this bride's way. Lim Boon Heng's proposal to the Karnataka State Electronics Development Corporation to let Singapore manage integrated industrial and residential estates for the international investment community was favourably received in principle, but Bangalore officials maintained that the terms and conditions for land use would have to be discussed separately. Yeo's request for a pair of white tigers, to be returned after mating in Singapore zoo which would keep the cubs, outraged Sanjay Gandhi's combative widow, Maneka. 'How would you like to be put in a cage and have all the animals come and stare at you from outside?' she snapped aggressively. But Yeo thinks Kamal Nath, minister for the environment and forests, did not accede to the request not because of Maneka's shrill intervention, but because 'he wanted a more attractive return.' At a more serious level, Singapore did not get all the Straits Settlements documents it wanted: India would not part with records relating to Malacca and Penang which had merged with Malaysia.

What did the tour achieve? Not a great deal physically. 'Narasimha Rao was unable to respond very enthusiastically or positively, so the

Singaporeans left knowing they had quite of lot of work still to do to move New Delhi. But they were not put off, and were willing to persevere. The high commissioner in India (Lam) and Kishore (Mahbubani) were willing to bet on India and they were to be proved right.'[28] The most significant achievement was intangible. The mission cleared the way for Prime Minister Goh's ceremonial visit eleven months later. It fostered a wider awareness in Singapore of India's business and investment potential and a surprise meeting in Bombay helped to demolish popular myths about Indians being obsessed with protocol and procedure.

A courtesy call on Maharashtra's chief minister, Sudhakarrao Naik, turned into an animated discussion of business propositions. As it showed no sign of abating, Yeo invited the Maharashtrians to continue the talks a couple of hours later at the Taj Hotel, where he was staying. A delegation led by the chief secretary did so, shocking Tiwari who had not expected the state's senior-most bureaucrats to turn up in a hotel at short notice. 'In the old days this would have been unthinkable.' Yeo's conclusion was that, if Narasimha Rao could stay in office and sustain the reforms programme, the powerful vested interest of India's emerging 200 million middle-class consumers would create a political process that would counter the communal tensions that had surfaced with the destruction of a medieval mosque by Hindu militants. 'We took an early bet on India and I think we were justified,' is Yeo's verdict.

Will Singapore's 'Second Wing' Fly?

Deputy High Commissioner Balakrishna Shetty in India's mission in Singapore excitedly telephoned friends after Goh's 1993 National Day Rally speech to ask if they had counted the number of times the prime minister mentioned India. In this first public response to Narasimha Rao's Look East policy announced two years earlier, Goh acknowledged that 'even Indian businessmen who are used to a protected market realize that India must open up and welcome foreign investments in order to progress'. He mentioned collaborating with a major Indian company to set up a software park in Bangalore and promised to take a business delegation to India and 'spark off a mild

"India fever"'. India would be Singapore's 'second wing' and give it 'a strong lift'.

Many who were unaware of Mission India contrasted the speech with Lee's silences and cryptic comments. Goh's caveat, repeating Lee's apprehensions, that India would not take off unless the government succeeded in changing public thinking and getting the bureaucracy to actively promote a free market passed unnoticed: 'The main obstacle to reform in India is the mindset of the people. In other words, the people must create their own wealth; the government can only create the conditions for them.'

Lee knew that Narasimha Rao's minority government might have to make concessions to its allies, and after two earlier short-lived coalitions, no one knew who would take over if Congress was dislodged. Tamil Nadu's Chief Minister J. Jayalalitha was dragging her feet over the Madras Corridor. When a reporter asked in Davos if India was an alternative to China where Singapore businessmen were facing difficulties, Lee retorted, 'India's got even more difficult problems. India's a thicket of rules and regulations and bureaucracy that you have to find your way through.'[29] All difficulties disappeared in China if businessmen touched base with the mayor or party secretary and established a good *guanxi*. 'That is not the case in India.'[30]

Indians read the comment as an unintended compliment to legal proprieties that mattered more than connections but that was not how Singaporeans, concerned only with getting a job done, saw it. 'I remained sceptical,' Lee says candidly. 'I did not express it because I wanted the thing to succeed. So I encouraged Goh Chok Tong. I said, you press on.'[31] With his intimate knowledge of Indian society, Lee told the Second World Entrepreneurs Convention in Hong Kong that Indians might be able to match the ethnic networking that had mobilized capital worldwide to transform China. Indian Singaporeans, especially, could benefit from opportunities elsewhere in the diaspora—'South Africa when that country resolves its political problems'—as India moved towards a free market:

> This is an updated version of the old networking when the Sindhi merchants in Singapore reached out to other Sindhi merchants all over the world, from the South Pacific to India, to Pakistan,

to East Africa, and to Britain, not only to do business, but, more important, to find brides and bridegrooms for their children.[32]

He mentioned India's economic geography, and the appeal of 'select areas... like Bombay or Bangalore, and if the Sikh problem is resolved, then Punjab...' They are the more dynamic areas where opportunities will be better. In these areas, I think growth rates could be sixty to seventy per cent of East Asia growth rates.'[33]

If Lee still doubted the scope and extent of the reforms for which he had waited thirty years, some senior Indian officials also wondered if upstaging Pakistan might not be the Look East policy's prime driving force. They feared that being really focussed on America, South Block did not have a long-term vision of India's Asian role. The Look East policy was not supported by well thought-out strategies, adequate monetary allocation and the deployment of appropriately trained personnel. Less than 8 per cent of the ministry's budget was earmarked for economic affairs, and economists were in short supply among foreign service entrants. Linguistic skills were also limited. While the appointment of a Portuguese speaker to Bangkok exposed the problem of manpower planning, an Indian ambassador who actually spoke Vietnamese was a talking point in Hanoi. Ranjit Gupta, who succeeded Ram in Bangkok, lamented that in contrast China's huge embassies boasted fluent linguists, teams of experts, a comprehensive database and the backing at home of high-powered think tanks. 'India is not well served by her foreign service,' agrees Gopinath Pillai, who also heads the Institute of South Asian Affairs, referring not just to capability but also concept.

Some Indians were equally sceptical about South-east Asia. Singapore was seen as mercenary and Indonesia and Malaysia as unfriendly. The Tengku was long gone and for all that his father had reportedly migrated from Kerala—perhaps because of that— Mahathir Mohamad, who became prime minister in 1981, was never conspicuously friendly, not even after inaugurating, at India's invitation, the India-Asean Eminent Persons Lecture Series in 1996, with a speech on 'India-Asean Partnership in an Era of Globalization'. It was a major blow when Malaysian police rounded up nearly 300 Indian software professionals at dawn one day. 'We were handcuffed and made to kneel or sit in the police station car park and our passports and visas were seized,' said Nagaraju Cheekoti, an IT professional working for WWI Malaysia. 'Some of us were slapped and kicked.'[34] They might have fared worse but for the spirited intervention of Indian High Commissioner Veena Sikri. 'Singapore was our only friend,' says Ram, singling out Jayakumar, who became foreign minister in January 1994, for special compliment.

Gupta found Dixit less than enthusiastic when he called on the foreign secretary with glowing plans for India's role as a full Asean dialogue partner. The foreign secretary drew on his pipe before replying, 'Don't waste your time. It's not about to happen soon!' Eagerness undiminished, Gupta unfolded another suggestion: India should be linked economically to countries fringing the Bay of Bengal in order to develop her neglected north-east (bristling with secessionist movements) and cooperate with a difficult neighbour like Bangladesh under a multilateral umbrella. Dixit again poured cold water on his exuberance with a laconic 'It's an interesting idea!'[35] Attending the first meeting in Bali of the Asean-India joint sectoral cooperation, committee in January 1994, Dixit did, however, argue that 'geographical proximity, cultural affinity and a shared ethos' defined 'a distinct Asian personality' and that the coming together of 'two sub-regions of Asia'—India and Asean—affirmed 'recognition of a common destiny.'

It afforded Gupta considerable satisfaction when both his proposals materialized during his ambassadorship. Echoing the complaint of other diplomats in the field from Tyabji to Tiwari, he says there was no response when he sent New Delhi a detailed letter fleshing out his scheme for a Bay of Bengal economic community. However, Supachai Panitchpakdi, a respected economist who became Thailand's deputy prime minister and director general of the WTO, was enthusiastic, and what eventually became Bimstec (Bay of Bengal Initiative for Multisectoral Technical and Economic Cooperation, embracing Bangladesh, India, Myanmar, Sri Lanka and Thailand) was launched in Bangkok five months before his accreditation ended.³⁶ Gupta could get appointments with top Thai officials at a few hours' notice. 'Half the Cabinet came to my farewell. Only American ambassadors get this kind of send-off.'³⁷

Meanwhile, Singapore's President Ong Teng Cheong, accompanied by Wong Kan Seng, was the guest in November 1993 of Maharaja Gaj Singhji II of Jodhpur, Babji to intimates, who celebrated his fiftieth birthday with a durbar in the Umaid Bhawan Palace. I suggested that the *Straits Times* send a photographer. Jodhpur's Arabian Nights palace would have made an exotic background for the bejewelled maharaja on his throne, and a couple of primly sedate Chinese in dark suits on upright chairs below, but the paper was coy about covering something that the government had not announced. A passing reference to Ong's private visit to India—he called it 'an enriching experience'—made no mention of Jodhpur but focused on Indian trade unionists wishing to learn from their Singapore counterparts.³⁸

'Giant Not Aware of Its Potential'

In January 1994 Goh became the first Singaporean to be chief guest at the mammoth Republic Day parade—the highest honour India bestows on a foreign dignitary. Jayakumar accompanied Goh who spoke at length to the *Hindu* before setting out. 'India is a giant which has not realized its own potential,' he said. Singapore expected to play the facilitator as India integrated her economy with a booming eastern Asia's, sought opportunities in property development, and hoped that at least 25 per cent of the output of its investment in India would be exported. He cited China, which had forced state enterprises to be more competitive by welcoming foreign investors, but tactfully shied away, unlike Lee or Yeo, from a question on Asia's balance of power, and said, 'I would not want to go into this geopolitics of balance. I will just simply say that India is a giant with tremendous potential, and if India realizes its potential, that is going to bring benefits for countries in the region. If you set out to try and encourage India to balance China, you are creating a huge problem when there is not any.'³⁹

However, his plea that India's new weaponry would not cause her neighbours to be 'overly concerned' if she became an economic giant and engaged with them implied that the hegemony fear still lurked somewhere in Goh's mind. But with eager Indian officials wanting 'to turn red tape into a red carpet',[40] there were no uncomfortable moments at a round-table discussion with the Confederation of Indian Industry or at Narasimha Rao's dinner at Hyderabad House. Singaporeans sought new reforms, speedier approvals and more power for state governments as in China. They also demanded a share of the property development pie. Property was becoming an obsessive interest, with the suggestion that India should grant NRI status to Singapore as a country so that it could buy, develop, sell and make a profit being bandied about only half in joke. But visiting Singapore, Najma Heptullah, chairman of India's Rajya Sabha, the upper house of Parliament, dashed hopes by warning that India's constitution would not allow foreigners to dabble in property. 'Real estate is basically a dead-end investment, a speculative business for an individual or a group. There's no benefit for the host country unless, of course, it is accompanied by a building industry in which case employment is generated.'[41] India did finally reduce the size of a plot that Singaporeans could develop from a hundred to twenty acres.

The *Straits Times* warned against excessive expectations from Goh's visit, stressing that Republic Day is an annual affair and that many guests of honour leave no imprint once the dust kicked up by marching soldiers has settled: 'If Prime Minister Goh Chok Tong's presence lent a new dimension to [the] celebrations, it was because the honour bestowed on him symbolizes India's own changing perceptions.' The occasion was meaningful because it was part of an integrated package and not just another ritual.[42] Nevertheless, it was a personal triumph for Goh. Narasimha Rao entertained him in his garden as another mark of friendliness. The official who took notes of the tête-à-tête told Tiwari that Goh 'spoke from his heart'.

Singapore was quick to try to seize on the promise of India. If property was out of bounds, tourism was not. Chandra Das, Mahbubani, every Singaporean who visited India, stressed the importance of open skies. After having to wait ten days for a flight, Mahathir caustically told Gujral at a NAM meeting that India 'wanted an open society with closed skies!'[43] Ron Somers, president of the United States–India Business Council, compared Delhi airport to a 'country bus station at best, after two years of reconstruction.'[44] Goh's Jet Airways flight from Ahmedabad arrived before schedule because of favourable tailwinds, and had to circle for an hour 'for a landing slot after being stacked twenty-second in the approach queue.'[45]

Singapore floated three relevant propositions. With surveys claiming that tourist traffic would treble in five years, the Tourist Promotion Board presented an ingenious airbridge plan for an all-inclusive SIA package direct from Europe or America to relatively small Indian airports serving clusters of sightseeing places. Second, several Singapore companies sought a bite of the new international airport planned for Bangalore when at last India was forced to accept that facilities were inadequate. Finally, the end, in May 1994, of the state-owned Indian Airlines's forty-year monopoly encouraged SIA (with Pillay as chairman) and Tata to set up a company in Mauritius and make a S$846-million bid for a joint venture domestic airline.

All three plans failed like the Madras Corridor (at least in its original incarnation), though Lee Hsien Loong isn't sure whether that was because of high visibility or inherent difficulties. 'We don't need flagship projects,' he says. Though Singaporean businessmen also prefer less publicity (not being part of a national project gives them greater flexibility and room to manoeuvre), they do agree that a special economic zone in India, like, the Suzhou Industrial Park in China or the Vietnam–Singapore Industrial Park in Ho Chi Minh City, would be a useful model for the future. Lee Hsien Loong says his government is still pursuing the idea, but quietly. 'If it gets politicized, then hard positions have to be taken and they can't negotiate.'

That's what happened with the three ambitious schemes. Some Indians fumed that an airbridge would reduce India to a suburb of Singapore. 'If it's Monday, it's Haw Par Villa. If it's Tuesday, it's the Taj Mahal!' Others growled that it was dangerous to allow foreigners to prowl around Bangalore cantonment. Though three prime ministers, Narasimha Rao, Deve Gowda and Gujral, favoured a Tata–SIA airline, it stirred depths of patriotic passion. Yogesh Chandra, secretary in the civil aviation department, hinted darkly at treason. 'Would you like an airline owned by China in your domestic sector? What if there's a war tomorrow?'[46] As a throwaway argument, he added that Indian airports were not equipped to take SIA's wide-bodied aircraft. He was at one with Civil Aviation Minister C.M. Ibrahim who thundered patriotically, 'Nowhere in the world are foreigners allowed to enter the domestic sector!'[47] Carefully choosing his words, Gujral admits that he and Ibrahim 'did not see eye to eye'.[48] Both Yogesh Chandra and Ibrahim supported—or were supported by—Naresh Goyal who had been SIA's Indian GSA and then helped to break IA's monopoly with Jet Airways. Business is like migration: the pioneers seldom want others to follow in their wake.

There is no such episode without the smoke of corruption. But the bigger explanation behind the bureaucrat's conservatism, military nervousness, fears of India's identity being submerged, or a politician's greed, is the suspicion of foreigners that Mukherjee described. Manmohan Singh says there is no need any longer to fight the East India Company, but the shade of the enterprise that came to trade and stayed to rule has not been exorcised.

The exception was the one-stop S$250-million Bangalore Information Technology Park housing international high-tech companies involved in computers, electronics and telecommunications. It is still the relationship's principal showpiece. A Singapore consortium took 40 per cent of equity, the Tatas another 40 per cent, and Karnataka state 20 per cent. Laying the foundation stone two days after the Republic Day parade in New Delhi, Goh announced prophetically, 'If India's reforms stay on course, I am sure that Indian companies which are already household names in the domestic market will soon be well known abroad.'[49]

The EDB's effervescent chairman, Philip Yeo, who identified the fifty-eight acre site eighteen kilometres east of Bangalore city, and was responsible for creating the park, was at hand. Conception to ground-breaking had been covered in a record six months. Philip Yeo got on famously with Ratan Tata on whom he lavishes high praise. Both are engineers. They are the salt of the earth for Yeo who plays down his Harvard MBA while stressing his applied science (industrial engineering) degree from Toronto University. 'Who built Machu Picchu?' he asks, 'Or the Taj Mahal?' Who else but engineers!'[50]

Supervising the industrial park was a trying business for High Commissioner Ong who had to fly down to Bangalore every month so that the project did not grind to a halt—or rather, dry up, water being the main problem at that stage. Chief Minister Veerappa Moily gave way in December 1994 to the Janata Dal's Deve Gowda, and when Deve Gowda became prime minister in 1996, J.H. Patel, also of the Janata Dal, took over. Since all the clients had to draw water from the same reservoir, no one was assured of a regular supply. Ong had no end of a problem with Patel's Cox and Box jugglery: 'The only way was to go and work on him, and then his officials would make sure our pipeline was open. If we turned our face and went back to New Delhi the pipeline to the Singapore park was closed and opened to another consumer! That's how he worked. There was great juggling on Mr Patel's part.'

Patel's secretary was helpful. The chief minister was coming to New Delhi, he told Ong on one critical occasion, and made an appointment for the next morning.

> So at nine o'clock sharp I went to Karnataka House and Patel's secretary took me to the chief minister's private room. The guy had just woken up, I could see him sitting by his bed. I think he probably had a couple of drinks the night before because he still had very bloodshot eyes. There was a big sitting room where the private secretary asked me to sit, and the bed was at the end of the room. I guess he met his own people there.

An embarrassed Ong—the Chinese respect privacy unlike Indians—sat down near the door but Patel waved him forward and asked why he had come. Ong explained that the park would have no water unless the last stretch of pipe was laid quickly. Ong goes on to say, 'I do not know whether he was awake or not, but he said, "Where is the paper? Where is the paper?" I gave it to him. He scribbled something and gave it to his secretary who was standing beside him with tea. Then he said, "OK, Excellency, you can go, don't worry about it."'

Ong asked the secretary if he should follow up, write a letter or pay anything, 'but he said, "No, he's already written his instructions and I'll follow up."' Ong again called the secretary who assured him he had telephoned the IT park and been told that the last stretch was being completed. It was a bizarre experience for Ong to conduct official business with a chief minister 'sitting next to the bed in his pyjamas, or whatever you call it, and I in my suit in a chair next to him'.

By the time work was completed, Philip Yeo was convinced—as he keeps repeating in bubbling Singlish—that India's government is her biggest enemy. Manmohan Singh wanted him to build a second park. 'Thank you, Prime Minister,' he laughs, miming the conversation, right hand held to one ear, thumb and little finger sticking out in a typically Singaporean gesture indicating a telephone, 'but not again!' The prime minister despatched, the engineer turns back to me to repeat, 'India's government is the biggest enemy of the Indian people. Businessmen are their best friend!'[51]

Beating China with Asean

Entertaining Asean Secretary-General Ajit Singh, an ethnic Indian from Malaysia, with drinks at home, three days before the Bangkok summit in December 1995, Gupta asked about India's prospects. 'None,' Ajit Singh replied. But the secretary-general, for whom Manmohan Singh professes 'great admiration' and calls 'a great friend of India', had been discreetly working the ground. India was 'a very quiet uncirculated point on the Asean agenda'.[52] Thailand's prime minister, Chuan Leekpai, who passed the baton to Banharn Shilpa-Archa seven months before the decisive meeting, was also very supportive. But it was a surprise when it did happen for Goh had given no warning he would raise the matter at the last session.

> I got a call from Ajit Singh around ten o'clock at night and at once sent the first secretary to the press conference where there was a casual announcement about India having been invited to become a full dialogue partner. No questions were asked. Next morning I rang up the Thai foreign ministry's permanent secretary and asked for an appointment which I was promptly given. I had to wait about twenty-five minutes when the door opened and an extremely angry Chinese ambassador burst out. He had dropped in without an appointment and spent half an hour with the foreign secretary.[53]

When the decision was formally conveyed to him, Gupta 'was specifically told that though Asean countries were quite unhappy about India's past attitude and her policies towards South-east Asia, and disappointed at the tardy pace of substantive interaction and lack of focussed interest even after India was made a sectoral dialogue partner, Asean had nevertheless decided to upgrade India's status in the expectation that India would be more proactive in the future.'[54]

Despite its far more substantive involvement with Asean, to which Lee had drawn attention, China was not accorded full dialogue status until six months later. Gupta says, 'China had conveyed its unhappiness and displeasure to Asean countries in no uncertain terms' about India's promotion.

India did some rather circuitous lobbying of her own the following year to join the ARF. Instructed by New Delhi, Ambassador Naresh Chandra in Washington approached the state department and messaged back six hours later that the United States would not oppose Indian membership. That also took care of strong Japanese reservations. China was privately assured that the word 'Taiwan' would never be uttered. But, once more, it was Goh's initiative that made the difference. The Asean post-ministerial conference in Jakarta in July 1996 was a jovial jamboree with each delegation presenting a skit and a sing-song, and Gujral, external affairs minister in Deve Gowda's United Front coalition, gamely sang a Hindi film song, '*Savan ka mahina*'. Faithful Singapore was India's country coordinator.

Singapore sponsored India, says Jayakumar, because it was no longer productive for Asean to confine itself to only its seven, nine or ten members. 'Singapore felt that for Asean to be a key player, it must play a facilitator role, a catalytic role in engaging the entire region.' Lee sees this as the only way of avoiding domination by a single or even two players. After failing to persuade Indira Gandhi, Singapore thought of an American–Chinese–Japanese triangle until evidence of India's interest and ability to engage changed the picture. Jayakumar does not deny that some members did not like this, but 'strangely, they were not at the leaders' level but at the officials' level'. He recalls Asean officials arguing that bringing in India would mean Pakistan, and meetings would then be bedevilled by wrangling over Kashmir. He is not sure whether this was a genuine concern or an excuse to keep India out. Or, whether officials were proxies for their political masters. As foreign minister, he had not attended the summit meeting where India was accepted. However, Jayakumar recounts meeting Gujral later: 'I once explained to Gujral after he thanked me for Singapore's quiet role behind the scenes in making India a full dialogue partner that I would have been very pessimistic if the process had been from bottom up, with officials making recommendations to foreign ministers, and foreign ministers to heads of governments.'[55]

A combination of political and personal factors, both hinging on China, explains Singapore's sustained commitment. 'We in Southeast Asia have no wish to become an adjunct to China's economy,' says George Yeo sounding like Lee.[56] Leifer indicates a personal angle: 'It was almost certainly to counter any impression of any undue dependence on China that Prime Minister Goh Chok Tong, not known as a fluent Chinese speaker, has encouraged a countervailing economic interest in India with a corresponding search for opportunities expressed in investment.'[57]

Leifer agrees that Suharto decisively supported Goh's initiative because his 'government had long held an apprehensive view of China's regional intentions.'[58] Lee elaborates, 'It's only now with China entering the region that the Indonesians have decided better have India in, too. China is now unstoppable! They can see that. So have the Indians in, besides the Japanese, because the Americans are really not part of the region. One day they will go home.'[59]

Indonesia initially thought 'it could dominate this region' after the Americans left, which explained the protest when Singapore let the United States use its bases for logistics.[60] But Lee feels the team that a shrewd politician like Ali Alatas had left behind worked out that this was not a viable long-term proposition: 'When they discovered they were not going to dominate the area when the Americans left or were displaced, and that it would be China or even Japan, they changed their minds (about India). I mean they calculated not what is going to happen next year but in the next ten, twenty or thirty years.'[61]

That reasoning shaped the East Asia summit when it was launched in December 2005. Abdullah Badawi, who succeeded Mahathir in October 2003, suggested an Asean plus Three—China, Japan and

South Korea—summit in Kuala Lumpur. Chinese Premier Wen Jiabao offered to host the second summit. 'That would move the centre of gravity away from South-east to North-east Asia and make some countries anxious,' Lee says and adds, 'We agreed that we should also invite India, Australia and New Zealand and keep the centre in Asean. India would be a useful balance to China's heft. This is a getting-together of countries that believe their economic and cultural relations will grow over the years. And this will be a restoration of two ancient civilizations: China and India.'[62]

Lee's dream is that Chinese and Indian 'influence will again spread into South-east Asia' as their economies grow. It will mean greater prosperity for the region, 'but could also mean a tussle for power.' Hence, a bigger group right from the beginning in which tensions and rivalries can be subsumed.

> It's not Asians versus Whites. Everybody knows Australia and New Zealand are close to the US. There shouldn't be any concern that this is an anti-American grouping. It's a neater balance.[63]

Mahathir was not amused at China being neutralized. Asean plus Six did not serve his vision of 'a consultative group where people of East Asia can sit around the table and take a common stand on WTO and globalization'. India being Asian was 'fine' he conceded, but Japan was too close to the Americans to represent East Asia's point of view. His real ire was directed at Australia and New Zealand. They offended his 'Caucus without Caucasians' ideal: 'Australia is basically European and it has made clear to the rest of the world that it is the deputy sheriff for America.'[64]

But Vietnam and Japan supported Singapore. So did Indonesia. Eventually. 'It was only when the Indonesians did their calculations that they said yes!'[65] Suharto's successors looked ahead to India holding the balance when the United States turns its back on Asia because its economy cannot afford the cost of international engagement. 'But it may be a different world with global warming. All kinds of things can happen to us then,' says Lee.[66]

Too Much or Too Little Democracy?

No one could have been more gracious than Lee when Narasimha Rao returned Goh's visit in September that year to deliver the Singapore Lecture, the first Indian prime minister to visit Singapore since Indira Gandhi, twenty-six years earlier. Introducing him, Lee reminded listeners that 'the *Economist* wrote in June 1991: "no one believes that his political future will extend very far."' He added his own corrective, 'India is fortunate that this conventional wisdom was wrong. Instead of acting as a stop-gap leader, Prime Minister Rao has launched fundamental changes that can be as lasting as those of Deng Xiaoping's in China'.

A writer in the *Hindu* gushed that Narasimha Rao's 'much acclaimed' speech 'ushered in a new era in India's relations with South-east Asian countries'.[67] The invitation, the circumstances that accounted for it and Narasimha Rao's deportment counted for more than what he actually said. He was the first Indian to be invited since the series had started in 1980 under the auspices of Singapore's Institute of South-east Asian Studies. It was a rare honour, too, for Lee to take the chair, which he did not do for President Kalam, Prime Minister Vajpayee, or international celebrities like Nelson Mandela, Chancellor Gerhard Schroeder or even China's Premier Zhu Rongji. His description of Narasimha Rao as someone who looked both East and West was more apt than he may have known, for the Indian premier was, indeed, looking East to look West. The Asia-Pacific was India's springboard for the 'leap into the global marketplace'.

Narasimha Rao made a point of addressing Goh's sensitivities, quoting American and South-east Asian strategic thinkers as well as the Australian Senate report of 1991 which had all absolved India of any ambition of replacing the United States as the region's principal power. The plea that India did not have the capability did not make him popular in nationalist circles at home but may have been necessary in Goh's less secure Singapore. There was 'no cause whatsoever for the alarmist views propounded about India's alleged expansionist designs, or its blue-water navy', he said, adding that it was difficult 'to conceive of a navy that does not sail in blue waters'. He spoke of 'the magnitude of India's territory; the distance of its island territories from the mainland; its maritime boundaries which are demarcated with those of Asean; and the enormous resource base which has to be protected, whether it be our fisheries, offshore oil and gas or even under-sea mineral deposits in the area we have been allotted in the Indian Ocean, as a pioneer investor recognized under the United Nations Convention on the Law of the Sea.'

Singaporeans were relieved when he quashed reports of Indian businessmen objecting to multinationals. They were not really opposed, he said, they were only trying to nudge him a little. They knew they could also invest overseas and form multinationals 'so the word "multinational" is no longer a bad word'. He could have quoted the foremost of them, eighty-eight-year-old JRD, who denounced critics of liberalization in a stirring *Times of India* article titled 'Berlin Walls Should Fall'. JRD ended dramatically, 'A new tiger has emerged in Asia—a tiger uncaged.'

The polite firmness with which Narasimha Rao despatched Pakistan's high commissioner who stood up to ask a question and plunged into a rambling tirade impressed the gathering. Lee's repeated angry orders to the diplomat to sit down conveyed its own message. When a South Asian put up his hand to ask a question after the high commissioner had been silenced, Lee barked, 'Not another Pakistani, I hope?'

But clouds streaked the horizon when, responding to a question on development and democracy, Narasimha Rao replied, 'I have said often that the remedy for the ills of democracy is more democracy, not less.' The packed Conference Hall burst into spontaneous applause but Lee was not amused. A reply that seemed to smack of tub-thumping populism confirmed that there was little meeting ground between the two old political warhorses. Lee confirmed his displeasure two years later.

{11}

End of One Honeymoon,
Start of Another?

Lee accused Narasimha Rao of 'holding back Manmohan Singh'.[1] The finance minister had told him as much, he said. That was one reason why he visited India in 1996 when the BJP was gaining ground as the Congress government became bogged down in corruption scandals. He went back in 2005 when Manmohan Singh was prime minister, and twice in 2007. Keeping in close touch with Indian affairs all through those years, he was impressed by the spectacular strides India made in IT and space research but continued to regret the drawback of her poor infrastructure. He watched Rajiv Gandhi's son Rahul blossom into a political aspirant, and thought Bombay could match Shanghai as an autonomous growth centre. His regard for Manmohan Singh increased. But Lee is convinced that it was under Atal Behari Vajpayee that India at last forged ahead to provide the alternative that would ensure China did not 'squeeze' Singapore. Less logically, he is also convinced that Vajpayee opposed reform until he went to China.

The BJP was largely to blame for these misunderstandings. Lee found in 1996 that Advani and Vajpayee denied their own economic faith. Capitalizing on the realization that far from wishing away poverty overnight, liberalization entailed considerable hardship, the BJP leaders were accusing Congress of selling out to foreigners. When Manmohan Singh reported similar allegations in happier times, Narasimha Rao had shot back insouciantly, 'Who would want to buy this country anyway?'[2] Now he reacted with panicky gestures like a food grains subsidy which Lee deplored. Reports reached him of Manmohan Singh's unhappiness with his leader, and a worried Goh asked Lee to find out how things were shaping.³ 'I thought Narasimha Rao needed to be encouraged. So I went there,' Lee says.⁴ It was eight years since the last visit which he had made as prime minister.

High Commissioner Prem Singh, who was close to the BJP and toying with the idea of giving up diplomacy to stand for the Lok Sabha, thinks another reason for going was to get a feel of the BJP. Prem Singh's outspokenness about the government he represented riled Indians but Mahbubani thought him 'very active, very pro' because 'he believed in strong relations between India and Singapore'. Prem Singh had not forgotten his stint in Washington when the embassy's appeal for investment did not yield a cent. Nor did he forget the seminar where the George Washington University historian, Richard C. Thornton, invited as keynote speaker on India and Southeast Asia, said, 'I don't know why I am here because India is not a player in South-east Asia.'⁵

Embarrassed when New Delhi rejected Singapore's request for sand from the Andamans, the high commissioner had no answers when Nathan, Goh and Mahbubani asked, like Lee, why India was holding back. Prem Singh was particularly stung at a closed-door meeting in 1997 when George Yeo spoke scathingly of India's shoddy treatment of Singaporean investors, meaning Satpal Khattar, whose Radisson Hotel in New Delhi had brought only a pack of troubles. Bitter about India's 'rules and regulations', Khattar said, 'If there is a possibility of a bureaucrat (in India) saying "No", the answer will be "No".' He added, 'It took fifteen months after the hotel was ready to get a licence to open it! In no other country does one face such hassles.'⁶

There may not have been a licence at all if Prem Singh had not at once sent 'a very strong letter' to N.N. Vohra, Prime Minister Gujral's principal secretary, about the bureaucracy giving India a bad name. He also took Khattar to see Delhi's lieutenant-governor and a host of senior officials. Not everyone has this entrée, and Lee says that despite his urgings, only one Singaporean businessman risks India against five or six who go to China. The Gulf states, new and anxious to please, are also emerging as rivals, 'My secretaries asked Singapore businessmen with investments in India what, apart from infrastructure, they found as major constraints. To a man, they replied it was the bureaucracy.'

Prem Singh recalls the lunch at Hyderabad House where Lee, sitting between the prime minister and Vajpayee, told the latter. 'If your party comes to power, you will also waste four or five years discovering that socialism doesn't work!' Not so, Vajpayee retorted, pointing at Narasimha Rao, 'He has stolen our policies!'[7] Lee called at the BJP's Ashok Road office where he met Advani, Brajesh Mishra and others, five of whom returned his call at the Maurya Sheraton Hotel. There did not seem to be much communication. 'We are not going to learn anything from Lee Kuan Yew,' BJP's Sikandar Bakht bristled, earning Prem Singh's dismissal as 'Mister Know-All'. Lee himself misunderstood Indian opposition politics. He thought Vajpayee and Advani 'unreformed'. Lee says that 'They were not at all convinced that what Manmohan Singh and Narasimha Rao were doing was right. They said—wrong policies, giving away the country on the cheap. So I said, "Oh God! This is back to Square One again!" And I warned Goh Chok Tong. I said, "One step forward, one step back."'[8]

Advani knew Lee had got it wrong. But he could hardly explain that India's electoral style obliges the Opposition to oppose irrespective of substance. Or that the easiest way of demolishing an adversary is to accuse him of being in league with the Foreign Hand. Hindu nationalist circles were fiercely debating the respective merits of *swadesi* (national) and multinationals, and Advani thought it wiser not to commit himself. In any case, the BJP was always more anxious to talk about culture than economics. This provided more meaty fare for the media too. Lee was allowed to draw the wrong conclusion. Looking back, Advani says, 'We strongly opposed the Congress's licence–permit–quota raj. We were against a controlled economy, but we also felt that a fully free economy was not suited to a large country like India with a strong democratic tradition and large areas of poverty.'[9]

Lee addressed two meetings to drum home the message that India would have to open up to keep Nehru's Tryst with Destiny. One was a gathering of the country's most influential businessmen, the other of civil servants and professionals at the IIC. Narasimha Rao suggested the latter so that New Delhi's elite could hear the reforms mantra straight from the horse's mouth and gain a better appreciation of his task.

Speaking 'as a well-wisher of India', Lee argued in his sharply-worded sixteen-page address to businessmen, 'A Tryst with Destiny', that any pause in reforms would mean 'a drift back to the mediocre 4 per cent rate of economic growth.' China had demonstrated foreign direct investments' 'pivotal role in moving innovations around the world,' he said, sweetening the pill by calling India's achievement in software 'nothing less than staggering', commending the pharmaceutical industry's growth and reproving non-resident Indians for investing so little in the motherland. But Indian tariffs and corporate taxes were among Asia's highest and 'national interest was often subservient to special interests'. Lee found the infrastructure appalling: 'I understand that it takes seventy-two hours to move goods from Delhi to Bombay by containers and another thirty hours just to move the containers to the port railway line at Nhava Sheva. To realize India's potential for exports, it must dismantle the myriad of regulatory hurdles.'[10]

No foreign leader discusses the host country's domestic systems so minutely. He blamed self-reliance, preoccupation with fair distribution, economic populism and the public sector. It was ironical that the economy was being strangled in the name of social justice and democracy when both would perish if the economy languished. Far from growth taking toll of social or political development, growth alone could cure social and political ills. As for democracy, Lee reiterated that 'political systems that yield inferior economic performance will ultimately be discarded for those that are more productive'. He ended on a sentimental note, recalling the profound impression of Nehru's promise 'that at the stroke of the midnight hour, India had a Tryst with Destiny'. He urged in conclusion, 'Now is the time for India to keep its Tryst with Destiny.'

He was equally trenchant at the IIC where the theme, 'Survival through Remaining Relevant', allowed him to describe the challenges Singapore had mastered. He took the bull by the horns when an IIC sophisticate commented on Singaporeans' obsession with money. Yes, an unapologetic Lee agreed, it marked the nouveau riche, and many Singaporeans were nouveau riche. 'I would like to believe that in the next twenty-thirty years as we become "old rich", we will acquire the graciousness that comes with a cultivated society.' People who owned two-million dollar homes were naturally obsessed with their wealth because twenty years earlier they lived in hovels with a hole in the ground for a toilet. He added, 'The story of the last thirty years of Singapore is an account of how we improved the administration and made it an effective instrument to plan and execute our policies; how we educated our young in one common language, improved our infrastructure, and increased our economic actitivies in manufacture, services, banking and financial services, telecommunications and tourism.'

The international optimism that Narasimha Rao's reforms had generated five years earlier was ebbing. Companies like Merck had left India, and Lee hoped to motivate Indians by harping on China. But the tactic could go too far, as when, speaking at a dinner in Hong Kong on the eve of the colony's handover, he showered praise on China for its restraint. 'In 1961, China could easily have followed India's example of invading Goa on the perfectly legitimate ground that all such vestiges of colonial rule had outlived their time.'[11] It was comparing apples and oranges. British Hong Kong was a bustling commercial centre under an enlightened administration whereas Goa was a stagnant backwater under police rule. Moreover, Britain had readily discussed the colony's future with China's leaders and agreed as early as 1984 to hand over Hong Kong, as well as the New Territories which it had acquired through treaty and could have retained forever. In contrast, Antonio Oliveira Salazar's dictatorship angrily refused even to talk about Goa to which its only right was that of conquest, a fifteenth-century papal Bull and the fiction that parts of India comprised metropolitan Portugal.

Hoist with the Democratic Petard

Lee expressed his disappointment with Narasimha Rao more bluntly at a dinner with journalists at the Raffles Hotel six months after returning from India. Congress had been defeated at the hustings a month earlier, Vajpayee had been prime minister and gone after only fifteen days in office, and Deve Gowda was prime minister in the first of two ill-assorted coalitions. India was not on the agenda but when someone asked why Singapore 'had not thrown up a credible opposition', he launched into a dissection of Indian, Malay and Chinese psychology. While a poll among the Chinese or the Malays shows the majority on one side and a minority on the other, Indians are always evenly divided. 'Why? I will never know,' Lee chuckled. 'They just love an argument!'[12] This was a decade before Amartya Sen's *The Argumentative Indian,* but Lee's analysis made no allowance for Sen's thesis of a 'simultaneous flourishing of many different convictions and viewpoints' as the basis of the 'heterodoxy and dialogue' that animates Indian life. Lee's India was destructively contrary, 'So that's why it's such a wonderful time in India. You never get a consensus. What you have is more debate. All right. So it's supposed to be good, good for the soul, good for the system!'

He was scathing about the man he had compared to the revered Deng only two years earlier: 'You heard Mr Rao! He was prime minister, I was in the chair in the Conference Hall. He says, 'The failings of democracy, the answer is more democracy.' Well, he's got it now!'[13]

Lee meant that the defeated Narasimha Rao had been forced to quit also as party president and become a political outcast in New Delhi. Lee accused him of not standing up to voters and saying, 'This is going to make you a better India, you will have a better life,' instead of being defensive about liberalization: 'They were selling out India, they were killing Indian industries, causing unemployment, making Indians eat potato chips when what they want is computer chips. That's democracy. And they enjoyed [it]. I'm sure it was an enjoyable election. But I'm not sure that's what we need in Singapore.'

India was 'going to zig and zag' but would finally have to opt for the free market 'because there's no other route to prosperity'.[14] Twelve years later, Lee explained he was worried by the tentative nature of reforms and the estrangement between Narasimha Rao and Manmohan Singh. Narasimha Rao told him 'he was regretting this whole thing' because 'it wasn't producing results' which Lee blamed on inadequate back-up measures.

> The liberalization, because of your lack of infrastructure, did not bring in investments from manufacturers. So no new jobs were created. And even now you liberalize, you sell state-owned

enterprises but you say you cannot dismiss workers. How the hell are you going to make it profitable? How can you expand and make it productive and begin to employ workers on a different basis?[15]

High Commissioner Lam faced a dilemma when Deve Gowda took over from Vajpayee on 1 June 1996 with Chidambaram, who had left the Congress, in charge of finance. Lam's concern was the three-day Global Indian Entrepreneurs Conference that Lee Hsien Loong would inaugurate later that month. It was planned as a gala occasion, the first of its kind, an expression of Singapore's faith in 'New India', and an early attempt to reserve a slice of the expected economic cake. The Singapore Indian Chamber of Commerce was the official host but the government's entire resources were behind it. Manmohan Singh, slated as the star speaker, backed out when his government fell. Chidambaram, whom Lam approached, said he was too busy preparing his first budget. The high commissioner called twice on the former and the current finance ministers to no avail.

Appealing to Deve Gowda through the foreign office—as protocol demanded—would take time. An informal approach seemed impossible as the entire palace guard had changed and he had no contacts among the Karnataka men Deve Gowda had brought in. But Ng Lang, Lam's enterprising young first secretary, had made a friend in the prime minister's entourage who agreed to smuggle them in among the state governors who were calling on Deve Gowda that day. Lam and Ng went in and met a retired army general turned governor—'not a big burly boastful man like the usual run of generals but small and modest'—who allowed them to go into the prime minister's room before him.

> Deve Gowda was sitting with his bare feet, slippers off, on a table, reading a magazine. He looked up and was very surprised at suddenly seeing two Chinamen in his sitting room, but Ng's friend spoke quickly to him in Karnataka [sic]. I put on a sad face and said my job was on the line. As a good friend of Singapore, he would have to help me. Deve Gowda took pity on me and called Chidambaram. Then he told me in broken English that Chidambaram would go.[16]

Chidambaram was not happy at having his arm twisted. India's chief of protocol telephoned huffily to complain Lam had breached diplomatic propriety.

'So That China Doesn't Squeeze Us'

Gujral replaced Deve Gowda in April 1997, and the following year's election returned the BJP to power with Vajpayee again prime minister. Though he had stopped briefly in Singapore in the early 1990s, it was the impression gained from his first visit in October 1967 that was firmly lodged in Vajpeyee's memory. He couldn't get over his astonishment at the transformation when he paid his first and only official visit as prime minister to Singapore in April 2002. Attending a private dinner at the Shangri-la Hotel, he gazed transfixed through the plate glass walls, murmuring in Hindi, '*Yeh ek chamakar!*' (This is a miracle!) 'It used to be like Calcutta!'[17] Shourie, who accompanied Vajpayee, was equally enthusiastic: 'For India, Singapore is a catalyst. We really must learn their work culture. Every visitor to Singapore sees this.'

He is convinced that India should long ago have followed Lee's economic prescription. Vajpayee seemed to think so too. He delivered the Singapore Lecture, addressed the India–Singapore Business Forum, attended Prime Minister Goh's banquet, gave an interview to Channel NewsAsia and concluded agreements on a biotechnology park, combating terrorism, telecommunications, and leisure and conventions tourism. The most significant achievement was the appointment of a joint study group to report within a year on plans for an ambitious Comprehensive Economic Cooperation Agreement. Equally momentous plans were made for Singapore's defence minister, Teo Chee Hean, to visit India and sign a major framework defence cooperation agreement with his opposite number, George Fernandes. A defence policy dialogue was initiated, with the joint press statement describing the 'consolidation of defence ties as a mutual evolution of their excellent political understanding.'

Lee Hsien Loong says Singapore was 'astonished' not only at the readiness with which Vajpayee welcomed these pioneering measures but also his invitation to Singapore industrialists to invest in special economic zones. India's premier mentioned China in this context: 'What Singapore has done in Pudong outside Shanghai, we want you to replicate, in some places in India, by not just investing in SEZs, but in actually running them.'[18] By Pudong, Vajpayee obviously meant Suzhou, of which more later. Shourie had briefed him on China, Singapore's projects there and the SEZ concept. Actually, India set up SEZs—then called export promotion zones—long before China. The first was in Kandla in Gujarat in 1965. Falta in West Bengal followed. They failed to take off because of high indirect taxes, poor infrastructure and an insatiable but easily satisfied domestic market right at the gates. Though deeply suspicious of China's political intentions, Shourie reckons that India 'fell behind China by fifteen to twenty years' because she 'clutched on to the corpse of socialism.'[19]

China was also causing some concern to Singapore at this time, and Lee had to find another partner. He knew that Singapore had to 'diversify, we can't put all our eggs into China and it is bad for us. We want India to succeed and, anyway, if the Chinese know we have an alternative that will make sure they don't try to squeeze us.'[20]

The US$30-billion Suzhou industrial park, pride of the Sino-Singaporean connection, on which work had started in 1994, was intended to be a self-contained, manufacturing, urban and high-technology centre replicating Singapore's capitalist efficiency in Communist China's industrial heartland. It would also be a model to attract foreign investment, and that's where things went wrong because China created another park nearby, state-owned but with a similar name. To quote Lee, the Chinese were 'using us to get investors in, and when investors came in, they said: "You come to my park, it's cheaper."' The full scandal was exposed three years later when Suzhou's Singaporean CEO said it had lost an annual average of US$23.5 million since 1994 and that losses would reach US$90 million by the end of 2000.[21] But it was already clear in 1996 that China had taken Singapore for a ride. Lee badly needed to offset those losses but wasn't sure after visiting India in 1996 that she could provide either an alternative or the psychological restorative he also needed.

Referring to that visit, he says, 'I met Advani and Vajpayee in India and I said, "Oh dear, this is going to be one step forward, one step back." But I was wrong, because Vajpayee went to China and declared he will look, India will look. That was a very important change of mind.'[22] Lee repeats he 'remained sceptical until Vajpayee changed his mind' after going to China. 'Vajpayee went to China and he came back, and he came here [to Singapore] and made a speech. I knew he had changed . . . And I knew Advani had also changed. I subsequently met Advani here.'[23] When I asked if he was sure that China was the decisive factor in Vajpayee's thinking, Lee immediately replied, 'I am quite sure. Because that was visible demonstration of how liberalization has worked. If it can work for a Communist-run economy, why can't it work for India? You had a mixed economy and you had entrepreneurs, and most of your individual entrepreneurs and individual companies were more successful than any Chinese company.'[24]

This conversation took place at the Istana on 18 December 2006. On 7 January 2008, Lee again claimed at the ISEAS's fortieth anniversary dinner at the Shangri-la Hotel that China had changed Vajpayee who had accused Narasimha Rao of selling the family heirlooms. 'But he went to China thereafter and said, "Full steam ahead!"' Lee repeated this version at another interview at the Istana two days later.

> I remember I met Advani and they were against it (liberalization) until they took office and Vajpayee went to China and then he changed his mind. Then I was convinced, yes, this will change now because two major parties have come to the same conclusion. I was not convinced at the time I published my memoirs in year 2000. I thought there would be a u-turn because it (reforms) had slowed down.[25]

The credit Lee gives to China for India's policy is an extraordinary idée fixe. Discounting the first fifteen-day tenure, Vajpayee became prime minister in March 1998. He went to Singapore in April 2002 and announced or endorsed a slate of radical economic measures that confirmed his commitment to reform. His six-day trip to China—the first since the fiasco of his 1979 visit and also the first by an Indian prime minister in ten years—was fourteen months later, in June 2003, by which time the BJP government was set firmly on course. No announcements followed the China trip. Vajpayee did not go back to China. Nor did he visit Singapore again. The BJP lost power in May 2004, eleven months after the China trip. But Lee remains convinced that the BJP's epiphany was in China, that the party was anti-reform until Vajpayee went there, and that he visited Singapore *after* returning from China.

What matters more than the confusion is Lee's certainty that though attempts will be made to 'camouflage' reforms and execution may remain 'rather inefficient', there will be no serious backsliding: 'It will stay on course this time. Of that I am convinced. Therefore we are telling our investors to go in.'[26]

In some ways more perspicacious than his father, and certainly more *sympathique*, Lee Hsien Loong says that if there isn't the 'same degree of nationwide consensus for reform' in India as in China, it is because the benefits are less apparent. 'If you go to Uttar Pradesh or Bihar, they are in such miserable circumstances that you ask why should I support this when there is nothing in it for me?' It's enough, he says, to drive people back to caste-based politics, oppose the BJP's Sunshine policy and even vote out a reform-driven chief minister like Andhra Pradesh's N. Chandrababu Naidu.

Defence cooperation was discussed during Lee Hsien Loong's second visit to India in 2004 but was not at the top of the agenda. The economy was, because so much had changed since 1992 and Ceca negotiations were almost over. Singapore's prime minister knew that with elections ahead, finalization would take a bit longer. 'The reforms had started and then tailed off and run into a lot of difficulty with the political environment, until the BJP government came in and pursued reforms seriously. By 2004 India was opening up fast. Singapore and India were negotiating an FTA . . .'[27]

What struck him amidst India's myriad problems was that everyone he met was convinced there was no other option but to reform and move forward. Officials as well as businessmen agreed that while the pace might vary, the direction was irreversible. Lee Hsien Loong called on Rajiv Gandhi's widow, Sonia, where he also met Manmohan Singh, then shadow finance minister, and explained Singapore's agenda 'because if they (the Congress Party) came in—which at that time was hardly expected—we would like them to support it too'. Manmohan Singh was 'emphatic and categorical.

He said, "Absolutely we support this. This is not a partisan thing and if we come in, we will be fully behind it too.'"

'China and India Will Shake the World'

Congress did come in—'unexpectedly' says Lee Hsien Loong—but Manmohan Singh's position was anomalous when that happened in May 2004. Lacking a parliamentary majority, the Congress-led twelve-party United Progressive Alliance depended on the votes of about sixty Left Front (Communist) MPs who held the government to ransom by refusing to join the coalition. Also, as Congress Party president and UPA chairman, Sonia Gandhi was the obvious candidate for prime minister. Though she surrendered the position to Manmohan Singh, people regarded her as the power behind his throne. Sonia invited Lee to deliver the thirty-seventh Jawaharlal Nehru Memorial Lecture in New Delhi in November 2005.

The relationship had forged ahead by then and Lee Hsien Loong was back again at the end of June to sign the landmark Ceca. 'This is how countries merge seamlessly' commented one of Manmohan Singh's trusted aides. It was India's first Ceca and Singapore's first with a South Asian country. 'I collected the credit,' Lee Hsien Loong says with typical modesty, 'but, actually, my predecessor did most of the work. He started it and made it happen.'[28] Commerce Minister Kamal Nath also 'pushed very hard' to finalize the agreement: 'Six hundred pages and there is a picture of Kamal Nath bringing us the tome. He did a lot of heavy lifting and has helped to navigate and implement the Ceca commitments since then.'[29]

Lee had been away from India for nine years but India continued to occupy his thoughts. His keynote address at the Lee Kuan Yew School of Public Policy's inaugural conference in April 2005 opened on a dramatic note—'China and India will shake the world'—to trace how China had started with less but overtaken India in creating technological parks, transferring technology and—index of modernity—mobile phone penetration. Though still deploring India's bureaucratic delays, inertia, caste quotas and political pressures, Lee recognized the superiority of her private sector with 'world-class' companies like Tata Consultancy Services, Infosys and Wipro. He mentioned another asset that he had not always regarded as such—'India's system of democracy and rule of law gives it a long-term advantage over China, although in the early phases China has the advantage of faster implementation of its reforms.'

His analysis of Sino-Indian relations also held a new element. He still expected India to balance China's rapidly growing weight in Asia, and still looked in the longer term for a replication of the fusion that gave Indochina its name. But he also now expected the two giants to learn from and cooperate with each other. Chinese participants at the school's inaugural conference agreed. Professor Zhang Xiaoji of the department of foreign economic relations under China's State Council disputed Lee's claim that homogeneity gives China an advantage: 'India is very good at preserving the diversity of its cultures. Some people may argue that diversity can lead to low efficiency, but I believe it means dynamism and the blossoming of a lot of good ideas.'[30]

Xu Xin from Harvard's Olin Institute of Strategic Studies referred to 'China's attempts at mimicking India's IT successes' to argue it 'is already beginning to learn from India.'[31] It was left to Roderick MacFarquhar, a British academic familiar with both countries, to make the most telling comparison.

> One important thing China can learn from India is how to have a plural political environment with the exercise of democratic rights without destabilizing the country. China is obsessed with stability. Rightly so. India has, by some Chinese definitions, seemed to be very unstable. But it survives. I think the Chinese government is beginning to realize it needs to allow room for views, passions, grievances to be expressed. And India shows the way in which it is possible.[32]

Never before had India shone so brightly in discourses involving China with no hint of Tregonning's comment on the Chinese superiority complex. Lee extolled India's role in shifting the focus of attention from the Atlantic to the Pacific Ocean. He told the German magazine, *Der Spiegel*, that only India's infrastructure lagged behind China's, ' But I think they will join in the race, build roads, bridges, airports, container ports, and they'll become a manufacturing hub. Raw materials go in, finished goods go out.'[33] There may be an element of wishful thinking in the rosy picture he painted of an inevitable but peaceful transfer of the centre of gravity from the West, with the Chinese 'not asking for a military contest for power, but for economic competition.' China might confront the United States, which India 'will not even think of'.[34] But Sino-American or Sino-Indian rivalry need not mean hostility.

> The Chinese have spent a lot of energy and time to make sure that their periphery is friendly to them. So, they settled with Russia, they have settled with India [sic]. They're going to have a free trade agreement with India—they're learning from each other.

He stopped at Dubai on his way to India in 2005 to deliver a Citibank Legacies of Leadership lecture. The Middle East transformation was 'spectacular' and he didn't mind waiting for nearly thirty minutes because the sheikh he was seeing was busy with Richard Branson. But members of his entourage told Leslie Koh of the *Straits Times* who was covering the tour that it would never have happened in India where Lee was held in high esteem. He took the opportunity also to speak to 500 expatriate Indian professionals. He told them, 'You, more than anybody else, can be the catalyst for change in India. You know the country, you grew up there . . . you know the outside world, you've got links in America, in Europe, Australia, New Zealand, Japan, and soon China, the Middle East. What better input to get India growing?'[35]

Why was India not moving faster when she had the talent, he asked rhetorically. His audience also wanted to know what was holding India back. What advice would he give Manmohan Singh in New Delhi? How did he see India and China growing in the future? With a few hours left for his Emirates flight to Hyderabad, dubbed Cyberabad, Lee reiterated that India should liberalize her banking and retail sectors to weed out weak over-protected operators: 'With so many Indians in multinational banks across the globe, what are Indians afraid of? Bring them back, they know how to run a big bank. Without the competition, Indian banks will always be sub-par. You cannot play in the US Open, whether it's golf or tennis, if you're always playing by yourself in your own class.'[36]

Indians abroad were soaring to great heights, especially in banking and finance. Yashwant Sinha, who succeeded Jaswant Singh as the BJP government's external affairs minister in 2002, pointed out in Melbourne that 'a thousand Indian professionals' had saved 'the giant Long Term Credit Bank of Japan' from collapse at an implementation cost that was 90 per cent lower than estimated: 'The Indian company provided a complete solution, reorganizing the bank's functions around a fresh business model based on their knowledge of financial markets, of new financial products, of modern commercial banking and accountancy, and of the complicated software and hardware to go with the new functions.'[37]

Lee's point was: would they be able to repeat the feat in India? He was not a disinterested observer. After nearly two years of wrangling, the Reserve Bank of India had told DBS it could open eight additional branches in India, providing four were in what Indian officialese called 'underbanked' areas. This was a touchy subject. Ceca allowed Singapore banks to open fifteen Indian branches in the first three years alone and also entitled three Indian banks in Singapore to qualifying for full banking status. Both sides complained of delays in clearing applications.[38] When the RBI did announce its verdict, Lee Hsien Loong said it 'was not exactly in accordance with the letter of the Ceca' but DBS 'accepted' the ruling and would 'take full advantage of' it. The happy state of affairs Rajaratnam had spoken of, when there were no differences because there were no stakes, was over.

Surfing the Future with Jet

After half a day in Hyberabad, much of it spent at Cyber Pearl, a 500,000 square foot technology park developed by Singapore's Ascendas and the Indian infrastructure company L&T Infocity, Lee flew to Bangalore. There, he visited Infosys Technologies, described as India's version of Microsoft, and the Indian Space Research Organization whose unassuming premises, modest budget and relatively small staff of 16,500 people offered little clue to its success in launching thirty-seven satellites (seventeen from India) or the help it gave Germany, Belgium, South Korea and other countries with their space programmes. India's first unmanned lunar spacecraft Chandrayaan I planted a probe on the Moon's surface in December 2008. Lee noted India had a 'large field of talented people' who can devote their lives to space research, and was pleased with the director-general's assurance, in answer to his query, that Isro scientists speak among themselves in English.³⁹

The chaotic thirty-five-kilometre Hosur Road out of Bangalore with its potholes, dusty pavements, untidy construction sites and overladen trucks 'gave way to manicured gardens, well-stocked canteens and dozens of gleaming modern buildings' when they reached Electronics City technology park and Infosys. Koh, the *Straits Times* reporter, knew from Lee's body language, the questions he asked, and the respectful silence in which he listened to replies, that Infosys impressed him profoundly. Seven men had started the company in 1981 with a budget of US$300. Now, with a market capitalization of US$20 billion, Infosys competed with IBM and Accenture. 'I have two heroes,' said founder-chairman N.R. Narayana Murthy, welcoming Lee. 'One is Mahatma Gandhi, and the other is you.'⁴⁰

Lee believed that men like Narayana Murthy could 'transform India' and find jobs for everyone if they multiplied Infosys's culture of excellence. It was back to his lament that good men shun politics. 'When will we have people like you going for elections?' he asked in all seriousness.⁴¹ Back in Singapore, he told a forty-two-year-old businessman, R.K. Misra, who had flown in from Bangalore to seek his advice about giving up his business 'to do something for his country', that Narayana Murthy had laughed at his suggestion: 'He's reached the apex and he's dealt with the government. He knows that this gargantuan bureaucracy moves in a very measured elephantine way . . . so thinking it over it would have been quite a sacrifice for him.'⁴²

If politics was Misra's goal, Lee warned, he should think very carefully about his affiliation and be prepared 'for a very long and rough ride because there's no guarantee that the Congress can win the next election'. Joining the wrong party could mean the wilderness for five years. When Misra said the answer was 'not very encouraging', Lee retorted, 'If I encourage you, you'll hold me to blame.'

His skill at handling informal exchanges was again apparent that quiet Saturday afternoon in Bangalore when he dropped in on 100 young students from China on a seven-month internship with Infosys and drew applause by greeting them in Mandarin before switching to English. He urged them to learn from their Indian hosts as well as countries like the United States. 'China needs to catch up on IT,' he said, reminding the students that Narayana Murthy had acquired his knowledge in the United States which led the world.[43] Koh reported, 'More students needed to come from China to India and the US, Mr Lee added, to learn about this culture of physical and mental openness that encouraged innovation.'[44]

Bangalore had deteriorated since George Yeo was so taken with the yuppie town. Lee found the one-time garden city that some say inspired the original blueprint for Singapore 'dysfunctional'. It was in far worse shape than Hyderabad and not at all a worthy setting for Infosys. Lee was surprised that Karnataka's new government was spending its resources on the countryside (a concomitant of electoral politics that he deplored) when the city needed attention so badly. 'You have one Silicon Valley, build it!' he urged, but was told that neglect would encourage new centres like Pune to open up. It was the price of diversity. His son, too, found Bangalore 'bursting at the seams' without adequate housing, commercial space and infrastructure. 'If you could get developers in, I am sure that the money will flow and the urban fabric will improve,' Lee Hsien Loong says, making another pitch for allowing Singapore into real estate which he calls 'potentially a major interest.'[45]

Like the flight from Hyderabad to Bangalore, the one from Bangalore to New Delhi (where Lee also rode the brand new Metro) provided him with more heartening evidence of 'New India'. Further proof also that Air India cannot stand up to competition. He flew Jet which had broken the Air India/Indian Airlines monopoly on both laps and found it—high praise coming from him—as good as SIA. 'When I went up the aircraft, all the girls were smartly dressed like Singapore Airlines girls and the seat in front of me had that Sunday's *Straits Times*.'

Anyone else would have seen through Jet's little ploy—Jaswant Singh teased him about it—but Lee is convinced he received normal service. 'They can compete with SIA. And why not? They have retired SIA staff working for them, so picking up all the tips on how to do it.' The wheel had turned full circle. But Lee is not sure yet whether Jet's success does reflect the future. 'I don't know,' he says, 'it is very difficult to predict how it will unfold with free enterprise not really given full rein yet'. It would be an altogether different India 'if you allow enterprise to take over'. If he were in charge, he would wind up the red tape and 'give Indian entrepreneurs full rein'.[46]

In New Delhi, he delivered the 2005 Jawaharlal Nehru Memorial Lecture. The first speaker in 1967 was the Nobel Laureate scientist, P.M.S. Blackett; Desmond Tutu and Vladimir Putin have spoken since. Lee's speech was polite, even complimentary, but not one warning was left out. He spoke of the judicial backlog of twenty-six million cases, antiquated labour laws and losses caused by congestion on poor roads. He warned again against using democracy as an excuse for inertia. An official who was present says no one else could have got away with questioning the wisdom of India's founding fathers. Not normally regarded as very forthcoming, Sonia Gandhi spent more than seventy minutes talking to Lee. Maybe it was because of her European birth that she was able afterwards to drag into the open something (Lee's criticism) that Indians only grumbled about in private: 'Lee Kuan Yew has been a friend and well-wisher of India. As a friend, he has also occasionally criticized us, but we have always listened to what he has to say with great, great respect.'[47]

Indirectly, she was chiding all those who accuse Lee of lecturing and compare him unfavourably with Goh. Manmohan Singh was more conventionally complimentary in introducing Lee as 'a visionary statesman, a towering Asian leader . . . who had become a legend in his own lifetime.'

Did the Young Lions Impress?

Lee speaks with circumspection about the bright young hopes of India's political future who were trotted out for his benefit at lunch at the Taj Hotel. A cynic suggests that he cannot but admire someone who is wise enough to seek his approval but no folie de grandeur can impair his judgement. Though he recognized the undoubted popular appeal of these six or seven MPs, he himself valued systems more than personalities, and told a TV interviewer that India needs more than leadership to catch up with China.

Being in his fifties, Marxist MP and politbureau member Sitaram Yechury was odd man out among the highly-connected young sparks, but High Commissioner See Chak Mun insisted on including him. He and Lee discussed the economics of growth with surprisingly little disagreement during a forty-minute tête-à-tête afterwards. Yechury felt but not did not say that Singapore was looking for a buoyant economy to park its surplus funds. Visiting Singapore, he was much taken by a museum depiction of the evolution from communalism to Communism to capitalism.

Rahul Gandhi, heir to the Nehru–Gandhi mantle, alumnus of Doon School (like his father) but also educated in England and America, was the star of the lunch. Harvard-trained Jyotiraditya Scindia, whose engaging father, Madhavrao Scindia, Maharajah of Gwalior, had been talked of as a future prime minister before his private plane crashed, killing him, and twenty-eight-year-old Milind Deora, a Boston-educated MBA and the son of a tycoon who had joined the Cabinet, provided the setting. Being so fresh-faced, Deora, who had been India's youngest MP the previous year, was asked his age as soon as he entered the room. 'He's our youngest!' the Singaporeans exclaimed, pointing to thirty-six-year-old MP, Chong Weng Chiew.

Indira Gandhi may not have thought Singapore relevant to India's needs but Sonia Gandhi obviously did so. The woman who once 'fought like a tigress'[48] to keep her husband out of politics thought exposure to Singapore would further her son's political career. Though unsure how relevant the experience would be to Amethi, Rahul's constituency, Lee invited him to be his guest for a week. They were looking for a different dividend in New Delhi. 'This trip is very crucial. Rahul himself, his mother and others expect a lot from this visit,' a family aide was quoted saying. 'Besides being a learning process, they feel it would make him more confident and capable of taking on tougher assignments.' What assignments? There was no beating about the bush. 'Well, it's not a secret that he is being prepared to be the future prime minister. I do not think the family wants to be secretive about it. He is being prepared for the top job.'[49]

It was a busy week for the blandly handsome young man with the dimpled smile and firm handshake, the burden of destiny weighing upon him betrayed only by the occasional slight facial tic. Rahul and the bright and faithful Kanishka Singh, son of a foreign office veteran, who left the World Bank to be his aide and seems to play the part Natwar Singh did to his father, stayed at the Shangri-la Hotel. They visited the port and airport, colleges, public corporations, an eye centre and even a beauty therapy course. If it was not Foreign Minister Yeo briefing him, it was Education Minister Tharman Shanmugaratnam. They made a special point of explaining that Singapore's Institutes of Technical Education and Technical and Vocational Education and Training might be relevant to India's skilled manpower shortfall.

Setting aside his habitual attire of politically correct white cotton kurta and pyjamas, Rahul donned the Singapore uniform of long-sleeved shirt, tie and dark trousers for a small interactive meeting at the Raffles Hotel that Gopinath Pillai and Kishore Mahbubani organized on behalf of the Institute of South Asian Studies and the Lee Kuan Yew School of Public Policy. The gathering was surprised when he revealed that unlike his father, he was not an accidental entrant into politics. 'I had consciously decided I would go into politics the day my father was assassinated to carry on with the work he was doing.'[50] He was then a month short of twenty-one.

There were discussions with Prime Minister Lee Hsien Loong and, of course, Lee who threw a dinner party at the Istana where the stern old man reportedly let his hair down. Amidst the marvels of Singapore, Lee seems to have dazzled Rahul most. 'I am not the kind of person who minds criticism,' he says. 'If somebody makes sense, I listen.'[51] Lee did. What struck Rahul most forcibly was how flexible—a favourite word—an experienced octogenarian could be. Discussing technology at dinner, Lee made a comment that one of the younger guests—a member of the computer generation, says Rahul—contradicted. Lee thought about it a bit, then completely accepted the young man's point of view. Rahul thinks him a better learner at eighty than many persons of twenty-five because his opinions are based on what works, not dogma. He did not find Lee abrasive in the least; on the contrary, Lee's devotion to precision resembled his father's. Of himself he says, 'I listen. I am not judgemental.'[52] Lee is flexible, so is he.

Rahul repeats 'flexible' in many contexts. He saw the Singapore experience as an opportunity, and despite huge differences of scale—which he stresses—not altogether irrelevant to India. 'You can't have the same kind of control,' he admits, but sees resemblances in Singapore's sensitivities over language which Lee explained in detail, or the impact of Oxford and Cambridge graduates, which Tharman mentioned. 'There's a lot we can learn if we are flexible'.[53] An academic who attended the Raffles session thinks Rahul projected a 'positive' picture of 'the political rookie out to learn.' He was pleasantly unassuming.

Lee took a practical view of the dynastic heir. The 'name recognition of his ancestry' gives Rahul 'an enormous advantage' in the age of television and the Internet but drawing votes is not enough.[54] Neither is 'just looking good'.[55] You can be very bright and able but in a large country like India you also need luck. 'If you're not lucky, you don't end up at the top.'[56] Rahul would have to prove himself. The first thing he and the other young eagles should remember was 'not to promise something they couldn't deliver.' Lee had learnt the hard way by being knocked about by Communists and having nasty conflicts with communalists that credibility is crucial to leadership. Looking beyond the glamour, Lee warned that implementing policy was more difficult than mobilizing support for it. 'To get the policy implemented, you must have a strong administrative machine, an apparatus. In China, they have a very powerful administrative capability.'[57] Rahul should prepare carefully for the future he sought: 'If he is wise, he should not take the lead position until he is fully equipped to understand all parts of the complex and very intricate whole of India. Because his drawing power is very big and can vanish in one term at the helm, he should not take over until he has had enough experience to understand how it all works, and surrounds himself by very able people to run it until then.'[58]

Singapore may have influenced two of Rahul's decisions. First, he slapped a legal notice on *Newsweek* for suggesting he had not completed his studies at Harvard and Cambridge, forcing the magazine to apologize and qualify its earlier statements.[59] Lee and Goh have ruined political opponents through many defamation suits but such litigation is rare in India where slander and snide remarks are part of the political game. Second, though made a party general-secretary in September 2007, Rahul did not join the government the following April when Scindia became a junior minister. Nor after the Congress Party's return to power in 2009 when many well-wishers from Manmohan Singh down tried to persuade him to accept a berth. He holds no ministerial office at present.

Lee turns to the subcontinent's other young hopefuls. Rahul's first cousin, Feroze Varun, son of Sanjay and Maneka Gandhi, is a 'supplementary player' and not a 'contender' since 'he won't be given a chance to take over the BJP' which he has joined. But the real interest is next door, in Pakistan suffering yet another periodic spell of turmoil, with no hope in sight, and an onerous responsibility thrust upon a nineteen-year-old Oxford undergraduate, Bilawal Bhutto Zardari. Lee sympathises with his situation and says, 'I feel very sad for him and Pakistan. How can it change the destiny of Pakistan? It's just clutching at a straw going back to Zulfiqar Ali Bhutto. This is a Pakistan that has become radicalized and has so many madrassahs and all these jihadis! And this young man can't even speak Urdu as fluently as English!'

After listening to snippets of a BBC interview, Lee thought from his accent that 'he could pass off as an Englishman . . . How can he lead Pakistan?' In Pakistan as in India, stable policies and less regulation matter more than individual charisma. You have to put your seat belt on if you do business in India, Lee says, not because policy changes but because the government does. India's bureaucracy and her politics are still the biggest obstacles to growth, but perhaps not for long. He sounds upbeat. 'I believe it's only a matter of time before the bureaucrats get the message . . . They have to get the economy going. You do that by freeing the marketplace.'[60]

He still sees the federal structure as an impediment. 'Each state has its own state system' whereas in China, orders 'run through seamlessly' because of the 'very powerful administrative capability'.' Now that India is growing, the way to accelerate the process is 'for the Centre to go down to the state . . . it will take off faster then.' Only a uniform centralised decision-making and executing process can deliver. Reminded that some states are making progress on their own, he says it will be patchy, a hotch-potch, 'not on a comprehensive scale.' Central planning would allow investments to be moved inland when highly developed coastal provinces underline disparities. 'And every coastal province and city can adopt a city in the interior and support it.'[61]

Lee returned to the comparison in December, telling a business leaders' forum in Hong Kong that by 2050, India and China, 'old civilizations that have survived for millennia', would account for 40 per cent of the world's GDP. The first East Asia Summit prompted a fresh bout of comparisons. Kuala Lumpur was not Messina, where in 1955 European politicians had laid the foundations of today's European Union but some called it 'the first stage of an ever-enlarged series of free trade areas, leading to one big free trade area within ten to fifteen years'. Manmohan Singh spoke of 'the forerunner of an economic community in the region' and 'an arc of advantge and prosperity across Asia' that will lay the foundations 'of an Asian economic community.'[62] It's the 'Asian Way', he says, to avoid confrontation and build trust, confidence and consensus.[63] In his view a coalition of Asean, India, China, Japan and South Korea can compete with the European Union or the North American Free Trade Association.

Lee makes a rare reference in this context to the politics of Sino-Indian relations. The Chinese have accepted the American presence in Asia but 'not quite accepted Japanese supremacy over them'. 'There is [also] India. They know India will come back. We want India to come back.'[64]

India is still a bumpy ride. SIA dropped out of the bidding in 2001 when Air India hoped to recoup its US$70 million debt and raise money for the long overdue upgrading of its fleet of twenty-seven aircraft through partial privatization. Lee felt there was 'too much vested interest' for a slightly diluted ownership to make any difference to Air India's operations. SIA could not 'change the culture, it is too ingrained'. There would be 'too much opposition all down the line, within the company and in the government, in the civil aviation department and ministries, because this is the airline that services them.'[65] Many heads would be broken and life would be miserable. Nathan agrees that buying some equity would be throwing good money after bad.

Four years down the road, Lee was sorry when a wholly-owned subsidiary of the Civil Aviation Authority of Singapore withdrew from a multi-billion-dollar tender to upgrade New Delhi airport. Caas's Indian partner, Bharti Enterprises, believed it could do the job in fifty months and promised to indemnify Caas from penalties should the job take longer. But Caas insisted on a minimum of seventy months. The withdrawal disappointed Singaporeans who wanted a major visible project. Lee's advice was that Singaporeans must learn to take more risks. 'I think if we went upfront and said we think this is a seventy-month job but our partners think it can be done in fifty months with Indian labour working round the clock, well, we could risk it. They're indemnifying us. They would have protected their reputation.' Still, Lee added with a shrug, the case was over. 'We press on, there'll be other projects. This is a very big country.'[66]

'I See India on a Roll'

Lee went to India twice in six weeks in 2007. The first visit was for the JP Morgan International Council conference; the second to attend the Citigroup Asia Pacific Business Leaders Summit. He mingled with the world's great (United States Treasury Secretary Henry Paulson, George Shultz, Henry Kissinger, Time Warner's Richard Parsons and Lloyd Blankfein of Goldman Sachs), talked privately with Manmohan Singh and Sonia Gandhi, and ribbed Advani, four years his junior, on the meditation and vegetarian food that made him look so fit. Watching the top brass of Indian business and industry crowding round Lee at a reception under a marquee in New Delhi's Imperial Hotel, Kissinger murmured, nibbling smoked salmon, 'He does love to hold forth, doesn't he?' Brajesh Mishra and Arun Shourie also had much to say at interactive sessions organized by High Commissioner Eu.

Indians did not bristle any longer at Lee's 'lectures'. Nor did they counter with boasts of what they had achieved. Instead, they flooded him with their own complaints so that it was Lee who rose to India's defence with 'You haven't done too badly!' To the *Straits Times* he said,

'I see India definitely on a roll. I have never seen a bigger J.P. Morgan board than the one assembled this week in New Delhi. It's an Indian season. To use a phrase translated from Latin: "Seize the day."'[67]

India did not have more than five years to restore her infrastructure if she wanted to match China as a global player. 'If you don't, you risk losing out in the global economic sweepstakes.' Investments would come in and India would catch up very fast the moment her infrastructure was in place. 'What India needs is a more liberalized system which allows more international competition. Then they will be able to play to the level of international companies.'

Lee looked out from his twenty-first-floor suite at the Oberoi Hotel at Bombay's Nariman Point on the Indian offices of several global banks in one of the world's most highly priced locations where the TDB once had its office. But prosperity has its pitfalls. Maharashtra's chief minister, Vilasrao Deshmukh, told him that 300 migrant families move to Bombay every day in search of a livelihood, and Mayor Shubha Raul complained that thanks to archaic tenancy laws, it can take twenty years to acquire a piece of land for a public purpose. Struggling with a creaking infrastructure, squatters and bulging numbers, Bombay's leaders sought his advice. Lee thought Singapore's national development ministry which had sent experts to China and the Gulf might be able to help though numbers made Bombay a mind-boggling challenge: 'We were asked to look at Shanghai. We said no and chose to go to Suzhou because that was more manageable. You have sixteen million people!'

Lee had a taste of the power of India's poor when several thousand villagers marched on New Delhi to object to land being acquired for industrial use. The answer lies, he explained, in ensuring that the benefits of growth are seen to percolate down to the poorest sections. One 'solvent to soften feelings' is for industry to share profits by opening schools and hospitals, as American, German and Japanese companies do routinely.[68] He also underlined the importance of basic requirements like uninterrupted power, assured Internet access, First World banking, financial and transport systems, and—above all—a minimum traffic speed even at peak hours. His listeners knew what Lee was talking about. Many had taken the precaution of starting out more than an hour earlier for the lunch meeting. They knew it can take two hours to reach the airport during peak hours. Otherwise, Lee thought, Bombay, which contributes 40 per cent of India's income tax, has the potential to develop into a future New York, a suitable commercial capital for a nation that produces more than US$1 trillion in goods and services, but needs to ensure connectivity in all respects, from easy access to the airport to modern, fail-safe communication. Bombay could be a self-governing enclave like Shanghai whose mayor has the same powers as the provincial governor of Jiangsu, he said, recalling his earlier comparison of the two cities, 'You could make a case for this separate entity to govern Bombay and share revenue with the rest of the state of Maharashtra as a fair percentage.'

Lee also told Maharashtra's legislators, administrators and top tycoons that Singapore had done away with emblems of rank for cars. He felt that ruling parties whose leaders are recognizable from special number plates, bonnet pennants and red lights tend to lose elections in the capital, and Singapore is its own capital. Calculation apart, there is a puritanical streak in the man who drove his own Mercedes Benz 6566 up to the Istana in 1959 to be sworn in as prime minister. He abhors ostentation for 'Familiarity breeds contempt. So in Singapore no minister goes with the flag and our cars are not specially numbered. We share the trials and tribulations of the populace'.

The high-powered audience 'listened with rapt attention' and applauded fervently. Then they drove away in their chauffeur-driven official cars with distinctive number plates, flags fluttering bravely in the sea breeze, red lights flashing above and, in many cases, sirens also screaming. India is 'incredible' and 'shining' but also in some respects unchanging.

{12}

Shaping the Asian Century

The prince of Denmark was back in *Hamlet,* as Mukherjee might have said, by the time an Afro-American president made history in the White House exactly fifty years after a thirty-six-year-old Lee Kuan Yew, the unknown overseas Chinese prime minister of a self-governing colony, his government threatened by malcontents and his artificial country by hostile neighbours, watched Nehru drive up in an Ambassador to the jurists' conference. India was moving towards her Asian destiny. As the previous chapters have shown, Lee played a not inconsiderable part in the process. Yechury accused India's rulers of aspiring to become America's 'new Pakistan'.[1] Lee helped to awaken in them a realistic awareness of the need to renew India's ancient footprints in Suvarnabhumi. He also convinced Singapore's sceptical Asean partners of how much they had to gain from a modern revival of the old alliance with an India that had reformed her ramshackle politics, restored her bureaucracy, repaired a creaking infrastructure and was set again on the path to becoming a global powerhouse.

'It doesn't make sense for India not to be part of this region,' agrees Lee Hsien Loong as the contours of a new Concert of Asia, in which India, China, Japan and South-east Asia can set aside differences to engage in cooperative exercises, begin faintly to unfold. The life force that determined India's links with the region at least a thousand years before the first European appeared 'is flowing again', exulted George Yeo.[2] India did not let fears of a darkening global recession, the devastation of Islamist guerrilla attacks on Mumbai at the end of November 2008 or Chinese ambivalence over her emergence on the world stage distract her. On the contrary, the phenomenal expansion of Sino-Indian trade was one of the era's success stories. Yashwant Sinha reminded the Institute of Strategic and International Studies in Kuala Lumpur in September 2002 that India's engagement with South-east Asia over two millennia can be divided into three stages.[3] It began as a civilizational connection 'based on maritime interactions, trade, and some intermingling of people leading to a broad synthesis: of language, culture, religion and world view'. India exported thought, ideas and culture but never unleashed armies or promoted any destabilizing ideology. In recent times—and this is the much later second phase Sinha describes—India and Asean 'have worked together in several areas including search and rescue, sea piracy and disaster relief'. They have also started cooperating 'in many other areas, notably terrorism, small arms proliferation and their links with drug-trafficking'. The third and future phase highlights the economic interaction that became Lee's first priority when he realized India could not fill a quasi-imperial military role. Visualizing a wider Asian free trade zone, Sinha returned to Lee's early concern: 'We need to complement our economic exchanges with a more active dialogue on political and security issues at all levels—official as well as non-official.'

For Sinha, the ARF is 'an experiment for fashioning a new, pluralistic, cooperative security order, in tune with the diversity of the Asia-Pacific region, and in consonance with transition from a world characterized by balance of power and competing military alliances'. India's participation in this security dialogue can only contribute to the stability of the wider region.[4] With so many flashpoints in Asia, and China prone to taking provocative unilateral action as in the Paracel and Spratly Islands, the hope is that the ARF might one day operate as an effective damage control mechanism which, too, can benefit from a mature India's experience of statecraft.

If India has come a long way in this half a century, Lee has moved on, as Maharashtra's finance minister, Jayant Patil, told an interactive session in Bombay, 'beyond the domestic confines of Singapore'. He is now the world's Minister Mentor. Lee's persistent courtship of India over the decades was driven by the knowledge that Suvarnabhumi was the creation of Hindu merchants and mariners, not poets and philosophers. He deplored the factors that kept the new generation of merchants and mariners in chains, and welcomed any movement towards realizing the vision that had impelled Nehru to speak of 'economic diplomacy' when he handled foreign affairs in the interim government under Wavell, and set up an economic affairs division in the new external affairs ministry.

The mandarins from the political branch of the ICS, the crème de la crème of British Indian administration, who manned the new ministry may have felt that Nehru's new-fangled notions would legitimize the 'rentiers' and 'Dalda salesmen' whom South Block despised so heartily. Reigning over those pink sandstone halls half a century later, Jaswant Singh found that Indian diplomats had not outgrown the era when Whitehall did all the thinking for India, and foreign policy meant little more than managing subordinate potentates.[5] Another decade went by, and an indignant Kamal Nath witnessed a meeting with the European Union petering out in fifteen minutes because the Indian side held forth on Iraq and Afghanistan while the Europeans wanted to discuss trade and investment.[6] Those South Block officials must have squirmed when Manmohan Singh told the Asia Society's sixteenth Asian Corporate Conference in Bombay on 18 March 2006 that 'India is a vibrant marketplace'.

Lee was so impressed by Nehru's planning because he knew even then that India's capacity to play an active part in Asia depended on her economic muscle. Economics is even more the determinant today, making ties with Singapore uniquely an extension of what happens in India. It fell to Narasimha Rao, the Brahmin who reinterpreted Manu, to restore respectability to Nehru's concept of wealth generation. The philosopher in Nehru declared that 'the objectives of our foreign policy are the preservation of world peace and the enlargement of human freedom', as Yashwant Sinha told India's National Defence College in November 2002. 'Idealism formed the bedrock of Indian foreign policy'. But Nehru also condemned poverty as 'an evil thing which must be fought and stamped out'.[7] His Five-Year Plans and giant projects like the Damodar Valley Corporation modelled on the Tennessee Valley Authority, were geared to this purpose. So were the Indian Institutes of Technology started in the

1950s as a result of the recommendations of Nalini Ranjan Sarkar, an outstanding Calcutta businessman and industrialist, and the Indian Institutes of Management a decade later. Investment in heavy industry that was beyond the capability of any private capitalist was expected to give a fillip to growth and to create jobs. The IITs and IIMs would ensure that suitably trained manpower was available.

The purpose of all this integrated planning was never explained to voters. As a result, dams and factories were worshipped as the 'temples of modern India' (Nehru's phrase) while the public sector was revered as a sacred cow. Thus exalted, both were denuded of practical purpose. They were assessed not by their contribution to national productivity but by the number of people they employed. Trimming state enterprises was not seen as promoting efficiency, but as cutting jobs. Public ventilation in India of Lee Hsien Loong's view that 'the easier it is to sack somebody, the more people will be hired' would provoke riots. Reminiscent of Lee's strictures about Air India, the vast state-owned enterprises were treated as the bureaucracy's fiefdom, vesting a huge army of civil servants, heirs to a distorted ICS legacy, with the formidable power of veto. This perversion of Nehru's philosophy paralleled the story of Marie Stopes, the scientist, feminist and advocate of birth control, distributing strings of beads among Indian women to avoid conception by keeping track of the menstrual cycle. She found on a subsequent visit that the beads were worshipped as a magic talisman against childbirth.

Singapore inherited the same bureaucratic tradition and Fabian state-planning model, says Lee Hsien Loong, but tempered it with rational inputs and emphasized approvals: 'We have, over time, gone for more of a free market, laissez-faire approach, not totally hands off but the default position is "Yes", and as few signatures and approvals are necessary as possible.' As Khattar discovered during his difficulties over the Radisson Hotel, India's default position is 'No'.

Asked how Singaporeans would react if there was no scope for doing business in India, the seemingly other-worldly George Yeo exclaims in astonishment, 'But that is the substance of the relationship! The life blood is economics.'[8] His optimistic conclusion is that the process of people on the move, trading, visiting, working and investing that created Singapore is being replicated with Singapore's cable to Madras, more flights to several Indian towns,

Ceca, India's free trade agreement with Thailand and proposed FTA with Asean which Manmohan Singh pushed through at the end of August 2009 in the teeth of considerable opposition but thereby stealing a march over China whose similar agreement still hangs in the balance. 'The blood is moving. The links are opening up, re-harmonising, and all the meridians are reopening.'[9] Singapore is the constant factor in the equation, India still the Great Uncertain.

Lee's son too shares the paternal caution. Growth might taper off under the pressure of electoral compulsions, xenophobia, terrorist threats or just inertia. Businessmen tell Lee Hsien Loong, 'Well, frankly, nothing has happened and in some instances, even backward steps are being taken'. Indian ministers say they are doing what is politically feasible: Kamal Nath's explanation that reforms are being carried out in a 'calibrated manner' is almost an apology for inaction.[10] Singapore's prime minister sounds like his father as he regrets 'that generally, in the last one or two years, the pace of reforms has slowed down.' They are actually being reversed in telecommunications: 'So, you are not really going as fast as you can. If you could overcome these in a more systematic way, then growth wouldn't be 8 per cent. It may be 10, 12 per cent, what the Chinese have been doing.'[11]

He also fears that India is still 'not actively enough interested' in South-east Asia because of Pakistan and Bangladesh.

There was a flash of hope at the third India-Asean business summit in New Delhi in 2004 when Manmohan Singh approvingly quoted Sinnappa Arasaratnam, author of *Maritime India in the Seventeenth Century*, to recall that India profited from the autonomy enjoyed by littoral states 'with little interference from groups that would not have understood the needs and demands of the predominant activity of commerce'. He argued that 'mutually beneficial business links' between India's coastal states and South-east Asia would lend meaning to the Look East policy and 'eventually give shape to the idea of an Asian Century.'[12] This suggested a major break with the rigidity that had eleven years earlier killed an initiative by Kerala's industries minister, P.K. Kunhalikutty.

Kerala is a state with hoary maritime traditions. Moynihan told a congressional committee that it had supplied teak for King Solomon's palace. Legend has it that when Thomas the Apostle landed at the Roman staging post of Muziris in Kerala to found the world's oldest

Christian church, a Jewish girl played the flute to welcome him. Cochin's Jews claim descent from refugees who fled Nebuchadnezzar's sacking of Jerusalem and founded the world's first Jewish state centuries before Israel was a gleam in Chaim Weizmann's eye. China's Zheng He, the fourteenth-century Muslim eunuch admiral whose treasure ships made several voyages to the Malabar Coast, left behind the giant cantilevered fishing nets (*cheena vale*) that Malayali fishermen still use. Kunhalikutty was not boasting, therefore, when he went to Singapore in November 1993 with a brochure that claimed 'Setting up business in Kerala is an old European custom. Ask Vasco da Gama . . .' After talks with TDB and EDB officials, he announced that Kerala would be the first Indian state to station an official in Singapore 'to woo investors throughout the Asean region.'[13]

New Delhi scotched the plan, feeling Trivandrum was getting above itself. Commercial representation abroad could nurture ambitions of a political nature. Despite Manmohan Singh's assurance, no other Indian state has taken up the lead Kerala was forced to abandon. Yet, international interaction is not always a prerogative of sovereignty. Several Australian and Canadian states have long pursued their individual commercial stars in foreign capitals. Western Australia opened an office in Bombay some years ago. At the the end of 2008, Governor Qin Guangrong of China's Yunnan province visited Calcutta on an aggressive trade and tourism mission directed at West Bengal state but the Kunming–Calcutta link has yet to develop.

'Reform, Perform or Perish,' Says Buddhadeb

The paradox of West Bengal, ruled by Marxists since 1977, but now courting capitalists, intrigues both the Lees. Indonesia's Salim Group, founded by Liem Sioe Liong, the country's 'richest and most influential Chinese businessman',[14] was one target, Ratan Tata, JRD's successor as chairman of the Rs 790-billion Tata Group, the other. Apart from being an honorary citizen of Singapore, Tata is—unusual honour for an Indian—honorary economic adviser to China's Hangzhou city. His other distinctions include being named by *Time* as one of the world's 100 most influential persons and by *Condé Nast Portfolio* as one of the world's Best Business Brains. Lee Hsien Loong was especially impressed when West Bengal's second Marxist chief minister, Buddhadeb Bhattacharjee, told him in Singapore in August 2005 that his motto was, 'Reform, perform or perish'. Memorable words that Lee Hsien Loong hasn't forgotten.

Bhattacharjee failed to persuade populist opposition politicians to let the Salims set up the state's first special economic zone and chemical hub, and Tatas to produce a cheap people's car. But Lee Kuan Yew had anticipated the turnaround in Marxist thinking that Bhattacharjee's efforts signified when he visited India in 2005 and reported that 'all parties, even the Communists, both in Kerala and West Bengal, know they have to go the market route', though 'how they will distribute the benefits is another matter'.[15] He was confident that even if a 'Communist Bengal-type government' came to power in New Delhi, it would 'continue this open economy policy, maybe not as aggressively as the Chinese have done, but in the Indian way because of the constraints of the political parties, coalition politics and the states-versus-the-union equation'. But the process would still move forward. 'I don't see it moving back, at least in the next twenty-five years.'[16]

When he realized that the Left Front was thwarting Manmohan Singh, Lee made an effort to understand the reason by asking Yechury, with whom he has had three meetings, to explain their position. The Marxist leader answered that 'the present phase of globalization is not sustainable'. They would welcome foreign capital providing three conditions were met. First, FDI must augment existing productive capacity. Second, it should upgrade industry technologically. Third, and probably most important for Yechury, it should enlarge employment opportunities.[17] It sounded reasonable enough but Lee was not to know how obstructive on the ground Communist politicians could be. Three of the legislative measures that Left Front MPs thwarted were intended to enhance the voting rights of foreign players in proportion to their stake in private sector banks, raise the cap on foreign equity in insurance firms from 26 to 49 per cent and allow private sector participation in the pension sector. The Left Front also fanned fears of foreigners plundering India's resources, of indigenous skills and entrepreneurial ability being driven to the wall, and of widespread retrenchment. 'They wanted me to behave as their bonded slave,' was Manmohan Singh's anguished cry.[18]

China too, had to overcome contradictions, says Lee Hsien Loong, but can move more decisively partly because the custodians of ideology are also leaders of government and responsible for welfare which ensures a national political consensus. 'So, when you go to the Chinese cities and provinces, even inland, and talk to their leaders, mayors and party secretaries, you'll be amazed how entrepreneurial-minded they are. When the rules are awkward, they find ways around them so as to bring you in.' He speaks with respect of Chandrababu Naidu who 'transformed Hyderabad and would have transformed the state but the rural population voted him out', and expects flexibility from Bhattacharjee whose government allowed Changi Airports International an 18.4 per cent stake in the proposed 'aerotropolis' (airport-city) for the Durgapur industrial hub without public bidding, and sees the project 'as a matter of prestige' for the state.[19]

Bhattacharya also entrusted Calcutta airport's modernization to the Thais after Bangkok's showpiece and tellingly named Suvarnabhumi airport became operational. Like his father's reading of Vajpayee, but with greater justification, the younger Lee attributes Bhattacharya's pragmatism to China's example. He is a mini-Deng Xiaoping. 'He sent his party secretary [Biman Basu] to visit China and said you learn from them. He came back and he is trying to do the right thing in West Bengal, including having a big industrial park.'[20]

Bhattacharya told a Singapore audience that India would have to compete with China, but 'what we have learnt from them (the Chinese) is: don't stick to dogmas, learn the truth from the facts'.[21] When he also said that he 'didn't see the colour of capital', echoing Deng, an Indian newspaper columnist sneered, 'It seems that Buddhadeb is leading Bengal the Chinese way.'[22] Singapore is familiar with revisionist Communists, and the prime minister mentions 'hard-liner' Lim Chin Joo, younger brother of the charismatic Barisan leader, Lim Chin Siong, who spent so many years in jail. After visiting China, Chin Joo 'wrote a very poignant piece' in *Lianhe Zaobao*, Singapore's premier Chinese daily:

> He went there and saw the country. He asked the tour guide, 'What do you learn in university? You learn Marxism-Leninism-

Maoism?' 'Yes, of course. It's a compulsory subject.' So he asked her, 'So, what do you think about Marxism-Leninism-Maoism?' She said, 'The kind you practise in Singapore is the best kind.' So, Lim Chin Joo, the old Communist activist, said, 'I didn't know whether to cry or to laugh.' And Buddhadeb sent his people there to learn what's happening in China and did that in West Bengal. But they have to get that through also nationally which is very hard.

He knows of Bhattacharya's difficulties. 'There's no responsibility, they just take a hard line,' he says of the party's central leadership whose cussedness is all the more reprehensible when contrasted with the values and ideals now seeping through government corridors.

Lee Hsien Loong is philosophical about these hitches and accepts that change will vary from state to state. It would be unrealistic to expect every state to carry out decisions made in New Delhi. Even the Cabinet's formal approval of some course doesn't necessarily mean it is executed in full spirit by all the agencies down the line, particularly in banking where the supervisor with discretionary authority always stands on his prerogative. 'What to do? That's the way the society works. It is not just the political system, but also a very diverse country, diverse linguistically, diverse religiously—you've got a big Muslim minority in a Hindu country—and diverse in terms of the circumstances in different states.'

China may not have suffered battles like Nandigram and Singur—where Salim and Tata were foiled—but has known political problems with victims of exploitation not being properly compensated, land grabbers and corrupt officials who abetted them. All old agricultural societies resent land acquisition as unjust and resist it vigorously: 'I imagine that one of the reasons why in India it's a problem is because you have not been able to have a proper way of acquisition and compensation, and people don't see it as fair.'

Again, the contrast with China where Deng said, 'Let some people get rich first and then when they get rich, they will move the whole society and the rest will follow.' It became China's slogan. Lee Hsien Loong thought it a 'remarkable' thing for a Communist to say, 'Let some people get rich first.'[23] It worked.

Two Perceptions of India

There are differences as well as similarities in how the two Lees conceptualize India's Asian role. Whereas Lee senior thought of India as the region's most decisive force, evolving a modern coefficient of the part she once played in Suvarnabhumi, his son's more prosaic perception hinges on contemporary connectivity and formal structures. Lee saw India's regional role as an extension and consequence of Singapore–India ties. His son reverses that order to envisage a bilateral relationship 'within the context of India's relations with Asean and East Asia'. He wants India to be part of South-east Asia together with China, the United States and the European Union. But though the EU is economically (though not strategically) involved, it is too 'distracted with European integration and America and Russia' to be an effective partner. India's more positive interest would strengthen what the younger Lee calls Singapore's 'omni-directional linkages'.

Unlike his father in the 1960s, he does not see India as part of a defensive system. Instead, he describes her as a natural complement to Singapore's relations with China, giving three reasons why Singapore pushed hard at the Vientiane summit (Asean's tenth, in November 2004) for the bigger Asean plus Six grouping. First, including India, Australia and New Zealand 'reflects the actual pattern of cooperation which is developing in Asia'. Second, a more balanced group gives additional force to Asean. 'Our weight would otherwise be a lot smaller'. Third, this configuration cannot become a closed bloc since India has her own interests elsewhere, while Australia and New Zealand have links with America, Britain and Europe. 'I think it's good for India too, to be part of this, because as India looks outwards, one very big scope for expansion for markets and for investments is East Asia, and this is one way you can participate. That is why you wanted to join as an Asean dialogue partner. We thought it was important that you join East Asia too, and so we pushed hard for it.'

Like Lee and Jayakumar, he admits that not all participants were keen on India. Mahathir's Asean plus Three plan 'to keep the white man out' also excluded India. But Abdullah Badawi and his colleagues don't share Mahathir's 'very strong antipathy against Australia and New Zealand'. They may not share Mahathir's complex about India either: 'Some still think we should go with a smaller group because with a smaller group, it's more coherent and easier to make progress. So, now we have both—Asean plus Three and the East Asia Summit.'

It is necessary to inject substance into both, using the smaller organization in areas where fast movement is possible, while ensuring that the bigger group does not stagnate or merely lumber along. It, too, must have substance and make progress. Despite powerful political considerations in some Asean countries ('It has to do with palm oil, the crude version as well as the refined version, and tariff escalations between them'), his goal is an FTA encompassing the entire Asean plus Six. But Lee Hsien Loong recognizes the difficulties of achieving Manmohan Singh's 'Asian economic community' since an FTA even between China and Japan, leave alone China and India, is fraught with difficulties. 'But if we have that as an aspiration and meanwhile work on enhancing trade and trade facilitation, other areas of cooperation, financial services, and there is some interest in energy security, energy cooperation, environmental issues, then we put substance on this skeleton which is already in the right shape and then it will grow.'

Lee Hsien Loong's economic expectations from India are the same as his father's. 'We see India as a big economy,' he says, 'and if it lives up to its potential and develops the same dynamism as China has developed, then it is a tremendous plus for us because we are in Southeast Asia and will feel the radiance the same way.' That's the big picture, the 'vastness of the universe' that Zheng Bijian, whose calligraphy adorns Lee's anteroom, visualized. Lowering his eyes to Zheng's 'intricacies of things', Dr Balaji Sadasivan, Singapore's senior minister of state for foreign affairs, told the Pravasi Bharatiya Divas in January 2008 how each evening when he finished surgery while practising as a doctor in the United States, he would pick up the telephone and dictate the operating notes which an army of transcripters then typed. 'Today,' says Sadasivan, 'the telephone recording is sent electronically to India where it is transcribed and the reports are typed and sent electronically back to the US to be printed. What is more, the English is perfect and even the most complex medical term is spelt correctly—

a testimony to the high standards of English in India and the willingness of the Indian work force to continuously work at improving their skills.'

Another example was of Singapore clinics sending X-ray images to India where they 'are read by radiologists who send a report back within an hour', cutting down time and expense. 'At the same time, it frees our radiologists to concentrate on more complicated procedures like angiograms and MRI- or CT-scan directed interventional procedures.'[24]

This burgeoning connection has added to the consequence of Indian Singaporeans who were previously chary of being heard on the subject. Lee Hsien Loong calls them 'a natural link' with India. Lee, too, now acknowledges the importance of the human connection. 'Over 3000 Indian businesses have set up operations here in the last five years to join the many Indian shops and enterprises that have been here since the nineteenth century when the British brought them. Over 78,000 Indian citizens are permanent residents in Singapore, most of whom are tertiary educated. They have comfortably adjusted to life in Singapore.'[25]

Despite the nuances discussed in earlier chapters, Indians feel more comfortable in Singapore than in many other countries. Shared British institutions and the English language create a sense of familiarity. The imprint of colonial Calcutta has not been wiped out altogether. A growing number of non-Indians—meaning ethnic Chinese—are joining Khattar and Chandra Das to invest in India, says Lee Hsien Loong. 'Our interest is to fly the flag where there is commercial opportunity for our economy, which there is in India.'

Temasek Holdings, an 'Asia investment house' that manages a portfolio of more than US$134 billion, is the leading player.[26] Dhanabalan is chairman but the prime minister's wife, Ho Ching, who runs Temasek as executive director and CEO, amazes Indians by flying in and out of India without ceremony, impervious to the sights, smells and sounds that many foreigners find disturbing. Lee reacts angrily to the suggestion that some Indians might think Temasek is buying too much stock too quickly. 'Do you want us to hold back?' he asks angrily, implying that the objections are not economic but ethnic, and adding tellingly that Indians 'would have been very happy' if the British or Americans had taken up the maximum share option. He may be right. Lee's own yardstick is commercial: 'If the companies we invest in are unhappy that's a different matter. That means we are clashing with their management. But we are leaving that in your hands, right? We are not taking control of the company. We are saying this is my vote of confidence in your government and your management and your economy.'[27]

Singaporeans were disappointed when India lumped Temasek and the Government Investment Corporation, a global investment company set up in 1981 and with a portfolio of 'well above US$100 billion',[28] together as a single entity. But the ruling was reversed so that each can enjoy a foreign corporate investor's full quota. That is as it should be under Ceca, says the prime minister, but distancing his government from his wife's business operations. Opinion differs on whether Ho Ching is influenced by her father-in-law or whether her enterprise shapes her husband's policy. Lee Hsien Loong firmly denies any connection saying, 'No, no, she has her job to do, I have my job to do. We can't short-circuit the process. Temasek operates commercially, their board supervises them. Even the Ministry of Finance, which is the parent ministry and ultimate shareholder, does not get involved in what Temasek does. I think we have to keep it that way.'[29]

However, the government will follow any successful company's lead. 'It has a responsibility to pursue the interest or to foster the interest of Singapore companies, which includes Temasek.' It also has a responsibility not to favour Temasek. 'So, we have to be very careful.'[30] The rules are transparent, transactions are at arm's length. And when Temasek or government-linked companies deal with the government, whether for tenders or contracts, the process has to be especially transparent. He mentions China's Huaneng Group outbidding several Temasek subsidiaries to buy a privatized power company and says, 'We have to operate like that. Sometimes, it's not understood in India that this is how Singapore functions. Frankly, in Singapore, sometimes it's not understood either!'

Ascendas' president and CEO, Chong Siak Ching, is another Ho Ching. Chandra Das calls her 'Miss India'. Other architects and builders are snapping up contracts all over India. The involvement of Sats (Singapore Airport Terminal Services) in airport catering and support services can be guessed only from glimpses of the white vans with the telltale logo wheeling away from runways. PSA's imprint is evident in the container terminals at Tuticorin, Pipvov and Hazira ports, and in Kakinada port's upgrading programme. Gopinath Pillai's Gateway Distripark is the largest private sector provider of port-related logistics and support. Singapore's presence in India is understated but growing.

Lee is understandably gratified. For many years he 'saw no desire to change, to open up the system', and told High Commissioner Jaishankar at their first meeting in 2007 that 'without opening up you cannot progress as fast as you can if you open up'. India's telecom market is the fastest-growing in the world with seven million connections every month only because the government 'did not stifle the development,' says Lee Hsien Loong. Other areas need the same freedom. Financial services can be upgraded to become competitive only if India's prudential concerns are balanced with pragmatic considerations.

'Hallmark of Quality'

Having taken Singapore *From Third World to First*, the title of the second volume of his memoirs, Lee is convinced that his country—'the only former colony to make a success of independence' according to Jagat Mehta—can make a substantial contribution to India's growth. Singapore 'has the highest per capita income in Asia, short of Japan, and the most dissatisfied people,' Lee boasted in 2007.[31] Delighted to find so many ethnic Chinese chief financial officers in the Gulf, he asks with a flash of race pride, 'Why don't they get the British? Or Americans or Europeans? Because we deliver. Because we have integrity. They know we are trustworthy. Our law firms are just. Why? Because they are part of the system.'[32] Singapore carries the hallmark of quality. 'If we do not deliver, we will ruin Singapore's brand name.' He nods, unsurprised, when told that even some Indian building promoters use the Singapore label, not necessarily with justification, to advertise their condominiums and adds, 'The premium that we command today after forty-plus years of effort is not (because of) our size but our standard of construction and our high quality both in executing the project and managing it. And it's not just the government. Our companies have also imbibed that culture because many of them are run by former government servants.'[33]

Foreigners know within fifteen minutes of landing at Changi how efficiently the place is run. 'By the time a passenger gets off the plane, his luggage is cleared.' An Australian journalist told this writer of seeing Lee in shorts and sports shirt at the airport late one night with only a Gurkha guard in attendance, checking and re-checking the time it took a newly-installed conveyor belt to deliver baggage. He was prime minister then, surely the only one in the world to supervise such minutiae. After baggage collection, a passenger gets another impression of Singapore from the orderly taxi queue. He reaches the city in twenty to twenty-five minutes because the traffic system works. Singapore taxis 'can try and take you in a roundabout route if you are a stranger and they think they can put one on you,' Lee admits, 'but they don't con you. They don't tinker with the meter or say there's no meter.' Drivers who try that lose their licence.

'What's our limitation?' Lee answers his own question. 'Size. A market of only four million people. So how much can you do?' Singapore has therefore made the world its oyster. 'We have to, we have no choice.'[34] Some might say that far from being a disadvantage, size is his main asset—Singapore works so smoothly because it's so small. The miracle is that a tiny country with no natural resources and so few people, without historical antecedents or a unifying culture, should become such a powerful economic dynamo. Singapore is the world's most efficient middleman, witness Ceca which Lee Hsien Loong thought 'unimaginable' even in 2002. Largely responsible for India–Singapore trade rising to S$20 billion in 2006, Ceca encourages the world to invest in India through Singapore on the most advantageous terms for all three parties.

Lee credits a mix of luck, pluck, hard work and rational policies like adopting English or linking up with distant developed countries for Singapore's success. Being 'a nation of migrants or sons of migrants drawn from various parts of the British empire' helped because a rootless population does not resist change.[35] 'To understand Singapore, you have to understand it as a people with their backs to the wall,' he explains. The ensuing prosperity has created an altogether new civilization with the means and leisure to sponsor art, music, sports and the sciences. But while Singapore may have arrived, it could all go wrong too easily. 'I say if you aren't careful, you disarrive tomorrow!' He has seen empires rise and fall. One of Singapore's biggest challenges today is to produce a committed leadership with the passion and drive to guide voters who take prosperity for granted.

Singapore must, therefore, continue to integrate its fortunes with established societies whose past and future are for eternity. It 'already has several billion dollars of investments in India,' Lee Hsien Loong says (cumulative investments stand at US$1.6 billion, S$2.3 billion[36]) but this can and should grow with better banking, telecommunications, civil aviation, infrastructure, access to real estate and streamlined laws. 'There have been some improvements in the rules and some going around them, but a lot more could grow,' is Lee Hsien Loong's view. 'If you make your rules more flexible, a lot more investment will come.'

Real estate is still a major interest. 'You need the urban development desperately,' Lee Hsien Loong says. Companies like CapitaLand, Keppel and CitiDev develop commercial and residential properties and operate hotels in China and Vietnam. Tourism's enormous two-way potential has not been tapped either, though more than a million Indians visit Singapore annually. 'With the IRs (integrated resorts with casino and Formula One racing) coming up, even more [Indians] would be interested.' The potential is enormous 'in the opposite direction, too'. He speaks of India's history, culture and scenic attractions. 'If you opened up, if the flights were convenient, if the tourist infrastructure were built, and you have the hotels, tours and the packaging, a lot of people would go.' Air services, which remained static to protect Air India even if it meant discomfort and 'ungodly' hours for passengers, should be improved. Now, many of the travellers from Singapore are ethnic Indians but huge numbers of 'high-class tourists, not just hippies,' would go from other South-east Asian countries and China as well. The Ceca effect in short.

Narayana Murthy told Yeo in 2002 that Singapore might become a major disaster recovery centre for Indian software companies. Five years later Mahendra K. Sanghi, president of India's Associated Chambers of Commerce and Industry, announced that more than

300 Indian IT companies had already set up software development operations in Singapore where about, 1500 Indian companies had bases. 'Every year around 150 new companies set up their operations.'[37] Even Ramachandran, who had assured Indira Gandhi in 1968 that Indian industrialists 'with their fund of technical and technological skill and expertise' would receive 'active assistance and cooperation' from Singapore businessmen, would have been surprised.

Ceca has been reviewed, enhanced and widened but not enough, says Lee Hsien Loong. 'We don't have the Mauritius treatment and, therefore, although we have a double taxation agreement with India, it is meaningless because Singapore investments are going through Mauritius.' (Such investments were estimated in 2002–03 at US$534 million, roughly one-third of the total India received.[38]) Singapore wants the same facility so that every investing company doesn't have to 'go and put a few people in Mauritius and set up a little outfit down there'. It is not the only aspect of doing business in India that irks him, and he narrates what an Indian businessman told him: 'I met an Indian businessman once who told me that India is completely open, it's totally transparent. Then he added, but, of course, you need to know where to go.'

There lies the rub. Whom you know makes all the difference. India opens all doors to those who have the magic contacts. Hindrances remind him of Manmohan Singh's 'very powerful and heartfelt speech' on the sixtieth anniversary of independence, explaining 'how far India still has to go in its reforms and the many urgent things which need to be done'. Lee Hsien Loong felt the oration was too sincere and convincing to have been left to any speech-writing hack. Manmohan Singh confirms this. He wrote the speech himself.[39]

India's sagging infrastructure is another major handicap. As Lee told a Bombay audience, ' You already have rule of law, a supporting cast of architects, accountants and lawyers. What you need is physical infrastructure.'

Japan is looking for investment alternatives to China. Vietnam isn't big enough. India would be the obvious destination but for a critical lack of quality. There has been some improvement with the Jawaharlal Nehru Port Container Terminal near Bombay loading a forty-five-wagon goods train in a record fifteen minutes, and the new Hyderabad and Bangalore airports taking the Airbus A380 so that travellers between Australia and Europe can break journey in India. But despite Gateway's spectacular success, Gopinath Pillai fears India is 'some distance away' from offering world-class facilities. The 'integrated infrastructure' is missing.[40] Former finance minister Chidambaram's promise of a five-year outlay of US$500 billion on cities, ports, roads and airports improved on previous estimates of US$150 billion and US$320 billion. But it's still a promise.

The relationship is now also characterized by second- and third-track linkages like strategic dialogues, joint working groups, joint ministerial committees and mechanisms to share intelligence on terrorism, transnational crime and piracy. Other linkages include a trilateral highway project between India, Myanmar and Thailand, and a commission to restore Cambodia's magnificent twelfth-century Ta Prohm temple (originally known as Rajavihara, Monastery of the King) that Vajpayee called an emblem of the 'common South Asian and South-east Asian heritage'. Many would like the popular 2004 India-Asean car rally (slogan: 'Networking People and Economies') whose sixty cars covered 8000 kilometres in six countries institutionalized as a regular event. George Yeo's fervour for a global university at Nalanda in Bihar's dusty outback underlines the Buddhist heritage that binds India with much of Asia.

This was the theme of two magnificent exhibitions in 2008 highlighting Singapore's role in the eastward spread of Indian culture. Visitors to the 'KaalaChakra' (Wheel of Time) display in Singapore's National Library were greeted with the mural inscription, 'The influence of Indian cross-cultural interactions was the major common factor across early South-east Asia.' The Asian Civilizations Museum's 'On the Nalanda Trail' traced Buddhism's path from India to China and thence to South-east Asia through a lavish display of rare artefacts from all over the world. The organizers complained, though, of the difficulties they faced in persuading Indian museums to lend exhibits despite their earlier enthusiastic support for the arrangement mentioned in Chapter 10. No such problems hampered a three-day conference on early Indian influences in South-east Asia organized by ISEAS at the end of November 2007 to examine past cultural and economic links in terms of future relevance.

When the Ganga and the Mekong Mingle

The Mekong–Ganga project is another such link. Two great Asian rivers inspired Jaswant Singh, for whom India's Look East policy reflects 'a certain historical inevitability', to propose economic cooperation among India, Thailand, Myanmar, Vietnam, Cambodia and Laos. His South-east Asian colleagues welcomed the idea when he mooted it on the sidelines of the Asean dialogue partnership meeting in Bangkok in July 2000, but demurred at his chosen name, Ganga–Mekong Suvarnabhumi cooperation. They wanted the order of rivers changed and had reservations about Suvarnabhumi. Jaswant Singh did not mind. 'Both rivers define civilizations', he says, 'and the Ganga is not diminished by following the Mekong which, I was told, was an *apabhransh*, distortion, of Mahaganga, Great Ganga.' As for Suvarnabhumi, the Laotians claimed it as their coinage (citing Suvannaphong, the so-called Red Prince, which could be another *apabhransh*) but Jaswant Singh sensed 'some simmering historical resentment at Siam's assertive conduct during those "Golden centuries" of the spread of Indian thought'. Thailand's 'self-image of a Suwannaphume (Golden Land, a word derived from Sanskrit)'[41] was a major hurdle. No one mentioned the possibility of any sublimal resistance to Suvarnabhumi's Indian (or Indic) roots.

The renamed Mekong–Ganga project was formalized in Vientiane later that year. Jaswant Singh flew to the inaugural in a special Gulfstream jet from Delhi which encouraged hopes of scheduled flights to South-east Asia from Imphal or Guwahati in India's north-east.[42] It was so long since India had made an appearance in what had once been her backyard that, inevitably, the project prompted allegations of grouping against China which was prominent in the older Greater Mekong Subregion scheme but was not invited to join the new organization. Jaswant Singh explained that the 'initiative was not aimed at China, nor a means of increasing India's power projection'. It was 'an affirmation of historical, cultural and geographical ties.'[43] His Laotian counterpart, Somsavat Lengsavad, added that the plan had no military dimension.[44] Slight though it was, the controversy underlined the sensitivities of any situation concerning India and China.

Given this interaction, it was not surprising when Lee wondered in an article in *Forbes* magazine why 'India's peaceful rise hasn't led to unease' whereas 'China's peaceful rise (has) raised apprehensions'.[45] The question was basically—but not exclusively—aimed at the United States. Though Lee (like George Yeo) had earlier acknowledged that some of Singapore's neighbours were also uneasy about China's growing power, it was the American reaction that bothered him. He was clearly addressing a sophisticated Western audience imbued with liberal political traditions when he asked whether the different response was 'because India is a democracy in which numerous political forces are constantly at work, making for an internal system of checks and balances'. Though the article discussed other possibilities *(were discussed)*, Lee answered himself. 'Most probably, yes—especially as India's governments have tended to be made up of large coalitions of ten to twenty parties.' He did not need to add that the contrary pulls to which coalitions are often subject can militate against decisive action.

It cannot have been an accident that the comparison with China occurred to Lee immediately after his two visits to India in 2007. Despite neither side giving up on the three chunks of disputed territory along the 2600-mile border, there may have been little reason for concern so long as the match was glaringly unequal. But as Lee saw, India was catching up. The high-powered Americans with whom he interacted in New Delhi and Bombay confirmed they shared India's enhanced confidence in herself: 'Two of the largest US banks consider India to be a growth story and are eager to service American and Indian companies. I did not detect any anxiety over India becoming a problem to the present world order.'[46]

The transformation encouraged the fear that India and China might be 'placed in opposing camps, one with the United States and the other against'. It was an understandable apprehension in the light of the June 2005 New Framework for India–US Defence Relationship formalizing a strategy for cooperation between the two militaries, and in defence, industrial and technological relations though Manmohan Singh declared and continued to repeat that there is no question of 'ganging up against any country, least of all China'.

Lee predicted that if confrontation is avoided and India persuaded not to abandon economic reforms, India and China can together regain the 45 to 50 per cent of the global gross domestic product they enjoyed before the West's Industrial Revolution stole a march on Asia. The two giants could then cooperate with Asia's third player— Asean—to strike an equilibrium that guarantees regional stability.

Sonia Gandhi's visit to China with Rahul in October 2007, just after China's seventeenth National Congress installed what Lee called 'a very competent and able team' of experienced leaders, sent a reassuring message. He thought the Chinese and the Indians knew they had much to learn from each other and would assiduously study each other's experiences, try to acquire each other's strong points and spur each other to excel. Lee's 'sense of the Indian position' (he voiced no sense of China's position) was that Manmohan Singh's 'strategic autonomy' meant India would defend her interests with Beijing as well as cooperate with it, depending on the situation. India's non-aligned record also told Lee that however close she moved to the United States, she would not surrender her independent foreign policy: 'Right from independence, India had its own separate policy. It created the Afro-Asian solidarity movement in Bandung, it formed the non-aligned movement to distance itself from the two power blocs. I don't see them being co-opted in one camp or the other. They will have their own camp and will strike common interest deals with one or the other as the case may be.' India could never be an American-camp follower.

He reasoned that even the United States might prefer it if, instead of growing in opposition to China, India provided another Asian pole so that Chinese power is not overwhelming. This has been Singapore's hope since the 1950s, and Lee thinks that this 'itself will bring [a] certain balance and perspective to the policies of each country'. But he also feared at the time that the Left Front would prevent India from achieving its hope of partnership with the United States to facilitate the transfer of higher-end military technology: 'Their civilian nuclear cooperation deal has already been checkmated by Communist parties. It will be a gradual process . . . There is no immediate strategic partnership to encircle China and even when the relationship grows, India will remain an independent player.'

The Communist stranglehold on the government of which Lee spoke was broken on 22 July 2008 when a parliamentary trust vote left Prime Minister Manmohan Singh free to press ahead with the civilian nuclear agreement with the United States and necessary economic reforms. Secretary of State Hilary Clinton's five-day visit to India in July 2009 saw the partnership strengthened further. But Lee is right in supposing that even without formal opposition, the temper of Indian opinion will never allow a government in New Delhi to be as closely allied to the United States as, say, Japan or the Philippines.

Nevertheless, Beijing expressed annoyance during the trilateral (India, United States, Japan) naval exercise off the Japanese coast in April 2007. Then it sent diplomatic memos to all four members of the Quadrilateral Initiative or Quad (the trio plus Australia), inaugurated on the sidelines of the ARF meeting in Manila a month later, seeking an explanation of Malabar '07, the thirteenth in the Indo-American series of naval exercises expanded to include Japan, Australia and Singapore. Chinese Foreign Minister Yang Jiechi conveyed his objections to Mukherjee when the latter broached the question of China's support for India's permanent membership of the Security Council.[47] When Chinese foreign ministry spokesman Qin Gang called on the Quad to be 'open and inclusive' about its actions, Manmohan Singh again announced that he had already told Hu Jintao 'that there's no question of ganging up against China'. The Quad wasn't 'a military alliance.'[48]

In Singapore, Mukherjee reminded a questioner that Manmohan Singh had endorsed Hu's comment that there is space enough for India and China to grow together, emphasizing 'together'. He added that India had adhered to principle even in 1962 when it had pushed, as in 1949, for China to replace Taiwan in the Security Council. But, of course, neither assurances nor Lee's musings would have been called for if scope for tension were not inherent in the situation, and if some European historians did not see the gentler Indian civilization receding as the Chinese surged aggressively forward over the submerged heads of the smaller and weaker peoples in between. Touchy on many points, China may also see in India's rise, no matter how peaceful, some ultimate curtailment of its own soaring ambitions. Chinese obstructiveness in the Nuclear Suppliers Group explained the otherwise unflappable Mukherjee's uncharacteristic testiness:

> We are today faced with a new China. Today's China seeks to further her interests more aggressively than in the past, thanks to the phenomenal increase of her capacities after 30 years of reforms. There are also new sets of challenges which China poses, such as the strategic challenge as China develops its capabilities in outer space; the geopolitical challenge as it reaches out to various parts of the globe in search of raw materials and resources.[49]

Beijing's complaint about an Asian version of Nato was obviously a grotesque exaggeration. Singapore strongly repudiates any suggestion of a watchdog role: its navy 'supports multilateral cooperation and participates in a number of exercises each year with navies from around the world' under the ambit of the Western Pacific Naval Symposium and FPDA. China, India, Australia, Indonesia, Japan, Malaysia, Pakistan, Thailand, Britain and the United States are participants. But Indian hawks may be tempted to see Malabar '07, especially roping in Singapore at the last minute, as one in the eye for China. Though the reason advanced for the exercise was 'looking at issues of common interest' like disaster management, it was not surprising that China saw a naval exercise held not far from the Straits of Malacca through which half of its oil imports pass as a reminder that its growing presence in the Bay of Bengal and the Indian Ocean has not gone unnoticed.

India and Singapore are not alone in rebutting any suggestion of targeting China. In fact, the anxiety of all Quad members to dispel suspicion with propitiatory references to China recalls the Greek practice of calling 'the Furies the Eumenides (the good-humoured ladies) in the hope that they might be flattered into being less furious.'

India's muted misgivings about rapid modernization of the People's Liberation Army (with a strength of two and a half million), military infrastructure build-up in Tibet and deep strategic links in

South Asia, were evident in a defence ministry presentation for the visiting American delegation, led by deputy under-secretary of defence for Asia and Pacific, Richard P. Lawless, during the first India-United States defence joint working group meeting.[50] Describing China's maritime strategy and growing naval expansion in the Indian Ocean, New Delhi's spokesman noted, 'China is rapidly increasing military and maritime links with countries like Myanmar, Bangladesh, Sri Lanka, Maldives, Seychelles, Mauritius and Madagascar.'

Lawless reminded his hosts that China's strategic forces modernization is 'altering the historical nuclear calculus'. He listed the development of DF-31 and DF-31A road-mobile intercontinental ballistic missiles, a new submarine-launched ballistic missile and 'qualitative upgrades' of older systems, and warned that China's anti-satellite weapon test in January 2007 posed a danger to the assets of all space-faring nations, including India. Indian concerns have extended since then to fresh Chinese claims on the Sikkim border, reports of renewed arms transfers to northeast insurgents, aggressive posture on India's Arunachal Pradesh state in violation of an agreement reached in 2005 and a nuclear submarine base in Hainan Island. However, another visit Mukherjee paid to Beijing in June 2008 helped to set at rest fears of the relationship drifting.

The new India's strategic initiatives are as omni-directional as Singapore's, embracing Burma, Thailand, Malaysia and Indonesia. But it says something for Lee's Mission India that the most significant of these partnerships is with Singapore. As Lee Hsien Loong pointed out, there was always some military cooperation like training in mountain warfare and artillery or use of the Integrated Test Range at Chandipur-on-Sea on the Bay of Bengal. But it was not until 9 October 2007 that the defence policy dialogue led to a formal agreement under the overarching 2005 pact and converted ad hoc cooperation into a permanent relationship whose specifics have not been divulged. The Singapore air force sends detachments to India for annual bilateral exercises and for training at the Kalaikunda air force base near Calcutta where upgrading, say the Singaporeans, 'is carried out on a cost-recovery basis.' Some Indians see Kalaikunda evolving into a future Okinawa. The defence relationship finally buries the suspicion

Goh expressed about India, and underlines Singapore's mediatory role in shaping the Asian Century.

Back to a Different Asian Past

When Manmohan Singh went to China in January 2008, the *Straits Times* pointed out that India and China 'have a critical modern role in a region that for millennia has felt their cultural and diplomatic influence'.[51] But Lee warns that future mingling will not be the same as in ancient times because history does not repeat itself exactly. All countries and cultures lose something of their individualism in the melting pot of globalization, and India and China will have to contend now with the impact of modernity and the competing influences of Europe, the United States and Japan. For the first time, too, Southeast Asia is also 'simultaneously influenced by the Christian West and Islam.' The region has the largest number of Muslims in the world, and Islamic society 'is in turbulent flux'. India and China may also have developed individual agendas that demand greater space for manoeuvre. Kesavapany explained to an Indian audience that a New Asia is emerging: 'The *newness* pertains to the fast-developing economies, starting first with Japan, then to the four Tigers, next the four Asean Second Wave (Thailand, Malaysia, Indonesia, Philippines), followed by the Chinese Dragon and the Indian Elephant and the Vietnamese Stallion.'[52]

A popular Hindi film, *Chak de India* (Go for it, India), uses a girls' hockey team as a metaphor for 'New India', a country of bursting ambition and opportunity in which many of the traditional values Lee and George Yeo hold dear are being jettisoned. Singapore's foreign minister ponders on these internal cultural shifts that also have a bearing on the emerging Asia: 'Are the Chinese in Singapore too Chinese or not Chinese enough? Are new Indians resensitising caste divisions among old Indians? What happens if the Malay community in Singapore becomes more Islamic in thought and practice? Are our young getting too Americanized?'[53]

The challenge of these and other changes is especially onerous for Singapore because, as Lee, apprehensive as always about the future, repeats, the city state has always found shelter in the shade of bigger players that underwrite its existence. 'Without the major powers we will not exist. It is the major powers plus the rule of the United Nations, the principles of state sovereignty, that forced Indonesia to give up East Timor. And forced the Vietnamese to quit Cambodia too.'[54]

These very valuable lessons warned the region that nobody could capture Singapore and hold on to it. 'You can hit Singapore, you can occupy us but you will have to leave, because that is the system.'[55]

Neither Japan nor the United States nor China would like it if, for instance, Indonesia occupied the entire region. 'I don't think India would be happy either to have both sides of the Straits of Malacca captured by Indonesians.' And if Singapore sank under the ocean tomorrow, Indonesia would suffer, for it would lose its financial channels, shipping connections and a whole range of efficient services. 'We survived Konfrontasi, but they had to reverse it for their own economic needs.'[56] Singapore's security and survival depend on being forever alert to winds of change. Lee foresaw this a lifetime ago, warning London's Malayan Forum in 1962 after his first official visit to India that Singapore would have to be 'an emerged nation, not an emerging one' by the time South-east Asia regained its poise. Otherwise—and he put it with appealing flippancy for adolescents—Singaporeans would find that 'the Indian boys were better clothed and shod and probably had better girl friends to take to better places.'[57]

That fear of being left behind haunts him still. So does the prospect of conflict. 'The Indian influence came from the west in Burma, Thailand, Laos, Cambodia, Malaysia, Indonesias. In the *Ramayana* classic you can see all the Indonesians dancing, and so on,' he says. 'The Chinese influence came through Vietnam and the city ports, the coastal ports of South-east Asia. The sunken ships with porcelain are testimony of that, way back—600-plus years from Zheng He's time and even beyond.' The nature of the interaction matters. 'I see now that with the revival of these two great powers, the same thrust is coming in again from the east and the west. If India is not here, I think there will be a lack of balance. But I think India will come.'[58] He said, 'Chinese and Indian influence will meet in South-east Asia, and they should meet in a cooperative and a positive competitive mode, not in an adversarial mode. Then all will prosper.'[59] Nehru too first articulated in Singapore the hope that 'free India and free China should work for the good and wear of the world'.

Like an ancient soothsayer, a Merlin of the Orient, Lee peers into the mists of the future to draw on a lifetime's experience to sum up the sweep of history:

> Indian civilization has had a profound influence on the cultures, religions and languages of many countries in Southeast Asia. The Ramayana classics, the vocabulary of many words in the region have come from India, especially Myanmar, Thailand, Cambodia and Indonesia. Buddhism and Hinduism have spread into the region, as seen in the temples at Angkor Wat and Borobudur, and in Bali. As the Indian economy revives and opens up to the globalised world, India's impact on the region and the world will grow. India-Singapore relations date from the days of the British Raj, when Calcutta was the seat of the government of the East India Company which ruled Singapore. India's engagement with the region has been episodic after World War II. Singapore will continue to facilitate India's links with the region. It is in Singapore's and Asean's interest that India succeeds and deepens its engagement with Asean.[60]

As High Commissiner Jaishankar reminded guests at his Republic Day reception in 2008, in India the little red dot is a token of lifelong commitment. Far from being only a stop on the way to the United States, Singapore is now India's gateway to the world. It is also the world's entry point into India. It is where the Concert of Asia is being forged out of the meeting of East and West. Lee's vision is the future Nehru predicted at the Ee Hoe Hean Club way back in 1946.

Notes

Introduction

1. Deep K. Datta-Ray, 'Securing India's Security', *Hindustan Times*, 16 October 2007.
2. Lee Hsien Loong, interview by author, Istana, 18 April 2008.
3. Jayan Jose Thomas, 'India-Singapore Ceca: A Step Towards Asian Integration?', *ISAS Insights*, no. 6, 5 September 2005.
4. Deep K. Datta-Ray, 'Securing India's Security'.
5. President S.R. Nathan, interview by author, Istana, 16 April 2007.
6. *Today*, 20 January 2006.
7. Rajabali Jumabhoy, in the Singapore Legislative Assembly, 10 January 1957.
8. Lee Kuan Yew, Interview IV by author, Istana, 12 March 2007.
9. Interview with Chandrasekhar Dasgupta, New Delhi, 12 June 2007.
10. *Time*, 24 August 1942.
11. Sunanda K. Datta-Ray, 'Chopsticks and Victorian Values', *Time*, 30 March 1998.
12. Loong, interview.
13. Lee Kuan Yew, Interview II by author, Istana, 18 December 2006.
14. See http://www.nerve.in/news:25350027296.
15. Lee Kuan Yew, Interview I by author, Istana, 11 November 2006.
16. Jaswant Singh, Interview by author, New Delhi, 30 May 2007.
17. Atal Behari Vajpayee, 'India's Perspectives on Asean and the Asia Pacific Region', The Annual Singapore Lecture 2002. See http://mea.gov.in/speech/2002/04/09spc05.htm.
18. *Straits Times*, 8 January 2007.
19. http://www.meaindia.nic.in/speech/2007/06/20ss01.htm
20. Public Record Office, Singapore, Ref. WO 203/3994 78314 Political Intelligence.
21. Kamal Nath, *India's Century* (New Delhi: Tata McGraw-Hill, 2008).
22. In *India's Century*, Nath mistakenly attributes the encounter to the non-aligned nations summit six months earlier which Lee refused to attend.

23. K.M. Panikkar, *The Future of South-east Asia: An Indian View* (New York: Macmillan, New York, 1943).
24. *Straits Times*, 1 September 1966.
25. *Straits Times*, 10 June 1995.
26. *Prime Minister's Speeches, Press Conferences, Interviews, Statements, etc.* (Singapore: Prime Minister's Office, 1959–90).
27. K.M. Panikkar, *India and the Indian Ocean: An Essay on the Influence of Sea Power on Indian History* (Bombay: George Allen and Unwin, 1945).
28. Interview with Shunmugam Jayakumar, Ministry of Foreign Affairs, Singapore, 22 June 2007.
29. George Yeo, interview by author, Ministry of Foreign Affairs, Singapore, 13 February 2007.
30. *International Herald Tribune*, 4 July 2001.
31. Lee, Interview I.
32. *Straits Times*, 1 February 1994.
33. *Telegraph*, 30 June 2007.
34. Conversation with Pranab Mukherjee, Ministry of External Affairs, New Delhi, 23 May 2008.
35. K. Kesavapany, *India's Tryst with Asia* (New Delhi: Asian Institute of Transport Development, 2006).
36. Lee Kuan Yew, Interview VII by author, Istana, 9 January 2008.
37. *Straits Times*, 3 March 2005.
38. *Straits Times*, 3 June 1959.
39. Lee Kuan Yew, *The Singapore Story: Memoirs of Lee Kuan Yew* (Singapore: Singapore Press Holdings, 1998).
40. Stan Sesser, *The Lands of Charm and Cruelty: Travels in South-east Asia*, New York: Alfred Knopf, 1993).
41. Nicholas D. Kristoff, 'Big Brother: Lee Kuan Yew tells how he transformed Singapore', *New York Times*, 5 November 2000.
42. Loong, interview.
43. Lee, Interview VII.
44. *Parliamentary Debates*, vol. 29, no. 3, 15 October 1969.
45. Singapore Government Press Statement, MC.MA.15/67(FOR).
46. *Straits Times*, 7 September 1959.
47. Loong, interview.
48. Badr-ud-din Tyabji, *Memoirs of an Egoist: Volume One, 1907–1956* (New Delhi: Roli, 1988).
49. Jaswant Singh, in conversation with the author, New Delhi, 26 May 2008.

Chapter 1: 'MM's Strategy, Goh Chok Tong's Stamina'

1. Alex Josey, letter to Dennis Bloodworth, 2 May 1962. Alex Josey Papers Collection, Courtesy of ISEAS Library, Institute of Southeast Asian Studies, Singapore.
2. Lee, Interview I.
3. Maurice Baker, interview by author, Singapore, 28 March 2007.
4. *Straits Times*, 28 March 2008.
5. Kripa Sridharan, 'Transcending the Region: Singapore's India Policy', in N.N. Vohra ed. *Emerging Asia: Challenges for India and Singapore* (New Delhi: Manohar, 2003).
6. Sridharan, 'Transcending the Region'.
7. K. Natwar Singh, *Profiles and Letters* (New Delhi: Rupa, 2004)
8. B.M. Oza, interview by author, New Delhi, 5 June 2007.
9. Melanie Chew, *Leaders of Singapore* (Singapore: Resource Press, 1996)
10. Tyabji, *Memoirs of an Egoist*.
11. R. Jumabhoy, *Multiracial Singapore* (Singapore: Tak Seng Press, 1970).
12. Sunanda K. Datta-Ray, 'Colombo Awaits Non-alignment', *Observer*, 2 August 1976.
13. Ong Keng Yong, interview by author, Singapore, 13 April 2007.
14. Ong, interview.
15. Baker, interview.
16. S. Dhanabalan, interview by author, Singapore, 19 December 2006
17. Natwar Singh, *Profiles*.
18. Han Fook Kwang, Warren Fernandez and Sumiko Tan, *Lee Kuan Yew: The Man and his Ideas* (Singapore: Singapore Press Holdings, 1998).
19. Lee, Interview I.
20. Lee, Interview IV.
21. Ibid.
22. Ibid.
23. Nathan, interview.
24. Alex Josey, *Lee Kuan Yew: The Struggle for Singapore* (Sydney: Angus & Robertson, 1974).
25. Lee Kuan Yew, Interview V by author, Istana, 21 June 2007.
26. *Legislative Assembly Debates*, vol. 2, no. 2, 5 September 1956.
27. Jaswant Singh, interview.
28. Lee, Interview II.
29. Kwang, Fernandez and Tan, *Lee Kuan Yew*.
30. Toh Chin Chye, *Speeches: A Monthly Collection of Ministerial Speeches*, vol. 2, no.1, Ministry of Culture, Government of Singapore, July 1978.
31. Israel Epstein, *Woman in World History: Soong Ching Ling (Mme. Sun Yat Sen)*, (Beijing: New World Press, 1995).
32. Kwang, Fernandez and Tan, *Lee Kuan Yew*.

33. Lee, Interview II.
34. Maurice Baker, *A Time of Fireflies and Wild Guavas* (Singapore: Times Heritage Library, 1999).
35. Lee, Interview II.
36. Josey, *Asia Pacific Socialism* (London: Snowdon Books, 1973)
37. K.M. Panikkar, *An Autobiography*, trans.K. Krishnamurthy (New Delhi: Oxford University Press, 1977).
38. Russell H. Fifield, *South-east Asia in United States Foreign Policy* (New York: Praeger, 1963).
39. Panikkar, *India and the Indian Ocean*.
40. Lee, Interview I.
41. Lee, Interview IV.
42. Lee, Interview I.
43. Ba Maw, *Breakthrough in Burma: Memoirs of a Revolution, 1939–1946* (New Haven: Yale University Press, 1968).
44. Lee, Interview I.
45. Lee, Interview I.
46. Avtar Singh Bhasin, ed., *India's Foreign Relations—2007, Documents Part II* (New Delhi: Public Diplomacy Division, Ministry of External Affairs and Geetika, 2008).
47. Jagat Mehta attended Leighton Park, a minor British public school, and would have gone to Cambridge but for the outbreak of the Second World War.
48. Jagat Mehta, in conversation with the author, New Delhi, 1 June 2007.
49. J.Y. Pillay, interview by author, Singapore, 13 March 2007.
50. Dhanabalan, interview.
51. Lee, Interview VII.
52. Jaswant Singh, interview.
53. Lee, Interview IV.
54. Maurice Baker in *The Singapore Foreign Service: The First 40 Years* by Gretchen Liu, (Singapore: Editions Didier Millet, 2005).
55. Lee, Interview II.
56. Lee, Interview IV.
57. Tan Siok Sun, *Goh Keng Swee: A Portrait* (Singapore: Editions Didier Millet, Singapore, 2007).
58. *Legislative Assembly Debates*, 29 November 1960.
59. Pamela Mountbatten, *India Remembered: A Personal Account of the Mountbattens During the Transfer of Power* (London: Pavilion; New Delhi: Roli Books, 2007).
60. Loong, interview.
61. *Straits Times*, 16 September 2005.
62. Lee Kuan Yew, 'East-West: the Twain have Met', The Dillingham Lectures 1970, East-West Center, Honolulu, 11 December 1970.
63. *Straits Times*, 14 December 1978.

64. See lky/1978/lky0316.doc.
65. Lee, Interview IV.
66. Lee, Interview IV.
67. *Straits Times*, 7 September 1959.
68. *International Herald Tribune*, 8 January 2003; *Telegraph*, 8 September 2007.
69. Sheikh Moinudeen Chisti Syed Abdul Kadir, Kimma, Kurma and Karma, http://www.malaysia-today.net/2008/content/view/3779/1/.
70. Jeffrey Finestone with Shahril Talib, *The Royal Families of South-east Asia* (Petaling Jaya: Shahidera Sdn. Bhd, 1994).
71. Anthony Spaeth, 'On the Road from Sapporo to Surabaya: A Heritage Denied', *Time*, August 21 2000.
72. Shriniwas Rai, *The Common Heritage: A Survey of Hindi Words in Malay* (Singapore: Malayan Law Journal Pte Ltd, 1987).
73. Jumabhoy, *Multiracial Singapore*.
74. Lee Kuan Yew, Address to students of Canterbury University, Christchurch, New Zealand, 7 February 1967.
75. *Legislative Assembly Debates*, Part I of Third Session, vol. 15, 8 December 1961.
76. Lee, Interview II.
77. Ibid.
78. Ibid.
79. Ibid.
80. *Straits Times*, 13 January 1959.
81. Loong, interview.
82. Lee, Interview I.
83. Ibid.

Chapter 2: Chinatown Spelt 'Singapur'

1. Jan Morris with Simon Winchester, *Stones of Empire: The Buildings of the Raj* (New York: Oxford University Press 1983).
2. Peter Chan Jer Hing, interview by author, Bangkok, 26 April 2007.
3. Singapore Government Press Statement, MC.MA.15/67(FOR).
4. Lee Kuan Yew, Speech at Kampong Sungei Tengah Community Centre, eighth anniversary celebrations, 22 May 1971.
5. *Straits Times*, 24 July 1953.
6. Chew, *Leaders of Singapore*.
7. George L. Peet, *Rickshaw Reporter*, (Petaling Jaya: Eastern Universities Press, 1975).
8. *Telegraph*, Calcutta, 10 April 2004.
9. R.C. Majumdar, H.C. Raychaudhuri, Kalikinkar Datta, *An Advanced History of India* (London: Macmillan, 1960).
10. A.L. Basham, *The Wonder that was India* (Calcutta: Fontana, 1971).

11. Morris with Winchester, *Stones of Empire*.
12. *Singapore, The Encyclopedia* (Singapore: Ministry of Information, Communication and the Arts and Editions Didier Millet, 2006).
13. C.M. Turnbull, *Dateline Singapore: 150 Years of The Straits Times*, (Singapore: Singapore Press Holdings, 1995).
14. Peet, *Rickshaw Reporter*.
15. *Legislative Assembly Debates*, vol. 2, no. 18, 10 January, 1957.
16. United States State Department, *Foreign Relations of the United States, Volume VI, Part: Asia and the Pacific*, (Washington D.C., 1951)
17. *Legislative Assembly Debates*, vol. 2, no. 28, 16 October 1957.
18. Kernail Singh Sandhu and A. Mani, eds., *Indian Communities in South-east Asia* (Singapore: Institute of Southeast Asian Studies, 1993).
19. Lee Khoon Choy, *On the Beat to the Hustings* (Singapore: Times Books, 1988).
20. C.P. Fitzgerald, *The Third China: The Chinese Communists in South-east Asia* (London: F.W. Cheshire, 1965).
21. FitzGerald, *The Third China*.
22. Lee Su Yin, *Rock Solid: The Corporate Career of Tan Chin Tuan* (Singapore: Landmark, 2006).
23. Sunanda K. Datta-Ray, 'World War II Legacies for India', in *Legacies of World War II in South and East Asia*, ed. David Koh Wee Hock (Singapore: Institute of Southeast Asian Studies, 2007).
24. Lee, *Singapore Story*.
25. K.G. Tregonning, 'Tan Cheng Lock: A Malayan Nationalist', *Journal of South-east Asian Studies*, vol. x, no. 1, March 1979.
26. Tregonning, 'Tan Cheng Lock'.
27. *Indian Daily Mail*, 27 May 1937.
28. Jumabhoy, *Multiracial Singapore*.
29. Public Record Office, Ref. WO 203/3994 78314 Political Intelligence.
30. Record Office, Ref. WO 203/3994 78314.
31. Vice-Admiral the Earl Mountbatten of Burma, *Post Surrender Tasks, Section E of the Report to the Combined Chiefs of Staff by the Supreme Allied Commander* (London: HMSO, 1969).
32. Lee, *Singapore Story*.
33. Record Office, Ref. WO 203/3994 78314.
34. Philip Ziegler, ed., *Personal Diary of Admiral The Lord Louis Mountbatten: Supreme Allied Commander, South-east Asia 1943–1946* (London: Collins, 1988).
35. Dorothy Norman, *Nehru: The First Sixty Years* (London: John Day, 1965).
36. Ray Murphy, *Last Viceroy: The Life and Times of Rear-Admiral the Earl Mountbatten of Burma* (London: Jarrolds, 1948).
37. Ziegler, *Personal Diary*.
38. Philip Ziegler, *Mountbatten: The Official Biography* (London: Collins, 1985).
39. Bhasin, *India's Foreign Relations*.

40. Pamela Mountbatten, *India Remembered*.
41. Murphy, *Last Viceroy*.
42. Record Office, Ref. WO 203/3994 78314.
43. Ibid.
44. *Straits Times*, 7 September 1959.
45. Ziegler, *Personal Diary*.
46. Pamela Mountbatten, *India Remembered*.
47. S. Gopal, *Jawaharlal Nehru: A Biography* (Bombay: Oxford University Press, 1976).
48. Pamela Mountbatten, *India Remembered*.
49. Ibid.
50. Lee, *Singapore Story*.
51. F.J. George, *The Singapore Saga* (Singapore: Society of Singapore Writers, 1985).
52. Joan Bieder, *The Jews of Singapore* (Singapore: Suntree, 2007).
53. Yeo Kim Wah, *Political Development in Singapore, 1945–55* (Singapore: Singapore University Press 1973).
54. Yeo, *Political Development*.
55. Anthony Short, *The Communist Insurrection in Malaya, 1948–1960* (London: Frederick Müller, 1975).
56. *Tribune*, Sydney, 14 August 1948.
57. Richard Clutterbuck, *Riot and Revolution in Singapore and Malaya 1945–1963* (London: Faber and Faber, 1973).
58. *Statesman*, 7 May 1949.
59. Sinnappah Arasaratnam, *Indians in Malaysia and Singapore* (London: Oxford University Press, 1970).
60. Yeo, *Political Development*.
61. Ibid.
62. Lee, *Singapore Story*.
63. *Progressive Party Newsletter*, no. 10, December 1952, and no. 17, February 1954.
64. Han, Fernandez and Tan, *Lee Kuan Yew*.
65. Lee, *Singapore Story*.
66. *Indian Daily Mail*, 29 September 29 1947.
67. Arasaratnam, *Indians in Malaysia and Singapore*.
68. Yeo, *Political Development*.
69. Ibid.
70. Godfrey Robert, ed., *Passage of Indians, 1923–2003* (Singapore: Singapore Indian Association, 2003).
71. *Straits Times*, 10 September 2007.
72. Han, Fernandez and Tan, *Lee Kuan Yew*.
73. Salil Tripathi, 'Business: Singapore's feuding Jumabhoys', *Asia Inc*, June 1996
74. Jumabhoy, *Multiracial Singapore*.

75. Ibid.
76. Chan Heng Chee and Obaid ul Haq, *S. Rajaratnam: The Prophetic & The Political* (Singapore: Graham Brash, 1987).
77. *Straits Times*, 30 October 1959.
78. *Straits Times*, 3 November 1959.
79. Part III of First Session, *Parliamentary Debates*, vol. 26, 8 September 1967.
80. Bieder, *Jews of Singapore*.
81. Jean Marshall, personal message to author, 19 March 2008.
82. See lky\1965\lky1008a.doc.
83. *Straits Times*, 9 December 1955.
84. *Straits Times*, 3 December 1955.
85. *Legislative Assembly Debates*, vol. 2, no. 20, 5 March 1957.
86. Ibid.
87. Introduction to *Challenge of Citizenship*, speech by George H. Thomson, director of information, delivered at Singapore Rotary Club, 11 December 1957.
88. Memorandum Paper S.C. (Singapore Citizenship Bill) No. 7, *Report from the Select Committee on the Singapore Citizenship Bill*, Legislative Assembly Sessional Paper no. L.A. 18 of 1957.
89. Peet, *Rickshaw Reporter*.
90. *Legislative Assembly Debates*, vol. 2, no. 2, 5 September 1956.
91. Ibid.
92. *Straits Times*, 1 June 1959.
93. Joyce Chapman Lebra, *Women against the Raj: The Rani of Jhansi Regiment* (Singapore: Institute of Southeast Asian Studies, 2008).
94. K.P. Nayar, 'Passage to China: A New Group of Indians in China Can Improve Sino-Indian Relations', *Telegraph*, 9 January 2008.
95. Lee Geok Boi, *Colony to Nation: Pieces of Singapore History* (Singapore: Ministry of Information and the Arts, 1998).
96. *Statesman*, 20 December 1948.
97. *Statesman*, 7 May 1949.
98. *Statesman*, 20 December 1948.
99. *Statesman*, 7 May 1949.
100. *Statesman*, 20 December 1948.
101. Harry Miller, *Prince and Premier: A Biography of Tunku Abdul Rahman Putra* (London: Harrap, 1959).

Chapter 3: Asia's 'Coca-Cola Governments'

1. Thomas Abraham, interview by author, Tiruvananthapuram, 4 April 2007.
2. *Time*, 24 August 1942.
3. Sarvepalli Gopal, *Jawaharlal Nehru, Volume I: 1889–1957* (Delhi: Oxford University Press, 1986).
4. John Connell, *Auchinleck* (London: Cassell, 1959).

5. K.S. Sandhu, Sharon Siddique, Chandran Jeshurun, Ananda Rajah, Joseph L.H. Tan and Pushpa Thambipillai, *The Asean Reader* (Singapore: Institute of Southeast Asian Studies, 1992).
6. Indonesia India Friendship Association, *India's Participation in the Indonesian Struggle for Independence, 1945–1949* (Jakarta: Indonesia India Friendship Association, 1995)
7. *BusinessWeek*, 3 December 2007.
8. Elpidio Quirino, *The Memoirs of Elpidio Quirino* (Manila: National Historical Institute, 1990).
9. Lee Kuan Yew, *South-east Asia in Turmoil* (Auckland: Auckland University, 1965).
10. Ronald Steel, *Walter Lippmann and the American Century* (London: Bodley Head, 1981).
11. Russell H. Fifield, 'The Concept of Southeast Asia: Origins, Development, and Evaluation', *South-East Asian Spectrum*, vol. 4, no. 11, October 1975, pp. 42–51.
12. Prince Norodom Sihanouk with Bernard Krisher, *Charisma and Leadership: The Human Side of Great Leaders of the Twentieth Century* (Tokyo: Yohan, 1990).
13. *Hindustan Times*, 21 July 1954.
14. Han Suyin, *Eldest Son, Zhou Enlai and the Making of Modern China, 1898–1976* (London: Jonathan Cape, 1994).
15. Maharaj Krishna Rasgotra, in conversation with the author, New Delhi, 11 October 2007.
16. Sarvepalli Gopal, *Jawaharlal Nehru: A Biography, Volume II: 1947–1956* (New Delhi: Oxford University Press, 1979).
17. Tyabji, *Memoirs of an Egoist*.
18. J.N. Dixit, *Makers of India's Foreign Policy: Raja Ram Mohun Roy to Yashwant Sinha* (New Delhi: HarperCollins, 2004).
19. Tyabji, *Memoirs of an Egoist*.
20. J. Bandopadhyaya, *The Making of India's Foreign Policy: Determinants, Institutions, Processes and Personalities* (Bombay: Allied, 1971).
21. *Times of India*, 23 April 2007).
22. Josey, Letter to Bloodworth.
23. Lee Kuan Yew, *From Third World to First: The Singapore Story 1965–2000* (Singapore: SPH, 2000).
24. Fali S. Nariman, 'We'll miss you, Dr Kalam', *Indian Express*, 23 July 2007.
25. Sunanda K. Datta-Ray, 'Chopsticks'.
26. Ch'ng Jet Khoon (Tiong Bahru), *Parliamentary Debates*, vols 27–28, Third Parliament, 20 December 1968.
27. Part I of Fourth Session, *Legislative Assembly Debates*, vol. 20, 8 April 1963.
28. Josey, letter to Bloodworth.
29. *Statesman* (Calcutta and Delhi editions), 22 April 1962.
30. Lee Kuan Yew, Interview VI by author, Istana, 21 June 2007.

31. Deep K. Datta-Ray, 'Darkness Visible and Beckoning', *(The) Telegraph*, 10 January 2007.
32. Lee, Interview I.
33. Lee, Interview IV
34. *Legislative Assembly Debates*, vol. 2, no. 15, 5 December 1956.
35. *Sunday Mail*, 30 September 30.
36. Josey, *Asia Pacific Socialism*.
37. Lee, Interview V.
38. Ibid.
39. Lee, Interview II.
40. Lee, *From Third World to First*.
41. See LKY/1962/LKY0520.doc.
42. Josey, Letter to Bloodworth.
43. Josey, Letter to Bloodworth.
44. *Straits Times*, 2 and 3 October, 1962.
45. *Straits Times*, 31 October 31.
46. *Straits Times*, 28 October 1962.
47. *Sunday Times*, 11 November 1962.
48. Lee, Interview II.
49. Chan Heng Chee and Obaid ul Haq, *The Prophetic and the Political: Selected Speeches and Writings of S. Rajaratnam* (Singapore: Graham Brash, 1987).
50. Chan and Haq, Prophetic and the Political.
51. Lee, Interview II.
52. Ibid.
53. Ibid.
54. Ibid.
55. Dhanabalan, interview.
56. Lee, Interview II.
57. Ibid
58. Lee, Interview II.
59. 'India Redefining China Ties', *Iran Daily*, 4 August, 2007.
60. Lee, Interview II.
61. Ibid.
62. Dennis Bloodwirth, *The Reporter's Notebook* (Singapore: Times Books, 1988).
63. Lee, Interview II.
64. Abraham, interview.
65. See Lky\1965\lky1008a.doc.
66. *Straits Times*, 25 July 2007.
67. Lee, Interview I.
68. A.J. Stockwell, *Malaysia in British Documents on the End of Empire, Series B, Volume 8* (London: The Stationery Office, 2004).
69. K. Natwar Singh, letter to author, 13 September 2008.
70. Lee, *The Singapore Story*.

71. Lee, Interview VII.
72. Lee Kuan Yew, Interview III by author, Istana, 2 March, 2007
73. Josey, *Lee Kuan Yew.*
74. Abraham, interview.
75. Ibid.
76. Ibid.
77. Former Indian diplomat, confidential conversation with author New Delhi, 15 June 2007.
78. Abraham, interview.
79. Ibid.
80. Lee, Interview IV.
81. *Straits Times*, 31 December 2007.
82. Muhammad Ghazali Shafie, *Ghazali Shafie's Memoir on the Formation of Malaysia* (Bangi: Penerbit Universiti Kebangsaan Malaysia, 1998).
83. *Far Eastern Economic Review Yearbook*, 1963
84. *Indonesian Herald*, 28–29 January 1963.
85. Lee, Interview IV.
86. Peter Boyce, 'Policy without Authority: Singapore's External Affairs Power', *Journal of South-east Asian History*, vol. 10, March 1969
87. Lee, *Singapore Story.*
88. Abraham, interview.
89. Josey, *Lee Kuan Yew.*
90. Lee, Interview IV.
91. Lee, Interview IV.
92. Josey, *Lee Kuan Yew.*
93. Ibid.
94. Lee Kuan Yew, 'Future of Malaysia, Institute of International Affairs', Melbourne, 24 March 1965, in *Malaysia—Age of Revolution* (Singapore: Ministry of Culture, 1965).
95. *Asian Almanac,* 20 December 1963, p. 318.
96. Ministry of External Affairs, *Foreign Affairs Record*, vol. x, no. 4, April 1964.
97. *Times of India*, 26 November 1995.
98. Dixit, *Foreign Policy.*
99. *Asian Almanac*, 25–31 October, 1964, p. 833.
100. V.P. Dutt, *India's Foreign Policy* (New Delhi: Vikas, 1984); also published as 'India and South-east Asia: Prospects and Problems' by Baladas Ghosal in *India and South-east Asia*, ed., Baladas Ghosal (New Delhi: Konark, 1996).
101. Lee, Interview III.
102. Hubert H. Humphrey, *The Education of a Public Man: My Life and Politic*s (New York: Doubleday, 1976).
103. Lee, *Third World to First.*
104. *Straits Times*, 10 May 1965.

105. *Sunday Times*, 9 May 1965.
106. *Statesman* (Calcutta and Delhi editions), 12 May 1965.
107. *Malay Mail*, 8 May 1965.

Chapter 4: 'An Absolute Pariah in the Whole World'

1. Abraham, interview.
2. See lky\1965\lky0809b.doc.
3. *Straits Times*, 10 August 1965.
4. Lee, Interview III.
5. Lee Kuan Yew, unpublished communication to Lal Bahadur Shastri, 9 August 1965.
6. Thomas Abraham, unpublished communication to Lee Kuan Yew, 11 August 1965.
7. Abraham, interview.
8. Ibid.
9. Lee, Interview IV.
10. See http://en.wikipedia.org/wiki/Lal_Bahadur_Shastri.
11. *Time*, 19 February 1965.
12. Lee, Interview III.
13. *Keesing's Contemporary Archives*, 7–14 August 1965.
14. Nathan, Interview I, Istana, Singapore, 2 April 2007.
15. Han, Fernandez and Tan, *Lee Kuan Yew*.
16. *Time*, 19 February 1965.
17. *Vietnam Courier*, vol. 6, no. 28, 1979; *Foreign Affairs Record*, New Delhi, November 1985.
18. Lee, Interview III.
19. *Legislative Assembly Debates*, Second Session, First Series, volume II, 10 August 1960.
20. Nathan, Interview I.
21. Abraham, interview.
22. Nathan, Interview I.
23. Chan and Haq, *S. Rajaratnam*.
24. *Straits Times*, 11 November 1965.
25. Lee, Interview III.
26. Michael Leifer, *Singapore's Foreign Policy: Coping with Vulnerability* (London: Routledge, 2000).
27. Amnon Barzilai, 'The Singapore Armed Forces: An India Defence Consultant's Analysis', 18 August 2004, http://www.singapore-window.org/sw05/040818id.htm.
28. Lee, *From Third World to First*.
29. Lee, Interview III.

30. Tan Siok Sun, *Goh Keng Swee: A Portrait* (Singapore: Editions Didier Millet, 2007).
31. Tan, *Goh Keng Swee*.
32. Ibid.
33. Nathan, Interview I.
34. Ibid.
35. Ibid.
36. Abraham, interview.
37. Dhanabalan, interview.
38. Leifer, *Singapore's Foreign Policy*.
39. Lee, Interview III.
40. Lee, Interview V.
41. Bloodworth, *The Reporter's Notebook*.
42. *Asian Almanac: Weekly Abstract of International Affairs*, Singapore, 1964, p. 810.
43. Ibid., p. 1166.
44. *Far Eastern Economic Review Yearbook 1966*, Hong Kong, p. 277.
45. M.C. Chagla, *Roses in December: An Autobiography* (Bombay: Bharatiya Vidya Bhavan, 1973).
46. *Straits Times*, 11 September 1965.
47. T.J.S. George, *Lee Kuan Yew's Singapore* (London: Deutsch, 1973).
48. Abraham, interview.
49. Ibid.
50. Lee, Interview III.
51. Ibid.
52. Nathan, Interview I.
53. Lee, Interview III.
54. Nathan, Interview I.
55. Lee, Interview III.
56. Lee, Interview III.
57. Abraham, interview.
58. Nathan, Interview I.
59. Ibid.
60. Bloodworth, *The Reporter's Notebook*.
61. Lee, Interview V.
62. Tommy Koh and Yeo Lay Hwee, 'Size is not Destiny', in *Singapore: Re-engineering Success*, ed. Arun Mahizhnan and Lee Tsao Yuan (Singapore: Singapore Institute of Policy Studies and Oxford University Press, 1998).
63. *Parliamentary Record*, Third Parliament, vols 27–28, 13 May 1968.
64. 'Bashing Singapore', *Economist*, 8 February 2007.
65. Lee, Interview III.
66. George Yeo, Foreword in *The Little Red Dot: Reflections by Singapore's*

Diplomats, ed. Tommy Koh and Chang Li Lin (Singapore: World Scientific, 2005).
67. Chan Chin Bock, *Heart Work* (Singapore: Economic Development Board, 2002).
68. *Singapore: The Encyclopedia*.
69. *Hindu*, 27 January 1994.

Chapter 5: India's 'Monroe Doctrine for Asia'

1. Oza, interview.
2. *Straits Times*, 2 September 2007.
3. *Straits Times*, 3 September 2007.
4. Lee, Interview VI.
5. Han, Fernandez and Tan, *Lee Kuan Yew*.
6. Lee, Interview III.
7. *Asian Almanac*, vol. 4, no. 11, 1967.
8. Lee, Interview III.
9. Lee, Interview V.
10. Mahbubani, interview by author, Singapore, 22 April 2007.
11. Lee, Interview V.
12. Ibid.
13. Ibid.
14. Maharaj Krishna Rasgotra, in conversation with the author, New Delhi, 17 October 2007.
15. Lee Kuan Yew, Lecture I, Jacob Blausten Lectures delivered at Lehigh University, 30 March–2 April 1973.
16. Jagat Mehta, in conversation with the author, 26 June 2007.
17. Lee, Interview VI.
18. Oza, interview.
19. Lee, Interview VI.
20. Oza, interview.
21. Lee, Interview VI.
22. *Straits Times*, 5 September 1966.
23. *Asian Almanac*, vol. 4, no. 11, 15 October 1966.
24. Lee, Interview III.
25. *New York Times*, 8 May 1988.
26. Lee, Interview III.
27. Oza, interview.
28. Rodolfo C. Severino, *Southeast Asia In Search of an Asean Community: Insights from the former Asean Secretary-General* (Singapore: Institute of Southeast Asian Studies, 2006).
29. Somkiat Omniwon, 'India's Relations with the Asean Countries, 1966–1975:

A Transaction Analysis'. A Dissertation in South Asian Regional Studies presented to the Graduate Faculties of the University of Pennsylvania in partial fulfilment of the requirements for the degree of doctor of philosophy (Ann Arbor: University Microfilms Dissertation Information Service, 1981).
30. *Foreign Affairs Record*, vol. XII, no. 6, June 1966.
31. Gretchen Liu, *The Singapore Foreign Service: The First 40 years* (Singapore: Editions Didier Millet, 2005).
32. *Statesman* (Calcutta and Delhi aditions), 19 June 1969.
33. Indira Gandhi, *India Speaks: Selected Speeches of Prime Minister Indira Gandhi on Her Tour Abroad, September–November 1971*, (New Delhi: Publications Division, Ministry of Information and Broadcasting, Government of India, 1971).
34. Dixit, *Makers of India's Foreign Policy*.
35. Chagla, *Roses in December*.
36. *Foreign Affairs Record*, vol. XII, no. 6, 9 May 1967.
37. Nathan, Interview II, Istana, 16 April 2007.
38. *Nation*, Bangkok, 6 August 2007.
39. *Parliamentary Debates*, vol. 27, no. 1, 6 May 1968
40. Unpublished note by C. Gunasingham, Singapore, 6 November 1996.
41. Ibid.
42. Ibid.
43. *Times of India*, 8–10 October 1967.
44. Lee, Interview III.
45. Nathan, Interview II.
46. Liu, *The Singapore Foreign Service*.
47. Thanat Khoman, 'Reminiscences', *Contemporary South-east Asia*, vol. 10, no. 1, June 1988.
48. D.R. Sardesai, 'India and Asean—An Overview', in *Yearbook on India's Foreign Policy, 1987–88*, ed. Satish Kumar (New Delhi: Sage, 1988).
49. Chintamani Mahapatra, *American Role in the Origin and Growth of Asean* (New Delhi: ABC, 1990).
50. Olaf Caroe, *Wells of Power* (London: Macmillan, 1951).
51. *Hindu*, 27 January 1994.
52. Retired Indian diplomat, in confidential conversation with author, New Delhi, 31 May 2007.
53. *Sunday Times*, 23 July 1967.
54. *Straits Times*, 24 July 1967.
55. Edward Tang, in conversation with the author, Singapore, 11 January 2008.
56. Chan, 'A Jonah in Diplomacy', in *Little Red Dot*.
57. *Straits Times*, 22 September 1993.
58. Baker, interview.
59. Baker, interview.
60. Maurice Baker, 'Impressions of Diplomatic Life', in *The Little Red Dot:*

Reflections by Singapore's Diplomats, ed. Tommy Koh and Chang Li Lin (Singapore: World Scientific, 2005).
61. *The Indian Political Science Review*, vol. III, nos. 1 & 2, October 1968–March 1969.
62. Baker, interview.
63. Indian diplomat, confidential conversation with the author, New Delhi, 31 May 2007.
64. *Straits Times*, 7 November 1967.
65. Baker, interview.
66. Lee, Interview I.
67. Ibid.
68. *Prime Minister's Speeches, Press Conferences, Interviews, Statements, etc.* (Singapore: Prime Minister's Office, 1959–90).
69. Lee, Interview II.
70. Lee, Interview IV.
71. Ibid.
72. Lee, Interview IV.
73. George Yeo, interview by author, Singapore, 13 February 2007.
74. Lee, Interview I.
75. *Straits Times*, 10 June 1995.
76. V. Suryanarayan, *Looking Ahead: India and Southeast Asia in the 1990s: New Perspectives, New Challenges* in *India and Southeast Asia: Challenges and Opportunities*, ed. Baladas Ghoshal (New Delhi: Konark, 1996).
77. Lee, Interview II.
78. Andrea Hamilton, *Asiaweek*, 16 October 1998.
79. Chandrasekhar Dasgupta, interview by author, New Delhi, 12 June 2007.
80. Dasgupta, interview.
81. Han, Fernandez and Tan, *Lee Kuan Yew*.
82. Chagla, *Roses in December*.
83. *Straits Times*, 24 June 1971.
84. Prem Bhatia, *Of Many Pastures* (Ahmedabad: Allied, 1989).
85. Rodriguez, ed., *Lee Kuan Yew, In His Own Words, Book I 1959–1970* (Singapore: SJ and Gavin International, 2003).
86. Rodriguez, *Lee Kuan Yew*.
87. *Straits Times*, 10 June 1995.
88. *Straits Times*, 10 June 1995.
89. Ibid.
90. S. Rajaratnam at the International Conference on the Future of Asia, Singapore, 23 August 1980.
91. Lee, Interview VII.
92. *Straits Times*, 10 June 1995.
93. *Straits Times*, 20 May 1968.

94. *Straits Times*, 20 May 1968.
95. Lee, Interview IV.
96. Lee, Interview V.

Chapter 6: 'India Alone Can Look China in the Eye'

1. Lee Kuan Yew, *From Third World to First: The Singapore Story 1965–2000* (Singapore: Times, 2001).
2. Eu Mun Hoo Calvin, in conversation with the author, Singapore High Commission, New Delhi, 27 May 2008.
3. Pranab Mukherjee, in conversation with the author, Ministry of External Affairs, New Delhi, 4 June 2008.
4. George Yeo, interview by author, Ministry of Foreign Affairs, Singapore, 13 February 2007.
5. George Yeo, interview.
6. Dhanabalan, interview.
7. Lee Kuan Yew, 'South-east Asia in Turmoil', *Malaysia—Age of Revolution, Singapore's Prime Minister in New Zealand and Australia, March–April 1965* (Singapore: Ministry of Culture Publication, 1965).
8. Lee, Interview VII.
9. Xuan Thuy, 'Chinese Expansionism in South-east Asia', *World Marxist Review*, Prague, vol. 24, no. 3, March 1981.
10. *Ministerial Speeches, Press Conferences, Interviews, Statements, etc., Singapore*, vol. 17, no. 1, January–February 1993.
11. Lee, Interview V.
12. *Straits Times*, June 10 1995.
13. Ibid.
14. *Straits Times*, 10 June 1995.
15. Varindra Tarzie Vittachi, *The Brown Sahib Revisited* (New Delhi: Penguin, 1987).
16. All Ewing, 'Administering India: The Indian Civil Service', *History Today*, vol. 32, no. 6, June 1982.
17. Lee, Interview I.
18. James Cameron, *An Indian Summer* (London: Macmillan, 1975).
19. Han, Fernandez and Tan, *Lee Kuan Yew*.
20. Lee, Interview I.
21. Lee, Interview VII.
22. Lee, Interview II.
23. Ibid.
24. Ibid.
25. Michael Leifer, *Selected Works on South-east Asia*, compiled and edited by Chin Kin Wah and Leo Suryadinata (Singapore: ISEAS, 2005).
26. Josey, *Lee Kuan Yew*.

27. Lee, Interview VII.
28. *Straits Times*, 2 February 1995.
29. Josey, *Lee Kuan Yew*.
30. *Straits Times*, 2 February 1995.
31. *Straits Times*, 12 January 2008.
32. Lee, Interview IV.
33. Lee at multi-party symposium organized by Historical Society, University of Malaya, Kuala Lumpur, 28 August 1964.
34. Ibid.
35. *Straits Times*, 25 August 2007.
36. Lee, Interview IV.
37. Ibid.
38. B.M. Oza, interview by author, New Delhi, 16 June 2007.
39. Lee, Interview IV.
40. Lee, Interview I.
41. Lee, Interview IV.
42. *Straits Times*, 18 August 2007.
43. Rodriguez, *Lee Kuan Yew*.
44. Han, Fernandez and Tan, *Lee Kuan Yew*.
45. Arun Shourie, interview by author, New Delhi, 1 June 2007.
46. *Straits Times*, 10 June 1995.
47. Lee, Interview I.
48. Ibid.
49. Rahul Mukherji, 'India's Aborted Liberalization—1966', *Pacific Affairs*, vol. 73, 22 September 2000.
50. Alex Josey, 'The Return of the Rosebud', *Time*, 28 January 1966.
51. Senior Minister's Press Club Address, 7 June 1996. Unpublished *Straits Times* record, trq8a.
52. Nathan, Interview I.
53. Lee, Interview II.
54. Lee, Interview V.
55. Confidential briefing by member of the Prime Minister's Office, New Delhi, 13 June 2007.
56. Lee, Interview V.
57. *Straits Times*, 10 May 1965.
58. Nathan, interview I.
59. *Straits Times*, 21 May 1968.
60. Alastair Buchan, 'An Asian Balance of Power?', *The Australian Journal of Politics and History*, vol. 12, no. 2, August 1966.
61. Morarji Desai, *The Story of My Life* (Oxford: Pergamon, 1979).
62. Russell H. Fifield, *South-east Asia in United States Policy* (New York: Praeger, 1963).
63. *Asian Almanac*, Singapore, vol. 6, no. 31, 3 August 1968.

64. *Asian Almanac*, Singapore, vol. 4, no. 11, 15 October 1966.
65. Lee, 'South-east Asia in Turmoil'.
66. *Indian Express*, 29 May, 2006.
67. *Foreign Affairs Record*, vol. XIV, no. 4, April 1968.
68. Confidential briefing by former Indian foreign secretary, New Delhi, 1 June 2007.
69. *New Straits Times*, Kuala Lumpur, 17 June 1967.
70. *Singapore Legislative Assembly Debates*, Second Session, First Series, vol. 2, 18 December 1968.
71. Confidential conversation with Indian diplomat, New Delhi, 31 May 2007.
72. Ong, interview.
73. Shunmugam Jayakumar, interview by author, Ministry of Foreign Affairs, Singapore, 22 May 2007.
74. Lee, Interview V.
75. Ibid.
76. Bhatia, *Of Many Pastures*.
77. *Straits Times*, 11 April 1968.
78. Lee, Interview IV.
79. *Sunday Times*, 28 March 1965.
80. *Straits Times*, 11 April 1968.
81. Lee, Interview IV.
82. Jagat Mehta, letter to author, 11 December 2006.
83. Ibid.
84. Kawin Wilairat, 'Singapore's Foreign Policy: A Study of the Foreign Policy System of a City-State', Thesis 4563, unpublished dissertation, Graduate School of Georgetown University, Washington DC, 1975.
85. Shakuntala Bhatia, interview by author, New Delhi, 3 June 2007.
86. Dasgupta, interview.
87. Lee, *From Third World to First*.
88. *Straits Times*, 12 January 2008.

Chapter 7: Goh's Folly to Goh's Glory with Tata

1. Shakuntala Bhatia, interview.
2. Lee Kuan Yew, Jacob Blausten Lectures, Lecture I.
3. Lee Kuan Yew, Jacob Blausten Lectures, Lecture II.
4. United States National Archives, Nixon Presidential Materials, NSC Files, Box 643, Country Files, Middle East, India/Pakistan, July 1971. Secret.
5. United States National Archives, Nixon Presidential Materials.
6. Lee, Interview II.
7. Ibid.
8. Ibid.

9. Low Choon Ming, 'Reflections of 33 Years in Diplomacy', *The Little Red Dot*, ed. Koh and Chang.
10. *Business Times*, 19 April 1990.
11. Prem Singh, interview by author, New Delhi, 5 June, 2007
12. Ibid.
13. George Yeo, interview.
14. *Sunday Times*, 11 August, 1968.
15. Nathan Interview I.
16. Chan Heng Chee and Obaid ul Haq, eds, *S. Rajaratnam: The Prophetic and the Political* (Singapore: Graham Brash, 1987).
17. *Statesman*, 4 September 1970.
18. *Eastern Sun*, 8 October 1970.
19. Shakuntala Bhatia, interview.
20. Prem Bhatia, *Of Many Pastures* (New Delhi: Allied, 1989).
21. *Times of India*, 20 September 1971.
22. *Straits Times*, 16 September 1971.
23. Ameer Jumabhoy, in conversation with the author, 7 February 2007.
24. *New Nation*, 1 August 1978.
25. Philip Ziegler, ed., *From Shore to Shore: The Final Years, The Diaries of Earl Mountbatten of Burma, 1953–1957* (London: Collins, 1989).
26. Gabriel Tan, Singapore Government, http://infopedia.nlb.gov.sg/details/SIP_544_2004-12-18.html.
27. *Parliamentary Debates*, Third Parliament, Vol. 27, 11 January 1968.
28. Ibid.
29. *Malay Mail*, 21 March 1968.
30. Lee Hsien Loong, interview by author, Istana, 4 April 2008.
31. Colin N. Powell (with Joseph E. Perisco), *My American Journey* (New York: Random House, 1995).
32. Abraham, interview
33. Interview with V.K. Rajan, Singapore, 18 March 2008.
34. Rajan, interview.
35. Lala, *The Romance of Tata Steel*.
36. *Strategic Pragmatism: The Culture of Singapore's Economic Development Board* (Cambridge, MA: MIT Press 1996).
37. *Straits Times*, 10 June 1995.
38. DS599.63 L471 1979.
39. Lee Kuan Yew, 'Managing Globalization: Lessons from China and India', inaugural speech at Lee Kuan Yew School of Public Policy, Singapore, 4 April, 2005.
40. E-mail communication from Syamal Gupta, 5 December 2006.
41. Dhanabalan, interview.
42. Syamal Gupta, interview by author, Singapore, 9 December 2006.

43. Gupta, interview.
44. Ng Pock Too, interview by author, 16 January 2007.
45. Gupta, interview.
46. Chan Chin Bock, Foreword to Indian edition of *Heart Work* (Singapore: Tata McGraw Hill, 2002).
47. Chan, Foreword.
48. http://www.thaindian.com/newsportal/uncategorized/singapore-confers-honorary-citizenship-on-ratan-tata_10090289.html.
49. Syamal Gupta, conversation with author, Calcutta, 26 December 2008.
50. *Straits Times*, 10 June 1995.
51. *Straits Times*, 10 June 1995.
52. Dhanabalan, interview.
53. Lee, Interview III.
54. Ibid.
55. *Asian Almanac 1973*, vol. II, no. 36, 8 September 1973.
56. *Parliamentary Reports*, vol. 30, 2 September 1978, p. 168.
57. *Parliamentary Reports*, vol. 34, 27 February 1975 p. 152.
58. Ibid.
59. Dhanabalan, interview.
60. *Straits Times*, 17 September 1998.
61. Ibid.
62. *Straits Times*, 14 November 1978.
63. *Bangkok Post*, 15 November 1978.
64. Lee, Interview II.
65. Lee, Interview V.
66. *Straits Times*, 7 October 1978.
67. *Straits Times*, 1 January 1979.
68. LKY/1978/LKY1206.DOC
69. Lee, Interview V.
70. Ibid.
71. Subramaniam Swamy, 'Vajpayee's China Fiasco', Institute of Peace and Conflict Studies, article no. 151, 12 November 1998.
72. Brajesh Mishra, interview by author, New Delhi, 6 June 2007.
73. LKY/1978/LKY1214.DOC
74. Lee, Interview II.
75. LKY/1978/LKY1206.DOC
76. Dhanabalan, interview.
77. LKY/1978/LKY1206.DOC
78. *New Nation*, 1 August 1978.
79. *New Nation*, 1 August 1978.
80. Lee, Interview V.
81. Kishore Mahbubabni, interview by author, 8 May 2007.

82. DS599.63 L471 1979.
83. *Straits Times*, 11 January 1980.

Chapter 8: 'The Lowest Point in Bilateral Relations'

1. Ministry of Foreign Affairs, *Havana and New Delhi: What's the Difference?* (Singapore: Ministry of Foreign Affairs, 1983).
2. Joint Communiqué of the Thirteenth Asean Ministerial Meeting, Kuala Lumpur, 25–26 June, 1980, http://www.aseansec.org/1243.htm.
3. *Times*, London, 21 June 1980.
4. Dasgupta, interview.
5. Oza, interview.
6. Ibid.
7. *Statesman*, 16 June 1980.
8. *Bangkok Post*, 18 May 1980.
9. Oza, interview
10. Ibid.
11. Lee, Interview V.
12. Ibid.
13. Ibid.
14. Ibid.
15. Inder Malhotra, *Indira Gandhi: A Personal and Political Biography* (London: Hodder & Stoughton, 1989).
16. Jayakumar, interview.
17. Norodom Sihanouk, *Charisma and Leadership*.
18. Sihanouk, *Charisma and Leadership*.
19. Lee, *From Third World to First*.
20. Thailand: Potential External Threats, CIA World Factbook, http://www.photius.com/countries/thailand/national_security/thailand_national_security_potential_external_t~2376.html.
21. *Far Eastern Economic Review*, 30 May 1980.
22. Lee, Interview VII.
23. *Time*, 24 June 2001.
24. Lee, Interview VI.
25. Tommy Koh, *Asia and Europe, Essays and Speeches* (Singapore: World Scientific, 2000).
26. Mahbubani, interview.
27. Ibid.
28. Ibid.
29. Ibid.
30. Kishore Mahbubani, 'Pol Pot: The Paradox of Moral Correctness' in *Can Asians think?* (Sinagapore: Times International, 1998).

31. Mahbubani, interview.
32. Ibid.
33. *Business Times*, 13 March 1984.
34. Yes Lay Hwee and Asad Latif, eds, *Asia and Europe: Essays and Speeches by Tommy Koh* (Singapore: World Scientific Publishing, 2000).
35. Lee, Interview V.
36. Oza, interview.
37. *Asian Almanac*, 1980, pp. 10075, 10076.
38. Natwar Singh, *Profiles and Letters*.
39. *Far Eastern Economic Review*, 22 September 1980.
40. *Straits Times*, 9 September 1980.
41. Lee, Interview I.
42. Ibid.
43. Ibid.
44. Lee, *From Third World to First*.
45. Dasgupta, interview.
46. Lee, Interview V.
47. Dasgupta, inteview.
48. Brajesh Mishra in *Across the Himalayan Gap: An Indian Quest for Understanding China*, ed. Tan Chung (New Delhi: Gyan Publishing House, 1998).
49. Lee, Interview VI.
50. Lee, Interview V.
51. Lee, Interview VI.
52. Ibid.
53. Ibid.
54. Ibid.
55. Ibid.
56. Lee Kuan Yew, Lecture II, Jacob Blausten Lectures, 2 April 1973.
57. Lee, Interview I.
58. Ibid.
59. Lee, Interview VI.
60. Ibid.
61. Lee, Interview II.
62. Ibid.
63. Dasgupta, interview.
64. Lee, Interview II.
65. Ibid.
66. Lee, Interview III.
67. *Sunday Times*, 28 October 1984.
68. *Straits Times*, 25 April 1985.
69. *Sunday Times*, 28 October 1984.
70. *Straits Times*, 29 April 1982.

71. Ibid.
72. *Straits Times*, 28 March 2008.
73. Lee, Interview V.
74. Ibid.
75. Ibid.
76. *Straits Times*, 9 October 2006.
77. P.N. Balji, *Today*, 1 December 2007.
78. Ibid.
79. Lee, Interview IV.
80. *Straits Times*, 3 March 2007.
81. Suresh Kumar, 'Different but Not Apart', *Today*, 15 March 2007.
82. Lee, Interview V.

Chapter 9: 'Scent of the S'pore Dollar'

1. *Parliamentary Debates*, vol. 59, no. 9, Tuesday, 10 March 1992.
2. Michael Richardson, 'City Built by Immigrants Ponders Job Curbs: Singapore's "Foreigners"', *International Herald Tribune*, 30 March 1999.
3. *Straits Times*, 28 February 2007.
4. Singapore Public Service Commission interview, 1950, http://app.psc.gov.sg/ctb/chapter2-01.asp.
5. Confidential interview with Singaporean politician, 13 February 2007.
6. Harry Chan, 'A Jonah in Diplomacy'.
7. Ibid.
8. *Legislative Assembly Debates*, vol.11, part I, First Series, 2 September 1959.
9. Rodriguez, *Lee Kuan Yew*.
10. *Tamil Murasu*, 14 June 1984.
11. *Tehran Times*, 13 June 1984.
12. Confidential briefing at Internal Security Department, Singapore, 25 September, 2007.
13. *Straits Times*, 19 June 1984.
14. *Straits Times*, 19 April 1985.
15. *Sunday Monitor*, 21 April 1984.
16. *Straits Times*, 20 April 1985.
17. Ibid.
18. 'Visas—What's At Issue', *Business Times*, 25 September 1986.
19. *Straits Times*, 18 May 1985.
20. *Straits Times*, 24 September 1986.
21. Press Trust of India/Reuters, 28 April 1989.
22. Shashank, interview.
23. Natwar Singh, interview.
24. *Straits Times*, 14 May 1989.

25. *New Paper*, 5 May 1989.
26. *Statesman*, 6 May 1989.
27. *Indian Express*, 23 May 2007.
28. *Sunday Times*, 25 November 2007.
29. *Straits Times*, 18 May 1989.
30. *Straits Times*, 14 May 1989.
31. *Indian Express*, 23 May 2007.
32. 'Inconvenient, but Necessary', *Straits Times*, 25 September 1986.
33. *Financial Express*, 20 November 2003.
34. Shashank, interview.
35. 'Visas—What's At Issue', *Business Times*, 25 September 1986.
36. Shashank, interview.
37. Ibid.
38. Rodriguez, *Lee Kuan Yew*.
39. *International Herald Tribune*, 30 March 1999.
40. Rodriguez, *Lee Kuan Yew*.
41. *Parliamentary Debates*, vol. 59, no. 9.
42. *Straits Times*, 29 November 2007.
43. *Straits Times*, 1 July 2003.
44. Edward Tang, interview, Singapore 12 February 2008
45. *Straits Times*, 18 March 1988.
46. Shashank, interview.
47. Ibid.
48. Ibid.
49. Interview with Lam Peck Heng, 26 January 2007.
50. Lee, Interview II.
51. Lee, *From Third World to First*.
52. Shyam Goenka, *Eternal Rajiv: Epitome of Humanity* (New Delhi: Resurgent India Publications, 2003).
53. Natwar Singh, interview.
54. *Parliamentary Debates*, vol. 45, no. 12, 22 March 1985.
55. *Straits Times*, 7 August 1985.
56. Mimi Ho, Christina Aw, Ng Yew Kwong, Tang Ming Yang, Gene Wong and Mindy Han, 'Case Study on Pan-Electric Crisis', MAS Staff Paper No. 32, Singapore, July 2004.
57. Pushpesh Pant, 'India and South-east Asia', in *Yearbook on India's Foreign Policy, 1985–86*, ed. Satish Kumar (New Delhi: Sage, 1988).
58. Lee, *From Third World to First*.
59. Lee, Interview II.
60. Lee, *From Third World to First*.
61. Kunwar Natwar Singh, conversation with author, New Delhi, 31 May 2007.

62. Patrick Daniel, 'PM begins visit to India and Pakistan', *Straits Times*, 15 March 1988.
63. Lee Kuan Yew to AIR's Deepankar Mukhopadhyay, 11 March 1988.
64. *Straits Times*, 15 March 1989.
65. Lee, Interview V.
66. Lee Kuan Yew to AIR.
67. Lee, Interview II.
68. Ibid.
69. P.N. Haksar, *India's Foreign Policy and its Problems* (New Delhi: Patriot, 1989).
70. Speech by I.K. Gujral, External Affairs Minister of India, at Chatham House, London, on Foreign Policy Objectives of India's United Front Government, 23 September 1996.
71. Lee, Interview II.
72. *Straits Times*, 18 March 1988.
73. http://socrates.berkeley.edu/~basc/pdf/articles/Aggarwal_ Mukherji_ ANIA_Ch9.pdf
74. *Canberra Times*, 25 May 1988.
75. *Straits Times*, 26 February 1990.
76. *Straits Times*, 6 March 1990.
77. Lee, Interview V.I
78. Lee, Interview II.
79. Lee, Interview VI.
80. *Straits Times*, 27 August 1989.
81. *Time*, 3 April 1989.
82. *Straits Times*, 3 March 1986.
83. *Keesing's Record of World Events 1990*, News Digest for November 1990.
84. Syamal Gupta, in conversation with the author, Calcutta, 26 December 2008.

Chapter 10: Singapore's 'Mild India Fever'

1. Described in detail in Sunanda K. Datta-Ray, *Waiting for America: India and the US in the New Millennium* (New Delhi, HarperCollins 2002).
2. Yogendra Mohan Tiwari, interview by author, New Delhi, 5 September 2007.
3. Lee, Interview I.
4. E-mail from Krishnan Srinivasan, 12 February 2007.
5. Tiwari, interview.
6. Ibid.
7. *Indian Foreign Policy: Challenges and Opportunities* (New Delhi: Academic Foundation, 2007).
8. *Business Times*, 19 October 1991.

9. Lee, Interview V.
10. Sridhar Krishnaswamy, 'Singapore PM sees a new dawn in ties with India', *Hindu*, 154 January 1992.
11. Lee, Interview VI.
12. K.K. Katyal, *Hindu*, 19 January 1994.
13. *Hindu*, 19 January 1994.
14. *Straits Times*, 28 February 1992.
15. *Straits Times*, 22 January 1994.
16. A.N. Ram, http://www.google.com/search?q=cache:yzFcIZrlQO0J:www.india-seminar.com/2000/487/487%2520ram. htm+a.n.+ Cram& hl=en&ct=clnk&cd=1&gl=sg.
17. *Straits Times*, 13 August 1991.
18. Lee, *From Third World to First*.
19. *Straits Times*, 24 March 1992.
20. *Straits Times*, 26 March 1992.
21. Tiwari, interview.
22. *Straits Times*, 3 December 1993.
23. Ong, interview.
24. Ibid.
25. George Yeo, interview by author, Ministry of Foreign Affairs, Singapore, 13 February 2007.
26. George Yeo, interview.
27. Lam, interview.
28. E-mail from Srinivasan.
29. *Straits Times*, 1, February 1994.
30. Ibid.
31. Lee, Interview II.
32. *Straits Times*, 23 November 1993.
33. *Straits Times*, 1 February 1994.
34. *Asia Times Online*, 13 May 2003.
35. Ranjit Gupta, interview by author, New Delhi, 1 June 2007.
36. Ranjit Gupta, interview.
37. Ibid.
38. *Straits Times*, 7 December 1993.
39. *Hindu*, 19 January 1994.
40. *Straits Times*, 25 January 1994.
41. *Straits Times*, 9 January 1994.
42. *Straits Times*, 28 January 1994.
43. I.K. Gujral, interview by author, New Delhi, 6 June 2007.
44. *Telegraph*, 14 May 2008.
45. *Straits Times*, 24 January 2006.
46. Rediff on the Net, 23 April 1997.
47. Ibid.

48. Gujral, interview.
49. *Straits Times*, 29 January 1994.
50. Philip Yeo, interview by author, Singapore, 9 July 2007.
51. Philip Yeo, interview.
52. Confidential interview with Indian diplomat, New Delhi, 27 May 2007.
53. Gupta, interview.
54. See *Indian Foreign Policy*.
55. Jayakumar, interview.
56. *Wall Street Journal*, 5 April 2004.
57. Michael Leifer, *Singapore's Foreign Policy* (New York: Routledge, 2000).
58. Leifer, *Singapore's Foreign Policy*.
59. Lee, Interview VI.
60. Lee, Interview VII.
61. Lee, Interview VI.
62. *Time Asia*, 15 May 2001.
63. Ibid.
64. *Taipei Times*, 8 December 2005.
65. Lee, Interview VII.
66. Lee, Interview VI.
67. *Hindu*, 20 January 2004.

Chapter 11: End of One Honeymoon, Start of Another?

1. Lee, Interview II.
2. Datta-Ray, *Waiting for America*.
3. Lee, Interview VII.
4. Ibid.
5. Prem Singh, interview by author, New Delhi, 5 June 2007.
6. *Hindu BusinessLine*, 4 July 2006.
7. Prem Singh, interview.
8. Lee, Interview II.
9. Advani, interview.
10. Release no: 04\JAN 02-2\96\01\05.
11. *Straits Times*, 28 June 1997.
12. 'trq8a', 8 June 1996.
13. 'trq8a'.
14. Ibid.
15. Lee, Interview II.
16. Lam, interview.
17. Arun Shourie, interview by author, New Delhi, 1 June 2007.
18. *Visit of Prime Minister Shri Atal Bihari Vajpayee to The Republic of Singapore and The Kingdom of Cambodia, April 7–13, 2002* (New Delhi: Ministry of External Affairs, 2003 New Delhi).

19. Arun Shourie, *Will the Iron Fence Save a Tree Hollowed by Termites?* (New Delhi: ASA Rupa,2005).
20. Lee, Interview II.
21. Michael Richardson, 'Singapore Industrial Park Flounders: A Deal Sours in China', *International Herald Tribune*, 1 October 1999.
22. Lee, Interview II.
23. Lee, Interview II.
24. Ibid.
25. Lee, Interview VII.
26. Ibid.
27. Lee Hsien Loong.
28. Interview with Lee Hsien Loong.
29. Interview with Lee Hsien Loong.
30. *Straits Times*, 6 April, 2005.
31. Bhagyashree Garekar and Tay Hwee Peng, 'India, China learning from each other now', *Straits Times*, 6 April 2005.
32. *Straits Times*, 6 April 2005.
33. http://infoproc.blogspot.com/2005/08/lee-kuan-yew-interview.html
34. Lee Kuan Yew at Institute of Southeast Asian Studies' fortieth anniversary dinner at Shangri-la Hotel, Singapore, 7 January 2008.
35. *Straits Times*, 18 November 2005.
36. Ibid.
37. Yashwant Sinha, Asia Society AustralAsia Centre, 29 August 2003, http://www.asiasociety.org/speeches/sinha03.html.
38. *Straits Times*, 5 November 2007.
39. *Straits Times*, 21 November 2005.
40. *Straits Times*, 20 November 2005.
41. *Straits Times*, 20 November 2005.
42. *Straits Times*, 20 October 2007.
43. *Straits Times*, 21 November 2005.
44. Ibid.
45. Lee Hsien Loong, interview.
46. Lee, Interview II.
47. *Straits Times*, 23 November 2005.
48. Sonia Gandhi, *Rajiv* (New Delhi: Penguin, 1992).
49. 'Rahul learns governance in S'pore', *Times of India*, 5 June 2006.
50. Confidential conversation with one of the participants at the Raffles Hotel session on 9 June 2006.
51. Rahul Gandhi, interview by author, New Delhi, 1 December 2007.
52. Rahul Gandhi, interview.
53. Ibid.
54. Lee, Interview VII.
55. *Straits Times*, 26 November 2005.

56. *Straits Times*, 24 November 2005.
57. *Straits Times*, 26 November 2005.
58. Lee, Interview VII.
59. *Indian Express*, 17 January 2007.
60. *Straits Times*, 26 November 2005.
61. Lee, Interview II.
62. http://www.nerve.in/news:25350027296
63. *Times of India*, 15 January 2008.
64. Lee, Interview VII.
65. Lee, Interview II.
66. *Straits Times*, 24 November 2005.
67. *Straits Times*, 2 November 2007.
68. *Straits Times*, 1 November 2007.

Chapter 12: Shaping the Asian Century

1. Yechury, interview.
2. George Yeo, interview.
3. http://www.meaindia.nic.in/speech/2002/09/26spc01.htm
4. Ibid.
5. Jaswant Singh, interview.
6. Kamal Nath, interview.
7. Speech in Calcutta, 22 September 1928. Jawaharlal Nehru, *Thoughts*, Jawaharlal Nehru Memorial Fund, New Delhi, 1985.
8. George Yeo, interview.
9. Ibid.
10. Nath, interview.
11. Lee Hsien Loong, interview.
12. http://www.ficci.com/media-room/speeches-presentations/2004/oct/asean04/oct19-asean-pmspeech.htm
13. *Straits Times*, 11 December 1993.
14. Leo Suryadinata, *The Culture of the Chinese Minority in Indonesia* (Singapore: Times Books International, 1997).
15. Lee, Interview I.
16. Lee, Interview V.
17. Sitaram Yechury, interview by author, New Delhi, 27 May 2008.
18. *Telegraph*, 23 July 2008.
19. Avijit Ghosal, 'Changi may get Charge of New Durgapur Airport', *Hindustan Times*, 15 May 2008.
20. Lee Hsien Loong, interview.
21. *Hindu*, 25 August 2005.
22. Dina Nath Mishra, *Pioneer*, 22 April 2008.
23. Lee Hsien Loong, interview.

24. http://app.sprinter.gov.sg/data/pr/20080108994.htm
25. E-mail from MM's office, 31 March 2008.
26. http://www.temasekholdings.com.sg/
27. Lee, Interview V.
28. http://www.gic.com.sg/aboutus.htm
29. Lee Hsien Loong, interview.
30. Ibid.
31. *Straits Times*, 31 October 2007.
32. Lee, Interview VI.
33. Lee, Interview V.
34. Lee, Interview VI.
35. *Straits Times*, 31 October 2007.
36. *Straits Times*, 3 November 2007.
37. *Hindu BusinessLine*, 30 June 2007.
38. *Frontline*, 8–21 November 2003.
39. Manmohan Singh, in conversation with the author, New Delhi, 21 May 2008.
40. *Economic Times*, 24 April 2008.
41. Kishan S. Rana, Asian Diplomacy: The Foreign Ministries of China, India, Japan, Singapore and Thailand (Malta: Diplo, 2007).
42. *Frontline*, 25 November–8 December 2000.
43. *Hindu*, 9 November 2000.
44. *Hindu*, 10 November 2000.
45. *Forbes*, 24 December 2007.
46. Ibid.
47. Sudha Ramachandran, 'India promotes "goodwill" naval exercises of the "Axis of Democracy"', Asia Times Online, 14 August 2007.
48. http://larouchepac.com/pages/breaking_news/2007/06/29/no_gang_china.asp
49. *Times of India*, 5 November 2008.
50. *Times of India*, 10 April 2007.
51. 'China, India look Ahead', *Straits Times*, 17 January 2008.
52. K. Kesavapany, 'An Assessment of India's Role in New Asia', Centre for Indian Ocean Studies, Hyderabad, 12 February 2007.
53. *Straits Times*, 1 May 2001.
54. Lee, Interview III.
55. Ibid.
56. Ibid.
57. Speech to Malayan students in London on 14 September 1962. *Prime Minister's Speeches, Press Conferences, Interviews, Statements, etc.* (Singapore: Prime Minister's Office, 1959–90).
58. Lee, Interview I.
59. *Straits Times*, 18 November 2005.
60. Lee, e-mail, 7 July, 2009.

Index

Abdul Kalam, A.P.J., 79, 291
Abraham, George, 147
Abraham, Thomas (Tom), 11, 13, 88–93, 95, 101–03, 111–12, 114–16, 118, 121–22, 124–25, 130, 141, 144, 147, 150, 167, 179, 194, 203, 214
Abdul Rahman, Tengku, 12, 72, 84–85, 88, 90, 93, 102, 115, 120, 122–24, 131, 136, 142, 150–51, 167–68, 177, 230, 260, 280
Advani, Lal Krishna, 272, 293, 295, 301–02, 316
Air India, 8, 36, 50, 62, 98, 120, 129, 154, 158, 173–74, 309, 315, 322, 334
Alirajpur, Surendra Singh, 124–25, 139, 141, 148, 150, 155
Annadurai, C.N., 167
Arasaratnam, Sinnappa, 323
Ascendas, Singapore, 307, 331
Asia and Pacific Council, 139
Asian and Pacific Regional Commonwealth Conference (CHOGRM), 201, 220–24, 253, 256
Associated Chambers of Commerce and Industry, India, 334–35
Association of South-east Asian Nations (Asean), 5–6, 8, 11, 81, 139–45, 160, 176–78, 181–82, 190, 192, 207, 218–22, 226, 249, 252, 259, 268, 272, 280, 292, 319, 323–24, 328–29, 336–37, 339, 343
    India relations, 208–17, 266–71, 281, 287–90, 315, 320, 328, 338, 345

Aung San Suu Kyi, 99
Azad Hind (Free India) government, in Singapore, 33

Baker, Maurice, 19–20, 24–25, 29, 36, 146–51, 180, 183, 240
Bandaranaike, Srimavo, 78, 93, 143
Bangalore Information Technology Park, 266, 285
Barisan Socialis (Socialist Front), 32
Barker, E.W. (Eddie), 168, 201
Barzilai, Amnon, 115
Bay of Bengal Initiative for Multisectoral Technical and Economic Cooperation (Bimstec), 281
Bharatiya Janata Party (BJP), 171–72, 207, 218, 271–72, 293–95, 300, 302–03, 307, 314
Bhattacharya, Buddhadeb, 16, 324–27
Bhumibol Adulyadej, King, 41, 271
Bhutto, Zulfiqar Ali, 107, 109, 314
Birla, Aditya, 38
Bose, Subhas Chandra, 32–35, 51–52, 56, 59, 65, 74
Brezhnev, Leonid, 216
Bush, George W., 214

Cambodia
    Asean and, 209
    Vietnam intervention in, 48, 185–86, 203, 206, 209, 211–12, 215–20, 226, 252, 255–56
Carter, Jimmy, 198
Chagla, Mahommedali Currimbhoy, 120,

140–41, 145–46, 148, 155, 177–78, 189, 230
Chandrababu Naidu, N., 303, 326
Charan Singh, 186, 206, 210, 217
Chiang Kai-shek, 51
Chidambaram, Palaniappan, 256, 271, 299, 336
China
  Asean and, 160, 287–90
  development projects in, 163–67
  India relations, 84–88, 251–53, 287–90, 305–06, 315, 320, 338–43
  Lee Kuan Yew visits to, 159–60
CHOGRM, see Asian and Pacific Regional Commonwealth Conference
Civil Aviation Authority of Singapore, 316
Clinton, Hilary, 340
Coca-Colonialism, 78
Colombo Plan, 4, 35, 114, 191
Comprehensive Economic Cooperation Agreement (Ceca), 2, 303–04, 307, 322, 331, 333–35
Concert of Asia, 5–6, 10, 16, 32, 152, 201, 319, 345
Condé Nast Portfolio, 324
Congress Party, 19, 22, 25, 52, 63, 73, 81, 97, 113, 134, 140, 172, 174, 195, 203, 210, 256, 264, 275, 279, 297, 303–04, 308
Coomaraswamy, Punch (Punchardsheram), 147, 181, 186, 191

Das, S. Chandra, 64, 91, 157, 174, 182, 246, 253–54, 256, 273, 283, 330–31
Dasgupta, Chandrasekhar, 4, 154, 183, 213, 224–25, 244
Deng Xiaoping, 28, 38, 158, 183, 202–03, 206, 216, 226, 266–67, 291, 298, 326–27
Deora, Milind, 311
Desai, Morarji, 38, 97, 140, 151, 156, 169, 172, 176, 180–81, 183, 186, 203, 205–207, 210
Deve Gowda, H.D., 284–86, 297, 299–300
Dhanabalan, Suppiah, 24, 33, 35, 38, 62, 64, 86–87, 91, 118, 129, 139, 144, 157, 159, 163, 187, 196–200, 202–03, 205, 207–08, 210, 213–14, 220, 223, 273, 330
Dixit, J.N. (Mani), 140, 144, 179, 268, 281
Dravida Kazagham, 66

East Asia Economic Caucus, 268
East Asia Summit, 11, 289, 315, 329
Economic Commission for Asia and the Far East (Ecafe), 109, 111, 178–79, 190
Ee Hoe Hean Club, 5, 57, 345
Escap (United Nations Economic Commission for Asia and the Pacific), 178
Eu Mun Hoo Calvin, 158, 316, 328

Federation of South-east Asia, 74
Fernandes, George, 300
Fifield, Russell H., 31, 76, 139, 143–44, 176
FPDA, 192, 260, 341
Free trade agreement (FTA), 160, 306, 323, 329

Gandhi, Indira, 7, 10, 22–23, 26, 66, 72, 78, 82, 99, 109, 120, 124, 129, 151, 155–56, 192, 194, 202, 205, 210, 212–17, 234, 243 257–58, 288, 311, 335
  CHOGRM and, 221–24
  emergency imposition, 23, 186, 203, 205, 223
  foreign policy, 23, 135
  Lee Kuan Yew relationship, 12, 15, 22–23, 134–38, 158, 174–81, 185–89, 207, 224–25
  on South-east Asia, 139–41
  visit to Singapore, 53, 149, 174–81
Gandhi, M.K., 20–22, 51, 61, 71, 170
Gandhi, Rahul, 19, 38, 253, 257, 311–14, 339
Gandhi, Rajiv, 213, 239, 241, 252–54, 256–57, 259–64, 266–67, 293, 303
Gandhi, Sanjay, 213, 277
Gandhi, Sonia, 252, 260, 303–04, 310–11, 316, 339
Giri, V.V., 190–91
Goh Chok Tong, 1–3, 7–8, 9, 15, 23, 93, 130, 220, 239, 260, 266, 268–272, 279, 289, 295

Goh Keng Swee, 36–38, 68, 103, 116–17, 128–30, 141, 170, 193, 195–96, 260
Goho, S.C., 61
Goyal, Naresh, 285
Greater East Asia Coprosperity Sphere, 181
Greater India Society, 48
Greater Mekong Subregion scheme, 337
Gromyko, Andrei, 133, 215
Gujral, Inder Kumar, 38, 179, 259–60, 262, 283–85, 288–89, 300
Gunasingham, Canagaratnam, 92, 141–43
Gupta, Ranjit, 280–81, 287–88
Gupta, Syamal, 194–95, 197–200

Haksar, P.N., 134, 259
Harry Chan Keng Howe, 147, 239–41, 245, 251, 257
Head, Anthony, 121–22, 124
Henderson, Loy W., 50, 75, 144
Heng Samrin, 9, 209–10, 212–13, 220–21
Ho Chi Minh, 29, 111, 159
Ho Ching, 24, 330–31
Hon Sui Sen, 196, 198, 205, 260
Hua Guo Feng, 7, 202
Hu Jintao, 11, 27, 340
Hussain, Zakir, 148

Ibrahim, C.M., 284–85
Immigration Act, Singapore, 245
Immigration Affairs Committee (Imac), 236
Immigration (Prohibition of Entry) Order of 1966, Singapore, 146
Inche Rahim bin Ishak, 114, 126
Indian Association, 58, 63, 65, 95, 234
Indian Chamber of Commerce, 51
Indian National Army (INA), 33–35, 51, 53–55, 57, 59, 61, 65, 68, 71
India–Singapore Business Forum, 300
Indonesia, 2, 16, 17, 29, 31, 41, 42, 43, 57, 60, 71, 73–75, 78, 80, 81, 85, 86, 93–94, 110, 113, 119, 137, 140, 143, 150, 162, 174, 207, 212, 245, 259–62, 270, 280, 289–90, 324, 341, 342, 343, 344, 345
Infosys Technologies, 159, 197, 304, 307–09
Institute of Southeast Asian Studies, Singapore (Iseas), 291, 302, 336

International Commission of Supervision and Control for Indochina, 77
International Press Institute, 166
International Union of Students, 60
Intraco, Singapore, 183

Jagjivan Ram, 195, 206
Jaishankar, Subramanyam, 204, 332
Janata Dal, 285–86
Jayakumar, Shunmugam, 8, 155, 179, 215, 273, 281–82, 288–89, 328
Jayalalitha, J., 279
Jayewardene, J.R., 221, 240, 259, 261–62
Jemaah Islamiya, 230
Jemayat Islamiyah, 43
Jeyaretnam, J.B., 165
Jeyaretnam, Philip, 8, 20–21, 165
Jha, Chander Sekhar, 89
Jha, Lakshmi Kant, 110, 134, 172, 186
Jigme Singye Wangchuck, King, 240, 274
Jinnah, Mohammed Ali, 29, 52, 120
Johor, Sultan of, 26, 41
Johnson, Lyndon B., 100, 135
Josey, Alex, 19, 30, 79, 83, 99, 118, 152, 165–67, 172, 179
Jumabhoy, Ameer, 190–91, 258, 272, 277
Jumabhoy, Jumabhoy Mohammed, 67
Jumabhoy, Rafiq, 64
Jumabhoy, Rajabali, 3, 22, 51, 54, 64–65, 67, 86, 191

Karunanidhi, Muthuvel, 187
Kaul, T.N., 140, 150, 179
Kausikan, Bilahari, 201
Kennedy, John F., 158, 216, 254
Kesavapany, K., 11, 268, 343
Keskar, B.V., 61
Khalsa Dharmak Sabha, 242–43
Khan, Ayub, 102, 107–09, 120
Khan, Liaquat Ali, 29
Khattar, Satpal, 64, 294, 322, 330
Khruschev, Nikita, 135
Kidron, Mordecai, 116–117
Kidwai, Mustapha Kamal, 115, 124
Kissinger, Henry, 110, 127, 186, 257, 316
Koh, Leslie, 306, 308–09
Koh, Tommy Thong-Bee, 126, 217, 219

Konfrontasi, 73, 93, 110, 122, 137, 149, 215, 344
Kosygin, Alexei, 109, 135
Ko Teck Kin, 114
Krishna Menon, V.K., 37, 73, 76, 99, 134
Kwa Geok Choo, 19

Labour Front, 22, 62
Lam Peck Heng, 253, 273–74, 278, 299
Laski, Harold, 37
Lawless, Richard P., 342
Lee Hsien Loong, 2, 4, 8, 13, 16, 38, 137, 193, 266, 270, 272, 284, 299–300, 303–04, 307, 309, 312, 319, 322–327, 329–35, 342
   on real estate interest, 273, 283, 309, 334
Lee Kuan Yew
   on Afro-Asians, 94–98
   on apartheid in South Africa, 24
   on Bengalis, 39–40
   on Brahmins, 23–27, 179, 267, 274, 321
   British Indian bureaucracy, 161–63
   on caste and class, 25–27
   on China, 227–31
   concern for security and economics of South-east Asia, 78–82
   criticism of United States, 12
   culture from India, 48–49
   damage control after debacle, 91–94
   on democracy, 25, 30, 84, 96, 103, 107, 112, 152–53, 162, 231, 291–92, 296, 298, 304, 310, 338
   on democrats, 27–30
   on development projects in India and China, 163–67
   for English as common language, 167–70
   familial links with Nehru–Gandhis, 19
   on foreign training, 28–29
   gamble of Independence, 88–90
   on Hindu civilization, 39–40
   on Hindu Indian lineage in Malaya, 40–43
   on Indian politics and politicians, 25
   on India–Pakistan war, 107–10
   on India role in South-east Asia, 13–16, 344–45
   for India's support to build up Singapore's military, 102–07, 110–13
   Indira Gandhi relationship, 12, 15, 22–23, 134–38, 158, 174–81, 185–88, 224–25
   on Kavalam Madhava Panikkar, 30–32
   on media responsibilities, 165–66
   military assistance from Israel, 115–19, 128
   Mission India, 1–2, 6, 21, 35, 247, 256, 264–65, 269, 279, 342
   on Muslims, 227–31
   on/and relations with Nehru 16, 27–30, 82–84, 94–98, 168
   non-Communist and anti-Communist states, 111–12
   on old socialism, 98–100
   perception of India, 16, 19–22, 27, 328–32
   personal and political relationship, 12, 15, 22–23, 134–38, 158, 174–81, 185–88
   on press freedom, 166
   on Rahul Gandhi, 19, 311–14
   rule of law and life, 43–45
   as salesman for Malaysia, 78–82
   on Shastri, 106–07, 168
   on Sino-Indian relations, 338–43
   spiritual values and material facts, 170–73
   on Subhas Chandra Bose, 32–35
   on tourism potential, 174, 186, 204, 231, 236, 257, 263, 269, 283, 297, 300, 324, 334
   visits
      China, 159–60
      India, 35–40, 78, 185–90, 256–60, 293–94
      Jakarta, 12
Lee Siew Choh, 80, 86, 89
Lee Siong, Vladimir, 60
Leifer, Michael, 9, 114–15, 165, 289
Lenin, Vladimir, 60
Le Tam, 61
Liem Sioe Liong, 324
Lim Boong Heng, 255, 277
Lim Chee Onn, 205
Lim Chin Joo, 326–27
Lim Chin Siong, 72, 91–92, 326
Lim Choon Mong, 68–70
Lim Ek Hong, 245

Lim Hock San, 154
Lim Kim San, 66, 177, 205
Lim Yew Hock, 22, 67–68, 137
Lingham, S.V., 65–66
Lin Yu-tang, 14, 194
Little India, 20, 53, 60, 145, 178, 236, 239
Liu Shao-chi, 87
Loke Wan Tho, 51, 204
Lotus Club, 53, 58
L&T Infocity, India, 307

Madras Corridor, 258, 272, 277, 279, 284
Mahabharata, 37
Mahbubani, Kishore, 133, 147, 204, 207, 210, 214, 217–19, 276–78, 283, 294, 312
Majumdar, Ramesh Chandra, 48
Malabar '07 naval exercise, 176, 340–41
Malayan Chinese Association (MCA), 52
Malayan Communist Party (MCP), 59–62
Malayan Democratic Union (MDU), 59, 66
Malayan Forum, London, 20, 25, 28–29, 344
Malaysia, 1, 40–43
  Singapore relations, 121–26
Malaysian Federation, 72, 80, 90
Malaysia Singapore Airlines, 154
Malik, Adam, 140–41, 144
Mallik, Preet Mohan Singh, 62, 71, 269, 274
Mandela, Nelson, 291
Mansingh, Lalit, 267
Mao Zedong, 27, 81–82, 86–87, 135, 159–60, 215
Marshall, David Saul, 10, 22, 47, 59–60, 62, 85, 89–90
Marshall Plan, 66–72
Maxwell, Neville, 7, 87, 138, 202
Mehta, Asoka, 10, 36, 152, 170–73
Mehta, Freddie A., 36, 195, 199–200
Mehta, Jagat, 35, 135, 171, 181–82, 228, 332
Meir, Golda, 117
Mekong–Ganga project, 337–43
Menon, Lakshmi N., 78, 80, 90, 94
Mishra, Brajesh, 206, 212, 217, 220, 226, 295, 316
Mishra, Shyam Nandan, 210
Mittal, Lakshmi, 71
Mohamad, Mahathir, 268, 280, 283, 289–90, 328–29
Mohammed Hatta, 29

Moily, M. Veerappa, 276, 285
Moolgaokar, Sumant, 195–96
Moses, Catchick, 49
Mountbatten, Edwina, 55–58, 250
Mountbatten, Louis, 31, 33–34, 53–58, 70
Mountbatten, Pamela, 57
Moynihan, Daniel Patrick, 156, 323
Mukherjee, Pranab, 4, 6, 8–9, 34, 39, 56, 159, 185, 191, 277, 285, 319, 340, 342
Mukhopadhyay, Deepankar, 36, 71, 256
Murdoch, Rupert, 235
Musharraf, Pervez, 108, 228–29

Naicker, E.V. Ramasami, 65
Naik, Sudhakarrao, 278
Naipaul, V.S., 71, 230–31
Nair, B.M.C., 220
Nair, Devan, 11, 21, 28, 91–92, 112, 157, 214
Namboodiripad, E.M.S., 111
Narasimha Rao, P.V., 2, 4, 9, 23, 38, 163, 213, 229, 245, 257, 266–69, 271–73, 275, 277–78, 280, 283–84, 291–95, 297–98, 302, 321, 323, 337, 345
Narayan, Jayaprakash, 155, 203
Narayan, R.K., 148
Narayana Murthy, N.R., 308–09, 334
Naresh Chandra, 288
Nasser, Gamal Abdel, 118–19, 137
Nath, Kamal, 6, 153, 221, 275, 277, 304, 321
Nathan, Sellappan Rama, 3, 33–35, 43, 53, 57, 91, 109, 112–14, 117–18, 122–23, 125, 139, 142–43, 154, 173, 179, 187–88, 193, 199–200, 202, 217, 225, 294, 315
Nefo (New Emerging Forces), 119, 121
Nehru, B.K., 97
Nehru, Jawaharlal, 43–45, 67, 70, 76, 85, 118, 132, 153, 180, 319, 321, 345
  and bureaucracy, 161–63
  for common nationality, 74
  on deployment of Indian troops against Indonesian and Vietnamese, 74
  and Edwina Mountbatten, 55–58
  foreign policy, 23, 70, 72, 77, 142, 321
  Lee Kuan Yew relations, 16, 19, 27–30, 82–84
  and Mountbatten, 53–58

on Singapore–India relations, 14
visit to Singapore, 53–58, 74
Nehru, Kamala, 58
New Delhi Commonwealth summit, 6
Ng Pock Too, 13, 196, 198
Nguyen Co Thach, 174, 216, 218
Nixon, Richard, 257
Nomura Asia Equity Forum, 264
Non-aligned nations movement (NAM), 10, 14, 73, 80, 88, 93, 112–115, 117, 119, 137, 139, 210, 212, 219–20, 222, 258, 262, 272, 283, 339

Oil and Natural Gas Commission (ONGC), India, 254, 263
Oldefo (Old Dying Established Forces), 119, 121
Ong Keng Yong, 7, 23–24, 179, 273
Ong Teong Cheong, 24, 282, 286
Operation Badr, 108
Operation Blue Star, 241–42
Operation Cactus, 262
Operation Cold Store, 86
Operation Gibraltar, 108
Operation Grand Slam, 108
Overseas Chinese Association, 52
Oza, B.M., 93, 136, 138, 148, 169, 203–05, 213–14, 220

Pandit, Vijayalakshmi, 66, 125
Panikkar, Kavalam Madhava, 7, 19, 30–32, 77, 149, 177
Parfitt, Tudor, 59
Parsons, Richard, 316
Partai Komunis Indonesia (PKI), 137–38
Parthasarathi, G., 217
Parti Islam SeMalaysia, 42
Patnaik, Bijayananda (Biju), 47, 74
People's Action Party (PAP), 13, 21, 24, 32, 36, 59, 62, 64–65, 67–70, 72, 86–87, 91–92, 128, 145, 192, 202, 237, 239, 261
Peter Chan Jer Hing, 46, 147, 219, 253, 263, 350
Pillai, A.N. Gopalakrishna, 244, 246
Pillai, Gopinath, 61, 64, 280, 312, 332, 336
Pillay, J.Y. (Joe), 35, 116–18, 130, 260, 275

Prasad, Rajendra, 66
Progressive Party, 59
Puri, Yogendra Krishna, 89, 91, 115
Puthucheary, Dominic, 68, 128
Puthucheary, James, 68
Putin, Vladimir, 310

Quadrilateral Initiative, 340–41
Quirino, Elpidio, 75

Radhakrishnan, Sarvepalli, 100
Raffles, Stamford, 13, 47, 49, 58, 123, 128
Rajan, V.K., 195
Rajaratnam, Sinnathamby, 14, 31, 36–37, 46, 64–65, 79, 84–85, 87, 109, 111, 114, 133, 141–42, 148, 150–51, 156, 167, 170, 181, 189–90, 193, 201, 210, 214, 244, 307
Ram, A.N., 139, 269, 280–81
Ramayana, 13, 37, 41, 344–45
Ramphal, Shridath (Sonny), 24
Rasgotra, Maharajkrishna, 225–26, 253
Raul, Shubha, 316
Razak, Najib Tun, 90
Razak bin Hussain, Tun Abdul, 90, 150
Registration of Foreigners Act, 52
Romulo, Carlos P., 75, 142
Royal Singapore Flying Club, 50
Rushdie, Salman, 231

Sadat, Anwar, 241
Sandhu, K.S., 50
Sankaran, Ayyavier, 26
Schroeder, Gerhard, 291
Scindia, Jyotiraditya, 311, 314
Scindia, Madhavrao, 311
Selkirk, Earl of, 86, 106, 121–24
Selvadurai, Pathma, 192
Sen, Amartya, 39, 298
Senanayake, Dudley, 142–43
Sharif, Nawaz, 108
Shashank, 248–50, 252–53
Shastri, Lal Bahadur, 1, 7, 38, 97, 99, 102–03, 106–09, 111, 116–17, 119, 122, 168, 192
Shourie, Arun, 171, 174, 300–01, 316
Siddharthachary, Venkata, 192, 203, 208
Siddique, Kemal (Tony), 187, 217–18, 237

Index 383

Sihanouk, Prince Norodom, 76, 215, 222, 241
Singapore Airlines, 14, 154, 309
Singapore Citizenship Bill, 69–70
Singapore Indian Chamber of Commerce, 147, 299
Singapore Indian Regional Congress, 63
Singapore–India Partnership Foundation, Calcutta, 3
Singapore Industrial Promotion Board, 68
Singapore Labour Party, 59
Singapore Pledge, 37
Singapore Union of Journalists, 167
Singh, Ajit, 287
Singh, Arjun, 275–77
Singh, Dinesh, 14, 84, 89, 99, 124
Singh, Jaswant, 5, 17, 28, 35, 61, 88, 155, 158, 261, 307, 309, 321, 333, 337
Singh, Manmohan, 5–6, 9, 38, 71, 140, 159, 163, 206, 269, 271–72, 275, 277, 285, 287, 293, 295, 298–99, 303–04, 306, 310, 314–16, 321, 323, 325, 335, 339–40, 343
Singh, Natwar, 15, 46–47, 82, 88–90, 92, 110, 134, 136, 149, 172, 219, 222, 230, 245, 253, 257, 260, 312
Singh, Prem, 201–02, 204, 294–95
Singh, Swaran, 12, 99, 114, 136, 151, 185
Singh, Zail, 241
Sinha, Satyaprasanna, 39
Sinha, Yashwant, 307, 320–21
Sino-American détente, 189
Sino-Indian dispute, 1962, 84, 252
Sirindhorn, Princess Maha Chakri, 40
Socialist International, 98, 118, 152
Solanki, Madhavsinh, 268, 271
Soong Ching Ling, 28
South Asian Association for Regional Cooperation (Saarc), 259
South-east Asia, 74, 78–82
  India role in, 13–18, 344–45
South-east Asia Friendship and Economic Treaty (Seafet), 76, 143
South-east Asian League, 74
South-east Asia Treaty Organization (Seato), 75–76, 132, 143–44, 182, 193
South-east Asia Union, 75
Sri Guru Nanak Sat Sangh Sabha, 247

Srinivasan, Krishnan, 268, 275
Sri Tri Buana, 41
Sri Vijaya empire, 31, 42
Statesman, 6, 13, 37, 50, 189, 221, 246, 310
State Trading Corporation, India, 183
Straits Settlements, 52, 58, 183, 277
Straits Times, 15, 20–21, 36, 44, 49, 67, 69, 79, 86, 132, 146, 204, 222, 231, 236, 244–45, 248, 250, 258, 261, 282–83, 306, 308–09, 316, 343, 345
Subandrio, 73, 80, 93, 137
Subramaniam, C., 191
Suharto, 12, 75, 137–38, 259, 289
Sukarno, 30, 42, 72, 75, 77, 93–94, 110, 119–21, 137–38, 178
Sultan of Johor, 26, 41
Sun Yat Sen, 28, 59
Surrender Chamber, in Sentosa island, 33
Sutan Sjahrir, 74
Suvarnabhumi, 1, 13, 16, 25, 31, 40, 46, 48, 139, 142, 231, 248–51, 267, 319–20, 326, 328, 337
Suzhou Industrial Park, China, 284, 301

Tagore, Rabindranath, 21, 39, 48, 67, 98
Tamil Murasu, 54, 69
Tan Cheng Lock, 52
Tan Chin Tuan, 51–52, 255
Tang I-Fang, 128, 196
Tang, Edward Yew Chan, 245, 251
Tanglin Club, 240
Tan Kah Kee, 54, 57
Tan, Keng Yam Tony, 51, 192
Tan Sew Sin, 52
Tan Siok Sun, 116
Tata, Jehangir Ratanji Dadabhoy, 7, 38, 153–54, 156, 160, 171, 173, 195–98, 200, 272, 292, 324
  role in technical development of Singapore, 194–200
Tata, Naval, 194
Tata, Ratan, 194, 198–99, 272, 276, 285, 324
Tata Consultancy Services, 197
Tata Engineering and Locomotive Company (Telco), 195
Tata Government Training Centre, Singapore, 194, 199

Tata Iron and Steel Company (Tisco), Jamshedpur, 194–95
Tata Motors, 195–96
Tata Precision Industries Pte Limited, Singapore, 194, 196, 198
Temasek Holdings, 17, 21, 139, 330–31
Teo Chee Hean, 300
Thakin Nu, 29, 74
Thanat Khoman, 74, 139–40, 142, 144
Tharman Shanmugaratnam, 312–13
Tharoor, Shashi, 20, 233–34, 237
Thatcher, Margaret, 180, 224, 245, 253
Thimayya, Kodandera Subayya (Timmy), 33
Thivy, John Aloysius, 59, 63
Time, 134, 263, 324
Times of India, 83, 98, 292
Tiwari, Yogesh Mohan, 204, 246, 267–68, 270, 272, 278, 281, 283
Toh Chin Chye, 36, 95, 114, 159, 170, 183
Tourist Promotion Board, Singapore, 284
Tregonning, K.G., 52
Tryst with Destiny, 5, 9, 29, 295–96
Tyabji, Badr-ud-din, 17, 22, 77–78, 281

United Front for National Salvation, Cambodia, 209
United Malays National Organization, 62
United National Party, 142
United Nations of South Asia, 74
United States–India Business Council, 283
University of Malaya Socialist Club, 59
University Socialist Club, 68

Vajpayee, Atal Behari, 5, 15, 38, 171, 206–07, 218, 224, 228, 291, 293, 295, 297, 299–303, 326, 336
Venkateswaran, A.P., 263
Vij, Kirpa Ram, 141, 193–94
Vittachi, Varindra Tarzie, 161
Vo Van Kiet, 216

Wavell, Lord, 51, 56, 321
Wen Jiabao, 289
Wilson, Harold, 12, 107, 115, 145
Winsemius, Albert, 82, 128
Wipro, 159, 197, 304
Wolfensohn, James D., 235
Wolpert, Stanley, 29
Wong Kan Seng, 199, 246, 252, 269, 271, 282
Woods, George, 172
Woods, Robert Carr, 49

Yang Jiechi, 340
Yang Sou Mer, 51
Yechury, Sitaram, 311, 319, 325
Yeo, Yong-Boon George, 8–9, 11, 34, 127, 130, 153–54, 159–60, 175, 187–88, 191, 232, 237, 266, 269, 274–78, 282–83, 289, 294, 309, 312, 319, 322, 334, 338, 343
Yeo, Philip, 199, 285, 287
Yogesh Chandra, 284–85
Yusof bin Ishak, 86

Ze'evi, Rehavam, 117
Zheng Bijian, 11, 15, 329
Zheng He, 324, 344
Zhou En Lai, 30, 54, 66, 71, 77, 84–85, 88, 113, 218, 251
Zhou Ziyang, 218
Zhu Rongji, 291
Zone of Peace, Friendship and Neutrality (Zopfan), 192, 207

www.ingramcontent.com/pod-product-compliance
Lightning Source LLC
Chambersburg PA
CBHW031959220426
43664CB00005B/73